BONUS **SIMCITY** EGUIDE WITH FREE UPDATES!

Login with the voucher code below *(DLC subject to game launch date)*

- **Make better decisions with updated information for RCI buildings, playables and upgrades**
- **Reap enormous profits from big business opportunities with expert strategies**
- **Access strategy anywhere you have an internet connection**
- **Enlarge screenshots, search tables, bookmark pages and so much more**

1. Go to www.primagames.com. Select "Redeem Code" located at the top of the page.

2. Enter the voucher code in the text field and click the "Submit" button.

3. You will be redirected to your content now.

VOUCHER CODE - DLC subject to game launch date

3yt7-hdbt-sbps-fkrw

 **Follow us** @PrimaGames

 **Like us on Facebook**

SIMCITY

OFFICIAL GAME GUIDE

WRITTEN BY:

David Knight & Dorothy Bradshaw

Prima Games | An Imprint of Random House, Inc.

3000 Lava Ridge Court, Suite 100 | Roseville, CA 95661 | www.primagames.com

GET YOUR UPDATES NOW!

Access your free eGuide
(voucher code on insert) on
www.primagames.com

Contents

HI EVERYONE. I'm Lucy Bradshaw and I lead the Maxis label here at EA. Over the course of the last year, we have been talking to fans about this new *SimCity*. We have received some great questions on a range of topics, including the city size, the GlassBox engine powering *SimCity*, and even how many splines we've reticulated over the years. (Short answer: a lot.)

One particular topic that comes up pretty regularly is our decision to require an online connection to play the game. I understand why this may be a concern for fans who have been playing *SimCity* for decades now. Like all of you, I'm a long-time *SimCity* fan. But it's not just me—we have several veterans from previous versions of the game here at the Maxis studio, and we are all proud and excited about the game we're making and we think you'll really love it.

Creating a connected experience has always been a goal for *SimCity*, and this design decision has driven our development process for the game. This is easily the most ambitious game in the franchise and we've taken great care to make sure that every line of code embodies the spirit of the series. To do this, we knew we had to make sure we put our heart and soul into the simulation, and the team created the most powerful simulation engine in its history—the GlassBox Engine. GlassBox is the engine that drives the entire game—the buildings, the economics, trading, and also the overall simulation that can track data for up to 100,000 individual Sims inside each city. There is a massive amount of computing that goes into all of this, and GlassBox works by attributing portions of the computing to EA servers (the cloud) and some on the player's local computer.

Perhaps Ocean Quigley, our Creative Director, said it best when he said that real cities do not exist in a bubble; they share a region and affect one another. GlassBox does more than just segregate computing tasks, it also allows us to make it so that you can create specialized cities that are visually unique and personalized, and that can be economically integrated into a larger region. You're always connected to the neighbors in your region, so while you play, data from your city interacts with our servers, and we run the simulation at a regional scale. For example, trades between cities, simulation effects that cause change across the region (like pollution or crime), as well as depletion of resources, are all processed on the servers and then data are sent back to your city on your PC. Every city in the region is updated every three minutes, which keeps the overall region in sync and makes your decisions in your city relevant to any changes that have taken place in the region.

Running the regional simulation on our servers is something we also use to support features that will make this *SimCity* even more fun. We use the Sim data to update worldwide leaderboards, where you get to see your city or mayoral standings as compared to the other cities in your region and between all of the regions in the world. And since *SimCity* is a live service, we're also using the data to create weekly global and local challenges for our players that keep the gameplay fresh and surprising.

We think this is the best *SimCity* ever and it wouldn't be possible without the technology that powers our game. *SimCity* was designed to be connected from the ground up. We built the game around GlassBox, which takes the game to another level. And, we've given the player control over how to play. You can set your region to private and never interact with other people, or you can play exclusively with friends or join a public region.

As I write this, we're entering the final stages of development. We're still tuning and refining the game, but already it has that special magic that sucked me into the franchise in the first place. We really look forward to seeing what you will create and how you will mayor come March 5th.

Thanks

Lucy Bradshaw

LUCY BRADSHAW, *SVP Maxis*

MILLIONS OF PEOPLE around the world have been playing *SimCity* since it first came out in 1989. It's been eight years since the release of *SimCity 4,* and Maxis is now ready to unveil the next chapter of the *SimCity* story.

SimCity is about solving puzzles. It is a game of strategy, experimentation, creativity, and fun. This version of the game keeps all the great elements that have kept fans engaged, and adds new elements that deepen engagement with the game. I'm excited to think that, with this version of *SimCity*, people who played the game as kids can now introduce it to their children. The game is easy to learn and immediately accessible, but not at all "dumbed down," making *SimCity* a delight to veteran players and those new to developing their own cities. I think one reason *SimCity* has endured over the years is that it's an antidote to the mindless, violent, and disposable games on the market today.

There is no "right way" to play *SimCity*. One player may decide that she wants to maximize her city's population, while keeping all systems in working order. Another may re-create his hometown or build a utopia of sustainable energy. You may wish to keep your Sims happy in such a paradise, or build a wildly profitable, crime-ridden city whose economy is based on casinos and oil refineries. With multi-city play, you can build both, and see how the two cities impact each other! There are no right answers, only different approaches. *SimCity* allows you to craft your own puzzles and try out different solutions.

One thing you'll notice right away, the game is constantly in motion. Sims travel to work and school, winds blow and carry pollution or provide an energy source, tourists arrive at ferry docks to spend Simoleons at your city's commercial and cultural hotspots, traffic waxes and wanes at different hours of the day, buildings erupt in fire, and waves lap against your city's shoreline. There are dozens of these systems, or flows, each moving at their own rate with their own internal purpose. To grow a prosperous region, a player endeavors to keep all of these flows open and dependable.

Each system in *SimCity* is clear and simple to understand. Build a Water Tower over that nice aquifer and, as long as everything is connected by roads, the Sims in your city will be able to water their lawns and the restaurants will be able to wash dishes. As you build up your city, more systems and services are needed to keep the residents happy. As one simple system feeds into another, the complexity of the game increases. An accident in a chemical factory contaminates the ground water and sickness spreads amongst the residents in your city. A new Hospital cures your sick Sims, but causes gridlock along a narrow access road. And these systems are now not confined to one city, but extend to the region and the world.

This is why *SimCity* never gets old, and why we never get tired of making it a new experience with each version of the game. *SimCity*, and everything you see in it, is responsive to your actions. At any level into the game, you are working to sort out cause and effect relationships and are able to observe the results of your decisions—for good or ill.

So jump right in and get building. I hope you enjoy playing the game as much as we've enjoyed designing it.

STONE LIBRANDE, *Lead Designer*

SIMCITY **IS ONE OF THOSE GAMES THAT TRANSCENDS GAMING. It's a game that is near and dear to my heart. It's a franchise that I grew up with and always came back to through the years. Ever since I discovered it those many years ago on my parents' computer, I had a love for this quirky little city builder.**

SimCity taught me about how cities work and I never looked at real cities in real life the same. Maxis gave me the tools to be anything I wanted, to construct my own beautiful worlds to control and manage. With a flick of my mouse, I was transformed into a mighty politician, planning highways, financial districts, and raising taxes. I was an artist, an architect, a city planner, a god. It was these memories that stuck with me throughout my life that steered me into the game industry and to ultimately come to work for Maxis eleven years ago.

Another memory I had of *SimCity* was one of solitude. Creating great cities, so full of life and stories, but always alone—no one to share them with or any way to play with others. This next chapter in *SimCity* was designed to change all of that. Cities are not isolated things that sit alone on chips in space, disconnected from the universe. They are connected living organisms, each with a purpose and a story of their own. In this *SimCity*, we wanted to capture the ways in which real cities work together with one another: How they share services, goods, jobs, people, and more.

In *SimCity*, you'll be able to create your networks of cities that work together in ways only you can imagine. Create your own bedroom communities, where the Sims that live in the city commute to a neighboring city that is full of high-tech jobs. Build a city of knowledge full of schools, universities, and libraries providing education to all Sims in the region. Experiment with strange combinations like a green city full of wind turbines powering its neighboring city, which is filled with dirty industrial companies. All of the simulation and gameplay you find in the city extends to other cities. The multi-city play adds an entirely new level of strategy to city planning. Once you've mastered the ins and outs to playing a single city, try to run two cities, three cities, or more. Anyone familiar to *SimCity* will appreciate the added depth that multi-city play brings to the franchise. Anyone new to *SimCity* will wonder how anyone could have played *SimCity* any other way.

The team here at Maxis has worked hard to bring you the next great city builder. Enjoy!

KIP KATSARELIS, *Senior Producer*

A Message from the Author

Welcome to the official game guide for *SimCity*! As Lucy and Stone have alluded, this is the most ambitious *SimCity* yet, giving players an unprecedented amount of access and control while encouraging the same level of creativity that has been a hallmark of this acclaimed series for more than 20 years. Personally, I spent days upon days nurturing my sprawling, imperfect cities on the Super NES version, released back in 1991—and no, I didn't use any cheats! So I jumped at the chance to work on the latest *SimCity*, knowing full well it wouldn't be easy. But thanks to my wonderful team at Prima Games and the gracious developers at Maxis, it's been well worth the long days and nights.

As all *SimCity* veterans know, there is no right or wrong way to play the game—formulate an imaginative vision and use it as your blueprint to create any city you'd like, defining your own goals along the way. During the creation of this guide we kept that in mind, with an emphasis on providing you with all the information you need to create the city and region you want. The organization of the guide reflects this, serving more as a reference tool than a linear step-by-step narrative. While we'd recommend reading every chapter, it's not necessary. Simply flip ahead to the topics that interest you, or read it cover to cover and digest every bit of detail. The choice is yours.

The *SimCity* development team at Maxis has taken an active role in the creation of this guide. In addition to ensuring the accuracy of the content, several developers have participated, writing various pieces scattered throughout the guide on a wide range of topics. Given the scope and complexity of *SimCity*, who better to offer insight than those who actually made the game? Be sure to read through the various Developer Cities in the next chapter, offering plenty of useful gameplay hints as well as some cautionary tales. Look for more nuggets of city-building wisdom in our Chat with the Developers sections found at

Now and beyond the release date, *SimCity* is a constantly evolving game, with the development team making occasional tweaks and updates to ensure a fun and balanced gameplay experience for all.

Every time you start *SimCity*, the game automatically searches for new updates. If a new update is found, it is automatically downloaded and installed. As information and data changes in the game, we'll continue to update this guide at www.primagames.com. As the owner of this guide, you have access to our updated eGuide—go to www.primagames.com and enter the provided voucher code to gain access to the eGuide. Here you can find the same information in the print guide as well as new content pertaining to recent updates. So check back frequently for updated stats, challenges, achievements, and more.

the end of most chapters. We're very excited about this collaborative effort and feel it provides a better understanding of how the game's various systems function and interact with one another. For example, did you know that uncollected garbage poses fire and health risks? Or that Sims will walk a maximum of 400 meters before relying on a car or mass transit to reach their destination? By understanding the various rules of the simulation, it's easier to craft the city you've envisioned.

Our team has had a blast playing *SimCity* and creating this guide. We hope you find this information helpful when developing your own cities and regions. See you online!

DAVID KNIGHT
February 2013

What's New?

SimCity has a loyal following that literally spans generations. Many of us who grew up with the game are now playing it side by side with our children, nephews, and nieces. While the essence of *SimCity* remains intact, the latest iteration adds several new and exciting elements even veterans of the franchise should be aware of. But don't worry, the game you know and love is still here. Instead of fundamentally changing the game, these additions merely enhance and expand the same gameplay experience we've enjoyed throughout the years.

MULTI-CITY PLAY

You're not alone. Look out beyond your city and seek opportunities to trade and collaborate with other mayors in the region.

The concept that "no city exists in a bubble" comes alive with multi-city play. While regions aren't new to *SimCity*, the way regions function has been completely overhauled with a heavy emphasis on cooperative gameplay. Now, up to sixteen players can occupy a region, each the mayor of their own city. Cities interact with each other in numerous ways. They can gift each other Simoleons and resources or share service vehicles such as garbage trucks, ambulances, and fire trucks. But cities can also collaborate on Great Works, donating money and resources to construct the Arcology, International Airport, Solar Farm, or Space Center—each Great Works project benefits all connected cities with a variety of perks. So don't get tunnel vision and focus only on your city. Zoom out to the Region View and see what your fellow mayors are up to. You can even visit their cities, learning from their successes and mistakes. Before long you'll begin thinking about the region as a whole, perhaps becoming the Mayor of multiple cities or collaborating with friends and strangers.

LIVE SERVICE

There's no need to manually save that masterpiece of a city—your game is automatically saved to the cloud.

As Lucy mentioned in her foreword, *SimCity* requires a constant online connection to play—like most video games in 2013. While this is a departure from past installments, the benefits far outweigh any drawbacks, providing a truly integrated gameplay experience. An online connection isn't only a necessity for the simulation to function, but it also allows for greater depth. One of the coolest features is the global market, a virtual marketplace where in-game resources are exchanged— the market value of each resource fluctuates based on real-time supply and demand! Cloud saves have also been integrated, meaning there's no way to revert back to an old saved game. This gives each decision you make greater weight, potentially having far-reaching consequences. But don't worry. You can always play in Sandbox mode if you're more interested in learning and experimenting—the cheats offered in Sandbox mode make the game much more forgiving.

CITY SPECIALIZATIONS

They're not pretty, but Oil Wells are a necessity if you're hoping to make millions in the petroleum business.

Tired of relying on taxes to fill your city's treasury? With the new city specialization options you can now turn to a variety of alternative sources of income. Have oil beneath your city? Pursue the petroleum business, pumping crude oil from the ground to export on the global market for a quick profit. Or take that oil and process it in an Oil Refinery to produce plastic and fuel for even larger profit margins. By specializing in petroleum, metals, trade, electronics, or gambling there's an exciting variety of potential revenue streams available. But you'll need to master supply lines, transportation, and other challenges to ensure a steady flow of revenue from these lucrative businesses.

MODULES

Each casino has a variety of modules useful for accommodating and luring more tourists into your city.

All non-RCI buildings in the game can now be customized with modules to better meet the demands of your growing city. Running low on power? Add a new turbine to your Wind Power Plant. Want to increase police coverage? Add more Patrol Car Lots to your Police Station or Police Precinct. This gives you much more control over how utilities and city services are implemented and expanded. But these modules aren't free. Just like buildings, each module has an initial cost as well as an hourly operational cost, cutting into the city's budget. Before you add a new module to a building, make sure your city can afford it, otherwise your good intentions may lead the city to a financial crisis.

SIMCITY WORLD

Check out the leaderboards to see how your cities and regions stack up against the competition.

SimCity World is the underlying network that ties everyone's gaming experience together through leaderboards, achievements, challenges, and the global market.

There are a total of fifteen leaderboards tracking data and ranking players through a variety of categories including wealth, crime, and pollution, as well as all five city specializations. This adds a competitive element to the game for players interested in climbing to the top of the rankings or at least nudging past their friends. Achievements and challenges offer optional goal-oriented tasks to complete, sometimes requiring the cooperation of other mayors in your region. The global market tracks the prices of resources based on real-time supply and demand. This makes the import/export game extremely addictive, allowing you to buy low and sell high through Trade Depots and Trade Ports. In all, *SimCity* World keeps the game fresh, always providing new tasks and experiences to enjoy with others or on your own.

Getting Started

So Mayor, are you ready to start building a city?

Nurturing a small town to life and watching it grow into a bustling metropolis is just one of the many appeals of the *SimCity* experience. But before you start paving roads, plopping utilities, and laying out zones, it's a good idea to establish a basic understanding of the interface and underlying gameplay mechanics. Even if you're a *SimCity* veteran there's plenty of new material to learn, particularly when it comes to multi-city play—the new feature allowing you to share resources with other cities and players while working toward common goals. Once you've grasped the basics, follow the easy ten-step tutorial on how to establish the basic infrastructure for any city, helping you get on the right track. Want to know how the developers play the game? Then flip ahead to the sample cities section to learn how the Maxis team creatively approaches different goals and overcomes challenges. By learning how the developers play, you'll see what's possible, inspiring you to create your own imaginative cities. After all, there's no right way or wrong way to play *SimCity*. So read up, and most importantly, have fun!

Interface

City View
MENUS

1. **Roads:** Select from a variety of streets and avenues to create your road network. In addition to carrying traffic, roads also serve as the circulatory system of the simulation, responsible for conveying power, water, and sewage beneath the surface. All zones, structures, and even parks must be built adjacent to a road.

2. **Zones:** Use the zoning tools to zone residential, commercial, and industrial zones within your city. Zones can be removed by using the Dezone tool.

3. **Power:** How will you power your city? Choose from Wind, Coal, Oil, Solar, and Nuclear Power Plants. Once a power plant is constructed, power can be seen traveling along your road system, represented as a yellow line. When

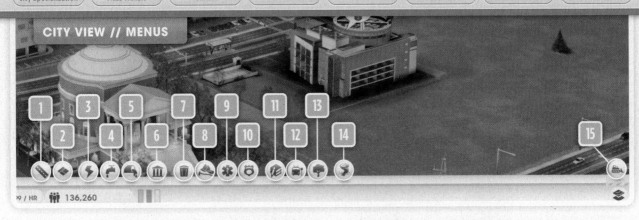

CITY VIEW // MENUS

the Power menu is open you can also see how much power is being generated and consumed.

4 Water: Whether you build a simple Water Tower or a Water Pumping Station, all cities require water. With a water source in place, water, represented by a blue line, flows along the city's road network. When the Water menu is open you can see the pollution level as well as how much water is being produced and consumed.

5 Sewage: Build a Sewage Outflow Pipe or Sewage Treatment Plant to deal with all the raw sewage building up in your city's pipes. Sewage appears as brown blobs beneath the surface of your city's road network—make sure it's pumped to a proper disposal area before it leaches to the surface and creates ground pollution.

6 Government: Access this menu to construct a Town Hall, Mayor's House, and Mayor's Mansion, as well as a number of departments. Departments must be placed adjacent to your Town/City Hall, so leave plenty of growing room.

7 Waste Disposal: All buildings in the city generate garbage. If left unattended, garbage can accumulate, spreading germs, lowering land value, and increasing the risk of fires. Construct a Garbage Dump and/ or Recycling Center to get a handle on your city's perpetual garbage problem.

8 Fire: The Fire Station and the Large Fire Station are your first lines of defense against small residential blazes and massive industrial hazmat infernos. Make sure your city has adequate fire coverage before the first fire breaks out—waiting to build a Fire Station until a fire spreads is risky and irresponsible.

9 Health: Even in the healthiest, pollution-free cities, Sims still get sick and become injured. Build a Clinic or Hospital to treat ailing Sims, returning them to full health. After all, Sims who are sick or injured do not go to work, potentially having a ripple effect on the city economy.

10 Police: If criminals have taken refuge in your city, building a Police Station or Police Precinct is the only way to get rid of them. Police actively pursue criminals immediately following a crime. Once jailed and rehabilitated, a criminal no longer poses a threat to your city. Deal with crime at its earliest, non-violent stages before it gets out of hand.

11 Education: Investing in education is costly but has many benefits. By building Grade Schools, Public Libraries, High Schools, Community Colleges, and Universities, you not only keep kids off the streets, but you also increase education and tech levels, eventually opening the door for clean and high tech industry.

12 Mass Transit: No matter how carefully you design your road network, it's difficult to avoid gridlock caused by too many cars. Alleviate road congestion by investing in mass transit. Utilizing buses, streetcars, trains, boats, and planes, an efficient mass transit system gives Sims other alternatives for getting around the city or commuting to neighboring cities.

13 Parks: Everybody wants to live next to a park. As a result, building parks immediately increases the surrounding land value, often attracting medium and high wealth Sims. Parks also help offset the negative affects of air pollution and increase the city's attraction rating, helping lure tourists.

14 Disasters: Choose from different disasters to unleash on your city. Disasters are not immediately available as they must be unlocked by completing specific achievements.

15 Bulldoze: Access this menu to demolish unwanted buildings and roads. Bulldozing roads destroys connected buildings and removes zones.

CITY VIEW // HUD ELEMENTS

HUD ELEMENTS

1 Neighboring Cities: The icons on the left side of the HUD represent neighboring cities in the region—the icon shown is the Origin avatar of each city's mayor. Click on these icons to view each corresponding city in the Region View.

2 Great Works: Choose to build a Solar Farm, International Airport, Space Center, or Arcology. Great Works benefit all cities in the region.

3 Region View: Switch to the Region View to see neighboring cities. From this interface you can also buy power, water, and sewage coverage from connected cities in the region. It's also possible to volunteer vehicles like garbage trucks, police cars, fire trucks, and ambulances to neighboring cities.

4 City View: When the Region View is open, click on the City View button to return to your city.

5 City Specialization: Here you can choose from a variety of city specialization opportunities. Specialize your city with mining, drilling, trading, electronics, culture, or gambling.

6 Pause/Play: Pausing the simulation stops time and all

movement within your city. You can still construct, zone, and make other adjustments while the game is paused. If the game is paused, click on this toggle button again to resume the simulation at the currently selected speed.

7 Time/Date: The current time is always shown here. Mouse over the time to reveal the current month and year.

8 Simulation Speed: Toggle between Turtle, Llama, and Cheetah speeds to alter the passing of time—Turtle speed is the slowest, and Cheetah speed is the fastest.

9 City Name: This is the name of your city. All cities have a default name, but names can be changed. Click on the city's name to change its name.

10 Mayor Rating: This colorful face icon represents the city's overall happiness and how you're doing as mayor—if the icon is a green happy face, you're doing a great job! If the icon is any other color, your city has problems. Click on the face icon to open the Mayor Rating panel. Here you can get a better idea of what your Sims are complaining about.

11 Budget Panel: This bar at the bottom of the HUD shows the amount of Simoleons in your city's treasury as well as how much money the city is bringing in per hour. Click on this bar to open the more detailed Budget panel. From the Budget panel you can adjust tax rates as well as view all income and expenses. If your city is strapped for cash, you can even take out loans from three different lenders.

12 Population Panel: This bar shows your city's current population. For a more detailed report, click this bar to open the Population panel. Here you can track your population across demographics, ideal for seeing how many low, medium, and high wealth Sims are living in the city. This is also a great place to view how many filled and vacant jobs are available in your city.

13 RCI Demand: These three green, blue, and yellow bars represent the current demand for residential, commercial, and industrial zoning—the higher the bar, the greater the demand. For greater detail on zoning demand, open the Zones menu.

14 **Data Map:** Choose from a variety of data layers, each represented by a different icon within this pop-up box. Each data layer reveals a wealth of information about your city, including the locations of natural resources, land value, crime, air pollution, and much more. Use the information provided in these data layers to plan your city, identify problems, and seek out new opportunities.

15 **Mission Tracker:** Missions are optional tasks that can be accepted and completed to earn rewards, paid in varying amounts of Simoleons. Current missions appear as icons on the right side of the HUD. Mouse over each mission icon to review their criteria and your progress toward completing them. You can only accept three missions at a time. Current missions can be canceled at any time in order to accept new missions in their place.

16 **Rotate/Zoom Controls:** Use these controls in the top, right corner of the HUD to zoom and rotate the

view of the city. Alternatively, you can use the mouse or keyboard to zoom and rotate your view.

17 **Achievements:** Click here to see all available achievements.

18 **Challenges:** Here you can see the current challenge available to the community.

19 **Leaderboards:** This button offers quick access to the leaderboards. Sort through all 15 to see how you stack up against your friends or the entire community.

20 **Friends Lists:** Here you'll find a list of your Origin friends who also have *SimCity*—send them invites, asking them to join your region. If you don't have any friends in your Origin friends' list, you can search for new friends with *SimCity* here. But you must know their Origin user name.

21 **Options Menu:** From this menu you can adjust the game's settings, access the game manual, enter the Help Center, view achievements, replay the opening tutorial, view the game's

credits, return to the main menu, or exit the game.

22 **Thought Bubble:** These bubbles project the citizens' positive and negative thoughts, giving you a peek into the public's attitude. Green bubbles are positive, orange bubbles are neutral, and red bubbles are negative.

23 **Request Bubble:** These blue bubbles appear when a Sim, company, or organization directly appeals to the mayor's office with a request.

24 **Region Wall:** This window can be opened to chat with other mayors in your region. This is a great way to communicate when attempting to build Great Works or negotiating gifts from neighboring cities.

25 **SimCity Wire:** All of the latest news for your city is displayed at the top of the screen. Events in the region are also reported, informing you when new mayors join the region or whenever a new government department module is constructed.

City Specialization

1 **Mining:** Choose from the Coal Mine, Ore Mine, or Advanced Coal Mine to start extracting raw materials from the ground. By building the Metals HQ and Smelting Factory, you can then refine coal and ore into metal and alloy. Metal and alloy are necessary for building Great Works. Alternatively, coal, ore, metal, and alloy also be sold to neighboring cities or the global market for a handsome profit.

2 **Drilling:** If your city has large deposits of oil beneath the surface, build an Oil Well to extract crude oil. With the construction of a Petroleum HQ and Oil Refinery, crude oil can be converted into fuel or plastic. All

CITY SPECIALIZATION

three resources—crude oil, fuel, and plastic—can be traded to neighboring cities or sold on the global market.

3 **Trading:** The Trade Depot is the central hub of all resources flowing in and out of your city. Here you can store, import, and export a variety of resources and freight—all imports and exports are carried by trucks. Building a Trade HQ and Trade Port allows you to import and export massive amounts of resources

and freight carried by trains and cargo ships.

4 **Electronics:** If your region already has a Community College or University and is producing a surplus of alloy and plastic, consider building a Processor Factory. A successful Processor Factory can lead to the creation of an Electronics HQ, which in turn unlocks the Consumer Electronics Factory, capable of producing TVs and computers.

CITY SPECIALIZATION (Continued)

5 Culture: Cultural buildings like the Expo Center, Pro Stadium, and real-world landmarks (like the Arc De Triomphe and Empire State Building) provide happiness for your city's Sims as well as attract tourists. Just make sure your city has plenty of mass transit options to accommodate the sudden influx of visitors. Surround these attractions with plenty of commercial buildings to encourage shopping by tourists.

6 Gambling: Casinos offer a quick way to earn a lot of revenue, attracting tourists from the region and beyond. Start small with a Gambling Hall, but make sure your city has police coverage to counter the criminal element. A successful Gambling Hall can lead to the construction of a Gambling HQ, followed by more lavish gaming palaces like the Sleek, Sci-Fi, and Elegant Casinos. Like cultural buildings, a good mass transit system is essential for handling the heavy traffic around casinos. A constant and robust police presence is also very important.

Region View

1 Region Name: The name of the region. Once established, regions cannot be renamed.

2 Region Population: This number represents the current population of the entire region, accounting for Sims in every city.

3 Region Treasury: The total amount of available funds in the region, accounting for every Simoleon in each city's treasury.

4 Great Works: Choose to build a Solar Farm, International Airport, Space Center, or Arcology. Great Works benefit all cities connected to them by road. Airports have additional benefit to cities connected by rail.

5 Workers: Shows the flow of workers commuting among the cities in the region. Unemployed Sims will look for work in neighboring cities. View the data maps to see total workers, total jobs, unemployed Sims, and open jobs.

6 Shoppers: Shows the flow of shoppers traveling throughout the region. Shoppers will travel by car, bus, train, and ferry to shop in neighboring cities. View the data maps to see total shoppers, total goods, unsatisfied shoppers, and unsold goods.

7 Freight: Shows the flow of freight throughout the region. Industrial businesses ship freight to commercial businesses in neighboring cities. View the data maps to see total freight, total freight orders, unsent freight, and unfilled freight orders.

8 Students: Shows the flow of high school and college students moving throughout the region. Grade school students travel to High Schools in neighboring cities by bus. College students use cars, buses, trains, or ferries to reach Colleges in neighboring

cities. View the data maps to see total students, total desks, uneducated Sims, and extra desks.

9 Transport: Shows the flow and use of mass transit throughout the region. Sims travel between cities using buses, passenger trains, and ferries. View the data maps to see the number of passengers, number of passengers waiting at stops, and the number of stops.

10 Power: Shows the flow of power traded between cities. You can also select a connected city and choose to buy power from it—the city requiring power must initiate the purchase. View the data maps to see power needed, power produced, power sold, and power deficits.

11 Water: Shows the flow of water traded between cities. A city creating water makes its excess water available to connected cities for a fee. You can buy water from any neighboring city with a water surplus. View the data maps to see water produced, water needed, water sold, and water deficits.

12 Sewage: Shows the flow of sewage traded between cities. A city providing sewage can take in sewage from connected cities. Select a neighboring city and buy sewage service. View the data maps to see sewage capacity, sewage produced, sewage treated, and sewage dumped.

13 Waste Disposal: Expand waste disposal coverage by volunteering garbage and recycling trucks to other cities in the region. Cities receiving garbage coverage get the service for free from neighbors willing to volunteer trucks. The city

REGION VIEW

receives income for the garbage it collects. View the data maps to see total number of garbage and recycling trucks, total number of garbage cans, and total number of garbage cans not picked up.

14 Fire: Expand fire coverage by volunteering fire trucks, hook & ladder trucks, hazmat tucks, fire marshals, and fire helicopters to neighboring cities. The city receiving the fire coverage gets it for free. The city providing the coverage receives income for each fire extinguished. View the data maps to see total fires, total fire trucks, fires extinguished, and unattended fires.

15 Health: Expand health coverage by volunteering ambulances and wellness vans to neighboring cities. The city receiving health coverage gets it for free. The city providing health coverage receives income for the sick and

injured Sims it treats. View the data maps to see total health vehicles, total health vehicles not giving services, total sick and injured, and total sick and injured not treated.

16 Police: Expand police coverage by volunteering police cars, detective cars, crime prevention vans, and police helicopters to neighboring cities. The city receiving police coverage gets it for free. The city providing police coverage receives income for criminals it catches. View the data maps to see total crimes, police on the beat, criminals apprehended, and criminals at large.

17 Gift: Cities can send resources and Simoleons to neighboring cities. To receive resources a city must have a place to store them. Resources are sent by truck, rail, or boat. Resources that can be gifted include alloy, coal, computers, processors, fuel, metal, crude oil, raw ore, plastic, and TVs.

HOTKEYS

Command	Keys
Control camera	W/A/S/D/number keys/arrow keys
Rotate camera	Q/E
Zoom camera	Z/X
Tilt camera up/down	END/HOME
Camera zoom in/out	+/- or PAGE UP/PAGE DOWN
Back out of current menu or tool	ESC (while tool or menu is open)
Options menu	ESC (while no tool or menu is open)
Population Panel	F2
Budget Panel	F3
Approval Rating Information	F4
Open chat/Region Wall	ENTER
Enter/Exit Region View	BACKSPACE
Screen capture	C
Video capture	V
Residential zoning tool	CTRL + R
Commercial zoning tool	CTRL + C
Industrial zoning tool	CTRL + I
Unzoning tool	CTRL + U
Upgrade road tool	R (Only works with Road Tool menu open
Bulldoze tool	B
Leaderboards	L
Achievements	;
CityLog	'

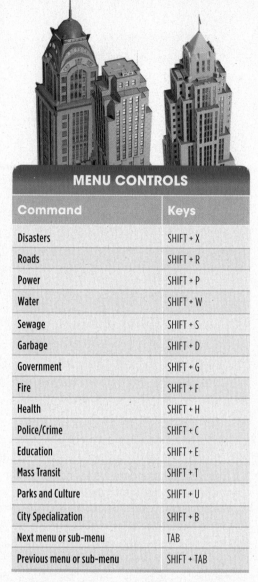

MENU CONTROLS

Command	Keys
Disasters	SHIFT + X
Roads	SHIFT + R
Power	SHIFT + P
Water	SHIFT + W
Sewage	SHIFT + S
Garbage	SHIFT + D
Government	SHIFT + G
Fire	SHIFT + F
Health	SHIFT + H
Police/Crime	SHIFT + C
Education	SHIFT + E
Mass Transit	SHIFT + T
Parks and Culture	SHIFT + U
City Specialization	SHIFT + B
Next menu or sub-menu	TAB
Previous menu or sub-menu	SHIFT + TAB

SANDBOX MODE

Command	Keys
Sandbox ModeToggle Fire On/Off Toggle Crime On/Off	ALT + F ALT + C
Toggle Health Issues On/Off	ALT + M
Toggle Air Pollution On/Off	ALT + A
Toggle Ground Pollution On/Off	ALT + P
Toggle Homeless Sims On/ Off	ALT + H
Add $100,000 to City Budget	ALT + W
Toggle Sewage On/Off	ALT + S

TIME CONTROLS

Command	Keys
Pause	~
Turtle	1
Llama	2
Cheetah	3

RESOURCE MAPS

Command	Keys
Water map	4
Coal map	5
Ore map	6
Oil map	7

DATA MAP CONTROLS

Command	Keys
Population	F5
Happiness	F6
Land Value	F7
Trade	F8
Building Density	F9
Residential System	F10
Commercial System	F11
Industrial System	F12
Tab through associated data maps (when a menu is open)	/

SimCity Terminology

→ **Approval Rating:** This communicates how happy your Sims are with how you're running the city.

→ **Building:** This describes anything you can place (or "plop"), which includes buildings, modules, and things like Water Towers. It does not include zones, roads, or things that are painted onto the terrain.

→ **Challenge:** This is a general term for the weekly/global challenges offered by the game.

→ **City Site:** This is a selectable area of a region in which a player can choose to build a city, before a city is built. Once a city site is claimed, it is simply referred to as a city.

→ **City Specialty:** This describes the way in which a city specializes, whether using city specialization (coal, tourism, ore) or a department of the government (education).

→ **Clean Industry:** Refers to tech level 2 industrial (I) buildings.

→ **Dirty Industry:** Refers to tech level 1 industrial (I) buildings.

→ **Edit Mode:** The mode in which you edit a building to add/remove modules.

→ **Factory:** This is what develops in industrial (I) zones, regardless of wealth level.

→ **Global Market:** Resources can be imported and exported through a Trade Depot or Trade Port. Resources are bought and sold at the current market rate as determined by real-time supply and demand.

→ **Great Works:** This is the term for the multi-city projects, including the Arcology, International Airport, Solar Farm, and Space Center.

→ **Great Works Site:** The area in a region in which you can build Great Works.

→ **High Tech Industry:** Refers to tech level 3 industrial (I) buildings.

→ **Highway:** The main regional thoroughfare that connects neighboring cities within a region.

→ **House:** This is what develops in residential (R) zones.

→ **Mission:** This is an optional objective, requiring you to complete a specific task as mayor.

→ **Module:** This is an additional structure/feature that can be added to a building to increase efficiency/output.

→ **Natural Resources:** A resource that is extracted from the map, such as raw ore, crude oil, or coal.

→ **Power:** The electricity or energy required to power buildings.

→ **RCI:** Short for Residential, Commercial, and Industrial zones.

→ **Region:** The area that contains your city, neighboring cities, and Great Works sites, connected by the regional highway.

→ **Resource:** Refers to any product that can be traded or sold on the global market. Resources include alloy, coal, computers, processors, fuel, metal, crude oil, raw ore, plastic, and TVs.

→ **Sims:** These are the citizens inhabiting each city in every region.

→ **Simoleon:** The global currency of SimWorld, it is represented in the game with the Ş symbol.

→ **Shop:** This is what develops in commercial (C) zones, whether they are shops, offices, big box stores, or gas stations.

→ **Upgrade:** The process used to change HQs (including Town/City Hall) or roads/bridges from one model to an improved version.

Getting Started Scenario: Summer Shoals

Can you save Summer Shoals? Learn the basics of city management by completing this step-by-step tutorial.

Jumping into the seat of a small town mayor is no easy task...especially when your predecessor didn't know what they were doing. Such is the situation in Summer Shoals, a quaint seaside community with big problems. The previous mayor has been run out of town and you've been brought in to clean up the mess.

When you first start *SimCity*, you're prompted to play through this short scenario, which takes you through a step-by-step process of getting Summer Shoals on the right track. In addition to familiarizing you with the basic controls, the tutorial also covers the fundamentals of establishing and maintaining a functional city. Here you'll learn the importance of connecting your city to the region's highway as well as providing vital utilities and city services. The scenario also touches on the interaction between neighboring cities in the region, giving you a glimpse at the nearby city of Lucky Shores. Overall, spending some time in Summer Shoals is a great idea whether you're a *SimCity* veteran or a rookie. The lessons learned here will carry over to your own cities, serving as a cautionary tale of what happens when a mayor neglects his or her duties.

Building Your First City

Saving Summer Shoals is just the first step in your *SimCity* adventure.

Once you've completed the tutorial you're free to start your very own city. But don't move too quickly. Rescuing an existing city like Summer Shoals is one thing—starting a city from scratch is an entirely different challenge with numerous (and potentially costly) pitfalls. If you don't approach your new city with proper planning and financial discipline, you might find yourself looking for a new line of work, along with Summer Shoals' previous mayor.

Create Game

If you prefer to join an existing game you'll enter a region already occupied by other players and cities.

Immediately following the tutorial you're returned to the game's main menu—choose the Play option. Now you can choose between joining an existing game or creating a new game of your own. If you choose to join a game, you're prompted to select a region. When joining a game, the regions available are already populated by other players. In fact, there could be up to a dozen other players playing in a single region. The prospect of playing with friends or strangers may be extremely compelling. But if you're new to *SimCity* it's recommended to create a new game of your own, where you can control access to the region. This is also the best way to learn the principles of creating a self-sufficient city without worrying about potential pollution and crime problems encroaching from other cities in the region.

Select Region

Some regions are huge, others are small. Try to find a region with plenty of open, flat space. Building in hilly or mountainous areas can be tricky.

Once you've chosen to create a game, the next step is to select a region. There are several different regions to choose from, each with its own distinct geographical features ranging from mountains, to rivers, to plains, to coastlines. The regions also differ in size, determining how many cities and Great Works it can support. Small regions can only support three cities and one of the Great Works, while large regions can support up to sixteen cities and four Great Works. Great Works are large structures, like the International Airport, which benefit all cities in a region. But as the name suggests, constructing Great Works is a large undertaking often requiring multiple cities to pool their money and resources. When starting out, don't worry too much about Great Works. Instead, pay more attention to the topography of the region. For beginners, regions with relatively flat and level terrain are ideal—constructing cities in hilly or mountainous regions is much more challenging.

In addition to topography, pay attention to the layout of the highway and railway systems—the highway appears as a yellow line while rails appear as white. All cities have access to a highway connection, but not all have railway access. Rail access is extremely important if you're hoping to ship large amounts of freight or raw materials—these resources can be sent to neighboring cities or sold on the global market. Or, if you're hoping to draw tourists into your city, trains are the perfect way to transport large numbers of visitors into your glitzy casino and commercial districts. Waterways, like rivers, are another way to transport a high volume of visitors and resources in and out of your city. So even at this early stage, it's important to sketch out the flow of goods and Sims throughout the region.

Set Up Region

Check the Private Region box if you want to control who can play in your region. Then send invites to friends, asking them to join your game—or send no invites to have the region all to yourself.

Now that you've selected a region that fits your grand vision, take a moment to give it a name and adjust a couple of settings. While the region already has a default name, you can give it a more personalized touch by naming it anything you like. However, when naming a region, remember that its name can be seen by other players. Avoid any names that may be embarrassing or reveal personal information.

Next, it's time to determine the region's privacy setting. By default, all regions are public, allowing other players to join your game by taking ownership of any unclaimed cities. Cooperating with friends and strangers alike to create a mutually beneficial region is extremely rewarding. However, if you prefer to have complete control of your region, check the Private Region box. When setting a region to private, you must send invites to players before they can claim a city in the region. This gives you much more control over who you are playing the game with. It also gives you the option to lock out all other players, simply by never sending any invites. Once an invited player has claimed a city in a private region, they can then send out invites to anyone.

Finally, choose whether you want to play in Sandbox Mode. In Sandbox Mode, you have access to all buildings as well as several cheats, giving you a distinct advantage. Random disasters are also turned off, ensuring your region never faces an existential calamity. However, when choosing Sandbox Mode, any gameplay conducted in the region is not eligible for achievements, challenges, or leaderboards. So if you only want to learn and experiment with the game, Sandbox Mode is good idea. But if you're more interested in the bragging rights associated with earning achievements, completing challenges, and climbing the leaderboards, steer clear of Sandbox Mode.

Claim City

Browse the available city sites in the region to find one that has the resources you're looking for. At the very least, make sure a city site has plenty of water.

You're almost ready to start building your first city! Once you've selected and set up the region, it's time to claim the plot of land where you'll build your city—this is called a city site. Each region has multiple city sites to choose from, so take your time browsing the options. Remember, pay close attention to topography—selecting a flat and even city site is recommended for beginners. In addition to the city site's topography, take note of its natural resources. Hover the mouse over each city site to bring up a small box revealing more information about each location. At the center of the box are five colorful meter-like icons representing the site's five natural resources: coal, raw ore, crude oil, water, and wind.

Coal, ore, and oil are all associated with the city specialization city specializations. By constructing mines and wells you can draw these resources from the ground and sell them for a big profit—coal and oil can also be used to fuel power plants. Or, you can take it a step further and refine coal, ore, and oil into metal, alloy, and fuel for even greater financial gain. But the buildings associated with these heavy industries are big polluters, decreasing land value and spreading sickness. So if you're looking at a city site rich with any of these resources, consider the benefits and drawbacks of building mines, wells, and their supporting infrastructure.

Of all the five resources, water is the most vital—Sims need water to survive and most buildings require water to function. Water is also essential for constructing a sewage system, a crucial element of any city's sanitation system. While glancing at the various city sites, make sure you find one that has plenty of water, as indicated by a full, green meter. By tapping into underground aquifers, you can supply your entire city with plenty of water. Surplus water can also be sold to neighboring cities in the region, netting your city a modest profit.

CLAIM CITY (continued)

Wind is less vital than water, but it still plays a significant role, particularly if you're interested in creating a green, environmentally friendly city. By constructing a Wind Power Plant, you can harness a city site's wind to generate power. Generally city sites in hilly and mountainous regions have the heaviest winds—the faster the wind blows, the faster the wind turbines turn, generating more electricity. However, even when placed in areas with moderate winds, a Wind Power Plant can still generate enough electricity to power a small city.

Once you've surveyed a city site's natural resources, look on the left side of the information box to determine whether the site has rail and waterway access. Here you'll find two icons: the railroad track icon represents rail access and the ship icon represents waterway access. If either of these icons are grayed out, access is not available. Rail and waterway access is important if you want to ship large amounts of cargo or if you want to bring in tons of tourists. Most city sites have rail access, but naturally only cities adjacent to rivers and coastlines have waterway access.

Now you have enough information to claim your first city. As you can see, there are many factors to consider before choosing a city site. But most importantly, stay focused on the city you want to create and don't let the terrain or natural resources compromise your vision. Harvesting a city site's natural resources can certainly be tempting, especially if your goal is making piles of money. However, there is no right or wrong way to play *SimCity*. So if you want to build a quaint low density burg atop a vast oil reservoir, go for it! Likewise, if you want to create city filled with factories, you can do that too. The future of your city is entirely up to you, so tap into your creative side and see where imagination takes you.

STARTING A NEW CITY:
10 STEPS TO SUCCESS

It's finally time to start building your city!

What kind of city will you make? Will you rely on green technologies to create a city free of pollution and waste? Will you create a small, self-contained community where most residents can walk to work? Or will you build a sprawling metropolis filled with skyscrapers and overlapping mass transit networks? These are just some of the questions you should ask yourself before you lay the groundwork of your city. Regardless of what kind of city you want to make, all cities share the same basic infrastructure. In this section we take a look at ten steps you need to follow to get your city functioning. Once you get your city humming along, you can then focus on carrying out your grand vision. So what are you waiting for? Get to work, Mayor!

1 SURVEY AND PLANNING

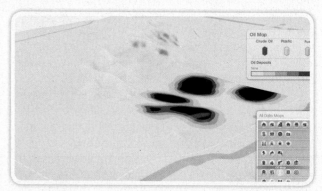

Use the data maps to locate a city site's resources. It looks like this city has a few oil reservoirs. How do you feel about drilling for oil?

In *SimCity*, the importance of planning cannot be overstated. Unlike previous installments, there is no going back once you've made a decision. The game is continually saved

2 CONNECT TO HIGHWAY

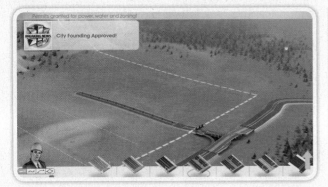

Use a Medium Density Avenue to connect to the regional highway. Once connected to the highway you can begin zoning as well as build vital utilities for your city.

Although you've claimed a city, the region does not recognize it until it's been connected to the regional highway. In fact, you can't build or zone anything until a highway connection has been established. Most cities have one, and only one, highway connection. The highway is the main thoroughfare in the region, connecting neighboring cities to each other. This is how construction trucks, moving vans, and even tourists will enter your city. Click on the Roads menu to choose from a variety of different roads. As the main entrance into your city, the highway connection will incur heavy traffic—the narrow streets offered here won't cut it. Choose the Medium Density Avenue to accommodate the numerous cars and trucks traveling in and out of your city. Later on, if congestion becomes a problem,

the Medium Density Avenue can be upgraded to handle more traffic. Both streets and avenues can be upgraded and downgraded, giving you better control over traffic and density. However, due to size differences, a street cannot be upgraded to an avenue and an avenue can't be downgraded to a street.

Constructing a road is as simple as drawing a line with your mouse. But pay close attention to the length of your avenue when connecting it to the highway—avenues are very expensive to construct and you don't want to blow all your money on this first step. When you're ready to draw your avenue, place your mouse over a starting location, then hold down the left mouse button. Drag the mouse in the direction of the highway connection, but don't release the mouse button just yet. Notice how the price of the avenue increases as you drag the mouse toward the highway connection—the longer the road, the higher the cost. Are you satisfied with the length/cost of the avenue? If not, while still holding down the left mouse button, click the right mouse button to cancel the avenue and try again—canceling is much cheaper than placing an unwanted road and bulldozing it. If you want to construct straight roads, hold down the SHIFT key while drawing your avenue. There are also a few line tools you can use to help construct curvy roads. Once you're satisfied by the length, shape, and cost of your avenue, release the left mouse button while hovering over the highway connection. At this point your city is connected to the region. But don't expect to see any traffic until you start zoning.

to the cloud—there are no saved games you can revert back to if you make a mistake. Therefore, every decision you make may have far-reaching consequences. To avoid blundering along, pause the game and take the first few minutes to familiarize yourself with the city site. Take note of the highway connection, as this is the area where your city will most likely start out. If available, also pay attention to rail and waterway access, as these transportation hubs are essential for trade and tourism.

Utilizing the data maps, quickly survey the city site's natural resources—click on the Data Maps button in the bottom right corner of the screen. The data maps give you access to a wide range of information pertaining to your city. Hover the mouse over the various icons in the Data Map window to view the names of the available maps. Start by clicking on the water data map. This shows the city's water table, revealing subterranean aquifers appearing as blue pools—the darker the blue, the more water available.

If water is scarce, you may need to construct a special Low Density Dirt Road to the nearest aquifer in order to build a Water Tower. Next, click on the coal, ore, and oil data maps to reveal the deposits of these natural resources. Knowing exactly where these resources are located can greatly impact the structure of your city. For instance, if you want to eventually mine ore, you'll want to avoid building directly over ore deposits. And since mines and wells lower land value and increase pollution, you'll want to place these heavy industries far from your residential areas.

After spending a few minutes surveying the city site and studying the data maps, you should have a general idea of how you want to proceed. But remember, you only have limited financial resources to begin with. It's important to start small and gradually work your way to greatness. The city you start with is rarely the city you end up with—keep that in mind as you begin building.

3 ROAD CONSTRUCTION

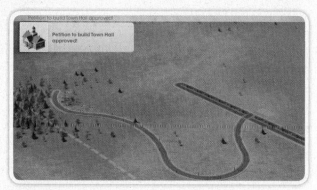

Constructing roads can be expensive, so don't let costs get out of hand. Only build the roads you need to construct vital utilities and a few zones.

As you can see, the mechanics of road construction is fairly simple. But laying out a congestion-free network of roads throughout your city is an ongoing challenge. In addition to serving as a means of transportation, beneath the surface, your road network is also responsible for carrying water, power, and sewage. Don't get ahead of yourself. For the time being, figure out what kind of roads you'll need and where they need to go. For example, where are you going to get water? Where is your power plant going to be located? Do you need any roads to reach distant coal, ore, and oil deposits? There's a lot to figure out, and you don't have a ton of money. Treat the Medium Density Avenue as your city's main thoroughfare, and then use smaller streets to branch off the avenue in different directions. Start with Low Density Streets to save money. You can even construct cheaper Low Density Dirt Roads if forced to reach distant aquifers for your Water Tower or high wind areas for your Wind Power Plant. Only construct roads on an as-needed basis. While it's important to keep a general plan in the back of your mind, there's no need to lay out your entire road network now. A road is only necessary if you're going to build something next to it.

4 WIND DIRECTION/POWER PLANT

Wind Power Plants are most effective in areas with high wind speeds. Before plopping it, move it around the city site to find the optimal location.

Although you have no buildings yet, there's a huge benefit to determining the direction of prevailing winds. Why is wind so important? All air pollution carries with the wind, across the city, and even across the region. Therefore it's important to know which direction the wind is blowing before you start zoning. After all, you don't want to build a residential neighborhood downwind from a heavy polluting industrial district, right? Pollution leads to sickness and angry Sims, a negative for any mayor. Open the Wind data map to see the direction the wind is blowing—the blue arrows represent wind blowing across your city site. Consider building a Wind Power Plant to generate cheap and clean power for your city.

Before placing a Wind Power Plant, available from the Power menu, drag it across multiple areas to see what kind of wind speed is generated at each location. Usually wind speed is relatively constant across flat, low lying terrain. But wind speeds pick up considerably on hills, mountains, and other high elevation areas. The stronger the wind is blowing, the more efficient your Wind Power Plant will be, generating more electricity per turbine. Figure out where you want to build your Wind Power Plant and plop it next to an existing road—if necessary, build a Low Density Dirt Road to reach a distant, but optimal location. Once the Power Plant is placed, the turbine will rotate, automatically facing incoming wind. Now that you know the wind direction and are producing power, you can better plan out the zoning of your city, ensuring your polluting industries are placed in areas where they won't negatively impact your residential and commercial zones. While the Power menu is open you can now see power flowing along your city's streets, appearing as yellow lines.

5 RCI ZONING

Keep your polluting industrial zones downwind from your residential and commercial zones. Air pollution spreads germs that can make Sims sick.

If you want Sims and businesses to move into your city, you need to set aside areas for them to begin the construction of houses, shops, and factories. This is accomplished through zoning. In the Zone menu there are three different zone types: residential, commercial, and industrial. You can only zone areas adjacent to existing roads. Simply select one of the zoning options and draw a zone along the side of a road. Before long Sims will appear in these zones and start constructing buildings. Once built and occupied, these buildings then begin generating revenue in the form of taxes, the lifeblood of your city's budget.

The density of a zone is directly governed by the density of the adjacent road. For example, if creating a residential zone next to a Low Density Street, only low density, single family homes will appear in that zone. If you want to create higher density housing, such as tenements or apartments, you'll need to upgrade the adjacent road to accommodate the heavier traffic associated with higher density housing. You can also dezone an area, preventing the construction of new buildings or the upgrade of existing buildings. Dezoning is a good way to freeze the density of an area regardless of what kind of road is adjacent to the zone.

So what is the relationship between these three zones? Your Sims have two basic needs: money and happiness. Sims live in residential zones and get money by working at jobs provided largely by factories in industrial zones. But Sims can also find work in the shops of commercial zones as well as at buildings, such as Coal Mines, Trade Depots, Grade Schools, and Hospitals. Once Sims have a way to earn money, they seek out happiness by shopping in commercial zones. There are many other factors that also affect happiness, but as long as Sims have a way to earn money and a place to spend it, you'll be on the right track when it comes to zoning.

Before zoning in your new city, plan out where you want certain structures to appear. Now that you know which way the wind is blowing, create industrial zones on the edge of your city, downwind from your other zones. This causes most of the air pollution to blow away from your city, and into the region—at least it's not your problem, right? Traditionally, commercial zones serve as a good buffer between residential and industrial areas. However, if pollution gets out of hand, even commercial buildings will experience difficulties when placed directly across the street from dirty factories. Consider building an isolated industrial district, using open space or parks to serve as a buffer. Consider placing commercial zones along your Medium Density Avenue while zoning residential along Low Density Streets branching off of the central avenue. As a basic rule of thumb, create two residential zones for each commercial and industrial zone. This 2:1:1 ratio is the best way to create a self-sufficient city with a stable tax base.

6 WATER

A single Water Tower is enough to quench the thirst of a small city. But as the city grows, you'll need to place more Water Towers or a Water Pumping Station to keep pace with increased demand.

As construction is underway within the newly created residential, commercial, and industrial zones, turn your attention to supplying the city with water, otherwise you'll have some thirsty Sims to contend with. If you haven't already, open the water data map to find a nearby aquifer with plenty of water—look for an area that is dark blue. Construct a small road out to the aquifer and construct a Water Tower, available from the Water menu. When you select the Water Tower, the water data map is automatically activated, helping you place the structure in an optimal location. Before placing the Water Tower, move it over different areas of land and notice how the water output changes. When placed over a white or light blue area, the Water Tower only produces a small amount of water. But when placed over a bright or dark blue area, water production increases significantly. If you place a Water Tower next to a river, it will have an endless supply of water. So find the perfect spot for your Water Tower, ensuring it's drawing an optimal amount from the aquifer. Once placed, the Water Tower immediately begins pumping water. While the Water menu is open, you can see the water flowing from the Water Tower and through your road network. As water coverage spreads, every building is automatically connected and begins receiving water. No more thirsty Sims!

> ☑ **TIP**
>
> Like power, any excess water produced can be bought by neighboring cities in the region. A neighboring city must first choose to buy your water to begin the transaction.

7 SEWAGE

Build a Sewage Outflow Pipe on the outskirts of your city, far away from your population and Water Tower.

Immediately after supplying the city with water, your Sims begin creating sewage. Left unattended, sewage builds up in the pipes and can eventually leach to the surface, creating nasty ground pollution—you don't want this to happen. Ground pollution isn't just disgusting, but it can also spread germs, making your Sims sick. As expected, ground pollution also lowers land value.

To avoid a public health crisis you need to act quickly to deal with the looming sewage problem. The cheapest and easiest solution is building a Sewage Outflow Pipe, available from the Sewage menu. But you need to be very careful of where you place this building. The Sewage Outflow Pipe pumps raw, untreated sewage out of the sewer system and dumps it onto an open piece of land, creating heavy ground pollution. Obviously, you don't want this anywhere near your residential or commercial zones. You also want to keep the Sewage Outflow Pipe far away from your Water Tower. Ground pollution is absorbed through the soil and can end up contaminating your water supply. If you're not careful, you may inadvertently pump contaminated water throughout your city leading to a massive germ outbreak, generating sickness on a grand scale. So find a remote area you're not planning to use for anything else and place your Sewage Outflow Pipe there.

8 TOWN HALL

Leave plenty of open space around your Town Hall. The blue dots indicate areas where department modules can be constructed in the future.

Soon after connecting your city to the regional highway and establishing power and water service, the Town Hall is available for construction from the Government menu. The Town Hall is the seat of local government, allowing you to adjust the city-wide tax rate while unlocking the Health, Fire, and Police menus. Constructing the Town Hall also gives Sims a place to gather and voice their concerns. If things aren't running smoothly, large groups of Sims will gather outside the Town Hall and protest, demanding action from their mayor.

As your city grows, the Town Hall can be upgraded at specific population thresholds. With each upgrade, a new department can be constructed, allowing access to advanced buildings. For example, you'll need a Department of Transportation before you can construct a Bus Terminal, or a Department of Education before you can build a High School. However, if these departments already exist in another city in the region, you don't need to build them at all. That's because each department is shared throughout the region, encouraging communication and cooperation with your neighbors. Before constructing a department, make sure one of that kind doesn't already exist in the region, otherwise you'll just be wasting money and valuable space.

Before placing your Town Hall, make sure you give it plenty of room for expansion. The additional department modules can eat up quite a bit of space. Consider creating a large town square-like block and place your Town Hall at the center, giving it plenty of growing room on all sides. The Town Hall, along with all government buildings, increases land value. This is beneficial to nearby residential and commercial zones, potentially leading to the construction of buildings that cater to medium and high wealth Sims.

ⓘ NOTE

You can adjust the city-wide tax rate by accessing the Budget panel. When the Town Hall is upgraded to a City Hall, you can adjust the individual tax rates for each zone, fine-tuning the rates for residential, commercial, and industrial. Building a Department of Finance gives you even more control, allowing you to tax each zone based on low, medium, and high wealth.

Like any structure, the Sewage Outflow Pipe must be placed adjacent to a road, but don't break the bank. Build a cheap Low Density Street to the desired location and build the Sewage Outflow Pipe. While the Sewage menu is open, you can now see sewage (brown blobs) flowing through the road network in the direction of the Sewage Outflow Pipe where it is unceremoniously dumped onto the land. Out of sight, out of mind.

✓ TIP

If you don't want to deal with the pollution caused by a Sewage Outflow Pipe, you can buy sewage services from a neighboring city in the region.

9   WASTE DISPOSAL

If no garbage trucks are volunteered by a neighboring city, building a Garbage Dump is the only way to empty the garbage cans lining your city streets. The facility can be expanded with modules to accommodate your growing city.

As your city slowly hums to life, each building outputs a steady flow of garbage. Like sewage, garbage accumulates over time and will eventually become ground pollution. Ground pollution caused by garbage spreads germs and can lead to widespread sickness. Furthermore, the accumulation of garbage in your city streets reduces land value and significantly increases the risk of fires.

It's important to deal with the garbage problem sooner rather than later. Open the Waste Disposal menu and select the Garbage Dump. Since you're already polluting an area with sewage, place the Garbage Dump along the same road as your Sewage Outflow Pipe—it's best to keep your ground pollution consolidated in one smelly area. The Garbage Dump automatically dispatches garbage trucks on a daily basis to collect garbage. When a garbage truck is full, it returns to the Garbage Dump and deposits the collected garbage, creating ground pollution. But as long as

the Garbage Dump is far away from your water supply and populated areas, there are no immediate negative impacts.

While the Waste Disposal menu is open, study the info tab on the right side of the screen to monitor the number of garbage cans collected each day out of the total number of garbage cans in the city—as long as this number is green, you're doing okay. At the beginning of the day, this number is red, indicating uncollected cans. Throughout the day, the color of the number changes, from red to yellow then from yellow to green, as more and more cans are collected. If the number is still yellow or red by the end of the day, you need more garbage trucks. Add a Garbage Truck Garage module to the Garbage Dump. This increases the number of garbage trucks dispatched every day, helping ensure each garbage can in the city is collected. As your city grows, so will the number of garbage cans. Periodically revisit the Waste Disposal menu to check up on garbage collection.

☑ TIP

If a neighboring city in the region volunteers its garbage trucks to pick up your city's garbage, you may not even need a Garbage Dump of your own. But even if such an arrangement is made, continually monitor the Waste Disposal menu to make sure the visiting garbage trucks are getting the job done. If not, you may need to augment services with a Garbage Dump and garbage trucks of your own.

10 CITY SERVICES

Providing health, fire, and police service is expensive, but don't wait too long. The rise of health and crime concerns are somewhat predictable, but there's no telling when your city will experience its first fire.

With a functioning Town Hall in place, you can now provide city services, including health, fire, and police. However, don't rush into providing these services immediately, as they are extremely costly and could potentially cripple your fledgling city's fragile budget. Furthermore, these services aren't crucial to your city's growth and development. It's best to spend the first few days expanding your tax base by zoning. The costs associated with providing power, water, sewage, and waste disposal are already a massive burden on your small city—open the Budget panel to see the precise cost. It's important to grow your residential, commercial, and industrial zones to offset for these costs. The more homes, businesses, and factories in your city, the more the city collects in taxes.

Before you construct any health, fire, or police buildings, make sure you can afford them. These city services have a high hourly operational cost. For example, opening a basic Clinic, Fire Station, or Police Station will each cost your city §400 per hour, or §1,200 per hour for all three. Can you afford that? There's an easy way to find out. Simply study your city's revenue in the Budget panel. This number shows how much money the city is generating per hour. If the number is green, and you're generating more than §400 per hour, you can afford one of these buildings. If your city is generating more than §1,200 per hour, you can afford one of each, instantly giving your city comprehensive health, fire, and police coverage.

Just because you can afford them, it doesn't mean you need to provide city services right away. Instead, these services are best constructed on an as-needed basis, otherwise you'll have a bunch of doctors, firemen, and policemen on the city payroll with nothing to do. Chances are Sims will begin complaining about lack of health coverage before anything else. When these issues arise, plop a Clinic to treat the sick and injured. It's difficult to predict when your city will experience its first fire, but it's better to be safe than sorry. When you can afford it, construct a Fire Station. Unless you've constructed a Gambling Hall, the rise of crime in your city is very gradual. But once a criminal has moved into your city and has committed the first petty crime, it's time to build a Police Station. Criminals are emboldened when they get away with committing a crime, so it's best to address this problem before it gets out of hand—you can see the number of crimes committed and criminals at large in the Police menu's info tab.

✓ TIP

Like garbage trucks, your ambulances, fire trucks, and police cars can be volunteered to other cities in the region. When volunteering these vehicles, your city does not lose any coverage—technically, the same vehicle can respond to emergencies in both cities simultaneously, so there's no down side to volunteering emergency vehicles to neighboring cities. It's a great way to build relationships and foster a greater sense of regional cooperation.

CHAT WITH THE DEVELOPERS

Massive Multi-City Scale

KIP KATSARELIS, LEAD PRODUCER

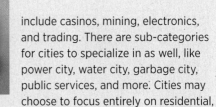

Hello everyone, I'm Kip Katsarelis, Lead Producer on *SimCity*. I'd like to let you know about multi-city play and why this feature takes city building to all new heights. Cities in the real world work together; larger cities support smaller surrounding cities by providing jobs, fire services, police services, education, and more. Cities everywhere in the world behave like this and we wanted to bring this experience into the new *SimCity*.

LAYING THE FOUNDATION

To fully understand the power of multi-city play, you must first understand the possibilities of what you can create in a single city. There is no single path for a given city—no rail or guide to follow. There are a number of factors and choices available to players as they set out to create their cities. Let's start with the choice on where to build your city. You'll have several Region Map options to choose from. Some may only have two city slots available to them and some can have as many as sixteen, and everything in between. The city location you choose can have a number of terrain formations and resources available to choose from. There are mountainous city locations rich with resources, like coal, ore, and oil. There are ones filled with water or wind. Others have many access points like rivers, bays, rails that run through, or large highways that connect them to the region. The conditions in each starting location will heavily influence the shape of your city, by supporting some industries to thrive and setting others to be less successful. We wanted to make sure there were plenty of options and a broad landscape for fans to be inspired by and create.

In this *SimCity* we've introduced city specializations into the game, which take advantage of the natural resources and landscape of the region. These city specializations

include casinos, mining, electronics, and trading. There are sub-categories for cities to specialize in as well, like power city, water city, garbage city, public services, and more. Cities may choose to focus entirely on residential, commercial businesses, or industrial. Within in each of the RCI types, each have their own wealth or tech types, which offers more directions to push your cities. When you start to think about all of these possibilities, plus all of the combinations, you start to realize the scope of gameplay a single city has to offer. I find new city combinations every day; the depth of the game continues to blow my mind.

CITY SYNERGY

Now that you have an idea of what a single city has to offer, let's talk about how these cities can work together and how these city specializations rely on one another to be successful. We had a few key design goals in mind when we set out to work on the multi-city play. We wanted to really push the amount of simulation that carries over across cities to epic proportions. The key goal is to give players control over what is shared, and making sure the experience holds up if it's one player playing multiple cities or multiple people playing multiple cities.

With the core RCI we share workers, jobs, shoppers, orders, freight, and students. These are "traded" automatically to take away some of the micromanagement. Workers will look within your city for jobs. If you have an excess of workers, these become unemployed Sims. If you are connected to a city that has excess jobs, then unemployed Sims from one city will commute to the neighboring city. The city with jobs receiving the workers will satisfy the needs of their shops and industries. The city with the residents will make its population happy, because they have money to pay their rent. It's a win-win. Workers will commute by car, but you can also set up bus routes, train connections, and ferry connections between cities. It's important that you are connected by road, rail, or water to trade with a neighboring city.

All of the core systems are shared, including fire service, crime, police coverage, medical coverage, garbage/recycling, classrooms, all public transportation, air pollution, water, power, sewage, and sewage treatment. Players have more direct control over where they send their services. We designed this system from the point of view of the player who is investing in a particular type of city. For example, if one player decides to build Fire Stations to protect not only that city, but the city's neighbors as well, the player should have the right to decide where to send the coverage. In the case of fire, a player can assign individual fire trucks and helicopters to serve specific cities. Just because a player assigns a vehicle to serve another city doesn't mean the player loses coverage in his or her own. This is asynchronous gameplay, so one fire engine can service both cities. The player receiving coverage will see fire engines come from a neighbor whenever there is a fire in the city. The player giving the coverage will earn money for each fire the fire engine puts out. Systems that have capacity, like a police station, will bring criminals back to house them in jail cells. If those jail cells are full, the criminals will be released into your city, which is an unexpected way to share criminals. The simulation extends beyond your city borders. Are you starting to get it?

BUILDING AND SHARING

Let me continue with how resource sharing works. Cities can gift one another coal, ore, oil, alloy, metal, fuel, plastics, processors, TVs, and Simoleons! This ability for cities to create a service and provide a role in the greater region adds a whole new micro-strategy to *SimCity*. To gift resources to another city you must have the resource in your city to gift. In the case of coal, this could be in your coal mine storage lot or in a Trade Depot storage lot. Resources and materials can be sent by truck, rail, or boat. The more options both cities have, the greater the throughput. Resources do take time to send and players can queue up orders, which are sent over

> The depth and scale of what we've delivered for this *SimCity* will amaze you. It amazes me! To think that all of the simulation you see inside your city works beyond the boundaries of your city, that your city and your actions influence and affect your neighbors. There are goals larger than simply building a single city and there are endless ways to build a city.

time. Players will be able to create port cities, establishing supply chains across the region, adding a completely new dimension to *SimCity*.

In addition to regional trading, we also wanted to give players new ways to play, and reasons why to create and push cities into different directions. Players will be presented with a variety of goals, which they can choose to opt into or not. These goals will require an entire region of cities to work together to complete. These include Global Challenges, like the "Lockdown!" challenge, where they to need arrest the most criminals possible in a specific amount of time. The top 10% of regions who successfully complete the challenge will earn an achievement. Leaderboards are another big motivator for me right now when I play the game. Each city specialization has its own leaderboard—the extraction-type leaderboards (coal, ore, and oil) seem to always suck me in. I'm always looking at who in the studio is at the top of the oil leaderboards and try to top them. We also have regional leaderboards for things like Highest Population or Most Simoleons. Here players are ranked on the total region's score and compete against other mayors and regions.

GREAT WORKS AND BEYOND

Great Works are the crowning achievement for any region, a major late-game reward. These are large collaborative civil engineering projects that multiple cities can work together to complete. In turn, they give a benefit to the cities connected to it. These include things like the Solar Farm that produces enough power to sustain a group of cities. It will also create jobs, which gives an economic boost to any city. We've left it wide open, and know players will come up with their own goals for how they want to play.

The depth and scale of what we've delivered for this *SimCity* will amaze you. It amazes me! To think that all of the simulation you see inside your city works beyond the boundaries of your city, that your city and your actions influence and affect your neighbors. There are goals larger than simply building a single city and there are endless ways to build a city. The sandbox just got a little bigger. I hope you enjoyed this deeper dive into multi-city play.

A Tale of Two Cities

Rome wasn't built in a day, and in *SimCity,* no city is built overnight. Instead, cities go through different stages of development, starting out as quaint small towns, and growing into sprawling urban centers packed with skyscrapers. In this section we take a look at the multi-stage development and specialization of two very different cities. As Mayor, it's your decision to choose how your city develops. Will you emphasize education and high tech? Or will your rely on natural resources and city specialization to develop an industrial juggernaut?

Berkeley: High Tech City

Berkeley is located on an relatively flat piece of land, making it easy to develop. However, other than wind and water, the city has no significant natural resources such as raw ore, coal, or crude oil. This city grows utilizing a balanced RCI approach, relying largely on tax revenue to pay for utilities and city services. Emphasizing education, the city builds a Community College, allowing for the growth of clean (tech level 2) industry, supplying the city with jobs. Later, the addition of a University spurs the growth of high tech (tech level 3) industry, offering even more jobs. With the increased tax revenue from more prosperous residential and commercial zones, advanced city services like the Hospital, Large Fire Station, and Police Precinct can be funded. By the final stage, the city can extend its fire, health, and police services to the neighboring city of Pittsburgh. In return, Pittsburgh supplies Berkeley with power.

STARTING CITY

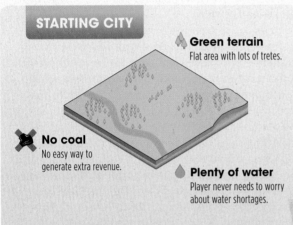

Green terrain
Flat area with lots of tretes.

No coal
No easy way to generate extra revenue.

Plenty of water
Player never needs to worry about water shortages.

STAGE 1

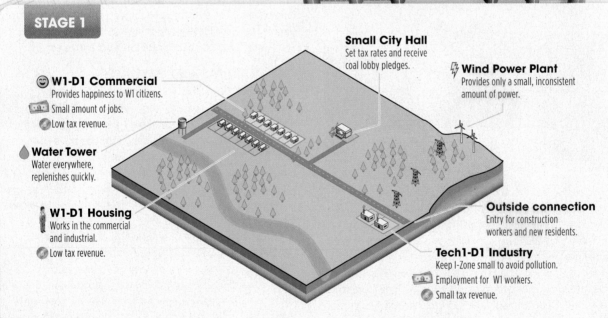

Small City Hall
Set tax rates and receive coal lobby pledges.

Wind Power Plant
Provides only a small, inconsistent amount of power.

W1-D1 Commercial
Provides happiness to W1 citizens.
Small amount of jobs.
Low tax revenue.

Water Tower
Water everywhere, replenishes quickly.

W1-D1 Housing
Works in the commercial and industrial.
Low tax revenue.

Outside connection
Entry for construction workers and new residents.

Tech1-D1 Industry
Keep I-Zone small to avoid pollution.
Employment for W1 workers.
Small tax revenue.

STAGE 2

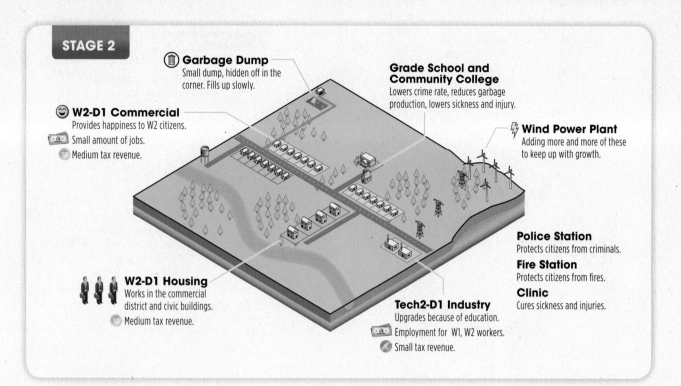

Garbage Dump
Small dump, hidden off in the corner. Fills up slowly.

W2-D1 Commercial
Provides happiness to W2 citizens.
Small amount of jobs.
Medium tax revenue.

Grade School and Community College
Lowers crime rate, reduces garbage production, lowers sickness and injury.

Wind Power Plant
Adding more and more of these to keep up with growth.

Police Station
Protects citizens from criminals.

Fire Station
Protects citizens from fires.

Clinic
Cures sickness and injuries.

W2-D1 Housing
Works in the commercial district and civic buildings.
Medium tax revenue.

Tech2-D1 Industry
Upgrades because of education.
Employment for W1, W2 workers.
Small tax revenue.

STAGE 3

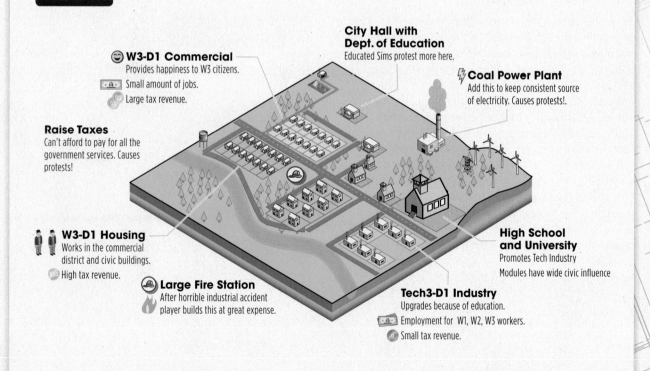

W3-D1 Commercial
Provides happiness to W3 citizens.
Small amount of jobs.
Large tax revenue.

City Hall with Dept. of Education
Educated Sims protest more here.

Coal Power Plant
Add this to keep consistent source of electricity. Causes protests!.

Raise Taxes
Can't afford to pay for all the government services. Causes protests!

W3-D1 Housing
Works in the commercial district and civic buildings.
High tax revenue.

Large Fire Station
After horrible industrial accident player builds this at great expense.

High School and University
Promotes Tech Industry
Modules have wide civic influence

Tech3-D1 Industry
Upgrades because of education.
Employment for W1, W2, W3 workers.
Small tax revenue.

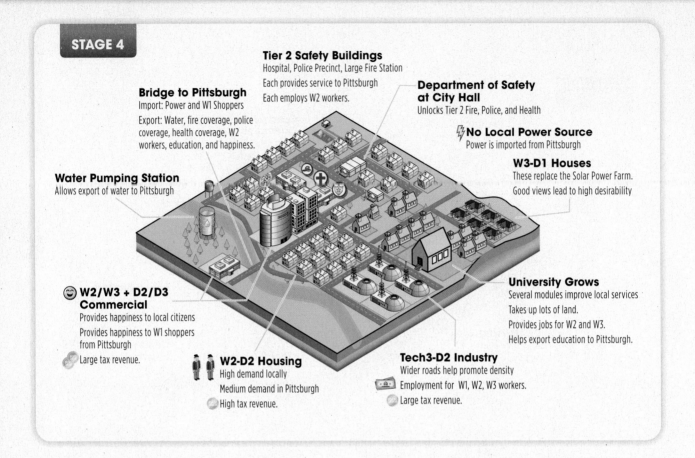

STAGE 4

Bridge to Pittsburgh
Import: Power and W1 Shoppers
Export: Water, fire coverage, police coverage, health coverage, W2 workers, education, and happiness.

Tier 2 Safety Buildings
Hospital, Police Precinct, Large Fire Station
Each provides service to Pittsburgh
Each employs W2 workers.

Department of Safety at City Hall
Unlocks Tier 2 Fire, Police, and Health

No Local Power Source
Power is imported from Pittsburgh

W3-D1 Houses
These replace the Solar Power Farm.
Good views lead to high desirability

Water Pumping Station
Allows export of water to Pittsburgh

W2/W3 + D2/D3 Commercial
Provides happiness to local citizens
Provides happiness to W1 shoppers from Pittsburgh
Large tax revenue.

W2-D2 Housing
High demand locally
Medium demand in Pittsburgh
High tax revenue.

Tech3-D2 Industry
Wider roads help promote density
Employment for W1, W2, W3 workers.
Large tax revenue.

University Grows
Several modules improve local services
Takes up lots of land.
Provides jobs for W2 and W3.
Helps export education to Pittsburgh.

Pittsburgh: Coal City

Pittsburgh is founded on a dry, uneven piece of land, with plenty of coal just beneath the surface. This presents the Mayor with a tempting economic opportunity. By mining coal, the city can provide a ton of low wealth jobs as well as fuel a Coal Power Plant. In addition to coal, the city invests in dirty (tech level 1) industry to supply more low wealth jobs while producing freight for commercial and increased tax revenue for the city. But the heavy emphasis on coal power and dirty industry results in heavy pollution, making it difficult to attract medium and high wealth residential and commercial buildings. By the end, the city generates most of its tax revenue from dirty industry while supplying its neighboring city Berkeley with power and freight. In return, Pittsburgh gets fire, health, and police services from Berkeley—ambulance coverage is essential for treating all those injured Sims working in the factories and the Coal Mine.

STARTING CITY

Rugged terrain
Little room for contiguous zoning

Lots of coal
Dig it up and sell it to maximize income.

Very little water
Player experiences water shortages in the mid to late game.

STAGE 1

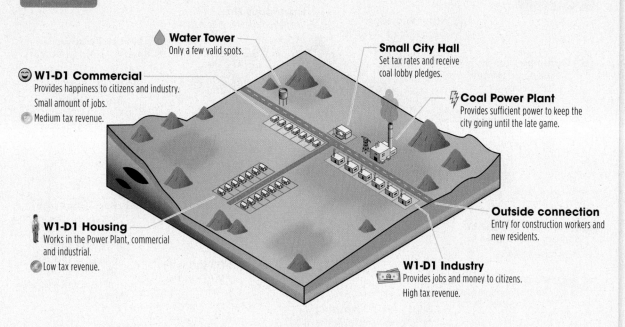

Water Tower
Only a few valid spots.

Small City Hall
Set tax rates and receive
coal lobby pledges.

W1-D1 Commercial
Provides happiness to citizens and industry.
Small amount of jobs.
Medium tax revenue.

Coal Power Plant
Provides sufficient power to keep the
city going until the late game.

W1-D1 Housing
Works in the Power Plant, commercial
and industrial.
Low tax revenue.

Outside connection
Entry for construction workers and
new residents.

W1-D1 Industry
Provides jobs and money to citizens.
High tax revenue.

STAGE 2

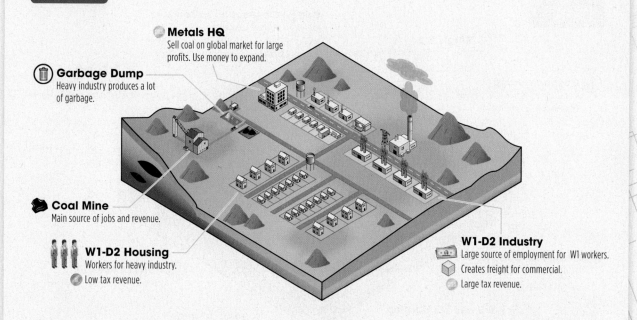

Metals HQ
Sell coal on global market for large
profits. Use money to expand.

Garbage Dump
Heavy industry produces a lot
of garbage.

Coal Mine
Main source of jobs and revenue.

W1-D2 Housing
Workers for heavy industry.
Low tax revenue.

W1-D2 Industry
Large source of employment for W1 workers.
Creates freight for commercial.
Large tax revenue.

STAGE 3

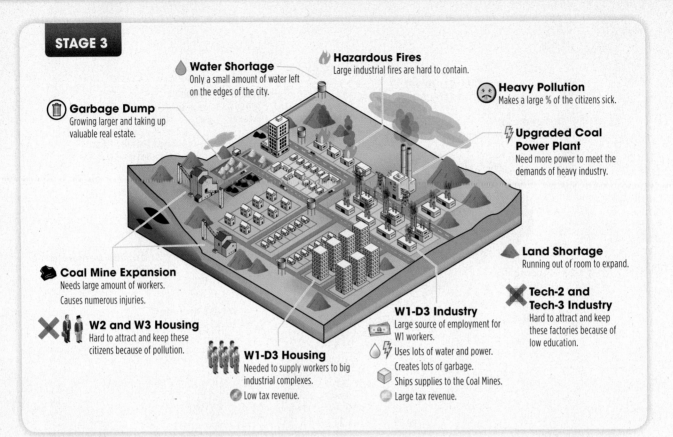

Water Shortage
Only a small amount of water left on the edges of the city.

Hazardous Fires
Large industrial fires are hard to contain.

Heavy Pollution
Makes a large % of the citizens sick.

Garbage Dump
Growing larger and taking up valuable real estate.

Upgraded Coal Power Plant
Need more power to meet the demands of heavy industry.

Coal Mine Expansion
Needs large amount of workers.
Causes numerous injuries.

Land Shortage
Running out of room to expand.

W2 and W3 Housing
Hard to attract and keep these citizens because of pollution.

Tech-2 and Tech-3 Industry
Hard to attract and keep these factories because of low education.

W1-D3 Housing
Needed to supply workers to big industrial complexes.
Low tax revenue.

W1-D3 Industry
Large source of employment for W1 workers.
Uses lots of water and power.
Creates lots of garbage.
Ships supplies to the Coal Mines.
Large tax revenue.

STAGE 4

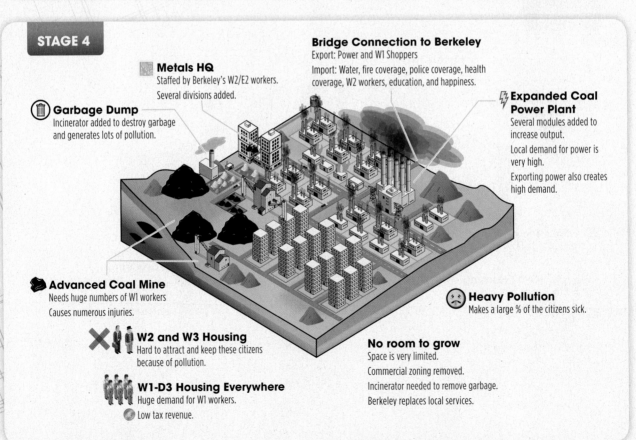

Metals HQ
Staffed by Berkeley's W2/E2 workers.
Several divisions added.

Bridge Connection to Berkeley
Export: Power and W1 Shoppers
Import: Water, fire coverage, police coverage, health coverage, W2 workers, education, and happiness.

Garbage Dump
Incinerator added to destroy garbage and generates lots of pollution.

Expanded Coal Power Plant
Several modules added to increase output.
Local demand for power is very high.
Exporting power also creates high demand.

Advanced Coal Mine
Needs huge numbers of W1 workers
Causes numerous injuries.

Heavy Pollution
Makes a large % of the citizens sick.

W2 and W3 Housing
Hard to attract and keep these citizens because of pollution.

No room to grow
Space is very limited.
Commercial zoning removed.
Incinerator needed to remove garbage.
Berkeley replaces local services.

W1-D3 Housing Everywhere
Huge demand for W1 workers.
Low tax revenue.

Developer Cities

Every *SimCity* player approaches the game with his or her own goals and gameplay style. If you're looking for new ideas, it's often helpful to see what other players are doing. Through the Region View, you can visit other cities in your region to see what your fellow mayors are up to. Who knows, they may have developed some cool ideas for their road network.

Or maybe they've overcome the supply chain challenges associated with city specializations. Feel free to take a look and learn from your neighbors' successes and mistakes. Want to know how the developers play? Here's a few cities created by members of the *SimCity* development team, giving you an idea of what's possible in the new *SimCity*.

High Wealth-High Tech: Where Self-Reliance is King (or Queen)

BY CHRIS SCHMIDT, TUNING DESIGNER

I wanted to develop a city that had high wealth joined with high tech industry. A place where you could go to the local coffee shop and meet the woman who invented a way to de-salinate ocean water based on the biology of penguins. That's my city.

I wanted to maximize the space in my city, because I knew I'd be building a University. I started with a standard grid layout for my roads, with a beltway loop that connected everything and could serve as the main artery for public transit. I filled the in-between spaces with smaller residential neighborhoods. To speed up the increase in land values, I placed the City Hall at the center of the city, and built schools at the edges of town. This way, I knew I was increasing land value and happiness for my entire city, and was ensuring that everyone was getting an education.

I checked the terrain for wind direction and resources, and zoned for industrial business in the optimum areas. I started small with industry, enough to generate some income, but not too much that my Sims were getting

sick from pollution. I planned to zone for more industrial development once I had an educated workforce, so the industry could be green and high tech.

I grew the city by zoning for residential development, and increased my land value with strategically placed parks and needed services. And when I say needed, I mean it. I really kept the services to a minimum: one fire station, one clinic. By starting out small, and with low industry, I didn't have much need for a lot of services. The schools and parks also kept the crime rate low. I also kept things at a low density at first, to keep the demands low. I took out bonds, and began to slowly accrue money, and then invested in building a University, along with the departments that allowed me to develop more high tech industry. I started with solar power, then, as the demand grew, had a more polluting power source. Once I had educated my Sims and built up some income, I built a Nuclear Power Plant.

I started this city as a self-sustaining metropolis, and for a long time it was. I had plenty of jobs, and my Sims were pretty happy. As the population grew, however, the challenges started growing too. At about 130,000 Sims,

CONTINUED ON NEXT PAGE...

HIGH WEALTH-HIGH TECH: WHERE SELF-RELIANCE IS KING (OR QUEEN)

(continued)

there were big problems with garbage, sewage, and water. I had run out of space. I was going to have to demolish a section of my city to deal with these issues.

I did put in a garbage incinerator, but that was a pollution nightmare. I realized I had not placed my water plant in an ideal spot, and could have avoided some of the problems with better placement when I first began development.

I'm still playing this city, two and a half years in (about 10 hours of play). The challenges keep changing. As soon as I solve one problem, another develops. I am building another city in the region, and have decided it is okay to rely on others for some things. A little.

Healthy, Pretty, Circle City

BY KYLE BROWN, LEVEL DESIGNER

I wanted to build a city that made my Sims happy. There would be huge tracts of green open space, lots of opportunities for intellectual and cultural advancement, good health care, and no belching smokestacks. Oh, and no grids. Everything in this city would be aesthetically pleasing, right down to the gentle curves of its transportation networks. And so Park It Up was born.

Of course, I had to build a big, dirty, industrial city up in those ore-filled hills first.

This is not as awful as it sounds. As I have played this version of *SimCity*, I think about resources and services on a regional, rather than city level. I knew where Park It Up would be sited, but spent some time first developing the Ore Town. I made sure I had a City Hall, a Department of Utilities that served the region, and exportable resources and services (power, water, sewage) before I started development of my healthy, pretty city.

The terrain of Park It Up already had an intrinsically high land value. I laid the city out in a circle with radiating spokes, and placed the Town Hall and some parks at the center of the city, so that they would radiate out to increase land values.

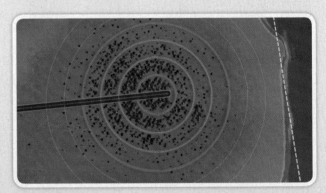

To get Park it Up started right, Ore City gifted 200,000 Simoleons, out of the goodness of their grimy hearts. This allowed me to zone mostly residential and commercial, and to build roads. I never over-build my roads, because they cost so much money. I start out with cheap roads, then upgrade as needed. With the spoke and wheel layout, traffic congestion has been low. The various connecting points give my Sims many alternate routes to avoid traffic jams.

I decided that tourism would be the major income source for Park It Up, so I added a Department of Transportation wing to my City Hall. I developed cultural attractions close to the train station and ferry dock, to minimize congestion in town. With placement of parks, educational buildings, and services, my land values stayed high, and my Sims stayed happy. I am able to keep my tax rates at about 10% across the board. Once the tax rates get to 11%, Sims start to fuss.

To develop high tech industry and jobs, I built a High School, because it can educate more students. A University is expensive, but if you want to go green, it unlocks the technology needed for clean power. I skipped building a Community College, because there are fewer benefits, and it also competes with the University for students.

At first, I didn't need many services, and what I did need was supplied by Ore City. As my population hit about 50,000, though, Park It Up needed to pony up. I didn't have enough water or power, and the garbage was not being picked up quickly enough by the Ore City volunteers. Park It Up citizens were getting a mite testy.

> I decided that tourism would be the major income source for Park It Up, so I added a Department of Transportation wing to my City Hall. I developed cultural attractions close to the train station and ferry dock, to minimize congestion in town.

I solved the water/sewage problem by placing my Water Pumping Station right next to my Sewage Treatment Plant. This may sound a bit risky, but if you make sure there is no disruption of service, you end up with an endless loop of clean water supply.

The power situation was harder to address. I had started with a Solar Power Plant, but it wasn't long before it could not meet the needs of the city. I ended up building a Coal Power Plant, because I did not have room for a Nuclear Power Plant. I have added a School of Science to the University, and students are researching the Concentrated Solar Array. This will add lots more power, using much less space than lower tech solar power collectors (25 MW vs. 8 MW). When space is at a premium, these things matter a lot.

Park It Up is doing well. I need to upgrade the Fire Department, but my Sims are so healthy that I don't need a big Hospital. Sims are just like people. They will complain a lot about things you can't fix, so sometimes you just have to ignore them. The Sims in Park It Up never complain about being sick, though, and that makes me happy.

Stadium City: GuiVille

BY GUILLAUME PIERRE, LEAD GAMEPLAY SCRIPTER

I wanted to turn my sleepy little town of GuiVille into a tourist mecca by building a Pro Stadium in town. Since this was an experiment, I was working in Sandbox mode and using money cheats.

Here's my little town of GuiVille, just as the sun rises over the hills beyond the river. The Pro Stadium takes up a pretty big piece of real estate, so I had to make space for it early in the development of my city. Even though the river offered a means of getting tourists to my city, I focused on getting as many tourists as possible to town by road, since the highway connection was so far from the water. I wanted to see if I could start right off with an event that would make money and not cause gridlock in GuiVille. This was a gamble. Events at the Pro Stadium are expensive to put on, but the potential profits make up for it, and can become a sustainable source of income for a city. One thing I like about Sandbox mode is that I can set up challenges like this, learn from them, and then bring what I've learned into conventional play.

For this challenge, I knew I needed a good bus system that could bring in tourists from the region and from the region and beyond. In the foreground, you can see a fully upgraded Bus Terminal, with all the Municipal Bus Garage modules built. In the background, there's my Pro Stadium, a large sporting complex with soccer fields and basketball courts, and you can also see a little bit of my Expo Center. These buildings sure were expensive to build, but I think they'll be worth it after a few successful events.

The other thing I needed to do was situate the Pro Stadium in my city so that the roads could handle a sudden influx of traffic. I built an avenue that provided direct access from the highway to the Pro Stadium, and built the Bus Terminal between the highway and the Pro Stadium.

I wasn't thinking much about GuiVille's neighboring cities at this point, so I didn't check to make sure that these cities had Bus Stops. I just scheduled my first event and hoped for the best!

Just as I feared, the flood of Sims from GuiVille and my neighboring city are clogging up the main avenue leading to the Pro Stadium. At least the tourists are able to take a different route to the Bus Terminal and aren't affected as much. But the traffic didn't keep people away. The event was a success! I turned a small profit and learned a lot about how to improve my city in the process. Next time, I'll make sure that my friend in the neighboring city has enough public transit options so her Sims can come into my city more easily, and I think I'll build a dock on the river so that cruise ships can bring in wealthy tourists as well.

It is also a challenge to build roads that limit how often cars have to stop, since traffic tends to get snarled up at stoplights. Here is another idea for how I would increase the flow of traffic, by flanking boulevards with local access roads. You can keep things looking nice and green with parks and trees.

> Just as I feared, the flood of Sims from GuiVille and my neighboring city are clogging up the main avenue leading to the Pro Stadium. At least the tourists are able to take a different route to the Bus Terminal and aren't affected as much.

Meltdown!

BY CHRISTIAN STRATTON, USER INTERFACE DIRECTOR

This is a sad story, sadder than it should be. One accidental nuclear meltdown is understandable. "Oh, he's a new Mayor. Cut him some slack. It'll be okay." But, two? Well, no one is around anymore to say anything.

My city was beautiful. It was one of the first cities I got really excited about playing. It had a grand boulevard, a glittering downtown complete with the Empire State Building, a great bridge, and a burgeoning, happy populace of 130,000 souls with lots of tourists. I wish you could have seen it.

As the tourists and high wealth skyscrapers came in, the city started having brown-outs. Wind power was not generating enough energy for all of the TVs, the computers, the nightlife. I wanted to keep the city as unpolluted as possible, but there was no room for solar power. I eyed the bluff. It looked about right for a Nuclear Power Plant. Perfect.

Nuclear power is great! I immediately had gobs of good, clean power. Then came the warning: I did not have enough educated workers. My plant was at risk. I was not going to take any chances with this city. I got right into the education business and built a University. I had the money. This was a really good city. You could tell my Sims were hungry for learning. The University ramped right up, and thousands of students enrolled.

I was so busy building Dormitories, I guess I assumed my graduates were going to work at the nuclear plant, but apparently the damage had already been done. Radiation was leaking. I started receiving health alerts. Not just any health alerts—1,400 Sims were getting sick every day! This was unprecedented!

I needed to cure my populace. I shut down the nuclear facility, and built an Oil Power Plant for a temporary power supply. The Hospital, complete with Diagnostic Lab, Wellness Center, and all the extra modules went in. At this point, my population had dipped down to about 90,000, but I knew we could recover. I was tackling an enormous health disaster, and was successfully treating 800 Sims a day. Phew! This in itself was an exhilarating crusade

My population recovered, and, although people were still getting sick (it takes a while for radiation pollution to diminish), my health care system had things under control.

A little more time went by. Hey, I thought, I still want to realize that nuclear dream! That bluff just begged for another plant. I built it. I was sure I had all the elements in place for success. This time the meltdown wiped out the city.

I'm not sure what happened, but the whole city, except for a little sliver in the farthest corner, is so polluted with radiation that nothing will grow.

All the RCI buildings were abandoned and turned to rubble. Everything is still zoned, but no one is moving in. The buildings remained. Services quickly drained what was left of the city's riches. I have since turned all the buildings off. What services it gets now come from the goodness of the neighbor cities. It has a trickle of revenue, and, for now, I am just letting it be—a gruesome, husk of a city in my region. I don't know, maybe I can salvage it. What's the half-life of uranium?

I am not a Square: Playing with Non-Traditional Layouts

BY JOHN SCOTT CLARKE, SENIOR JAVASCRIPT ENGINEER

I'm a big *SimCity* fan. I've been building cities since the first *SimCity* was released in the 1980s. Like most die-hard players, I was always looking for the most efficient way to lay out my city. Maximization was the name of the game—higher populations, higher profits, best use of resources. With this new game, however, I find myself taking a new approach. It's those curvy roads.

What could I do with those curves? Why not make a city that looks like a face? Yeah! Here are two of the face layout cities I built and played, viewed from above.

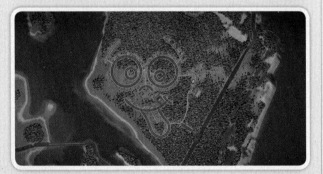

With these cities, I drew the faces with higher density roads, and then linked these with dirt or low density roads to connect the series of circles. I figured I could upgrade those roads later, and this was a good, cheap way to get going.

I found out that there are some real advantages to these unconventional, curvy layouts, besides the fact that they are really fun (watch those cars go around that guy's eyeball...). The flow of these cities, at lower populations, was very good. The circular structure of the city's roads worked like traffic circles. There were fewer stop lights and choke points to cause traffic jams.

I successfully played both of these cities, although with the lower density roads, population was limited to about 5,000 Sims. If I had made the low density connector roads long enough, I could have upgraded them and increased the city's density, but then I also ran the risk of traffic problems. With the higher density roads, there would be traffic lights at intersections instead of one-way stop signs.

With one-way stop signs on a circle with two roads connected to it on opposite sides, you can start to see an example of a single queueing node from queueing theory in action. Cars will enter the circle in a consistent rate, find where they need to go, and get out of the circle without getting held up by other traffic. The one-way stop sign ensures that the circle itself doesn't get backed by cross traffic like what would occur with a grid layout. If the circle does start to get backed up, that extra traffic will "queue" in the connecting roads instead of clogging up the circle. Also, by using a stop sign instead of a stop light, as soon as the circle has more capacity, cars will continue to enter it without having to wait for the light to change. Cars exiting the circle don't get held up either, provided there are at least two connecting roads on the circle. With just one road, traffic doubles back on itself and ends up constantly backed up. You can see this same theory in action at those big warehouse stores where they have one or two lines that feed into dozens of registers at checkout. Turns out to be much more efficient then having one line per cash register.

Traffic doubling back on itself on inside circles plus too short of a connecting road between the larger circles caused a lot of unnecessary backup that could be resolved with better placement of the connecting roads, but that wouldn't have looked as nice.

But the fun did not stop there.

There's another factor, besides those curvy roads, that has impacted my gameplay. I have a six-year old daughter, and we play together. This experience has radically changed my approach to city planning. I decided to build a test city that would be a place where I would like my daughter to live. Someday.

My goal was to make a working city that was high wealth and sustainable with almost no industry. Also no casinos, even though my daughter thinks the casinos are magic. Casinos also bring crime, and I want this place to be safe. I would keep my city sustainable with tourism and education. I was not in Sandbox mode for this city, so my eventual goals, once I had the money, were to build an Expo Center and some landmarks to cement it as a tourist center.

I found a city with boundaries that spanned several islands in an archipelago. After I checked out the placement of resources, I built some long, curving roads that linked the islands with really cool bridges. I built main branch roads off the curving road for city development. This created a really interesting aesthetic.

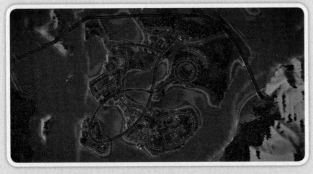

To make this city work, I developed two other cities in the region that provided services and jobs. One city was heavy industry, with bus, rail, and ferry connections to my archipelago. Another city had a lot of low wealth residential and commercial zoning, with industry and services. These cities provided employment, workers, and certain services for my utopia of tourism and education.

I invested in developing the educational system in the city to increase land values. I did zone a small industrial area at the beginning, to get some Simoleons in the city coffers. Once the city had other sources of income, I increased the tax rates on my industrial zones, and pretty soon the buildings were abandoned. I got rid of the rubble, and rezoned the area for residential and commercial use. I also used parks and other city services to increase my Sims' happiness levels and land values. When I could afford it, I placed landmarks that also generated income. The Edifício Copan is also an apartment building that housed 150 Sims. The Globe Theatre puts on events that bring in Simoleons, so I planned to build that when I had the money.

This city has been successful. I had to think about region play to make it work right from the beginning, and develop cities that work together. I left room for some of the landmarks I knew I wanted to place. Don't ever use up all your real estate until late in the game, unless you want to do a lot of destruction. And if you have a six-year-old child around, I recommend using them as advisors in your city planning process.

My Own Specialization City: Trash Town

BY JASON HABER, PRODUCER

Trash Town exists in the world for one purpose and one purpose only. We want your trash. And your sewage. We'll take anything smelly. My goal in developing Trash Town was to create a support structure for the other cities in the region: in this case, one city for all the bad stuff. This goal created its own interesting challenges in developing my city. Actually, running a garbage city is fun!

I knew right from the start that Trash Town would be accepting all the garbage and sewage from other cities in the region, so I wanted all these services to be close to the regional highway connection. To avoid congestion and traffic jams, I built a bunch of medium density loop roads off the main artery, and built my garbage dumps and sewage treatment facilities on these loops. This created a good traffic flow for all garbage-laden trucks and other regional traffic.

I had built up the other cities in the region first, so I gifted Trash Town some Simoleons at the outset to afford the needed facilities. My purpose here was not to make a city that made money hand over fist, but I did want it to be as sustainable as possible. I added Recycling Centers with all the modules, and built a Trade Depot. Trash Town's only source of income is, well, trash. Other cities in the region pay for each trip by a garbage/recycling truck and each piece of sewage that is sent to Trash Town. Recycled materials are traded on the global market, with a little bit of local industry on the side. There is no commercial sector. The other cities in the region still have to send funds (essentially, they are paying for the waste services), and I have to keep an eye on things to make sure Trash Town is not going down the toilet.

I freely admit that Trash Town does not think highly of my mayoral skills, but I don't care. If you live in Trash Town, you're on your own. There are no services. Other cities have to provide everything: water, power, police and fire protection, and health care. We can't use our own water because it is so polluted. Trash Town is home to about 6,000 low wealth Sims. There is a rail connection, so Sims can come to Trash Town for work, or the locals can look for work elsewhere.

It's a totally different experience to play a town like this—more strategic. I've started playing regions where one city will supply all of one certain resource to the region. It's fun to see the trade map of the region with Trash Town.

The point here is that you don't have to be limited to developing cities with the specializations that are in the game. You can make your own specialization. You don't have to follow our rules. You can make up your own.

Build it Up: Starting a City

CHRIS SCHMIDT, TUNING DESIGNER

When planning out how you want to begin building, you should first have a look at the resources available to you in the city by browsing through the data maps.

Once you've done that, all you need to do is figure out what kind of city you want to make. Various natural resources are available to exploit for additional Simoleons, and by taking a quick glance at the Land Value data map, you can get a sense of where the middle and high wealth Sims would prefer to live, provided you spruce up the place with parks. Additionally, it's important to make note of which way the wind is blowing, as setting up dirty industrial buildings upwind of the rest of your city will make your Sims sick from the air pollution. Instead, you should try and put them downwind so you can blow away all that nasty smog.

Fortunately, zoning and dezoning in *SimCity* is now free, in large part because the infrastructure cost that zoning used to represent is accounted for by tying zones to roads. But it's important to keep an eye on your Simoleons as you make new roads and to start small, particularly in your first city. Power, water, and sewage treatment will still need to be handled once your Sims have broken ground on their new homes. It's a good idea to start thinking about where you are going to put your dirtier services like garbage and sewage, as well as any city specializations you want to pursue. Specialization buildings (like the University, Gambling HQ, Trade HQ, etc.) also provide boosts and penalties to the area around them, and may have several buildings or modules that you'll need to accommodate, so make sure you leave room in your plan for where they can do the most good and the least harm. Once you have an idea of what you want to do, you'll want to start laying down your roads.

No city starts in a vacuum, so every new city begins by connecting a road to the highway (after all your people have to come from somewhere). Even though any road can be used, I generally like to start by building out a Medium Density Avenue as a main street coming into the city. This street lets you get up to medium density buildings, and has the flexibility to be upgraded to add an additional lane, and even add streetcar rails along the center. These roads are pretty expensive, so to save costs and keep my grid tight, I then like to use two-lane roads or dirt roads to start building out the side streets to maximize my space and keep my usable area compact.

Depending on what specialization I am going for, I can use an avenue to make a direct thoroughfare to my resources, or I can start building out a beltway around my city to better manage the flow of people within the city. Once I have a few blocks laid out, I will start putting down my zones, so my Sims can get building and generating tax revenue for me. Now that the city is underway, low wealth Sims will move in, but while they are eager to get a new start in your city, if you fail to get your basic services covered, they won't stay for long. If I was a little overzealous in my initial layout, I can also take out loans to make up for the cost of these services. These are a great way to get a little bit ahead when used wisely. Loan payments can take a real toll on your city as it's starting out, however, so make sure you keep an eye on your budget!

As my city grows, I will need to start thinking about density and traffic flow, so I will likely remove some of those two-lane roads to make larger blocks, and upgrade others to accommodate some of the larger high density buildings we have. Keep in mind that any high density road will get high density buildings, not just the avenues, so when you upgrade your roads you had better be prepared for it with mass transit options and plenty of services, or the city's demands will really start piling up! I hope this helped you get an idea on how to plan out your cities in *SimCity*. With a little exploration of your options and pre-planning I think you should have no trouble setting up a city from scratch.

PowerWaterTestville

BY DAN MOSKOWITZ, LEAD GAMEPLAY ENGINEER

I didn't plan on caring about these poor Sims. I didn't set out to build a dream city, or any city at all really. I just needed a way to test a certain power and water delivery issue to fix a bug. But while I played the city with the sole purpose of fixing the bug, it happened. The game made me care. I cared about my terrible city—my terrible city full of traffic congestion, pollution, crime, fires, and sickness.

The bug I was fixing had to do with delivery of water and power over long distances, so I created PowerWater-Testville to help me do the job. I built a giant grid city and immediately zoned everything with RCI. I needed to make sure all the buildings were getting water and power when they were supposed to. I did borrow a little money at the beginning of the game to build all those roads, but have not used any cheats or shortcuts since. As I was fixing the bug (and, yes, don't worry, it's all fixed), my city started to grow and I began playing the game.

It was fascinating to see what I had created. My poor Sims were miserable. I had dug a deep hole for this city, but I found I really wanted to make things better for my citizens. But that hole was really deep. I had taken a pristine coastline of glittering sands and turned it into an industrial wasteland. That's what happens when you build your sewage outflow pipes right on the beach.

I had become emotionally engaged with this city, but not just because my Sims needed me. A lot of people play *SimCity* with a goal of maximizing efficiency and minimizing mistakes. I am more interested in the creative aspects of the game. I'm not trying to "win", or see my name in lights on the leaderboards. I realized that in three years of working on this game, some of the stuff I was seeing in PowerWaterTestville was a first. One thing I love about this game, you don't have to fix all the problems if you don't want to. I got fascinated watching the city grow, seeing how the citizens and systems managed with the hand that was dealt them. It was not a very good hand, but they kept on going, and I wanted to help them.

PowerWaterTestville has tons of money—over 8 million Simoleons at last count, mostly from its tax base. While money was no issue, it was also not the answer to everything. The problems in my city were not going to go away immediately. I had to address the root problems to start heading in another direction. I started by upgrading some roads from medium density to high density, to change stop signs to stop lights. I had gotten fascinated in watching the traffic flows in town. There is no mass transit; I like watching everyone get around by car, but it did cause gridlock at times.

As part of the debugging process, I had built a Pro Stadium at the end of a long access road, with only one way in and out. Just for fun, I scheduled a rock concert, and watched the entire city line up at the choke point of the stop sign at the access road entry. I'm sorry, but it was hilarious. The event was poorly attended, due to traffic problems, but I still netted §29,000 in profit from the event.

The two big problems I worked on right away were fires and health. I had no services, and the fires were getting out of control, putting the entire city at risk. I built one small Fire Station, but that hardly made a dent. Once I added all the garages for more fire trucks, the fire situation started to calm down. I also became very handy with the Bulldozing tool, since I had so many abandoned buildings and rubble. Sims were leaving town because of the poor health conditions. I built a Clinic, and then I got lost watching my two ambulances navigate the city to pick up sick and injured Sims. You can zoom way out and still see the ambulances with the flashing lights. These poor guys were driving all the time! It would take forever to get to their destination, pick up the sick Sim, and get back to the Clinic, but they kept right at it. You can't keep a good Sim down.

The next big problem is the water. I have a slight ground pollution problem, so my water is compromised.

I barely upgraded my City Hall, and hadn't added any modules, so I couldn't build upgraded service facilities. When one water source became polluted, I would just build a new Water Tower in another spot. Once you have polluted ground and water, it is like a scar on your city. It is really hard to clean up, and takes a long time to dissipate. Besides that, I was going to run out of clean water! It was clear that I needed to get help from neighboring cities.

I have started building a city next door that is all about education, and I am setting up systems for my Sims to use to commute. This will take time, but it will hopefully bring some high tech, less polluting industry into town. I need a Department of Utilities in the region so that I can get a Sewage Treatment Plant and a better Water Pumping Station.

PowerWaterTestville is an impoverished rust belt of a city with decaying infrastructure and few services. Part of me has watched this city limp along, and I have wondered what it would take to have everyone leave. How much sickness? How much rubble? How many buildings would have to go up in flames? My city doesn't need an alien invasion or giant lizard to come along and wreak destruction. It is quietly struggling along; a sad city, and I love it. It has taught me all over again that there is no right or wrong way to play this game.

Roads

Roads are much more than a way to get around town—they're the essential building blocks your city is based on. In addition to serving as the backbone of your transportation network, roads also control density and supply all buildings with water, power, and sewage service.

Given their significance, nothing in the city can be built without proper road access. In this chapter we take a close look at the different roads available, as well as considerations relating to road construction, density, and congestion.

Don't forget to go to **www.primagames.com** to access guide updates free of charge with your voucher code.

Road Selection

There are two different types of roads to choose from: streets and avenues. Each road is designed to carry a specific volume of traffic, determined by how many lanes it offers. The flow of traffic is also affected by whether the road is equipped with stop signs or traffic lights at intersections. The roads also support different density buildings, giving you control over how quickly your city grows. Here's a quick look at the different roads available as well as some helpful advice on where to use each one.

 TIP

Follow road guides to maximize your city's density.

Low Density Dirt Road

Cost: §1

Number of Lanes: 1

Maximum Density Supported: Low

Description: This dirt-cheap narrow road supports low density zones with only stop signs at intersections.

This road is best reserved for areas where you're expecting little to no traffic. While you can construct zones along this road, it isn't recommended, unless you're going for that rustic shotgun shack appeal. Instead, consider building this dirt road out to your Sewage Outflow Pipe or your Wind or Solar Power Plant—these power plants require no deliveries, keeping traffic to a minimum. If necessary, this road can later be upgraded to a Low Density Street.

Low Density Street

Cost: §2

Number of Lanes: 2

Maximum Density Supported: Low

Description: This narrow two lane road supports low density zones with only stop signs at intersections.

Want to create that perfect suburban neighborhood? This is the street you want! The Low Density Street is the perfect choice when constructing low density residential areas filled with small single family houses. However, do your best to avoid creating too many intersections. The

stop signs on these streets interrupt the flow of traffic and may lead to congestion, particularly in the mornings and evenings as Sims travel to and from work.

Medium Density Street

Cost: §4

Number of Lanes: 4

Maximum Density Supported: Medium

Description: This narrow four lane road supports up to medium density zones with only stop signs at the intersections.

This street is very versatile, ideal for serving the transportation needs of a growing city. When starting out, these streets are great for connecting your commercial and industrial areas. With four lanes, the street doubles the capacity of the Low Density Street, allowing for medium density buildings and steadier flow of traffic. But like the Low Density Street, work to minimize intersections to avoid congestion caused by the stop signs.

High Density Street

Cost: §7

Number of Lanes: 4

Maximum Density Supported: High

Description: This narrow four lane road supports high density zones with traffic lights at intersections. This road cannot be upgraded further.

Although this street only has four lanes, identical to the Medium Density Street, the introduction of traffic lights greatly increases the flow of traffic, helping ease congestion in crowded corridors. Before building or upgrading to a High Density Street, pay close attention to the impact caused by increasing the density of adjacent zones. Creating this street may prompt the construction of high density residential, commercial, and industrial buildings, drawing more traffic and congestion to the area. If you're satisfied with the density of the adjoining zones, you may want to dezone those areas to prohibit growth.

Medium Density Avenue

Cost: §7

Number of Lanes: 4

Maximum Density Supported: Medium

Description: This wide four lane road supports medium density zones with traffic lights at intersections.

When beginning a new city, the Medium Density Avenue is the ideal choice when connecting to the regional highway. This avenue is capable of supporting the high volume of traffic coming off the highway, plus the tree-lined median is a nice, welcoming touch. Consider using this avenue as the main thoroughfare leading into your city. With a cost the same as a High Density Street, this avenue is often preferable because it can later be upgraded to accommodate heavier traffic as well as streetcars. But avenues are also much wider, making them difficult to build in already developed areas without bulldozing existing structures. Plan ahead and figure out where to build your avenues before zoning.

High Density Avenue

Cost: §9

Number of Lanes: 6

Maximum Density Supported: High

Description: This wide six lane road supports high density zones with traffic lights at intersections.

When experiencing gridlock on your Medium Density Avenue, consider upgrading it to this avenue to ease congestion. The addition of two extra lanes may not sound like much, but it can make all the difference during rush hour, even if it means the elimination of that quaint tree-lined median. But like the High Density Street, this avenue supports high density buildings. So before upgrading to this avenue, consider the consequences of increasing the density in the adjoining residential, commercial, and industrial zones. In addition to drawing more traffic, high density buildings often require more water and power while outputting more garbage and sewage.

High Density Streetcar Avenue

Cost: §12

Number of Lanes: 6

Maximum Density Supported: High

Description: This wide six lane road supports high density zones with traffic lights at intersections. Streetcar tracks running down the center provide support for streetcar stops.

This avenue performs identically to the High Density Avenue, but the addition of streetcar tracks down the center median allows more Sims to share the road. Before you can take advantage of streetcars you must first construct a Streetcar Depot—available in the Mass Transit menu—adjacent to this avenue. Streetcar stops can then be constructed along the avenue's median, giving Sims a place to board and disembark from the streetcar. As ridership increases, fewer and fewer cars appear on the avenue, reducing congestion. Running a streetcar system isn't cheap, but it's a worthwhile investment when attempting to counter gridlock due to high population and tourism.

> **ⓘ NOTE**
>
> Once constructed, roads incur no hourly operational cost. However, it does cost to upgrade streets and avenues.

Road Construction

Select the desired road type from the Roads menu to begin construction. Make sure the selected road can accommodate the traffic and desired density for the area.

Roads are purchased from the Roads menu. There are several types of roads available, and each serves a purpose. Hover over each option to view its name, a description, and how many Simoleons it takes to lay a single stretch of road. Select your preferred road, and then click the left mouse button and drag the road to where you'd like to place it. How much the total stretch of road costs is shown above your cursor. Release the left mouse button to build. Click the right mouse button to cancel. The type of road can drastically change the zoning density in the city. The wider the road, the more traffic it can handle, affecting how quickly your city can be populated. The higher your population, the more money you can acquire. Keep in mind the value and density of each zone as you lay down roads.

> **☑ TIP**
>
>
>
> Want to build a bridge? Simply draw a road across a body of water within your city site. Bridges can also be used to span canyons and other challenging geographical features. Tunnels are created in the same fashion when drawing a road through steep terrain.

Road Tools

Use the Circle tool to create to create ring-shaped road systems, using the road guides to determine proper spacing between each road.

You can lay curved, arced, rectangular and even circle roads. Click the Line, Curve, Arc, Rectangle, or Circle icons on the left side of the menu to adjust the shapes of the roads you can draw. The Curve and Arc tools allow you to build curved streets, while the Rectangle tool can lay down entire city blocks, perfect for creating a quick grid layout. The Circle tool is ideal for creating elliptical and perfect circular roads. Select the road type, then click and drag along the ground to pave the road. Press SHIFT to quickly toggle the selected tool—or simply click on the desired tool on the left side of the menu. Remember to leave enough space for houses, shops, and factories as you start creating city grids.

Road Guides

The white dotted road guides are helpful tools when creating new roads. Follow the guides to optimize spacing for zoning.

As you lay down roads, you'll see white dotted lines appearing nearby. Hover the mouse over a road to make the guides appear. These lines are suggested guides for additional roads. Use them to help with spacing. Spacing is particularly important when zoning residential, commercial, and industrial areas. If a zone is too cramped, there may not be enough room to build additional houses, shops, or factories within a block, resulting in empty unused space. It may not seem like much early on, but undeveloped space is essentially a wasted piece of land, generating no tax revenue for your city. The better planned out your roads are, the more organized your city. Press ALT to toggle the guides on/off, or simply click on the Guides box below the road tools options.

> ✓ **TIP**
>
> Start with cheaper streets, then use the Road Selector tool to upgrade as traffic increases.

> ✓ **TIP**
>
> Medium Density Avenues make a good region connection because they can be upgraded later.

Upgrading/Downgrading Roads

As traffic builds up, use the Road Selector tool to upgrade existing roads. There's no need to bulldoze unless you want to replace a street with an avenue.

As your city grows, traffic increases along your road network, leading to congestion. Upgrading your roads is important because cluttered streets can cause problems, including slowing down fire or police services or delaying assistance from neighboring cities. Fortunately, you don't have to bulldoze existing roads in order to upgrade or downgrade them. By using the Road Selector tool, also available in the Roads menu, you can select any road segment and determine its density. Simply click on the Road Selector tool and then select any stretch of road you wish to upgrade or downgrade. A small window appears above the selected road giving you options to upgrade or downgrade. Upgrades always cost more money, but downgrades are performed free of charge. Due to the difference in width, streets cannot be upgraded into avenues and avenues can't be downgraded to streets. If you wish to replace a street with an avenue, you'll need to bulldoze the existing street as well as any buildings that are in the way. For this reason it's a good idea to carefully plan the placement of your avenues, constructing them before you really need them. At the very least, set aside open land to construct avenues in the future. To avoid costly demolitions, make a habit of placing expensive buildings such as Hospitals, Bus Terminals, and landmarks next to avenues instead of streets. You can also use the Road Selector tool to upgrade bridges.

> ✓ **TIP**
>
> Roads equipped with stoplights allow for much smoother flow of traffic. All avenues and the High Density Street are equipped with stoplights.

TRAFFIC JAMS

Look for flashing yellow and red road segments to identify areas of congestion. Perhaps it's time to upgrade roads or roll out a mass transit solution?

If your road network is experiencing congestion, the Roads menu button will flash yellow or red, depending on the severity of the situation. Once the Roads menu is open, you can see certain segments of road in your city flashing yellow or red. Yellow segments indicate areas where congestion is becoming a problem. Red segments show areas where traffic has reached a gridlock state, with little or no movement. Take these warnings as a cue to upgrade these road segments to better accommodate high volumes of traffic. But even upgrading your city's roads may not be enough to completely eliminate congestion. As traffic increases along your road network, consider turning to mass transit options to reduce the number of vehicles on your roads.

> (i) **NOTE**
>
> During some hours of the day your roads can look deserted. But during the 6-8AM commute they can become gridlocked. When looking for upgrade opportunities, pay attention to the time of day.

Road Planning and Management

The construction of your road network is one of the most important elements of developing an efficient and prosperous city. Before you start randomly drawing roads across your empty city site, take some time to think things through and ask yourself a few basic questions relating to your city's infrastructure. Where will your city get water? Where will you build your power plant? What about sewage and waste disposal? Roads must be created to support these basic pieces of city infrastructure. Taking it a step further, consider what kind of city specializations your city can support by studying the data maps. If you plan to drill for oil or mine ore and coal, those facilities will also need to be connected to your road network. In a sense, each city site is a puzzle and, as Mayor, it's up to you to figure out where all the pieces go and how they fit together. A rudimentary plan of your road network at the outset can save you a lot of time and money in the long run. In this section we take a look at a few considerations to keep in mind while constructing and expanding your city's road network.

> ☑ **TIP**
>
> Dirt roads are useful for remote buildings that don't require many workers, like Water Towers.

Transportation Overview

Keep a close eye on your road system. In some instances road upgrades may not be enough to alleviate gridlock. It may be time for a mass transit system.

SimCity is all about movement, and the core function of your road network is to transport Sims resources throughout your city. To understand the significance of roads it's first important to grasp the interconnected relationships between the various RCI buildings in your city. Sims live in residential zones and must travel to industrial or commercial zones to work at a job. Factories in industrial zones create goods called freight. This freight must then be shipped to shops in commercial zones where these manufactured goods can be purchased by Sims with money they earned at their jobs. Roads are absolutely essential for carrying out this cycle, not to mention the intricate supply chain concerns associated with city specializations like drilling and mining. As Mayor, there's a lot of issues vying for your attention, but make a concerted effort to slow down and study the flow of transportation throughout your city. Interruptions in these critical cycles must be addressed quickly. Failure to address problems with the city's road network may lead to a serious economical downturn as shops and factories go out of business and Sims lose their jobs, all leading to lower revenue from taxes. So it literally pays to keep a close eye on your roads.

Highway Connection

Placing intersections too close to your highway connection can lead to major backups on the highway.

When starting a new city from scratch, your first line of business is connecting the city to the regional highway by constructing a road. The task is simple enough, but improper planning at this early stage may have dire consequences as your city grows. First of all, make sure you choose the right kind of road when making the connection to the highway. The Medium Density Avenue is the best choice for connecting your city to the highway. With four lanes and traffic lights, this avenue can handle the volume and keep traffic flowing in and out of your city at a steady rate. Plus, the avenue can later be upgraded to accommodate more vehicles and even streetcars. Next, avoid placing any cross streets too close to the highway connection. Even with traffic lights, intersections can become bottlenecks, potentially leading to backups on the highway. Instead, let traffic flow into your city with minimal interruptions. As your city expands, consciously limit the number of intersections along the avenue connected to the highway.

Grid Layout

When developing your road network, utilize a grid system to maximize space for development within RCI zones.

For beginners, an empty city site looks massive, with plenty of room to expand and experiment. However, as you begin zoning and placing buildings, the amount of available space quickly dwindles. Perhaps all those curvy roads weren't such a great idea after all? If your city site is relatively flat, the most effective use of space is a grid layout, similar to those used in all modern cities. This allows you to divide your city into numerous city blocks, with all streets meeting at 90-degree angles. It may look boring, but it's the most efficient solution when attempting to build a high density metropolis. While building your grid system, use the road guides to help determine the width of your blocks. Proper spacing is important to ensure every bit of space can be developed. Instead of creating square-shaped blocks, draw elongated rectangle-shaped blocks to reduce the number of intersections. Limiting the number of intersections greatly increases the flow of traffic, allowing vehicles to travel greater distances without encountering stop signs or traffic lights. However, a grid layout may not work in some areas due to challenging geographic features such as rivers and mountains. In such areas, consider using curvy roads to better follow the terrain. Using the road guides it's possible to create parallel curvy roads with optimal spacing for zoning.

 TIP

Hold SHIFT while drawing roads in arc mode to draw 90-degree arcs.

Density Control

All cities experience growing pains when increasing density. Make sure your roads, utilities, and city services are capable of handling a sudden population increase.

One of the most important functions of roads is their ability to control density in adjoining residential, commercial, and industrial zones. Unlike previous installments where this was controlled by zoning for different densities, this time around density is governed by the roads adjacent to a zone. This helps ensure the nearby roads are capable of handling the traffic associated with larger buildings. As previously discussed, each road can support different densities. So if you want to create a city with only low and medium density, only build roads that allow a maximum of medium density. This automatically puts on the brakes, preventing out-of-control growth, regardless of the demand.

There may be instances where you need the traffic benefits of a high density road, but want to maintain the current low and medium density buildings in the area. In such instances use the Dezone tool (in the Zones menu) to remove the zoning from the area you want to prevent from growing. This essentially freezes the buildings, preventing them from attaining the next level of density, regardless of which road is placed next to them. Before upgrading roads, always take into account the consequences of nearby buildings increasing in density. With greater density comes greater problems, such as increased traffic, power/water consumption, and garbage/sewage output. If you're not careful, upgrading multiple roads in a short span of time could lead to a massive increase in density, putting a sudden strain on city utilities and services.

Utilities

Nobody wants to get stuck behind a slow-moving garbage or recycling truck. Consider upgrading your two lane roads if congestion becomes an issue.

In addition to carrying your Sims around town, your city's road network is also responsible for conveying all crucial utilities to every building. Access the Power, Water, or Sewage menus to view these vital services circulating beneath the city streets. Because a road is required to construct any building or zone, all buildings are automatically connected to these utilities by default. There's no need to construct a separate pipe or power line system. However, deficits in these utilities can still lead to outages. Usually buildings farthest from the source are the first to be affected. For instance, a factory on the west side of town will likely be one of the first to lose power if the power plant on the east side of town is struggling to meet demands. Buildings closest to the utility source are less likely to be affected by such deficits.

Garbage and recycling trucks also rely on the road system to conduct their daily waste disposal duties. During collection, trucks stop at each building to dump trash cans and recycling bins. Any cars stuck behind these trucks may experience significant delays unless traveling along a road with four or more lanes. Avoid using the Low Density Street in high traffic areas lined with various buildings, otherwise the repetitive stop-and-go behavior of garbage and recycling trucks may lead to congestion.

 TIP

Use Esc to cancel using any tool, even while drawing roads or bulldozing.

Emergency Services

This building is burning down because fire trucks cannot reach it due to gridlock. Solve your traffic problems so emergency vehicles can respond to fires, crimes, and injured Sims.

The layout and efficiency of your road network is regularly tested by your city's ambulances, police cars, and fire trucks. If they're having trouble navigating your streets, imagine what it's like for the average Sim trying to get to work. When you hear a siren and see flashing lights, zoom in on one of these emergency vehicles and follow it as it races to the latest fire, crime, or injured Sim. Emergency vehicles automatically take the most direct route to their destination, blowing past stop signs and traffic lights. But even these emergency vehicles aren't immune to gridlock. As a result, they sometimes get caught in traffic, particularly if responding to an emergency during the morning or evening rush hours. For emergency vehicles, any delay can be deadly, putting the lives of Sims at risk. If your emergency vehicles are constantly getting caught in traffic, it may be time to rethink your road network. The easiest solution is upgrading roads so they can support more traffic. But in large cities, even High Density Avenues can become parking lots. In these situations, you may need to build additional roads to alleviate congestion, or turn to mass transit solutions like buses and streetcars in an effort to reduce the number of Sims traveling by car. The location of your emergency buildings can also make a big difference in response time. Try to keep these buildings located near the center of your city, along avenues, so they can quickly respond in any direction without traveling the entirety of your road network.

TIP

Hold SHIFT while drawing roads in curved mode to draw straight roads.

Tourism

Culture buildings like the Expo Center draw large numbers of tourists into your city. Implement a mass transit system before constructing these attractions or suffer the consequences of cars and taxis clogging your roads.

No matter how well planned or designed, even the most robust road network cannot handle a massive influx of tourists. If the highway is your city's only connection to the region, tourists can only arrive by car and taxi, often leading to backups on your roads and even the highway. Gridlock caused by the arrival of tourists can absolutely cripple your city, blocking emergency vehicles and preventing Sims from getting to work. Congestion may have a ripple effect on the local economy too, preventing factories from shipping freight to shops, leading to the failure of buildings in your industrial and commercial zones. Therefore, don't try to attract tourists until your city has the transportation infrastructure required to handle large numbers of visitors. Construction of a Bus Terminal or Passenger Train Station reduces the number of cars and taxis flooding your city streets while helping draw large numbers of tourists to your city's attractions.

Roads: Points to Remember

→ Roads carry traffic, water, power, and sewage.

→ A road's number of lanes impact traffic capacity.

→ Roads can be upgraded with the Road Selector tool.

→ Buildings won't upgrade in density unless they are in zones along roads which support that density.

→ Bridges and tunnels can be built over water or through mountains—just drag a road across them.

CHAT WITH THE DEVELOPERS

Road to *SimCity* Success

CHRIS SCHMIDT, TUNING DESIGNER

Hey everyone! My name is Chris Schmidt and I am a Tuning Designer here at Maxis. I work closely with the Scripting and QA teams to refine and improve *SimCity* by tweaking the gameplay and smoothing out the rough edges as we implement new systems. Additionally, I adjust the game balance in response to feedback, observation, and telemetry to try and maintain a good pace and feel to the experience as it comes to life.

I am here to talk about roads, zones, and density. We have ditched the grid in favor of our new agent-based system powered by the GlassBox Engine that allows us to take a more "ground up," road-centric approach.

To better get acquainted with how this works, let me first explain how roads affect density. With the new road-centric approach, players can get the same functionality they used to get by zoning by density, but instead of using different zone densities, we limit density by road type. Zones and player-placed buildings can only be created on this existing infrastructure, since our new agent system uses the roads to bring power, water, sewage, and the agents themselves to and from your buildings.

As for the roads themselves, we have two size categories of road, each of which has their own upgrade path. We have the small roads (which can start out as dirt roads and move on up through four lane roads with traffic lights), and we have the large roads (which start out with boulevards and can be upgraded up to avenues with streetcar tracks like you'd see in real cities like San Francisco). The dirt roads and two lane roads are limited to the lowest density buildings, and each upgrade thereafter gets you to the next density type, whereas the large roads start out able to support up to medium density buildings, and can be upgraded to support the large high density buildings in one step.

In addition to allowing higher density buildings to be built, upgrading your roads will also improve your intersections, as higher tier roads will create stoplight intersections, and lower tier roads will generally have stop signs to regulate traffic. Upgrading your infrastructure can be expensive, but it's important to keep your traffic flowing so your services can get where they're needed.

Since we no longer have a grid to work from, it was important to us to make sure that traditional *SimCity* players still had the tools they needed to make the most efficient use of their space, whether it be using a grid or taking advantage of the new Curvy Road tool to work around some of the more challenging terrain features. As a result we have a new road guide that appears once you have placed your first road to show you the optimal distance from an existing road for you to build without wasting any of the space between. The road guides make it easy to build out a grid or to draw parallel curves, and its distance is calculated based on the depth away from the road that the buildings can grow. Since larger buildings have larger depths, and the roads themselves are two different sizes, the Large Road tool and the Small Road tool operate at different scales. But to make the grids work out as nicely as possible, we have made it so that four small roads made with the guides will line up nicely with three large roads. This means that your main street might have a little extra space behind it at first, but don't worry, like those sweaters you'd get as a kid, your city will grow into it.

I hope this gives you a better sense of how much control you have over roads and density in *SimCity*. We've worked hard to make this system as friendly and intuitive as possible to both new players and city-building veterans. From making an optimized grid or concentric circles, to even guitar cities and M. C. Escher-esque configurations, we've had a blast coming up with new ways to lay out our cities, and I can't wait to see what you guys come up with.

> In addition to allowing higher density buildings to be built, upgrading your roads will also improve your intersections, as higher tier roads will create stoplight intersections, and lower tier roads will generally have stop signs to regulate traffic. Upgrading your infrastructure can be expensive, but it's important to keep your traffic flowing so your services can get where they're needed.

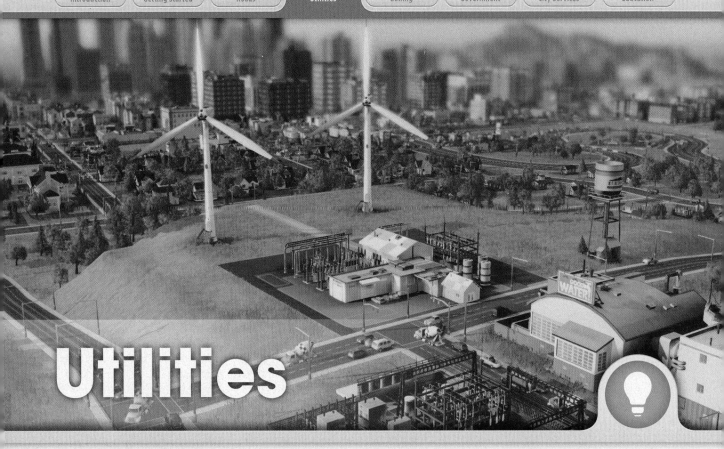

Utilities

Before you start zoning, take a moment to ask yourself a few basic questions pertaining to your city's infrastructure.

Where will your city get power and water? How will you dispose of sewage and garbage? As mayor, you need to address these issues soon after connecting your city to the regional highway. And since most utilities lower land value and spread pollution, it's a good idea to establish your utility infrastructure before you set aside land for houses, shops, and factories. In this chapter we take an in-depth look at power, water, sewage, and waste disposal, explaining how each system works, as well as detailing the differences between the various buildings and their associated modules.

Don't forget to go to www.primagames.com to access guide updates free of charge with your voucher code.

Power

The Power menu shows the flow of power beneath your city's road network. Study the info tab to determine current power production and consumption.

As the sun sets and the Sims in your city settle down for the evening, they'll expect the lights to turn on. As mayor, it's your responsibility to make this happen. Power is an essential utility for all cities. In fact, most buildings require power to function, including all Government buildings. You can supply your city with power by plopping a power plant adjacent to one of your existing roads. Alternatively, you can buy surplus power from neighboring cities, completely bypassing the challenges associated with power generation.

Regardless of how you get power, you need to constantly monitor the city's production and consumption rates, visible in the Power menu's info tab on the right. The analog gauge in this tab shows the surplus amount of power generated, measured in megawatts (MW) or, if facing a minor surplus or deficit, shown in kilowatts (kW). As long as the needle in this gauge stays within the green zone, you're doing okay. But if the needle dips into yellow or red territory, you need to address the power shortage immediately. To get a more precise reading of the city's power consumption, mouse over the gauge to trigger the appearance of a small blue window showing the exact numerical values of power needed and power produced, as well as any power bought or sold. Obviously, if your city needs more power than it's producing, you need to take action.

While the Power menu is open you can also see a graphical representation of power flowing throughout your city. Power is represented by yellow lines, branching off your roads and entering adjacent buildings. The yellow circles beneath each building represent its power consumption—the larger the circle, the greater the consumption rate. If at any point the yellow lines become red, it indicates a power outage due to insufficient production. Even without viewing the gauge and numbers in the info tab, this is a quick way to diagnose problems with power production and transmission.

Wind Power Plant

Cost: §8,000

Operational Cost: §80 per hour

Power Production Rate: 3 MW in 10 mph winds

Air Pollution Rate: None

Description: Harness the green energy of the wind by building a sprawling wind farm.

When starting a new city, the Wind Power Plant is the perfect solution. Not only is this power plant relatively cheap, it produces clean power, meaning you won't have to worry about the negative consequences of air pollution. The power plant is also expandable through the addition of turbines built along the Service Road—this road can

be lengthened free of charge to increase the footprint of your wind farm. To get the most out of your Wind Power Plant, construct it in areas with high wind speeds, usually along high elevations with wind speeds greater than 10 mph. By expanding the Service Road, you can scatter turbines over a wide area. Consider building turbines along slopes or other difficult terrain where it's impossible to zone or place other buildings. But a sprawling wind farm can eat up a lot of space, so place those turbines as close together as possible, ensuring they're each exposed to high wind speeds. But even when expanded to its maximum potential, the Wind Power Plant isn't a big power producer. So as a city increases in density, you'll need to look for other solutions to feed the increasing demand for power— consider augmenting your system by building a second power plant or buying power from a neighboring city.

 TIP

If you want to optimize your Wind Power Plant, complete the Vertical Turbine research project at a University and install these advanced modules.

MODULES

Wind Power Sign

Cost: §200

Operational Cost: None

Maximum Modules: 1

Description: Put down a sign so all the pizza delivery drivers stop going past you.

 TIP

Wind turbines are connected to Wind Power Plants by service road. That road can go up steep hills.

Service Road

Cost: Free

Operational Cost: None

Description: Allows workers to get out to the windmills. Has underground lines for power transmission. Extend the Service Road to fit more turbines if you need to.

Small Horizontal Turbine

Cost: §5,000

Operational Cost: §40 per hour

Power Production Rate: 3 MW in 10 mph winds

Air Pollution Rate: None

Maximum Modules: 24

Description: The Small Horizontal-Axis Wind Turbine produces a small amount of electricity. Must be built along a Service Road.

Large Horizontal Turbine

Cost: §10,000

Operational Cost: §60 per hour

Power Production Rate: 5.1 MW in 10 mph winds

Air Pollution Rate: None

Maximum Modules: 20

Description: The Large Horizontal-Axis Wind Turbine produces a moderate amount of electricity. Must be built along a Service Road.

Vertical Turbine

Cost: §20,000

Operational Cost: §170 per hour

Power Production Rate: 15 MW in 10 mph winds

Air Pollution Rate: None

Maximum Modules: 1

Prerequisites:

→ University in the region.

→ University with School of Engineering in the region.

→ Complete research project at a University in the region.

Description: It looks crazy! It also produces huge amounts of power. Service Roads only please!

> **(i) NOTE**
>
> The sign modules associated with the power plants and other buildings have no impact on gameplay. They're merely aesthetic touches you can use to decorate your city.

Coal Power Plant

Cost: §17,000

Operational Cost: §450 per hour

Power Production Rate: 75 MW

Coal Burn Rate: 4.32 tons/day

Air Pollution Rate: High

Description: Imports coal directly from the global market to generate enough power for even a large city. It also generates pollution. A lot of pollution.

When it comes to producing power, the Coal Power Plant offers a lot of bang for the buck. Even before placing any modules, this power plant cranks out a whopping 75 MW, enough to power most moderately sized cities. By adding additional generator modules this bad boy can produce more power than a stock Nuclear Power Plant. But few structures produce a higher volume of air pollution than the Coal Power Plant. If you choose to build it, make sure it's far from populated areas. Pay close attention to wind direction too, as you don't want the toxic smoke to blow across your city or neighboring cities in the region. To reduce air pollution consider building the Advanced or Clean Coal Generators. These costly modules significantly reduce the amount of pollution spewed into the air. If your city has a Coal Mine, make sure the power plant is open to local coal deliveries. It's much cheaper to use coal mined locally than to purchase it on the global market.

MODULES

Coal Power Plant Sign

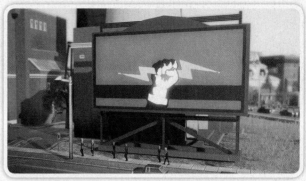

Cost: §200

Operational Cost: None

Maximum Modules: 1

Description: Someone has smeared "Clean coal my foot!" onto this sign.

Dirty Coal Generator

Cost: §5,000

Operational Cost: §425 per hour

Power Production Rate: 75 MW

Coal Burn Rate: 4.32 tons/day

Air Pollution Rate: High

Maximum Modules: 3

Description: For when all other considerations are secondary to cost. Requires a decent amount of coal to operate and pollutes a lot.

Advanced Coal Generator

Cost: §15,000

Operational Cost: §375 per hour

Power Production Rate: 75 MW

Coal Burn Rate: 8.64 tons/day

Air Pollution Rate: Medium

Maximum Modules: 3

Description: Costs more but produces less pollution as well as making decent levels of power. Y'know, for when you care about the environment a tiny bit.

Clean Coal Generator

Cost: §20,000

Operational Cost: §600 per hour

Power Production Rate: 75 MW

Coal Burn Rate: 5.76 tons/day

Air Pollution Rate: Low

Maximum Modules: 1

Prerequisites:

→ University in the region.

→ University with School of Engineering in the region.

→ Complete research project at a University in the region.

Description: This is as "clean" is it's going to get, bub. This is coal, after all.

Oil Power Plant

Cost: §27,500

Operational Cost: §856 per hour

Power Production Rate: 150 MW

Oil Burn Rate: 864K BPD

Air Pollution Rate: High

Description: Everything runs on oil, right? Imports crude oil directly from the global market. Converts crude oil into power...and pollution.

The Oil Power Plant performs much like the Coal Power Plant, albeit with a bigger price tag and greater hourly operational costs. However, in its stock state, this power plant also generates twice as much power as the Coal Power Plant, making it a serious contender, only outperformed by the Nuclear Power Plant. But like the Coal Power Plant, this facility pumps out a tremendous amount of air pollution, so keep it far away from major population centers and make sure the wind carries air pollution away from your city. Construction of the Combustion Turbine Generator or Clean Oil Generator modules help reduce air pollution output, but they don't completely eliminate it. If you have an Oil Well in your city, make sure the power plant is open to local crude oil deliveries. This helps keep operational costs down by consuming barrels of oil produced in your city instead of buying them on the global market. So if your city can tolerate the pollution, the Oil Power Plant is by far one of the most cost-effective solutions to meet your power demands.

> **TIP**
>
> Power plant not generating enough power? Add a module before plopping another power plant.

MODULES

Oil Power Plant Sign

Cost: §200

Operational Cost: None

Maximum Modules: 1

Description: This *cough* sign says *cough* "Dedicated to the Environment" *cough* *cough*.

Conventional Oil Generator

Cost: §7,500

Operational Cost: §756 per hour

Power Production Rate: 150 MW

Oil Burn Rate: 360K BPD

Air Pollution Rate: High

Maximum Modules: 4

Description: Crude oil is used to convert water into steam to produce power.

Combustion Turbine Generator

Cost: §20,000

Operational Cost: §1,185 per hour

Power Production Rate: 150 MW

Oil Burn Rate: 120K BPD

Air Pollution Rate: Medium

Maximum Modules: 3

Description: Crude oil is burned under pressure to produce power.

Clean Oil Generator

Cost: §27,000

Operational Cost: §1,295 per hour

Power Production Rate: 150 MW

Oil Burn Rate: 240K BPD

Air Pollution Rate: Low

Maximum Modules: 3

Prerequisites:

→ University in the region.

→ University with School of Engineering in the region.

→ Complete research project at a University in the region.

Description: After crude oil is used in a combustion turbine generator, excess exhaust is used to convert water into steam.

Solar Power Plant

Cost: §33,000

Operational Cost: §145 per hour

Power Production Rate: 4 MW during peak hours

Air Pollution Rate: None

Description: Collect the power of the sun itself to give your city clean energy. By day, solar panels absorb power. At night, they use power stored in batteries.

The idea of harnessing the power of the sun to generate clean electricity is extremely compelling. But in practice, running a Solar Power Plant can become extremely frustrating, particularly for a growing city. The initial cost of this power plant is quite high, particularly when compared to the cheaper and more efficient Wind Power Plant. And since the facility requires sunlight to function, it can only collect solar energy from 5AM to 8PM. As darkness falls, the power plant relies on power stored in batteries to light the city at night. You can increase the facility's power output by adding additional Fixed Solar Array modules. But the Fixed Solar Arrays are massive, quickly eating up precious space. If you're set on solar, hold off until you can build the smaller and more efficient Concentrated Solar Array. But to gain access to this advanced technology, you must first complete the associated research project at a University in the region. When operating at peak efficiency, the Solar Power Plant is still a low power producer when compared with the Coal, Oil, and Nuclear Power Plants. However, if you're only using it to power a small city with low power demands and strict growth limitations, it can certainly get the job done.

MODULES

Solar Power Sign

Cost: §200

Operational Cost: None

Maximum Modules: 1

Description: They'll see the sign. It'll open up their eyes. They'll see the sign.

Fixed Solar Array

Cost: §16,000

Operational Cost: §105 per hour

Power Production Rate: 4 MW during peak hours

Air Pollution Rate: None

Maximum Modules: 16

Description: Bulky but cheap, these panels are the bread and butter of solar power.

Concentrated Solar Array

Cost: §40,000

Operational Cost: §320 per hour

Power Production Rate: 12.51 MW during peak hours

Air Pollution Rate: None

Maximum Modules: 16

Prerequisites:

→ University in the region.

→ University with School of Science in the region.

→ Complete research project at a University in the region.

Description: These futuristic dishes are small, efficient, and expensive. They provide much more power than the basic panel, but take up much less space.

Nuclear Power Plant

Cost: §145,000

Operational Cost: §1,300 per hour

Power Production Rate: 300 MW

Air Pollution Rate: None

Description: Educated Sims and large amounts of water can create free, albeit radioactive, power. Careful! If this power plant is staffed with unskilled workers it may emit variable amounts of radiation.

If you're interested in building a city specializing in power production, the Nuclear Power Plant is the single best way to generate enormous amounts of power, capable of supplying multiple cities. However, the staggering costs and resources associated with generating safe nuclear power can be prohibitive. So even if you can afford it, never build a Nuclear Power Plant until you have the proper infrastructure in place. For one, these power plants require high volumes of water, serving as coolant. Those quaint Water Towers probably won't be able to keep up with the demand, so build a Water Pumping Station. Don't rely on other cities to supply water—a sudden and prolonged disruption in water supply can lead to the plant being shutdown. Secondly, these power plants require many educated, skilled workers, produced by Community Colleges and Universities. If the education level in your city is low or nonexistent, don't build this power plant. While the Nuclear Power Plant can function with unskilled workers, radioactive pollution will slowly spread along the ground, eventually seeping into the water table. There is also an increased chance of triggering a meltdown. But as long as you have enough money, water, and educated workers, nuclear power is completely safe and pollution-free.

⚠ CAUTION

Click on a Nuclear Power Plant to view the current education level of its workers. If the plant is deemed "unsafe" consider shutting it down until you can attract educated workers. Operating a Nuclear Power Plant with uneducated workers increases the chances of triggering a meltdown. Meltdowns are disasters resulting in widespread deaths, injuries, and sickness. The spread of radiation also leaves a large swath of your city uninhabitable for many years.

MODULES

Nuclear Power Plant Sign

Cost: §200

Operational Cost: None

Maximum Modules: 1

Description: When headless fish start showing up in the daily catch, this will show people where to go.

Gen I Thermal Reactor

Cost: §45,000

Operational Cost: §1,200 per hour

Power Production Rate: 300 MW

Air Pollution Rate: None

Maximum Modules: 3

Description: This standard reactor requires more water for coolant, but adds jobs and produces power that's almost problem free. Almost.

Gen II Thermal Reactor

Cost: §75,000

Operational Cost: §2,300 per hour

Power Production Rate: 400 MW

Air Pollution Rate: None

Maximum Modules: 3

Prerequisites:

→ University in the region.

→ University with School of Science in the region.

→ Complete research project at a University in the region.

Description: This mid-sized generator uses slightly more water and skilled workers, but produces slightly more power than the Gen I Thermal Reactor.

Fast Neutron Reactor

Cost: §130,000

Operational Cost: §3,200 per hour

Power Production Rate: 600 MW

Air Pollution Rate: None

Maximum Modules: 3

Prerequisites:

→ University in the region.

→ University with School of Science in the region.

→ Complete research project at a University in the region.

Description: Uses more water and skilled workers, but produces more power and three-eyed llamas.

Power: Points to Remember

→ Build power plants to provide power.

→ RCI buildings that don't receive enough power will go abandoned.

→ If a building doesn't get power it will stop providing services.

→ Power plants can import resources directly from the global market.

→ Local resources are cheaper than importing from the global market.

→ A city creating power makes its excess power available to its neighbors.

→ Power can be purchased from a neighbor in Region View.

→ Purchase power with the Buy button in Region View.

→ Cities pay a fee to their neighbors for power they purchase.

→ Cities only buy the amount of power they need.

→ Cities automatically increase the amount of power they buy as needs increase.

Water

The Water menu shows the flow of water circulating throughout your city while the Water data map shows the water table beneath your city.

Sims aren't the only ones who get thirsty. Without a constant and dependable water supply, many buildings will cease to function. You can pump water directly from the water table beneath your city—access the Water data map to see underground aquifers. Most city sites have plenty of water just beneath the surface. By placing a Water Tower or Water Pumping Station over an aquifer, you can supply your city with a steady supply of refreshing water.

All data relating to water production and availability is visible within the Water info tab, on the right side of the Water menu. The analog gauge here represents the surplus amount of water flowing through your system, measured in kilogallons (kgal). As long as the needle on this gauge stays within the green area, you have more than enough water. But if the needle moves into the yellow or red zones, you may be facing a water shortage. Build another Water Tower or purchase water from a neighboring city in the region— the amount of surplus water available in the region is also shown.

Water is susceptible to contamination, originating from ground pollution. The info tab also keeps track of how much pollution is in the water. If pollution gets high, you may see an increase in sick Sims due to germs in the water. Address pollution by keeping your water pumping facilities far from sources of ground pollution, like the Garbage Dump or Sewage Outflow Pipe. Pollution can also be filtered out of the system by constructing the Water Filtration module at a Water Pumping Station. Deal with polluted water as quickly as possible to avoid a massive germ outbreak.

While the water menu is open you can also view the water flowing beneath your city's streets. Water is represented by blue lines, with small branches entering buildings along each road. The blue circles beneath each building represent water demand—the larger the blue circle, the greater the demand. With a simple glance at your city you can quickly view usage and identify outages. If there's enough water in the system, all buildings are served. However, if there's a shortage, buildings farthest from your water source will be the first to suffer shortages. Act quickly to address deficits in your water system to prevent buildings from becoming abandoned due to lack of water.

Water Tower

Cost: §3,500

Operational Cost: §100 per hour

Average Water Pump Rate: 6 kgal/hr

Description: Pumps a decent amount of water from the water table to your city. Beware of ground pollution, which can carry sickness-transmitting germs.

The Water Tower is a simple, no-frills solution to your city's water needs. These structures are cheap and small, making it easy to expand your water coverage with the construction of additional Water Towers. When a Water Tower is selected from the Water menu, the Water data map is automatically activated, showing all aquifers beneath your city, appearing as blue pools—the darker the blue, the more water available. Before plopping a Water Tower, make sure you place it directly over a dark blue aquifer. Also, avoid placing the Water Tower anywhere near sources of ground pollution. This means keeping it far away from your Garbage Dump and Sewage Outflow Pipe. If placed in an area of high ground pollution, the water pumped is contaminated, spreading germs to all Sims who drink it. This can cause a massive public health crisis, leading to overfilled Clinics and Hospitals as sick Sims seek treatment for sickness.

TIP

Given their small footprint, Water Towers can be placed on steep, uneven terrain, unsuitable for zoning or other structures. If you can't place anything else there, you might as well build Water Towers.

Water Pumping Station

Cost: §24,000

Operational Cost: §400 per hour

Average Water Pump Rate: 80 kgal/hr

Prerequisites:

→ Town Hall in the region.

→ Town Hall upgraded to a City Hall in the region.

→ Department of Utilities in the region.

Description: Thirsty? Quench it with this large, expandable water production facility. With all the extra water, you could make a bit of extra income selling water to neighboring cities.

If your network of Water Towers isn't cutting it, consider upgrading to the far more efficient Water Pumping Station—you'll need a Department of Utilities in the region first. Although this facility is much larger than a Water Tower, it produces high volumes of water, capable of quenching the thirst of any sized city. Capacity can even be increased by adding extra Basic Water Pump modules. The Filtration Pump module can also be added to remove any contaminants caused by ground pollution. But don't bulldoze those old Water Towers just yet. It may take a while for the Water Pumping Station to reach peak efficiency. If you suspect ground pollution may contaminate your water supply, build the Water Pumping Station with a Filtration Pump module at the outset, removing the existing Basic Water Pump at the same time. The Filtration Pump filters out 100% of all contaminants, ensuring your city's water supply is safe. But if you're running a Basic Water Pump as well, contaminants may get through. So make sure you replace all Basic Water Pumps with Filtration Pumps.

MODULES

Basic Water Pump

Cost: §30,000

Operational Cost: §200 per hour

Average Water Pump Rate: 80 kgal/hr

Maximum Modules: 6 (one comes with base)

Description: If there's still water in the water table, add another Basic Water Pump to extract more to meet your city's needs or sell it to the region.

 TIP

Plop your Water Towers and pumps away from ground pollution.

 NOTE

Water Towers and Water Pumping Stations built next to rivers have an unlimited supply of water.

Filtration Pump

Cost: §60,000

Operational Cost: §400 per hour

Average Water Pump Rate: 80 kgal/hr

Maximum Modules: 6 (one comes with base)

Description: Everyone needs water, but if your ground is polluted, you don't want to drink germs! This filters out all contaminants as it pumps, sending mostly clean water to your city.

Water: Points to Remember

→ Place Water Towers to provide water.

→ RCI buildings that don't get enough water will go abandoned.

→ If a building doesn't get water it will stop providing services.

→ Dark blue areas of the Water map hold the most water.

→ Rain will replenish the water table.

→ Rivers and lakes supply unlimited water.

→ Water Towers on polluted ground will make many Sims sick.

→ A city creating water makes its excess water available to its neighbors.

→ Purchase water with the Buy button in Region View.

→ Cities pay a fee to their neighbors for water they purchase.

→ Cities only buy the amount of water they need.

→ Cities automatically increase the amount of water they buy as needs increase.

Sewage

The brown blobs beneath your city's road system are raw sewage. Don't let sewage build up in the pipes, otherwise it will become ground pollution.

It may be unpleasant to think about, but shortly after your Sims gain access to water, they'll begin converting it into raw sewage. This sewage builds up in the pipes beneath your road system, appearing as brown blobs when the Sewage menu is open. If ignored, the sewage will eventually back up, creating ground pollution all over your city. Not only are Sims disgusted by the sight of sewage pooling in their yards and streets, they can also get sick from it due to the spread of germs. So as Mayor, it's your job to make sure sewage is moved out of the pipes and into a designated disposal area. Build a Sewage Outflow Pipe to dump raw sewage onto an open piece of land far from your residents. Or collect it at a Sewage Treatment Plant and dispose of it properly. If you don't want to deal with sewage at all, simply buy service from a neighboring city in the region.

For all information relating to your city's sewage system, reference the info tab within the Sewage menu. The analog gauge here shows the excess capacity of your sewage system, measured in kilogallons (kgal). Keep the needle in the green to ensure sewage is flowing properly through the pipes with no backups. But if the needle moves into the yellow or red zones, you may be facing a flow or capacity problem—build another Sewage Outflow Pipe or add another Sewage Treatment Tank to your Sewage Treatment Plant to fix the problem. The info tab also shows the percentage of sewage being treated—make sure this reads 100% if you have a Sewage Treatment Plant. If it doesn't read 100%, your facility may be over capacity or under-staffed, resulting in ground pollution. You can also see the amount of sewage capacity available for purchase in the region, if you decide to send your sewage elsewhere.

While the info tab reveals a wealth of information, simply opening the Sewage menu and watching the brown blobs flowing beneath your city streets is usually adequate to spot deficiencies in your system. As long as these blobs

are moving at a steady rate, things are working well. But if movement of sewage is slow or stagnant, you need to address the problem quickly by increasing capacity. As your city grows, it will produce more and more sewage. As high density buildings start popping up, periodically click on the Sewage menu to ensure your system is still handling the increased flow streaming from new high rises.

Sewage Outflow Pipe

Cost: §3,500

Operational Cost: §100 per hour

Maximum Sewage Flow Rate: 11.7 kgal/hr

Maximum Ground Pollution Rate: 120,000 ppm/hr

Description: Converts sewage into ground pollution. Better in a spot you pick than backing up in John and Jane Q. Public's backyard.

Until a Department of Utilities has been built in the region, the Sewage Outflow Pipe is the only option for handling a city's sewage problem. This utility pumps raw sewage out of the pipe system and simply dumps it onto an open piece of land, creating plenty of icky ground pollution in the process. As a result, keep the smelly Sewage Outflow Pipe far away from your population centers to prevent the spread of germs. Speaking of germs, never build a Water Tower or Water Pumping Station near the Sewage Outflow Pipe. Ground pollution seeps into the water table and can contaminate your water source. Pumping polluted water throughout your city is a surefire way to trigger a massive public health crisis. To avoid water contamination, access the Ground Pollution data map to view the pollution surrounding the Sewage Outflow Pipe. Ground pollution spreads beyond the utility, but eventually stops—you don't need to worry about ground pollution spreading over a vast area. But no matter how crowded your city is, it's a good idea to keep some open space around the Sewage Outflow Pipe. This allows ground pollution to spread without serious consequences.

Sewage Treatment Plant

Cost: §64,000

Operational Cost: §400 per hour

Maximum Sewage Treatment Rate: 700 kgal/hr

Maximum Sewage Flow Rate: 300 kgal/hr

Ground Pollution Output: None

Prerequisites:

→ Town Hall in the region.

→ Town Hall upgraded to a City Hall in the region.

→ Department of Utilities in the region.

Description: What kind of civilized city dumps their waste into a field? Clean that sewage before disposing of it with this Sewage Treatment Plant. If you don't want a sewage spill, be mindful of its capacity!

If reducing ground pollution is a concern, and it should be, build the Sewage Treatment Plant as soon as possible—you'll need a Department of Utilities in the region first. Unlike the Sewage Outflow Pipe, this facility treats raw sewage in massive treatment tanks, removing all waste and contaminants. When functioning properly, the Sewage Treatment Plant produces no ground pollution, returning treated water to the water table. But if the facility loses power or water, is understaffed, or reaches capacity, raw sewage may spill from the tanks, creating ground pollution. Keep a close eye on this facility to ensure it's functioning properly. Click on the building to open its information window. Here you can see the current capacity of the facility. Hard data is also displayed showing the total amount of sewage processed, including sewage that has been treated and untreated. If any amount of processed sewage is going untreated, consider adding an additional Sewage Treatment Tank. Once your Sewage Treatment Plant is functioning, remember to turn off or bulldoze your old Sewage Outflow Pipes to stop polluting the ground.

MODULES

Sewage Treatment Tank

Cost: §40,000

Operational Cost: §200 per hour

Maximum Sewage Treatment Rate: 700 kgal/hr

Maximum Modules: 7 (one comes with base)

Ground Pollution Output: None

Description: Ew! Holds even more sewage water! Increase your Sewage Treatment Plant's capacity, so it doesn't overflow with human waste.

Sewage: Points to Remember

→ Sims create sewage.

→ Sewage Outflow Pipes collect sewage but don't treat it.

→ Uncollected sewage creates ground pollution.

→ Germs from ground pollution make Sims sick and unhappy.

→ A city providing sewage treatment can take in sewage from other cities.

→ Send sewage for treatment with the Buy button in Region View.

→ Cities pay a fee to their neighbors for sending their sewage.

 TIP

If your Sewage Outflow Pipe is clogged, plop another but be sure to keep your first one.

Waste Disposal

Keep an eye on the Waste Disposal's info tab to ensure all garbage cans and recycling bins are being collected each day. If not, it may be time to expand coverage with additional trucks.

Sewage isn't the only germ-spreading nuisance accumulating throughout your city. All buildings output garbage, appearing as garbage cans lining the streets. If you don't address this problem soon, the number of garbage cans will increase along with ground pollution. In addition to spreading germs, uncollected garbage also increases the risk of fires, potentially forcing you to expand fire coverage prematurely. Furthermore, garbage also attracts the homeless, making certain buildings less effective. So soon after starting a new city, construct a Garbage Dump to deal with this issue before it gets out of hand. Later on you can even construct a Recycling Center, reducing the amount of garbage collected while producing alloy, metal, and plastic for use in industry or for pure profit.

The info tab in the Waste Disposal menu displays all the information you need to know about your garbage and recycling services. The top number shows the daily number of garbage cans collected out of the total number of garbage cans in the city. If every garbage can has been collected by the end of each day, you're doing a great job. But if there are several cans not being collected each day, expand coverage with more garbage trucks—build additional Garbage Truck Garages at your Garbage Dump. The same goes for the second number in the info tab showing the number of recycling bins collected daily out of the total number of recycling bins. If some recycling bins are going uncollected each day, field more recycling collection trucks by building additional Recycling Collection Truck Garages at your Recycling Center.

When the Waste Disposal menu is open, you can see the various garbage and recycling collection trucks driving around the city, emptying garbage cans and recycling bins. A blue icon appears above each truck—garbage trucks are marked with a trash can icon and recycling trucks are marked with a recycle icon. Each truck leaves its respective facility at 6AM each day and begins its work. Monitor the trucks' movement along narrow two lane streets, as their stop-and-go movement may lead to congestion, with multiple cars lined up behind each truck. If your trucks are causing traffic problems, consider upgrading affected roads with the Road Selector tool.

Garbage Dump

Cost: §9,000

Operational Cost: §300 per hour

Waste Capacity: 40 tons

Ground Pollution Output: 7,000 ppm/hr

Description: Sims hate piles of garbage in front of their homes, so dump it all here! Add more garbage trucks to have garbage collected faster.

Unless receiving garbage coverage from a neighboring city, the Garbage Dump is the only way to remove trash accumulating in your city's streets. Like the Sewage Outflow Pipe, this building accumulates large amounts of ground pollution, so build it a safe distance away from your major population centers. Building it directly next to the Sewage Outflow Pipe isn't a bad idea, helping consolidate ground pollution in one area. The Garbage Dump dispatches a single garbage truck at 6AM every day to empty garbage cans. The garbage truck stops at every building in the city, emptying all garbage cans along its route. The single garbage truck included with this facility is enough to get started, but you'll need to build additional Garbage Truck Garages to expand coverage as your city grows. You can even volunteer these trucks to collect garbage in neighboring cities. Eventually the provided Dump Zone will reach capacity, requiring you to place another Dump Zone, connected to the Service Road. Extend the dump's existing Service Road to place additional Dump Zones. But if you're tired of accumulating mounds of trash, you could always burn it with the Garbage Incinerator. This is a very effective way to remove garbage, but it emits an enormous amount of air pollution, similar to a Coal or Oil Power Plant. If you build it, make sure the wind carries the pollution away from your city, otherwise the spread of air pollution will lead to sick Sims.

MODULES

Service Road

Cost: Free

Operational Cost: None

Description: Dirt road for garbage trucks to take garbage to dump in Dump Zones...and it smells nasty. Add more Service Roads to give you room to place more Dump Zones.

Garbage Truck Garage

Cost: §5,000

Operational Cost: §100 per hour

Vehicle Capacity: 1.5 tons

Maximum Modules: 8 (one comes with base)

Description: Add another garbage truck to your dump to speed up garbage collection.

Dump Zone

Cost: Free

Operational Cost: None

Waste Capacity: 40 tons

Ground Pollution Output: 3,500 ppm/hr

Maximum Modules: 8 (one comes with base)

Description: Designate more space for garbage dumping. Just avoid people's backyards, okay?

Garbage Incinerator

Cost: §25,000

Operational Cost: §300 per hour

Garbage Burn Rate: 6 tons/hr

Air Pollution Rate: High

Maximum Modules: 4

Description: Burn the garbage away! Air pollution? Nah, nobody cares about that.

Recycling Center

Cost: §111,000

Operational Cost: §700 per hour

Waste Capacity: 20 tons

Prerequisites:

→ Town Hall in the region.

→ Town Hall upgraded to a City Hall in the region.

→ Department of Utilities in the region.

Description: Educated Sims will want to recycle. Used alloy, metal, and plastic can be brought here to be reclaimed, to be used or sold on the global market via a Trade Depot. Does not replace the Garbage Dump.

If you have the money to spare, you can significantly reduce the amount of garbage collected by building a Recycling Center. This functions much like the Garbage Dump, dispatching trucks that collect recycling bins filled with alloy, metal, and plastic. These materials are then processed at the facility and converted into usable alloy, metal, and plastic, which can be sold or used by local industry. Initially the Recycling Plant is equipped with one Plastic Reclamation Line. If you wish to produce alloy and metal, you'll need to construct Metal and Alloy Reclamation Lines. Each line comes with one product storage lot, each capable of storing 10 tons of recycled products. The facility comes with one delivery truck which is responsible for delivering the recycled products to local businesses, Great Works sites, or Trade Depots and Ports—recycled products cannot be sold directly from the Recycling Center. Build additional Reclamation Delivery Truck Garages if any of the product storage lots are full—the facility automatically shuts down if all product storage lots are full. As with garbage collection, build additional Recycling Collection Truck Garages to expand coverage as your city grows. These trucks can also be volunteered to neighboring cities.

The amount of alloy, metal, and plastic generated through recycling is minuscule when compared to the output produced by the Smelting Factory and Oil Refinery, so maintain realistic expectations. The Recycling Center won't make you much money (if any), but it will reduce

the amount of garbage piling up in your Garbage Dump. Plus, recycling makes educated Sims feel good about themselves. Isn't that enough?

> **(i) NOTE**
>
> The amount of recyclable material collected is tied to education level—the higher the education level, the greater the recycling rate. Uneducated Sims recycle 20% of their garbage while highly educated Sims can recycle as much as 100% of their garbage. As the recycling rate increases, your garbage trucks will have fewer garbage cans to collect. So as recycling takes hold, scale back your garbage collection services to reduce costs.

MODULES

Alloy Reclamation Line

Cost: §25,000

Operational Cost: §400 per hour

Garbage Burn Rate: 0.1 tons/hr

Maximum Modules: 4

Description: Converts reclaimed alloy into usable alloy that your delivery trucks can deliver to Great Works projects, Trade Depots, Trade Ports, or local industry.

Metal Reclamation Line

Cost: §25,000

Operational Cost: §400 per hour

Garbage Burn Rate: 0.1 tons/hr

Maximum Modules: 4

Description: Converts reclaimed metal into usable metal that your delivery trucks can deliver to Great Works projects, Trade Depots, Trade Ports, or local industry.

Plastic Reclamation Line

Cost: §25,000

Operational Cost: §400 per hour

Garbage Burn Rate: 0.1 tons/hr

Maximum Modules: 4 (one comes with base)

Description: Converts reclaimed plastic into usable plastic that your delivery trucks can deliver to Great Works projects, Trade Depots, Trade Ports, or local industry.

Recycling Collection Truck Garage

Cost: §3,000

Operational Cost: §100 per hour

Vehicle Capacity: 4.5 tons

Maximum Modules: 8 (one comes with base)

Description: Increases your recycling collection rate with an additional truck for collecting raw recycled alloy, metal, or plastic.

Reclamation Delivery Truck Garage

Cost: §3,000

Operational Cost: §100 per hour

Vehicle Capacity: 1 ton

Maximum Modules: 4 (one comes with base)

Description: Houses a recycling delivery truck for delivering plastics, metals, or alloys that have been reclaimed to businesses that need them.

Waste Disposal: Points to Remember

→ Sims create garbage.

→ Garbage will become ground pollution if not collected.

→ Excess garbage drives customers away and increases injuries/sickness.

→ A Recycling Center will cause Sims to separate recycling from garbage.

→ A Recycling Center only picks up recycling— you will still need garbage collection.

→ Recycling reduces pollution, reduces garbage, and generates resources.

→ Homeless are attracted to garbage at buildings, making them less effective.

→ The Garbage Dump will fill with garbage and can be expanded with modules.

→ Any garbage vehicle can be volunteered to any connected city.

→ Cities receiving garbage coverage get it for free.

→ The city providing the garbage coverage receives income for the garbage it collects.

Utility Management

Providing power, water, sewage, and waste disposal services is a fundamental responsibility for all mayors. If you're not doing your job, you'll hear about it from angry Sims protesting outside City Hall. Red thought bubbles will also pop up all over the city, revealing the complaints of individual Sims. Failure to meet any utility demands could eventually lead to abandoned buildings as Sims pack up and leave the city. As the population drops, so does tax revenue. To avoid a massive exodus, stay on top of the ever-changing demands on your city's utilities.

Pollution and Land Value Concerns

Most utility buildings cause land values to plummet, as visible in the Land Value map.

Although they provide vital services to your city, nobody wants to live or conduct business next to your utility infrastructure. Why? Many of these structures emit some level of ground or air pollution. Plus, nearly all utility buildings reduce land value. Go ahead, activate the Land Value data map to see how these buildings bring down the neighborhood. As a result, it's a good idea to keep these buildings far from your residential and commercial zones. Industrial zones can tolerate the ill effects of pollution and low land value much better, but still, consider keeping these utilities somewhat isolated from the rest of your city. A classic *SimCity* strategy is to build these structures along the edge or corners of your city site, helping minimize the effects of pollution and low land value—when placed on a border, a portion of the negative footprint lands outside your city limits. But when doing this with a polluting power plant or the Garbage Dump's Garbage Incinerator, make sure the wind direction carries all air pollution away from your city, otherwise air pollution blowing over your city will lead to complaints and sickness. If you're running low on space and simply need to build closer and closer to utility buildings, consider building parks to serve as a buffer. Parks reduce air and ground pollution as well as increase land value, helping offset the negatives associated with utilities. Or dedicate an entire city to utilities, selling and

volunteering services to other cities in the region. This helps keep pollution consolidated in one city instead of spreading it throughout the region.

Expansion of Services

Most utilities can be expanded by constructing additional modules. This allows you to expand services as needed.

Once your utility infrastructure is in place and working splendidly, don't turn your back on it. As your city grows, so will the demand for more power, water, sewage, and waste disposal. Periodically open the associated menus and study the data in each info tab to ensure services are adequate—those analog gauges are a quick and easy way to analyze the situation. As a rule of thumb, check in on your utilities every time your City Hall earns an upgrade. City Hall upgrades are tied to increases in the population, a good indicator of increasing demand on your utilities. If you're seeing any deficiencies in service, expand the impacted utility buildings with additional modules to meet the increased demand. Also, keep an eye on your city's skyline. When high-rise residential and commercial buildings start popping up, take another look at the utility menus. The increased density of these structures can put a sudden strain on your utilities, potentially leading to shortages. As you can see, the demand on a city's utilities never ends. In fact, it only increases as the city grows. Keep this in mind when placing your utility buildings, leaving enough space around them so you can construct additional modules as needed.

 TIP

Most utility buildings require workers to function, so if a utility isn't operating at peak efficiency, you're probably facing a labor shortage. Zone more residential to attract more workers into your city.

Outsourcing Services

Open the Region View to buy power, water, and sewage service from neighboring cities.

Don't feel like supplying your city with utility services? You can always attain power, water, sewage, and waste disposal services from neighboring cities in the region. Open the Region View and look for nearby cities connected to the regional highway—all regional utility services are transmitted along the highway. If no cities are connected to the same highway, you're on your own. Open the Power, Water, or Sewage menu to open a new trade window, giving you the opportunity to buy services from any of the connected cities. Click the Buy button to begin buying services—you can stop the deal at any time by clicking the Stop button. All deals of this nature must be initiated by the city in need of services. Buying services from another city is easy, but it may not solve all your problems. For example, if a neighboring city is only supplying 15 MW of surplus power and your city needs 20 MW, you'll need to address the deficit by constructing a power plant or by purchasing additional power from another city. So even if you're purchasing utility services from another city, keep a close eye on the info tab within each menu to ensure demands are being met.

> **ⓘ NOTE**
>
> Purchased power and water must travel from a connected city to your city. This means it make take a few moments for power from a distant city to start flowing into your borders.

Volunteering Trucks

As you add new garbage and recycling collection trucks to your fleet, volunteer them to neighboring cities to generate extra income.

The sharing of garbage and recycling collection trucks works a little differently. You can't buy waste disposal services from a neighboring city. Instead, a city can volunteer its trucks to your city, free of charge. When receiving coverage in this fashion, you pay nothing, but have no control over the number of trucks charged with emptying garbage cans and recycling bins in your city. If some cans and bins are going uncollected, ask neighboring cities to volunteer more trucks, or build a Garbage Dump and Recycling Center of your own to handle the shortfall. If you already have a Garbage Dump and Recycling Center, open the Region View and click on the Waste Disposal menu. Here you can volunteer your own garbage and recycling collection trucks to neighboring cities. Click on the city you wish to assist, then adjust the number of trucks you wish to volunteer. Feel free to scatter your fleet of trucks among multiple cities. When volunteering vehicles, your city loses no coverage—the same trucks can service both cities simultaneously—so there's no reason not to volunteer every truck in your fleet. Each truck receives a small fee for collecting garbage cans and recycling bins in neighboring cities. This additional income can help offset the operational costs of running your Garbage Dump and Recycling Center.

UTILITY ACHIEVEMENTS

Icon	Name	Criteria
	2 Kilometer Island! (Secret)	Have a nuclear meltdown in your city.
	Aqua Max	Have a city that has over 100 kgal of water needed per hour.
	Blowin' in the Wind (Secret)	Have 24 Wind Turbines at Wind Power Plants in your city to gain access to the Tornado disaster.
	Dump City!	Have 560 tons of garbage in your Garbage Dumps.
	Garbage Man!	Pick up 10 tons of garbage in a day.
	Green Plumbobs	Pick up 10 tons of recyclables in your city in a day!
	Ick or Treat!	Treat 200 kgal/hr of sewage at a Sewage Treatment Plant.
	Make Sure You're Grounded...	Provide both power and water to a neighbor, at the same time.
	Mayor Yuck (Secret)	Have 500 Sims complaining about dirty water in a day.
	Sewage Stuffing	With 10,000 or more residents, prevent sewage issues using only Sewage Outlet Pipes.
	Sludge-free H-2-0!	Pump 500 kgal of fresh, clean water in an hour.
	Super-Powered	Have a city that has over 300 MW of power needed per hour.
	Time to Relocate	Have 200+ garbage issues at once in a region.
	What's Cookin'? (Secret)	Burn 100 tons of garbage in an Incinerator at the Garbage Dump to gain access to the Big Lizard disaster.

CHAT WITH THE DEVELOPERS

How I Mayor: Dirty Secrets of High Tech Industry

BRIAN BARTRAM, SENIOR GAME DESIGNER

Welcome, Mayors, to my high tech metropolis. Brian Bartram here, Senior Game Designer on *SimCity*, and I've been given the green light to show you how I built this city of the future. I've got a problem, though—investing deep in education has left my coffers nearly empty. But there's a clever solution here, a pro tip that I'm going to share with you. Pay close attention, I'm going to make gold out of garbage!

DAY ONE

When I founded Wintermute, I knew that I would need to plan ahead to create a high tech city. It took patience to build up a University to provide the strong education influence that I would need to convert dirty industry into clean (and profitable) high tech industry. But the result is worth it—I love the look of gleaming silver, clear blue, and bright yellow along with the interesting shapes and crazy structures of high tech industry.

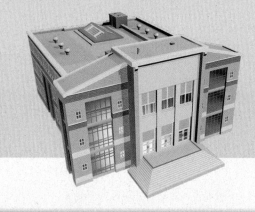

DAY TWO

It's no surprise that education doesn't come cheap, and my investment in this University has left me nearly broke. Luckily, there's a city specialization that fits my city perfectly—electronics manufacturing. The money is good, but the cost of raw materials is really cutting into my profits. Maybe there's another way to look at this problem...

DAY THREE

While considering how to handle my city's garbage problem, I noticed that recycling not only reduces garbage, but it also recovers alloy and plastic—which just happens to be the resources that I need to produce computer processors. Wait, this building will help me solve two problems at once? Gimme a loan, I need that Recycling Center right now!

> It's no surprise that education doesn't come cheap, and my investment in this University has left me nearly broke. Luckily, there's a city specialization that fits my city perfectly—electronics manufacturing.

DAY FOUR

It didn't take long to equip my new Recycling Center with modules to recover plastic and alloy for use in my electronics manufacturing city specialization I also make sure to provide my neighbors with recycling trucks to pick up their garbage—a win/win deal! I'm raking in so many resources that I'm able to stop importing them from the global market.

DAY FIVE

It almost feels like cheating—collecting other people's trash and turning it into the raw materials I need to make some of the most profitable goods available. But the results speak for themselves—my high tech city is clean, profitable, and full of smart, happy Sims. It was definitely a challenge, and required patience and planning. All the same, I'm delighted to show off my city to the other developers in the office, and a high tech city never fails to impress.

Zoning

Ready to populate your city and make some money?

Designating residential, commercial, and industrial zones spurs the construction of houses, shops, and factories, instantly creating multiple sources of tax revenue for your city. After plopping down all your utilities, you'll need plenty of income to offset those hourly operational costs. But there's more to zoning than setting aside plots of land for development. In this chapter we take a detailed look at how residential, commercial, and industrial zones function as well as offer some advice to help optimize happiness and profitability throughout your city.

> Don't forget to go to **www.primagames.com** to access guide updates free of charge with your voucher code.

RCI Overview

So how does zoning work? The accompanying diagram illustrates the basic symbiotic relationship between residential, commercial, and industrial zones. All Sims live in residential zones and they can work in commercial or industrial zones. The factories in industrial zones produce goods, called freight. The freight is shipped to shops in commercial zones where Sims can purchase these manufactured goods with money. By purchasing goods in shops, Sims gain happiness. Commercial and industrial zones also earn their own form of happiness, called profit. In turn, all zones pay taxes, supplying the city with vital revenue necessary to build infrastructure and supply utilities and services. Sims who have no job also have no money and cannot buy happiness—the same is true if there are no shops where they can spend their money. Industrial factories lose profit if they don't have an adequate outlet for their produced freight. Likewise, commercial shops have reduced profits if they don't receive enough freight from factories or shoppers from residential zones and tourism. As happiness and profits drop, so does tax revenue. It's all a very delicate balancing act. As Mayor, it's your job to provide the proper balance of zoning to ensure all Sims are happy and all shops and factories are profitable.

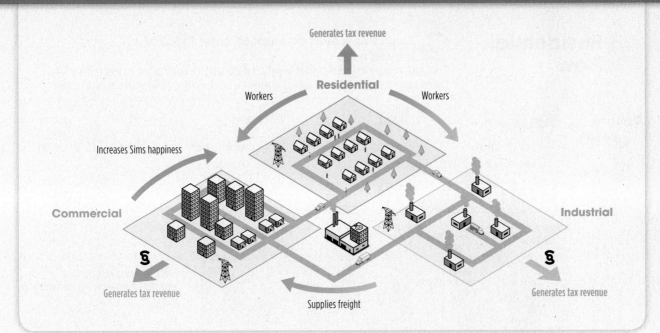

Residential Flow

Lead Designer Stone Librande designed this diagram to help explain the flow of activity in the residential zones. Think of the diagram as a Pachinko machine, with Sims entering through the top and filtering down into various residences. As the diagram illustrates, Sims enter your city based on the number of available jobs in your city and region's commercial and industrial zones. They will then occupy an available residence based on their wealth—low wealth Sims seek low wealth ($) residences, medium wealth Sims live in medium wealth ($$) residences, and high wealth Sims move into high wealth ($$$) residences. The type of residences available is based on land value. Density is then governed by happiness and access to roads with differing densities. By clicking on individual residential buildings you can determine the current needs/concerns of the Sims occupying it. A quick glance at a few residential buildings can reveal problems you can address to increase each Sim's happiness.

RESIDENTIAL: POINTS TO REMEMBER

→ Zone residential to attract houses.

→ Residents (workers, shoppers, kids) live in houses.

→ Workers earn money at factories and shops.

→ Shoppers spend money at shops to buy happiness.

→ Build parks and services to attract wealthy houses.

→ If a building can't pay rent it will go abandoned.

→ When low wealth Sims have no money to pay rent, they abandon their houses and become homeless.

→ Medium and high wealth Sims leave town when they abandon their homes.

Commercial Flow

The demand for commercial buildings is driven by shoppers. Shoppers are comprised of Sims living in a city as well as tourists visiting a city. Shops open throughout the city based on the demand (and wealth) of shoppers— low wealth shops ($) open to cater to low wealth shoppers, and so on. The land value and tax revenue of nearby residential buildings also influence the types of shops opening in an area—high-end shops will not open in areas with low land value, low tax revenue, or high crime and pollution. So if you're having trouble attracting shops catering to high wealth Sims, consider building parks nearby to increase land value (and decrease pollution) while expanding police services to deal with crime. Shops also have specific needs to stay in business, including workers, water, power, and most importantly, profit. Click on any commercial building to see if its needs are being met. Happy, profitable shops will increase in density when adjacent roads are upgraded to accommodate higher density buildings.

COMMERCIAL: POINTS TO REMEMBER

→ Zone commercial to attract shops.

→ Shops create jobs.

→ Shops sell goods to shoppers and tourists.

→ Higher wealth shops serve higher wealth customers.

→ If a shop can't sell enough goods it will go abandoned.

Residential Flow

 Happy new Sims attempt to enter the City at a fixed rate.

This rate can be increased (per wealth class) by transportation networks (roads connected to the edges of a region, boat docks, train stations and airports).

Demand

Low wealth jobs | Mid wealth jobs | High wealth jobs

The number of new residents allowed into the city is capped based on the demand for jobs.

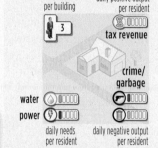

max residents per building | daily positive output per resident

tax revenue

crime/ garbage

water | power

daily needs per resident | daily negative output per resident

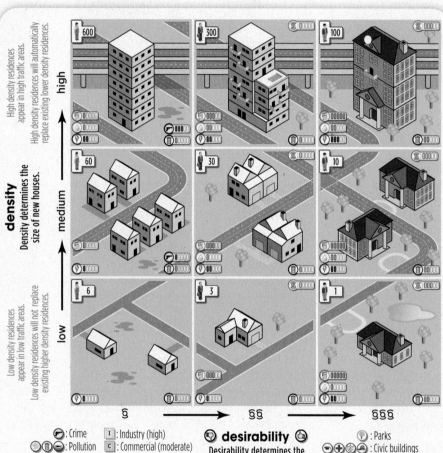

High density residences appear in high traffic areas.

High density residences will automatically replace existing lower density residences.

density
Density determines the size of new houses.

Low density residences appear in low traffic areas.

Low density residences will not replace existing higher density residences.

 : Crime
: Pollution

I : Industry (high)
C : Commercial (moderate)

desirability
Desirability determines the wealth level of new houses.

: Parks
: Civic buildings
: Residential tax income

Low wealth residences will not replace existing higher wealth residences.

High wealth residences will automatically replace existing lower wealth residences.

Every residential building contains the following information:

Needs

Job | Power | Water | Desirability

Every house keeps track of how many residents are employed and whether the building has enough water and power.

Unhappiness

Unhappy | Normal | Happy

Sims with unmet needs become increasingly unhappy.

Sims near Commercial entertainment buildings become increasingly happy.

Sickness

 =

As pollution grows the chance of sickness increases. Sickness will also be caused by random events.

Sick citizens are still employed. However, they don't contribute to their workplaces' production.

Sick citizens do not get any Commercial entertainment benefits.

Education

Low | High School | College | PhD

Residential buildings near schools increase in education level over time. (A lack of schools causes a decrease.) The education level determines the tech level of the industrial buildings.

New citizens enter the box with an education level that matches their residential building. (New buildings have an education value of 0.)

 Unhappy Sims abandon their houses and leave the city.

: Increased crime
: Increased fire hazard
: Counts as garbage

Abandoned houses decrease desirability.

You can bulldoze an abandoned house, wait for it to burn down, or fix the issues that caused the abandonment (this allows Sims to move back in).

C Commercial Flow

😊 Happy new commercial buildings attempt to enter the city at a fixed rate.

This rate can be increased (per wealth class) by transportation networks (roads connected to the edges of a region, boat docks, train stations and airports).

Demand

R

Low wealth shoppers   Medium wealth shoppers   High wealth shoppers

The number of new commercial buildings built in the box is capped based on the demand from shoppers

max workers per building | daily positive output per actual income
low wealth 6
mid wealth 3   tax revenue
high wealth 1

desired income 100
total for all sales

water   garbage
power   daily negative output per worker/shopper
daily needs per worker/shopper

Special Functions

🚩 **Attraction**
Increases visitors to the city.

👤 **Hotel**
Can house visitors
+1 income per low wealth, +3 income per mid wealth, +10 income per high wealth

😊 **Entertainment**
Distributes happiness to R .
+1 income per happiness.

🔫 **Crime**
Increases crime locally.

P **Parking**
Can hold cars.
+1 income per car.

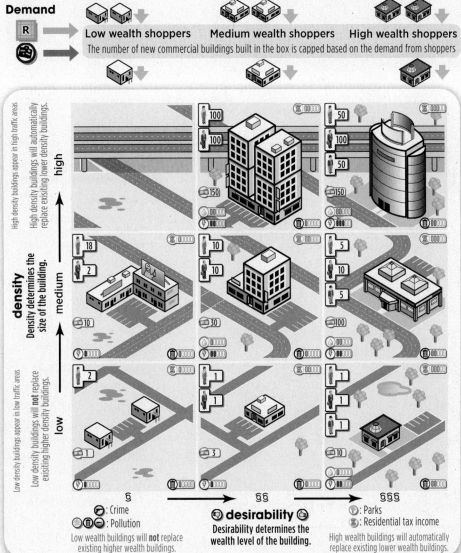

density
Density determines the size of the building.

High density buildings appear in high traffic areas

High density buildings will automatically replace existing lower density buildings.

Low density buildings appear in low traffic areas

Low density buildings will **not** replace existing higher density buildings.

high · medium · low

🔫 : Crime
: Pollution
Low wealth buildings will **not** replace existing higher wealth buildings.

😊 **desirability** 😊
Desirability determines the wealth level of the building.

🌳: Parks
: Residential tax income
High wealth buildings will automatically replace existing lower wealth buildings.

Every commercial building contains the following information:

Desired Income

20 Commercial buildings need to make a certain amount of money each day. Each building makes §1 each time it makes a sale.

A commercial building can make 1 sale per employee per day.

Low Wealth: All shoppers. §
Medium Wealth: Mid-wealth and wealthy shoppers. §§
High Wealth: Only wealthy shoppers. §§§

Needs

Workers   Water   Power   Desirability

Commercial Buildings without any workers, water, power, or in an undesirable zone will make no income.

Unhappiness

😞 Unhappy   😐 Normal   😊 Happy

Buildings that make less than the desired income become increasingly unhappy.

Desired income

Buildings that make more than the desired income become increasingly happy.

Workers/Shoppers
Employed Sims that don't work in a commercial zone will attempt to shop there.

Each morning workers leave the residential zones and go to work in nearby commercial zones.

R
Unemployed workers stay home for the day.

Visitors
Each visitor makes one purchase and then leaves the box.

The number of visitors in the city is capped to the number of hotel rooms.

New visitors enter the city at a fixed rate. Attractions and transportation networks increase the flow of visitors into the city.

 Unhappy commercial buildings become abandoned

🔫 : increased crime
: increased fire hazard
: counts as garbage

Abandoned commercial buildings decrease desirability.

You can bulldoze an abandoned or commercial building, wait for it to burn down, or fix the issues that caused the abandonment (this allows it to open again).

Industrial Flow

😃 **Happy new industrial buildings attempt to enter the city at a fixed rate.**

This rate can be increased (per wealth class) by transportation networks (roads connected to the edges of a region, boat docks, train strations and airports).

Demand

R ➡️

🎓 : Education

Low education | **High-school education** | **College education**

The number of new industrial buildings built in the city is capped based on the demand from residents.

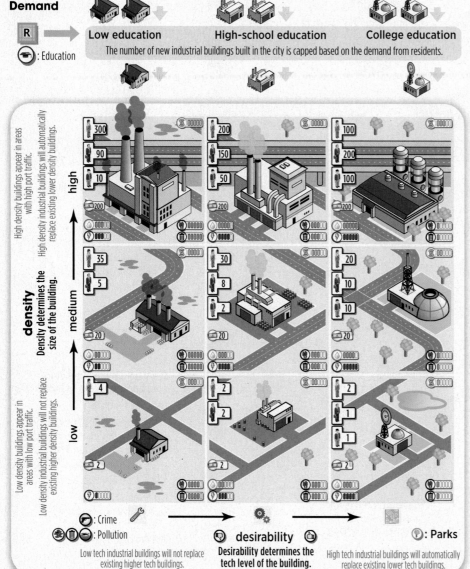

density — **Density determines the size of the building.**

High density buildings appear in areas with high port traffic.
High density industrial buildings will automatically replace existing lower density buildings.

Low density buildings appear in areas with low port traffic.
Low density industrial buildings will not replace existing higher density buildings.

💲 : Crime
🗑️ : Pollution

Low tech industrial buildings will not replace existing higher tech buildings.

⚙️ desirability — **Desirability determines the tech level of the building.**

High tech industrial buildings will automatically replace existing lower tech buildings.

🅿️ : Parks

Every industrial building contains the following information:

max workers per building
low wealth 6
mid wealth 3
high wealth 1

daily positive output per actual income
💲 tax revenue

desired income total for all shipments 💲 100

air pollution/garbage

water 💧
power ⚡

daily needs per worker

daily negative output per worker

Desired Income

💲 20 Industrial buildings need to make a certain amount of money each day. Each building makes money each time it makes a shipment

👥 An industrial building can make 1 shipment per employee per day.

Ⓒ Commercial Shipping
Every commercial building will buy shipments based on their density:

High Density: 200 units per day
Medium Density: 20 units per day
Low Density: 2 units per day

🌐 Global Shipping
Every time a transport unit arrives at a port it buys shipments from connected industrial buildings:

— Truck Stop: 10 units per truck.
🚢 Sea Port: 1000 units per boat.
🚃 Train Station: 100 units per train car.
✈️ Airport: 100 units per airplane.

Needs

 💧 ⚡ 🏭
Workers   Water   Power   Desirability

Industrial Buildings without any workers, water, power, or in an undesirable zone will make no income.

Unhappiness

😟 Unhappy   😐 Normal   😃 Happy

Buildings that make less than the desired income become increasingly unhappy.

Desired income

Buildings that make more than the desired income become increasingly happy.

Workers

Each morning workers leave the residential zones and go to work in nearby industrial zones.

R
🚫😟 Unemployed workers stay home for the day.

😟 Unhappy industrial buildings become abandoned.

🏚️
💲 : Increased crime
🔥 : Increased fire hazard
🗑️ : Counts as garbage

Abandoned industrial buildings decrease desirability.

You can bulldoze an abandoned industrial building, wait for it to burn down, or fix the issues that caused the abandonment (this allows it to open again).

Industrial Flow

Industrial zones are responsible for generating the bulk of jobs in a city and throughout the region. There are three tech levels of industry available based on the education level of the available workforce. Dirty industry is most common in areas with little or no education, resulting in factories that belch pollution into the air. Clean industry appears when an adequate number of Sims have a Community College education. High tech industry is only available after a University has been built. The growth and success of industry can be affected by other factors too, such as crime and pollution. So use parks to scrub out pollution and maintain a robust police presence to discourage criminals. Like their residential and commercial counterparts, industrial buildings have specific needs to maintain happiness and profitability. Basic needs include workers, water, and power. In addition, industry accrues profit by shipping freight to commercial shops—if there aren't enough shops to ship to, profits will decrease. Freight can also be shipped to the global market through Trade Depots, Trade Ports, and Cargo Terminals at Municipal Airports, serving as a secondary outlet when freight output exceeds local demand. Click on any industrial building to view its density, tech level, and needs.

> **INDUSTRIAL: POINTS TO REMEMBER**
> → Zone industrial to attract factories.
> → Factories provide jobs and make goods.
> → Factories ship freight to shops, Trade Depots, Trade Ports, and Cargo Terminals at Municipal Airports.
> → If a factory can't ship enough goods it will go abandoned.

RCI Management

Establishing and maintaining the proper balance of RCI zones throughout your city (and region) is a constant challenge. Keep an eye on that ever-changing RCI Demand meter to respond to the needs for more residential, commercial, and industrial zones. But if you want to really excel in your job as Mayor, it takes even greater involvement to keep up with the needs of the Sims living, working, and shopping in your city.

Smart Zoning

If you build zones close together, Sims can work and shop within walking distance of their house, cutting down on traffic and use of mass transit. Just be mindful of pollution generated by factories.

Designating residential, commercial, and industrial zones is easy—plus it costs nothing. Simply open the Zones menu, choose the desired zone from the tool bar, and draw the zone along an existing road. If you're planning to create a self-sufficient RCI system within your city, zone approximately two residential for every commercial and industrial zone—follow this 2:1:1 ratio to establish a stable tax base.

But before you start zoning, take into account the flow of activity between the different zones. For instance, where will your Sims live? Will they have to drive to work or can they walk to nearby factories and shops? How far will trucks have to drive to deliver freight to shops and Trade Depots? By keeping zones close together you can maximize efficiency and significantly reduce traffic. However, there are pollution concerns to take into account, especially if relying on dirty factories to supply most of the jobs. While keeping factories close to commercial and residential buildings is good for promoting pedestrian activity over vehicle traffic, the negative impact of pollution and low land value may lead to unhappy (and sick) Sims. Consider keeping your industrial zones a safe distance from the residential and commercial areas until you have an educated work force. Once you have enough high school and college educated workers, clean and high tech buildings will begin appearing in industrial zones, producing far less pollution than their predecessors. As these advanced facilities appear, consider shifting your commercial and residential zones closer to these cleaner buildings.

TIP

This Sim just got paid and is walking home from work. Sims will walk a maximum of 400 meters before relying on an automobile or mass transit to reach their destination. So the utopian goal is to create small self-contained modular communities where Sims can walk everywhere to fulfill their basic needs.

RCI on a Regional Scale

Don't have enough shops? The Sims in your city will go to other cities to buy goods. Workers, freight, and students are also shared between connected cities.

In previous *SimCity* games, all RCI activity occurred within one city, making it relatively easy to manage local demand. But with multi-city play, all cities linked by the highway or mass transit can participate in the process. In this sense, you no longer have to nurture that perfect RCI balance within the confines of your city. Instead, that balance must be accomplished on a regional level. Sims will freely travel to other cities in the region to work and shop. Freight produced at factories flows freely throughout the region too and is shipped to any connected shops in need of goods to sell.

The interconnection of cities allows you to take a more specialized approach when it comes to zoning. For example, you could build a city that's purely industrial as long as there are enough Sims in neighboring cities to

supply the workforce and enough shops to accept freight. Or you could create a quaint suburb consisting entirely of residential zones as long as the Sims living there have access to jobs and shops in neighboring cities—and a way to get there in large numbers without clogging local roads and the regional highway. Of course, such specialization requires a great deal of cooperation and communication between cities to ensure demands are being met. If you don't feel like working with other cities, simply stick to the tried and true methods of maintaining the proper RCI balance within your city. This is the easiest way to establish a self-sufficient city with a stable tax base.

Wealth and Demand

Plop an Urban or Formal park next to a residential zone and watch the mansions appear. Parks scrub away pollution and increase land value, making them a vital tool for attracting medium and high wealth Sims.

WEALTH DESIGNATIONS

Level	Name
W1	Low Wealth (Ⓢ)
W2	Medium Wealth (ⓈⓈ)
W3	High Wealth (ⓈⓈⓈ)

The population of your city is divided into three rigid classes, referred to as low wealth, medium wealth, and high wealth Sims. Although these Sims occupy the same city, they live, work, and shop in buildings that cater to their class. For example, a high wealth Sim will not shop or live in a building designed for low wealth Sims and vice versa. When zoning, you need to take into account your city's demographics, ensuring each class has enough jobs and shops to keep the population happy.

When the Zones menu is open, the info tab shows an expanded RCI chart displaying the current demand based on wealth. Here residential and commercial demand is broken up into three columns per zone: low wealth (Ⓢ), medium wealth (§§), and high wealth (§§§). Industrial demand is only represented by one column, since demand for factories functions independently from wealth. By studying this diagram you can better determine which types of zones need to be designated and where. For example, housing and shops attracting high wealth Sims must be zoned in areas with high land value—access the Land Value data map to view these areas. Based on geography, each city site has differing amounts of natural high land value areas.

To encourage the creation of specific residential and commercial buildings you can alter land value by placing parks or government buildings nearby. When building parks pay attention to which kinds of parks you create, because each type attracts different classes. Basic parks are popular with low wealth Sims while Sports and Nature parks attract medium wealth Sims. If you want to maximize land value, build Urban or Formal parks to attract buildings for high wealth Sims. Government and city service buildings like the Town Hall, Police Station, and Fire Station also increase land value. So before placing one of these buildings, be aware of its impact on the surrounding zones, otherwise mansions may spring up in a neighborhood you intended for low wealth Sims.

> ☑ **TIP**
>
>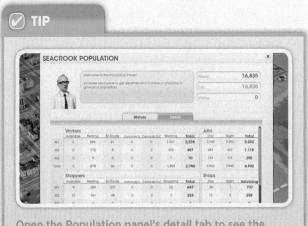
>
> Open the Population panel's detail tab to see the amount of low, medium, and high wealth Sims living in your city. You can even see the number of jobs and shops serving each wealth level. Use this info to fine-tune your approach when addressing demands.

Happiness and Density

Uh, oh. The wealthy residents of this high-rise aren't very happy. Address their concerns before the building is abandoned. You can gather a lot of information by clicking on any RCI building.

DENSITY DESIGNATIONS

Level	Name
D1	Low Density
D2	Medium Density
D3	High Density

As your city expands and space becomes limited, there's only one way to build—up! Density refers to how many Sims can live, work, or shop within a particular building. As a general rule, tall buildings support greater density than short buildings. There are three levels of density: low density, medium density, and high density. Density is affected by happiness and the type of road adjacent to a building. The happiness of a building is determined by how happy or profitable the tenants are. If the Sims living in a residential building are happy and have few complaints, the building is eligible for an increase in density. Likewise, the profitability of a commercial or industrial building determines when it can increase in density.

Click on any occupied building to open a window revealing more details about its current density. The meter at the top of this window shows the current density and its progress to reaching a higher density, as indicated by a face icon. If the Sims in the building are happy or profitable, a happy face icon is shown, with a green arrow pointing to the right, indicating a move toward higher density. If the Sims in the building have multiple complaints, they probably won't be too happy, represented by an unhappy face icon and a red arrow pointing to the left, indicating stagnation—once a higher density has been reached, a building will never reduce in size. For residential and commercial buildings this window also shows the land value, displaying which wealth class the building serves. In industrial buildings, instead of land value, the building's tech level is shown, displaying the education level of its workers. Review the comments at the bottom of each window to study what makes the building happy or unhappy. These comments can help guide your future decisions. For example, if a building is complaining about a lack of power, open the Power menu and make sure your power plant is generating enough power for the city. Do your best to address each complaint in an effort to increase a building's happiness.

No matter how happy or profitable, buildings can only grow if at least one adjacent road supports a higher density. For example, a happy low density building built next to Low Density Street can only grow if the road is upgraded to support medium or high density. If the happiness or profitability of a building is maxed out, upgrading the adjacent road will trigger an automatic increase in density, so keep this in mind when upgrading lengthy road segments. If multiple buildings along the road increase in density simultaneously, you may face sudden utility shortages, not to mention an increase in traffic.

ⓘ NOTE

Buildings automatically grow as the criteria for greater density are met. However, if happiness and profit wane, buildings will not downsize—they simply become abandoned, often requiring you to bulldoze them.

☑ TIP

Homeless Sims live in abandoned buildings, dine from uncollected garbage cans, and take up space in parks. To prevent your parks from being overrun by homeless Sims, bulldoze abandoned buildings or make sure all garbage cans are being collected every day. Without shelter and/or food, homeless Sims will leave your city.

Abandoned Buildings and Demolition

Abandoned buildings are often symptoms of bigger problems. Sims who run out of money were either unable to find a job or too sick to go to work. As a result, they can't pay rent and are forced out of their house.

Sometimes things just don't work out. Sims can't find work and run out of money. Shops and factories shut down due to low profits or lack of workers. And in some instances, Sims simply get disgusted by your city and move out. When a building becomes unoccupied, it's considered abandoned. All abandoned buildings in your city can be viewed by opening the Bulldoze menu—look for the flashing red icons to spot these troubled properties. It's a good idea to bulldoze these buildings quickly because they generate no tax revenue, lower land value, and simply take up space. But abandoned buildings aren't completely hopeless. After a building has been vacated there's a short span of time when new tenants can move in. So if a perfectly fine high density building goes abandoned, give it some time to recover. However, the longer a building is abandoned, the higher the risk for fires and crime—abandoned buildings house formerly low wealth Sims who have become homeless due to hard times. If an abandoned building is ignored, it will eventually collapse into a pile of rubble—flashing yellow bulldoze icons appear over rubble when the Bulldoze menu is open. Rubble serves no purpose at all, so bulldoze these unsightly piles of debris immediately. Immediately after an abandoned building or rubble has been bulldozed, a new building may pop up in its place, assuming demand is still high. Most tenants would rather move into a new building than occupy an abandoned one. So don't let those abandoned buildings sit around too long—you could be missing out on tax revenue.

Dezoning

If any area isn't developing well, or you simply need to create more space, use the Dezone tool to erase existing zones. This is also a handy way to prohibit new construction in already occupied zones.

Fluctuating demand and limited space may lead to situations where you need to alter your city's zones. Before a zone can be redesignated, it must be dezoned first, using the Dezone tool in the Zones menu. Dezoning erases the green, blue, or yellow colors associated with a particular zone, preventing further construction. However, dezoning does not demolish any buildings currently occupying a residential, commercial, or industrial zone—you'll need to bulldoze them to clear space. Since new buildings often pop up immediately after bulldozing, it's a good idea to dezone an area before demolition begins. Once dezoned and cleared of any unwanted structures, the area is eligible for new zoning or can simply remain undeveloped land.

In addition to returning land to its natural state, dezoning is also a powerful tool for controlling density. For example, if you want to maintain low density buildings in a particular zone, but need to upgrade the surrounding road network to increase traffic flow, dezone the area before upgrading the roads. Since dezoning prevents new construction, it prohibits those low density buildings from growing into medium or high density buildings, regardless of their happiness and access to higher density roads. This is a handy way to freeze growth, ideal when struggling to meet the needs of a city's existing population. RCI buildings left in dezoned areas function normally. However, if they ever become abandoned (or burn down) and require demolition, no new buildings will take their place until the area is zoned.

BULLDOZE: POINTS TO REMEMBER

➡ Abandoned buildings and rubble lower land value nearby.

➡ Homeless emerge from low wealth residential buildings when they go abandoned.

➡ Garbage in buildings will be converted to ground pollution if you bulldoze them.

➡ You can't bulldoze buildings that are on fire.

➡ You can close a building rather than bulldoze it, to save on expenses.

➡ Bulldoze roads by dragging along them. All buildings on that road will be destroyed.

➡ Instead of bulldozing, disasters can be used for clearing space.

➡ You can trigger disasters manually or they can appear randomly.

➡ Complete achievements to be granted access to disasters.

ZONING ACHIEVEMENTS

Icon	Name	Criteria
	Apartment Rows	Have 50 high density, low wealth residential buildings in your city.
	The Big (Insert Fruit Here)	Have 50 high density, low wealth commercial buildings in your city.
	Billionaire's Playground	Have 10 high density, high wealth residential buildings in your city.
	Elite Estates	Have 50 low density, high wealth residential buildings in your city.
	Office Parks	Have 50 low density, high wealth commercial buildings in your city.
	Skyscraper Magnet	Have 10 high density, high wealth commercial buildings.
	Technophile	Have 40 high density, high tech industrial buildings in your city.

CHAT WITH THE DEVELOPERS

Working Up *SimCity* Wealth

CHRIS SCHMIDT, TUNING DESIGNER

Hello again everyone! Previously, I talked to you about how roads affect density and how you get a city started in *SimCity*, so now I want to talk about how to make your city grow in wealth. Wealthy Sims bring with them high-rises and skyscrapers, as well as needs that others Sims will hardly complain about. Despite having a lower population density, these Sims are more demanding, and much harder to keep around. In the end, wealthy Sims can be a boon to your city, providing significantly more income than other Sims if managed well, or a burden if you aren't up to the task.

In *SimCity*, you'll find attracting high wealth Sims to your town and growing in wealth is fairly easy, however as I mentioned, the challenge comes in keeping wealthy Sims and businesses in your city. While all RCI buildings have basic needs, like water, power, sewage, and garbage, higher wealth Sims are more sensitive when their needs aren't met and will become more vocal and less happy the more you ignore their needs. Education, pollution reduction, better crime suppression, and consistency in all your services will become a priority as your Sims go up in wealth. Additionally, each RCI category has a service that becomes more important the more buildings of that type you have. Industrial buildings are more prone to fires, commercial buildings are more sensitive to crimes, and residents will go home and stay there if they get sick, demanding more health services.

Based on what your focus is, you'll want to make sure you have enough buildings to respond to their needs. Industrial cities will want to focus on fire and garbage services. Commercial cities will want to focus on police and transportation. Residential cities will want to focus on health and education. Individual services can cover a

> Based on what your focus is, you'll want to make sure you have enough buildings to respond to their needs. Industrial cities will want to focus on fire and garbage services. Commercial cities will want to focus on police and transportation.

fair amount of your city, but unlike the suppression radius of previous *SimCity* games, these units have to actually travel to the problem areas, so you need to keep your streets clear with public transportation and make sure to expand your services to cover multiple fires, crimes, or injuries, particularly as these buildings grow in density. As you place service and infrastructure buildings to meet your city's needs, you will see the land value of your city begin to change for better or worse, and in turn you will see some of your residential and commercial buildings upgrade to reflect these changes. Industrial buildings are less particular about where they like to be, and instead grow in tech level by having Community College or University education in the city. High tech buildings provide less air pollution, higher profit margins, and less of a negative impact on the land value of the neighborhoods that are nearby (though don't expect anyone to build mansions nearby).

Controlling your land value to attract specific wealth classes is an important part of managing your city, and while getting medium wealth residential and commercial buildings is a natural part of improving conditions in your city, getting more than a handful takes some sprucing up.

Players who decide they want to take on the challenges of higher wealth will mostly impact the wealth of their neighborhoods by improving them with parks. Parks come in a wide variety of flavors in *SimCity*, but can be generally broken into three categories: low wealth, medium wealth, and high wealth. Low wealth parks provide some happiness to the local Sims, and a place for Sims and their kids to hang out and keep out of trouble. Medium wealth parks attract medium wealth buildings, and are generally nature or sports themed. High wealth parks tend to revolve around sculptures and fountains and other expensive but nice to look at elements, and will attract high wealth buildings. Building parks in a neighborhood will spur the development of buildings of that wealth class in a radius around them, and building them in areas with a high natural land value, or overlapping the influence of another park will widen this effect. On the other hand buildings that are noisy, dangerous, or heavy polluters will decrease the land value around them, so be careful where you place them.

I hope this gives you a better sense of how you can attract and keep wealthy Sims and businesses in *SimCity*. The diversity and challenge of playing the wealth game means spinning a lot of plates, but I think you'll be happy with the results if you take on the challenge!

Government

Welcome to City Hall, Mayor.

As the head of local government it's your job to make numerous decisions that affect the lives of every Sim living in the city, as well as those visiting from the region and beyond. Are you up to the challenge? Here we take a close look at all functions of local government including the associated buildings and departments, as well as the importance of keeping your city's population happy. By studying the Population panel and various data maps, you have access to an enormous amount of real-time data, giving you everything you need to make informed decisions. Want to learn more about taxes and loans? All financial concerns are covered in a deep discussion of the Budget panel, helping you set tax rates and manage expenses in order to balance the city's budget. Take a moment to review this information, and then get back to serving the people, using your newly acquired knowledge to lead with confidence and wisdom.

Don't forget to go to **www.primagames.com** to access guide updates free of charge with your voucher code.

Government Buildings

Where are you going to plop that Town Hall? What about the Mayor's House? These are just a couple of the buildings associated with Government. You can also choose from a number of departments to unlock more buildings. And if you enjoy a high rate of success, the grateful Sims of your city may even award you with a Mayor's Mansion.

Town Hall/City Hall

Cost: Free

Operational Cost: §200 per hour

Description: This allows you to do business deals, manage systems, and start negotiating with neighboring cities.

CITY HALL UPGRADES

Level	Name	Population	Unlock
1	Town Hall	—	Fire, Health, Police buildings
2	City Hall	2,500	One department of your choice
3	City Hall	8,000	One department of your choice
4	City Hall	14,995	One department of your choice
5	City Hall	37,000	One department of your choice
6	City Hall	300,000	One department of your choice
7	City Hall	542,740	One department of your choice

Shortly after supplying your city with water and power, you're awarded a Town Hall, available in the Government menu. But don't just plop your Town Hall anywhere. This is prestigious building requiring plenty of space for expansion—up to six departments can be placed around the Town Hall. Consider cordoning off an entire city block and plopping your Town Hall in the center, with adequate space for growth on the sides and rear of the structure. The Town Hall serves as the centerpiece of all local government, giving Sims a place to voice their concerns and allowing you to set a flat city-wide tax. At certain population thresholds the Town Hall can be upgraded—the first upgrade converts the Town Hall into a City Hall. When the City Hall is unlocked you can individually adjust tax rates for residential, commercial, and industrial zones.

Each upgrade allows for the construction of one new department. Departments are specialized modules that grant regional access to new buildings like the Sewage Treatment Plant, Hospital, High School, Bus Terminal, and Recycling Center. Since each department unlocks these buildings across the region, there's no need to build more than one type of department per region. If all six departments have already been constructed by other cities, save your money and skip departments altogether. You don't even need to build a Town Hall as long as one exists in the region. Visit neighboring cities or communicate with other mayors in the region to coordinate the construction of specific departments you all can share.

 TIP

The Town Hall and its individual department modules increase nearby land value, so don't be surprised if medium and high wealth buildings pop up around your Town Hall.

 TIP

Leave room around your Town Hall for the inevitable upgrade to City Hall.

MODULES

City Hall Sign

Cost: §200

Operational Cost: None

Maximum Modules: 1

Description: What's the name of this town anyways?

Simcopter One

Cost: §6,000

Operational Cost: None

Maximum Modules: 1

Prerequisites:

→ City Hall

→ Municipal Airport in city or region

Description: For Mayors who like to make a big entrance.

DEPARTMENTS

Department of Education

Cost: §15,000

Operational Cost: §500 per hour

Maximum Modules: 1

Regional Access Granted:

→ High School

→ University

Description: If you believe the children are our future, then you need a Department of Education. With this City Hall department, you can add High Schools and your very own University!

Department of Finance

Cost: §15,000

Operational Cost: §500 per hour

Maximum Modules: 1

Regional Access Granted:

→ Tax Rate Control per Zone and Wealth

Description: Embrace your inner CPA! The Department of Finance grants the ability to tax wealth levels independently.

Department of Safety

Cost: §15,000

Operational Cost: §500 per hour

Maximum Modules: 1

Regional Access Granted:

→ Hospital

→ Large Fire Station

→ Police Precinct

Description: Maslow put safety at the second level of his hierarchy of needs pyramid. Give your Sims a sturdy foundation. Protect your populace with improved fire, health, and police city services.

Department of Tourism

Cost: §15,000

Operational Cost: §500 per hour

Maximum Modules: 1

Regional Access Granted:

→ Landmarks

→ Pro Stadium

→ Large Parks

Description: Turn your city into a tourist trap with the Department of Tourism. Tourist attractions like parks, stadiums, and landmarks will draw Sims to your city, ready to spend cash!

Department of Transportation

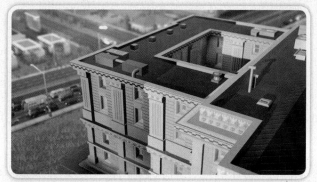

Cost: §15,000

Operational Cost: §500 per hour

Maximum Modules: 1

Regional Access Granted:

→ Bus Terminal

→ Passenger Train Station

→ Ferry Dock

→ Municipal Airport

Description: Address commuter or tourist traffic. The Department of Transportation will enable advanced transit options like streetcars, passenger rail, and even a Municipal Airport!

Department of Utilities

Cost: §15,000

Operational Cost: §500 per hour

Maximum Modules: 1

Regional Access Granted:

→ Water Pumping Station

→ Sewage Treatment Plant

→ Recycling Center

Description: Clean up your city, starting at the City Hall. The Department of Utilities gives you the ability to place advanced sewage, water treatment, and recycling buildings.

(i) NOTE

Stick around for the fireworks show every time you upgrade your City Hall. Also, remember you can build one new department with each new upgrade.

Mayor's House

Cost: §15,000

Operational Cost: §100 per hour

Prerequisites:

→ Population of 10,000

→ Town Hall

→ Moving In! mission: Approval rating of 70% or more

Description: For the neighborly, lend-a-cup-of-sugar, mow-their-front-lawn kind of Mayor. Raises medium wealth land value.

You can unlock the Mayor's House by completing the Moving In! mission, requiring you to reach an approval rating of 70% or higher. This mission is usually available soon after placing your Town Hall. Unless you've completely failed during the early stages of the city's development, you should already have a relatively high approval rating. Consider plopping parks and zoning the demanded residential, commercial, and industrial areas to push your approval rating above 70% or lower taxes to boost happiness. Regardless of city problems, if your tax rate is, around 3%, they just can't help but love you. The

Mayor's House increases medium wealth land value, so plop it in a neighborhood where you want to encourage medium wealth growth—everybody wants to live next door to the Mayor!

Mayor's Mansion

Cost: §30,000

Operational Cost: §100 per hour

Prerequisites:

→ Population of 40,000

→ Mayor's House

→ Mayor of the Year! mission: Approval rating of 75% or more

Description: Keep your Sims happy for long enough and you can move in. Sims all over the city will celebrate when you move into the city. As you run your city well, your Sims will even give you gifts to add to your Mayor's Mansion. Raises high wealth land value.

The Mayor of the Year! mission requires you to reach an approval rating of 75% or more. It's best to complete this mission as early as possible, soon after plopping the Mayor's House. Complications of a growing city can make it difficult to attain an 75% approval rating without some serious politicking. Don't be ashamed to win over the people by expanding city services, building schools, or even lowering taxes. You don't need to maintain an 75% approval rating for long to complete the mission, but you will need to maintain a high rating if you want to unlock the mansion's modules. This lavish piece of real estate increases high wealth land value, so place it in an exclusive part of the city and watch mansions and high-end shops spring up nearby. The mansion can be customized with a variety of modules. There are 16 different modules divided into four sets. A full set must be installed before a new set can be unlocked. For instance, once you've placed all four modules in the first set, the second set of four modules is unlocked, and so on. Each module also requires you to maintain a certain approval rating for a specific amount of time before it can be placed. These modules have no impact on gameplay, but instead serve as trophy-like flourishes, likely making other mayors jealous of your success. So don't be shy. You've earned this luxurious lifestyle! Flaunt it!

MODULES

Flag of the City

Cost: §200

Operational Cost: None

Maximum Modules: 1

Prerequisites:

→ Maintain 75% approval rating for 6 hours

Description: How can you not be proud when looking at your own city's flag? You know what it took to build this place!

Mayor's BBQ Pit Patio

Cost: §1,000

Operational Cost: §10 per hour

Maximum Modules: 1

Prerequisites:

→ Maintain 75% approval rating for 6 hours

Description: As Mayor, you have a lot at stake, but there's never a bad time to cook a great steak!

Circular Fountain

Cost: §1,000

Operational Cost: §10 per hour

Maximum Modules: 1

Prerequisites:

→ Maintain 75% approval rating for 6 hours

Description: If you look into the water long enough, you'll see your future. Nah, kidding. It's only water.

Mayor's Statue

Cost: §1,000

Operational Cost: None

Maximum Modules: 1

Prerequisites:

→ Maintain 80% approval rating for 6 hours

Description: Mayor, the whole city is proud of you. Proud, like...an eagle. Definitely not a peacock. Definitely not.

Balcony

Cost: §1,000

Operational Cost: §10 per hour

Maximum Modules: 1

Prerequisites:

→ Maintain 80% approval rating for 12 hours

→ Four upgrades of Mayor's Mansion

Description: Look upon your domain from here. Just be careful—it's the first place all the tomatoes get tossed!

Guest House

Cost: §1,000

Operational Cost: §10 per hour

Maximum Modules: 1

Prerequisites:

→ Maintain 80% approval rating for 12 hours

→ Four upgrades of Mayor's Mansion

Description: It's a known fact: visiting dignitaries, roaming rock stars, and famous movie stars love to hang out with cool Mayors. Serves as lodging for one high wealth tourist.

Guard Post

Cost: §1,000

Operational Cost: §10 per hour

Maximum Modules: 1

Prerequisites:

→ Maintain 80% approval rating for 12 hours

→ Four upgrades of Mayor's Mansion

Description: Make your mansion look even more menacing, Mayor. Maybe those protestors will think twice about bothering you. Or not.

Sports Car Garage

Cost: §1,000

Operational Cost: §10 per hour

Maximum Modules: 1

Prerequisites:

→ Maintain 80% approval rating for 12 hours

→ Four upgrades of Mayor's Mansion

Description: Complete with your new smokin' hot car! It's okay, break the speed limit...you're the Mayor!

Extension Wing

Cost: §1,000

Operational Cost: §10 per hour

Maximum Modules: 1

Prerequisites:

→ Maintain 85% approval rating for 24 hours

→ Eight upgrades of Mayor's Mansion

Description: What's better than having a giant mansion all to yourself? MORE giant mansion all to yourself!

Limo Garage

Cost: §1,000

Operational Cost: §10 per hour

Maximum Modules: 1

Prerequisites:

→ Maintain 85% approval rating for 24 hours

→ Eight upgrades of Mayor's Mansion

Description: You're Mayor. Why should you have to drive yourself? Have your driver bring the car around and travel in style.

Greenhouse

Cost: §1,000

Operational Cost: §10 per hour

Maximum Modules: 1

Prerequisites:

→ Maintain 85% approval rating for 24 hours

→ Eight upgrades of Mayor's Mansion

Description: You know how to grow a city, Mayor...but can you grow your garden? Just keep those pesky ants away...

Tennis Court

Cost: §1,000

Operational Cost: §10 per hour

Maximum Modules: 1

Prerequisites:

→ Maintain 85% approval rating for 24 hours

→ Eight upgrades of Mayor's Mansion

Description: Play tennis with your Mayor friends and keep fit so you can quickly jump into action when disasters strike!

Swimming Pool

Cost: §1,000

Operational Cost: §10 per hour

Maximum Modules: 1

Prerequisites:

→ Maintain 90% approval rating for 48 hours

→ 12 upgrades of Mayor's Mansion

Description: The life of a Mayor is never easy. That's why you need at least 18 hours a day of relaxing pool time. You're only human!

Lookout Tower

Cost: §1,000

Operational Cost: §10 per hour

Maximum Modules: 1

Prerequisites:

→ Maintain 90% approval rating for 48 hours

→ 12 upgrades of Mayor's Mansion

Description: Gaze down upon your city from the relative safety of your house's Lookout Tower!

> **ⓘ NOTE**
>
> If you apply the Mayor's Mansion modules at a steady pace, it will take a minimum of 408 hours (17 days) to place them all. So keep a close eye on the mansion and apply new modules as soon as they're available.

Party Wing

Cost: §1,000

Operational Cost: §10 per hour

Maximum Modules: 1

Prerequisites:

→ Maintain 90% approval rating for 48 hours

→ 12 upgrades of Mayor's Mansion

Description: Sometimes a Mayor just has to let loose! Throw your raging parties here with only the city's elite Sims!

Simcopter One

Cost: §6,000

Operational Cost: None

Maximum Modules: 1

Prerequisites:

→ Maintain 90% approval rating for 48 hours

→ 12 upgrades of Mayor's Mansion

Description: Real Mayors fly to work! Never be late to City Hall ever again!

City Management

Wondering what you've gotten yourself into? Don't worry. While running a city is challenging, you have a wide range of tools and advisors at your disposal to help ease the burden. The Mayor Rating, Population, and Budget panels all offer a wealth of information vital to keeping your city on the right track. If you need more information, turn to the data maps and advisors to respond to problems and discover new opportunities. Once you've gotten the hang of it all, complete missions offered by different Sims to earn your city some extra money. See, it's not that bad! So go out there and exude confidence. With so much information and data available at your fingertips, there's no challenge too daunting.

Want to know how well you're doing as Mayor? Look for the face icon on the bottom of the HUD, between your city's name and the Budget panel. This icon is a graphical representation of your current approval rating. If it's a green happy face, you're doing a good job—anything less, and you'll need to make some improvements. For a more detailed look at your approval rating, click on the face icon. This opens the Mayor Rating panel, displaying the percentage of Sims who approve of your leadership—the higher the percentage, the better your approval rating. The panel also displays three happiness meters, separating the citizens into residential, commercial, and industrial categories. The more each meter is filled, the higher your rating is for that category. If your Mayor Rating is low and your Sims are unhappy in a particular category, click on each individual meter to see more detailed comments from each wealth class. Address these comments and concerns to increase your approval rating.

Mayor Rating

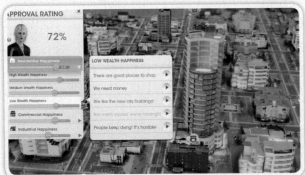

Uh, oh. Some Sims are complaining about a lack of jobs and your poor response to health concerns. Do something about it to improve your approval rating.

> ✓ **TIP**
>
> Click on individuals Sims and vehicles and follow them around to experience their life.

MAYOR RATING: POINTS TO REMEMBER

→ Sims can get happiness from visiting a park designed for their wealth level. Even Sims who have no money can gain happiness from a park.

→ Sims that can't get power or water will be unhappy.

→ Crimes and deaths at buildings will cause happiness loss.

→ Not having money to pay rent will cause happiness loss.

→ Medium and high wealth Sims are more sensitive to garbage or sewage issues.

→ Medium and high wealth Sims get unhappy due to sickness.

→ High wealth Sims are more sensitive to crime, pollution, and fire.

→ High wealth Sims need education to be happy.

→ Nobody likes high taxes. High wealth Sims don't like medium taxes.

Getting to Know Your Sims

Click on any building to view its current happiness as well as any complaints issued by the tenants. High wealth Sims have no shortage of complaints.

As Mayor, it's your job to keep the Sims and businesses in your city happy. It sounds simple enough, but it's no small task fulfilling the needs of a large and diverse population. Fortunately, Sims aren't exactly shy when it comes to providing honest feedback. There are several ways to tap into the word on the street. The best way to view a general consensus of public opinion is through the Mayor Rating panel. The comments and complaints shown here are shared by several Sims, helping you address the most pressing issues.

Also, be on the watch for green, orange, and red thought bubbles appearing over buildings. Click on these thought bubbles to get direct feedback on a wide range of topics, indicated by the icon within each bubble. When a thought

bubble is green, a Sim is happy about something—yes, you're doing something right! Orange thought bubbles indicate an issue of concern that should probably be addressed. But pay most attention to red thought bubbles, because they indicate a loss of happiness. If you're seeing a lot of orange and red thought bubbles, you've got some problems.

Click on colored thought bubbles to see what your Sims are thinking. This is a good way to diagnose problems with your city. Looks like your school buses are too full, so provide more to ensure all kids can make it to school.

You can also solicit feedback directly from individual Sims driving or walking around the city. Simply click on a walking Sim or vehicle to get a quick status update. A small window pops up next to the Sim or vehicle showing their name and a comment on what they're doing. Click on a Sim to see where they came from or click on the Follow button to track their movements through the city. When following a Sim, the camera automatically moves to keep the Sim centered in the middle of the screen. Following Sims is a good way to study the efficiency of your transportation system and layout of RCI zones. If Sims are stuck in traffic or have to drive across the city to reach their job or desired shop, consider making adjustments to make their lives easier.

SIM HAPPINESS

Events held at the Expo Center and Pro Stadium are likely to increase the happiness of attendees, as indicated by green thought bubbles.

EFFECTS ON HAPPINESS

Causes	Residential Low Wealth	Residential Medium Wealth	Residential High Wealth	Commercial Low Wealth	Commercial Medium Wealth	Commercial High Wealth	Industrial Low Tech	Industrial Medium Tech	Industrial High Tech
Low Land Value	–	☹	☹	–	☹	☹	–	–	–
No Power	☹	☹	☹	😐	☹	☹	😐	☹	☹
No Water	☹	☹	☹	😐	☹	☹	😐	☹	☹
Can't Pay Rent	☹	☹	☹	☹	☹	☹	☹	☹	☹
Uncollected Garbage	–	😐	☹	–	😐	☹	–	😐	☹
Sewage Back-up	–	😐	☹	–	😐	☹	–	😐	☹
Pollution	–	–	🙂	–	–	🙂	–	–	–
Germs	–	😐	😐	–	😐	😐	–	–	–
Sickness	😐	☹	☹	–	–	–	–	–	–
Injury	😐	😐	😐	–	–	–	😐	☹	☹
Death	☹	☹	☹	☹	☹	☹	☹	☹	☹
Successful Shopping	🙂	🙂	🙂	🙂	🙂	🙂	–	–	–
Tourist Shopping	–	–	–	🙂	🙂	🙂	–	–	–
Student Shopping	–	–	–	🙂	🙂	🙂	–	–	–
Visiting Parks	🙂	🙂	🙂	–	–	–	–	–	–
Lack of Any Education	–	😐	☹	–	–	–	–	☹	☹
Traffic	😐	😐	–	😐	😐	😐	–	–	–
Mass Transit	😐	😐	–	😐	😐	😐	–	–	–
Crime at Building	☹	☹	☹	☹	☹	☹	☹	☹	☹
Crime in Area	😐	☹	☹	😐	☹	☹	–	😐	☹
Crime Suppression	–	–	🙂	–	–	🙂	–	–	–
Low Taxes	🙂	🙂	–	🙂	🙂	–	🙂	🙂	–
Medium Taxes	–	–	☹	–	–	☹	–	–	☹
High Taxes	☹	☹	☹	☹	☹	☹	☹	☹	☹
Low Wealth Plops	🙂	–	–	🙂	–	–	–	–	–
Medium Wealth Plops	–	🙂	–	–	🙂	–	–	–	–
High Wealth Plops	–	🙂	🙂	–	🙂	🙂	–	–	–
Fire Marshal Visits	–	–	🙂	–	–	🙂	–	–	🙂
Health Outreach Visits	–	–	🙂	–	–	🙂	–	–	🙂
Police Outreach Visits	–	–	🙂	–	–	🙂	–	–	–
Homeless	–	–	–	–	😐	☹	–	–	–
Freight Deliveries	–	–	–	–	–	–	🙂	🙂	🙂

Legend:
 Complaints and happiness lost   Complaints but no happiness lost   Happiness gained and explained

So what exactly makes a Sim happy? What makes them unhappy? It depends on the Sim. But it's not just individual Sims who are affected by happiness. The happiness of businesses in commercial and industrial zones are also affected by specific events. The accompanying table shows the causes that affect happiness. As you can see, not every negative cause makes each Sim unhappy. Instead, they will complain about it without losing happiness. But don't take these complaints lightly. Complaints serve as warnings, giving you a chance to address issues before they become bigger problems.

> **✓ TIP**
>
> Sims get happy by spending money. If there are no shops, they can visit parks to become happy.

Demographics: Population Panel

Want more information about the Sims populating your city? Then open the Population panel. This handy panel does a lot more than just showing a city's current population. It also shows the population of the region as well as the number of Sims visiting your city. Not satisfied? Then dig a little deeper into this panel to reveal much more detail concerning wealth, jobs, education, shoppers, and freight.

HISTORY

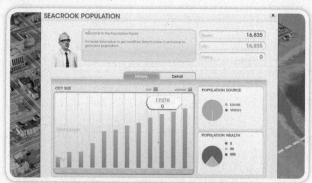

The Population panel's history tab tracks your city's population and wealth over a 12-month period. You can also see the number of Sims visiting your city.

At the top of the panel your city is described by two characteristics: size and wealth. Your city may be described as a Poor City, a Middle Class Metropolis, or any other moniker depending on the current size and wealth. The factors determining this description are shown in the City Size graph. This graph illustrates the rise and fall of your city's population. The green bars represent residents while the orange bars represent visitors. The Population Source pie chart shows similar data. In the background

of the graph are gray horizontal lines representing different population thresholds determining the type of city you have. The Population Wealth pie chart shows the proportions of low, medium, and high wealth Sims living in your city. How your city is characterized changes frequently and has no impact on gameplay, so don't get too obsessed with this title. But do pay attention to the activity in these graphs as well as the accompanying Population Density and Population Wealth pie charts, also in the history tab.

DETAIL

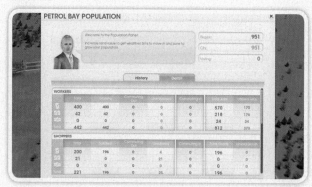

Access the detail tab for more hard data on your city's demographics. This is a great way to determine how many workers and jobs are available within the city.

The underlying numbers behind all this data are revealed in the detail tab. Here you can see the real-time number of workers, jobs, shoppers, shops, kids, and freight in your city, all shown in individual tables. When it comes to zoning, pay close attention to the Workers and Jobs tables, making sure you have enough jobs to accommodate the low, medium, and high wealth workers living in your city. Likewise, you'll want to make sure you have enough shops to accommodate shoppers of each wealth strata, shown in the Shoppers and Shops tables. But before rushing off and zoning, make sure the data you see here is backed up by current RCI demand and complaints within the Mayor Rating panel. Remember, if your Sims aren't finding jobs or shops in your city, they'll travel to other cities in the region. So even if you're showing a shortage of jobs or shops, RCI demand may be low. Study the "commute out" column in each table to see how many Sims of each wealth level are leaving your city to find jobs and shops. Likewise, look at the "commute in" column to see how many visitors are coming into your city for work and shopping.

Scroll down the detail tab to view the Students and Industrial Freight tables. The Students table shows the number of students in your city. It also shows the total number of desks in each school—you'll need a surplus of desks to accept more students, so consider expanding your schools if there's a shortage. The Industrial Freight table simply shows the current supply and demand of freight.

If there's a shortage in supply, consider creating more industrial zones to generate more freight. Scroll down to the bottom of the page to get an update on the number of tourists and homeless Sims in your city.

As you can see, the Population panel is filled with tons of useful data you can leverage to make informed decisions. But since the data is shown in real-time, it's always changing. Instead of relying solely on these figures, take into account feedback from Sims as well as current RCI demand to help influence your decision making.

City Finances: Budget Panel

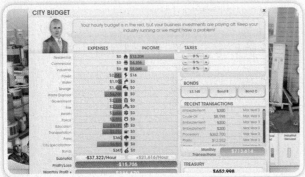

Access the Budget panel to make sure your city is bringing in more money than it's spending. If not, consider zoning, shutting down buildings, or raising taxes.

What kind of Mayor would you be without frequent visits to the Budget panel? This essential panel includes a ledger, detailing all hourly income and expenses, itemized in 16 different categories. Income is generated through taxing residential, commercial, and industrial zones. As a result, you should have a positive flow of income in all three categories at the top of the ledger, indicated by green bars. The remaining categories in the ledger show the hourly operational expenses associated with running buildings related to power, water, sewage, waste disposal, government, fire, health, police, education, transportation, parks, and city specialization—all expenses are shown as red bars. The last expense line in the ledger reports hourly costs related to paying back loans. The Subtotal line at the bottom of the ledger tallies all expenses and income while the Profit/Loss line subtracts total expenses from total income to report how much money your city is earning (or losing) per hour. If this line is green, you're doing fine. If it's red, indicating a loss, consider creating more residential, commercial, or industrial zones to increase tax revenue. If there's no demand for more zones and you're still operating in the red, consider raising taxes or cutting back on services.

But even if you're losing money every hour, it doesn't necessarily mean your city is facing bankruptcy. Transactions relating to city specialization and fees earned by providing services to other cities are not shown in the itemized list of the ledger. Instead, these all appear in the Recent Transactions window, on the right side of the panel. Here you can see recent sales of resources like crude oil, coal, and raw ore. Money earned from providing power, water, sewage, waste disposal, health, fire, and police services to neighboring cities is also shown here. Since these transactions are infrequent and difficult to predict, they're tallied monthly instead of hourly. So if you're relying on these transactions to keep your city's finances afloat, pay attention to the final Monthly Profit + Transactions line at the bottom of the ledger. This line calculates all profit/loss and transactions per month, providing a good overview of your city's current financial well being. If this line is green, you're doing okay. If it's red, it's time to start shutting down buildings/services, raising taxes, or taking out loans before your treasury is depleted.

> ⚠ **CAUTION**
>
> Are the numbers not adding up? You might have a white collar criminal embezzling money from your city to support a lavish lifestyle. Any embezzlement activity is shown in the Budget panel's Recent Transactions window. To catch embezzlers you must build a Police Precinct with a Detective Wing module. Do this at the first sign of embezzling, otherwise your city will continue losing money at a steady rate.

TAXES

Plop a Department of Finance next to your City Hall (or anywhere in the region) to expand your city's taxation capabilities as well as increase the size of loans you can acquire through bonds.

OPTIMUM TAX RATES

Wealth	Rate
Low	8-12%
Medium	7-11%
High	6-10%

GROWTH PROHIBITIVE TAX RATES*

Wealth	Density	Rate
Low	Low	19%
Low	Medium	18%
Low	High	19%
Medium	Low	17%
Medium	Medium	15%
Medium	High	12%
High	Low	14%
High	Medium	13%

New Sims stop moving into buildings at these rates.

HIGH WEALTH TAXES

Tax Rate	Happiness
0%	+3
2%	+2
5%	+1
8%	0
11%	-1
14%	-2
17%	-3
20%	-4

MEDIUM WEALTH TAXES

Tax Rate	Happiness
0%	+3
3%	+2
6%	+1
9%	0
12%	-1
15%	-2
18%	-3
20%	-3

LOW WEALTH TAXES

Tax Rate	Happiness
0%	+3
1%	+3
4%	+2
7%	+1
10%	0
13%	-1
16%	-2
19%	-3
20%	-3

Nobody likes taxes. But unless you have an alternate source of income, such as a specialization, taxes are necessary to keep your city functioning. Tax rates can be adjusted in the Taxes window within the Budget panel. Initially, with the Town Hall, you can only set one city-wide tax rate. But once you upgrade to a City Hall, tax rates can be set separately for residential, commercial, and industrial zones. If you build the Department of Finance, or one already exists in the region, you can adjust rates on the different zones as well as the different wealth/tech levels within each, giving you a total of nine rates to control.

By default, tax rates are set at 9%. This is a solid and fair rate for everyone, helping your city establish infrastructure and provide basic services. So when is it appropriate to raise taxes? If your city is facing a budget crisis, and there's no better solution, you may need to raise taxes to avoid financial collapse. But when raising taxes, do so gradually, at one percentage point per category. As you adjust tax rates, the income is adjusted in the ledger in real-time, giving you instant feedback. Simply bumping the tax rates up 1%

across all categories can have an enormous impact on your city's income, potentially restoring profitability. However, higher taxes can also lead to a loss of happiness among Sims and businesses. Sims perceive taxes in three brackets, low, medium, and high. Increasing taxes from a lower bracket to a higher bracket may result in a loss of happiness. As tax rates increase, Sims will stop moving into your city's residential buildings based on wealth and density. So if you want to attract new Sims, consider lowering taxes. To optimize tax rates for each category, study the accompanying tables. This will help you to set the highest rate possible without experiencing a loss of happiness or halting population growth.

If your city runs completely out of money, you have four options: turn off some buildings, increase taxes, take out a loan, or sneak out of town and start a new city.

In addition to raising taxes, look for other ways to increase revenue. Broadening your tax base through zoning is one of the easiest ways to bring in more money. Simply draw more residential, commercial, or industrial zones to encourage new construction. If you're out of room, encourage an increase in density by upgrading roads so they can accommodate medium and high density buildings. Of course, as more Sims flock to your city, you'll face an increased demand on utilities and city services, not to mention an increase in traffic, so keep this in mind before triggering a massive population explosion. Your efforts to broaden the tax base may backfire as you're forced to expand coverage of utilities and city services, leading to higher expenses.

 TIP

If your city is bringing in a tons of money from city specialization transactions, you can actually lower all tax rates to zero, using income generated from these transactions to cover all expenses. Setting tax rates to zero will spur a sudden burst in population as Sims rush to your tax-free city. Plus, everyone will be happy! But the population explosion also results in greater demand for city services, leading to higher expenses. You may need to raise taxes to offset these growing expenses.

LOANS

The Oil Refinery is very expensive but generates a lot of income when selling its products through a Trade Depot or Trade Port, so consider taking out a loan to build such big ticket buildings. With the extra income generated, you'll have that loan paid back in no time.

LOAN COSTS

Loan Amount	Hourly Cost	Total Cost
§25,000	§173	§27,880
§50,000	§347	§55,760
§100,000	§694	§111,520

Running low on money? No problem. Take out a loan! By issuing Bond A, Bond B, or Bond C you can fill your treasury with Simoleons in a flash. Within the Loans window of the Budget panel, click on any of the three lenders to select the loan amount—you can choose from loan denominations of §25,000, §50,000, or §100,000. But loans aren't free—a fixed interest rate is tacked onto each loan. Loans are automatically paid back in hourly installments, as shown in the ledger—it takes approximately seven days to pay back each loan. But if you have the money, you can pay back a loan in full at any time by clicking on the outstanding balance, shown in the Loans window. You can have a total of three loans out at any given time, one from each of the three lenders.

When should you take out a loan? Consider borrowing money when you need to make improvements to infrastructure or when constructing expensive city specialization buildings such as the Oil Refinery, Smelting Factory, Trade Port, or Processor Factory—taking out a loan so you can make more money is usually a safe and wise decision. Also, don't be afraid to take out small loans when starting a new city. Road construction alone can be costly, not to mention the cost of providing essential utilities. Plus, as your city grows and your tax base increases, you'll have no problems paying loans off. Avoid taking out loans during a budget crisis. The money you borrow may temporarily replenish the treasury, but it won't solve the root cause of your budget deficit. Instead, consider expanding your tax base through zoning, shutting down buildings, or raising taxes to balance the budget.

Data Maps

Reference the Land Value map periodically to view the negative impact of industrial and utility buildings on your city.

Numbers are nice, but if you prefer a visual representation of what's going on in your city, rely on the various data maps to reveal problems and potential opportunities. There are more than 30 data maps in all, covering a wide range topics including land value, wealth, population, happiness, mass transit, utilities, crime, resources, and pollution. To access all data maps, click on the Data Maps button in the bottom right corner of the HUD. Each menu also has a data maps tab, where you can access maps associated with the selected menu. For instance, the Crime map is available within the Police menu. Each data map includes a legend, explaining what the different colors and icons on the map represent.

While all of the maps reveal important information, you'll probably access some maps more than others. The Land Value map is extremely helpful when determining RCI zoning, as medium and high wealth buildings do not like the red areas representing low land value. If your city has a lot of factories or a Coal or Oil Power Plant, reference the Air Pollution or Wind maps to see where all that pollution is blowing. If your Clinics and Hospitals are seeing an uptick in patients, access the Germs map to see which areas of the city are a problem as well as what the source of the germs are—germs can spread through air pollution, ground pollution, sewage, water pollution, or garbage. When it comes to city specialization, don't forget to the check the Oil, Coal, and Ore maps, preferably before you start building a city. The Trade data map is also very helpful, showing the flow of resources throughout the city making it ideal for identifying kinks in your supply chains. If you recently built a Recycling Center, open the Garbage map to see the effectiveness of your recycling program—buildings with educated Sims recycle more than those with uneducated Sims. Before making a decision, reference the data maps on a particular topic to help guide your actions.

Advisors

If there's a problem in your city, advisors will let you know about it and offer solutions.

Feeling a bit overwhelmed, Mayor? Don't worry, you're not in this alone. In fact, you have a small army of advisors on your side, helping guide you through the challenges of managing a city. When a menu is opened, the advisor associated with the menu appears in the bottom left side of the HUD, sometimes dispensing helpful tips in a speech bubble. If you missed what they said, click on the red exclamation point icon above their head to restore the speech bubble. Advisors usually only offer advice when there's a problem. If an advisor has something to say, the menu buttons at the bottom of the HUD will turn yellow or red—yellow indicates a potential problem while red indicates a more serious matter requiring immediate attention. Keep an eye on all the menu buttons and address concerns as they arise before problem get out of hand. If you need more information about a particular topic, hover the mouse over the blue "i" icon just below an advisor's portrait. This reveals a list of helpful tips relevant to the current menu.

Missions

Accept and complete missions to earn some extra money for your city's treasury. Completing this particular mission unlocks the Mayor's Mansion.

Periodically Sims throughout the city will ask you to build a particular building or complete some other task. These are called missions. Missions first appear as blue request bubbles hovering above buildings. Click on a blue bubbles

to review the Sim's request and criteria for completing the mission. Missions usually offer a reward issued in Simoleons (to the city's treasury) when all required tasks have been completed. You can choose to accept, decline, or postpone any mission after reviewing it. If you're sure you can't complete the mission, decline it by clicking on the "No Thanks" button. If you'd like to do the mission, but the timing isn't right, choose the "Ask Later" button and the mission will reappear later. If you choose the "I'll Do It!" button, a new icon appears on the right side of the HUD serving as a reminder—this area is called the Mission Tracker. Here you can have up to three missions active at any given time. Hover over the icons in the Mission Tracker to review the criteria for completing each one. Early on, missions often serve as tutorials, helping you get your city functioning. But as your city becomes more established, a variety of missions will appear, including some your city may not be ready for. For example, Sims seeking entertainment options often want you to build an Expo Center, so they can attend local shows and sporting events. So before taking on a mission, make sure the request is feasible within a reasonable amount of time. Otherwise, consider postponing the mission until you can easily complete it.

> **(i) NOTE**
>
> For a list of all missions and their associated rewards, flip to the Quick Reference chapter at the back of the guide.

GOVERNMENT: POINTS TO REMEMBER

→ City Hall allows you to set tax rates.

→ Each City Hall upgrade grants your choice of one department module.

→ Most City Hall departments grant access to more buildings for all cities in the region.

→ Government buildings increase nearby land value.

→ Buildings start as low density but can grow if they are kept happy/profitable.

→ A building will only grow if the road it is on is big enough to permit the traffic.

→ Click on an individual building to see its progress toward the next density level.

→ Density is the building's size. Land Value relates to its wealth level.

→ If a building loses happiness/profit, it will eventually go abandoned.

→ An abandoned building may revive if its problems are resolved.

GOVERNMENT ACHIEVEMENTS

Icon	Name	Criteria
	Best Mayor Ever!	Have an approval rating of 95% or more.
	Big Government	Place one of each of the City Hall departments on a single City Hall.
	Bronze Anniversary (Secret)	Play a city for 10 years!
	Busy Downtown	Have at least 100 commercial buildings in your city.
	Dug Too Greedily and Too Deep (Secret)	Mine 100 tons of coal or raw ore in your city to gain access to the Earthquake disaster.
	Golden Anniversary (Secret)	Play a city for 50 years! Take a break!
	Good Credit	Pay off §1,000,000 in bond debt.
	Industrial Revolution	Have 100 industrial buildings in your city.
	Jumbo Region!	Have 1,000,000 residents living in a region.
	Mega-Region!	Have 2,000,000 residents living in a region.
	Metropolis!	Have 100,000 residents living in your city.

GOVERNMENT ACHIEVEMENTS

Icon	Name	Criteria
	Money Cube	Have a total income of §15,000+ per hour.
	Multi-Millionaire City	Have §10,000,000 in your treasury.
	My Favorite Mayor	Have 24 hours of a 75% or better approval rating.
	The Philanthropist	Gift §200,000 or more to a neighbor.
	Population Boom	Have 50,000 residents living in your city.
	Quid Pro Quo	Place one each of all the modules on a single Mayor's Mansion.
	Sand Through My Fingers	Have total expenses of §15,000+ per hour.
	Silver Anniversary (Secret)	Play a city for 25 years!
	Suburb City	Have 10,000 residents living in your city.
	Suburbtopia	Have 500 residential buildings in your city.
	Team Mayor	Grant approvals for 10 buildings for the region.
	Worst. Mayor. Ever.	Hold an approval rating of below 50% for 24 hours.

CHAT WITH THE DEVELOPERS

How We Sim our Sims

JEREMY DALE, ANIMATOR

Hey everyone! I'm Jeremy Dale and I'm an Animator here at Maxis. It's my job to make all the little Sims feel at home. Or at least act like they're feeling at home. Or maybe if they don't like their home, make them act like they don't like their home. Okay, the important thing is I make sure that what the Sims are doing makes sense and is relevant.

There is a tremendous amount of data being transmitted under the hood with the GlassBox engine. My job is to put a human face on these transactions, and make them entertaining. From the lowly surveyors that you see preparing for construction, to the chaos of a foiled bank robbery shootout, I utilize our vignette system to expose the simulation to the player using Sims rather than pie charts.

As you may read in Engineer Robert Perry's piece about physics, "what you see is what we Sim" is one of the core driving philosophies on *SimCity*. In my case, it's more "when you see your Sims, you're seeing your Sims' simulation." It's not enough to make a city feel alive. It has to be alive. If you see a Sim wearing scrubs walking down the street, that's not some random "extra," that's a nurse heading home from a shift at the hospital.

When Sims are at home, what do they do? What do Sims do when they're shopping at a boutique? How can I best leverage an opportunity to show what it looks like when workers at a warehouse

are on break? To answer these questions, I need to look at the data in the simulation and find out how many kids are present at a residence, how many workers are in a commercial building, or how many executives a manufacturing operation might support. In this way, I can surprise an observant player with a fact-at-a-glance while wandering around the city as I have surprised myself when I saw an injured Sim standing in front of his home, hoping an ambulance might arrive to speed him away to recovery. As any good mayor would, I quickly built a clinic nearby, and he was quickly retrieved and cared for.

You might see some shabby looking characters huddled around the entrance of a park, which will prompt you to check the deeper data on hand to see the extent of your homeless population. Seeing a mob of Sims outside City Hall might cause you to inspect your tax rates. If there are large groups of Sims gathered around bus stops for an extended period of time, you will know that you should add more buses to your transportation network.

> When Sims are at home, what do they do? What do Sims do when they're shopping at a boutique? How can I best leverage an opportunity to show what it looks like when workers at a warehouse are on break?

City Services

Mayor, don't you think it's time to provide fire, health, and police coverage?

What about parks? These city services help promote a safe and healthy community, where Sims can thrive...and feel they're getting a good return on the taxes they're paying. But city services are an all-expense, non-profit venture, requiring a great deal of fiscal discipline to avoid overextending services and bankrupting the city. Like all things in *SimCity*, start small and expand coverage of services as needed while keeping hourly operational costs within the constraints of the city's budget. By providing and carefully managing these city services you can take your city to the next level, enjoying an uptick in your approval rating along the way!

Don't forget to go to **www.primagames.com** to access guide updates free of charge with your voucher code.

Fire

A lack of fire coverage can lead to large fires that spread from one building to the next, potentially reducing a large portion of your city to ash and rubble.

Uh oh. Do you smell smoke? Maybe it's time to build that Fire Station after all. Providing fire coverage for your city is one of the most important aspects of establishing a safe living, working, and shopping environment for residents and visitors alike. It's impossible to determine when and where your city's first fire will break out, so once you have the money, plop a Fire Station in a central location. At the very least, ask a neighboring city to provide fire coverage until you can establish adequate fire protection for your city.

Fire Station

Cost: §20,000

Operational Cost: §400 per hour

Response Time: 12 minutes

Prerequisites:

→ Town Hall

Description: Stop the spread of fire across your city. Improve coverage by adding more fire trucks.

It may not look like much, but this little Fire Station is quite capable of serving the fire suppression needs of a small or moderately sized city. When you first build the Fire Station, immediately add the Fire Alarm module. This cuts the station's response time from 12 minutes down to 6 minutes, getting firefighters out the door and to the location of a fire before it can turn into a dangerous multi-structure blaze. The Fire Station comes with one garage and one fire truck, but the station can be expanded through the addition of up to three more Fire Station Garages, giving the building the ability to house a total of four fire trucks. The expandability and relative low cost of the Fire Station makes it an attractive alternative to the Large Fire Station—you can build three fully expanded Fire Stations, supporting 12 fire trucks, for less than one Large Fire Station, supporting only four fire trucks. So take into account the needs of your city and consider plopping multiple Fire Stations before dropping a lot of money on a Large Fire Station.

MODULES

Fire Station Sign

Cost: §200

Operational Cost: None

Maximum Modules: 1

Description: It's nice to have a sign, for when you're running around in a panic looking for the Fire Station.

Fire Station Flagpole

Cost: §100

Operational Cost: None

Maximum Modules: 1

Description: Wouldn't be a Fire Station without a flagpole, right? Hopefully the pole doesn't confuse any of the firefighters into sliding down it...

Fire Alarm

Cost: §3,000

Operational Cost: §75 per hour

Response Time Modifier: 1/2 the previous response time

Maximum Modules: 1

Description: Wake those sleepy firefighters from dreams of Dalmatians jumping over fences. Fire trucks are dispatched twice as fast.

Fire Station Garage

Cost: §15,000

Operational Cost: §200 per hour

Maximum Modules: 4

Description: Attach this garage to your Fire Station and gain an additional fire truck. And maybe your firemen can start a garage band during their time off?

> ### ⚠ CAUTION
>
> Don't wait until you have your first fire to build a Fire Station. Like most buildings, a Fire Station must be staffed before it can function, and the hiring process can take time. In the meantime, a large portion of your city could burn down while the new Fire Station sits unmanned.

Large Fire Station

Cost: §85,000

Operational Cost: §1,700 per hour

Response Time: 6 minutes

Prerequisites:

→ City Hall

→ Department of Safety in the region

Description: This Fire Station is hot stuff! Go all out with better trucks, larger fire coverage, the addition of Hazmat for those stubborn industrial fires, and a fire helicopter! That's right, we said helicopter.

Is your city experiencing more than its fair share of fires? Then consider building the Large Fire Station. This is a highly specialized facility capable of handling the most dangerous fires your city will face—it already comes equipped with two hook & ladder trucks. Soon after building the Large Fire Station, build the Fire Dispatch Tower module to decrease response time from 6 minutes down to 3 minutes. If you have the money, add on a Fire Marshal Office to prompt random visits by the fire marshal to various buildings—a visit from the fire marshal makes the building immune to fire for several days. If you have numerous mines or industrial buildings in your city, it's strongly advised to add at least one Hazmat Garage. Hazmat fire trucks are the only way to put out hazmat fires, caused by the combustion of toxic materials found in industrial buildings. Add more hook & ladder trucks to your fleet by building additional Fire Truck Garages—hook & ladder trucks can extinguish fires faster than their smaller fire truck cousins. Or take the fight to the skies by adding a Fire Helipad. The Large Fire Station is a very expensive facility to place and run on an hourly basis. Before building and expanding, make sure your city's budget can handle the burden of running a top-notch facility. Otherwise, stick with the smaller and more economical Fire Stations.

MODULES

Large Fire Station Sign

Cost: §200

Operational Cost: None

Maximum Modules: 1

Description: It should be pretty obvious from the sirens where the Large Fire Station is, but the sign makes it more official!

Fire Station Flagpole

Cost: §100

Operational Cost: None

Maximum Modules: 1

Description: Wouldn't be a Fire Station without a flagpole, right? Hopefully the pole doesn't confuse any of the firefighters into sliding down it...

 TIP

Abandoned buildings are a fire risk. There's a higher chance of fires in abandoned neighborhoods.

Fire Dispatch Tower

Cost: §10,000

Operational Cost: §525 per hour

Response Time Modifier: 1/2 the previous response time

Maximum Modules: 1

Description: This state-of-the-art dispatch tower communicates over satellite. Speeds up response time of all your fire vehicles. Fire trucks are dispatched twice as fast.

Large Fire Station Garage

Cost: §15,000

Operational Cost: §400 per hour

Maximum Modules: 4 (one comes with base)

Description: With all the capabilities of a regular fire truck, the hook & ladder that comes with this one extends its coverage by quite a bit.

Fire Marshal Office

Cost: §20,000

Operational Cost: §500 per hour

Fire Retardant: Adds 10 per house

Maximum Modules: 4

Description: The fire marshal drives around the city, visiting houses, factories, and shops. Places the fire marshal visits are immune to fire for several days.

Hazmat Garage

Cost: §40,000

Operational Cost: §250 per hour

Fire Retardant: Adds 10 per house

Maximum Modules: 4

Prerequisites:

→ University in the region

→ University with School of Engineering in the region

→ Complete research project at University in the region

Description: This hazmat truck puts out heavy industrial fires caused by hazardous materials. Without it, hazmat fires will burn unchecked!

Fire Helipad

Cost: §60,000

Operational Cost: §1,400 per hour

Fire Retardant: Adds 10 per house

Maximum Modules: 4

Prerequisites:

→ Municipal Airport in the city or International Airport in the region

Description: Put out fires in a blink of a helicopter blade. Make sure you have enough water towers, because this one uses a lot of water!

Fire Management

Building a Fire Station may not be enough to address all the fires breaking out across your city. Before investing a small fortune on fire services, it's important to understand how fires function and how they can be prevented. Once you've got a handle on the basics, gradually expand services as needed through the construction of additional modules or the Large Fire Station. But if you're not careful, the natural urge to provide fire protection could bankrupt your city.

UNDERSTANDING FIRE

Where there's smoke, there's fire. At least there will be if your fire trucks don't get there in time. As the diagram illustrates, fires don't just burst out without warning. Fires go through four stages of increasing intensity, beginning with smoke. When a building begins emitting smoke, an alarm is sounded and your fire trucks begin rolling out. While a building is emitting smoke, Sims can still escape without suffering injuries. However, as flames become visible, the risk for Sims trapped inside increases. Any Sim escaping a building in flames will be injured, requiring medical assistance from an ambulance—if no ambulance arrives, they will die. Meanwhile, your fire trucks are tasked with extinguishing the flames. As the fire consumes more fuel, it becomes larger, radiating heat to nearby buildings. As neighboring buildings absorb heat from the fire, they run the risk of catching on fire too. But as the fire truck pours water on the fire, the heat radiated drops signifi-

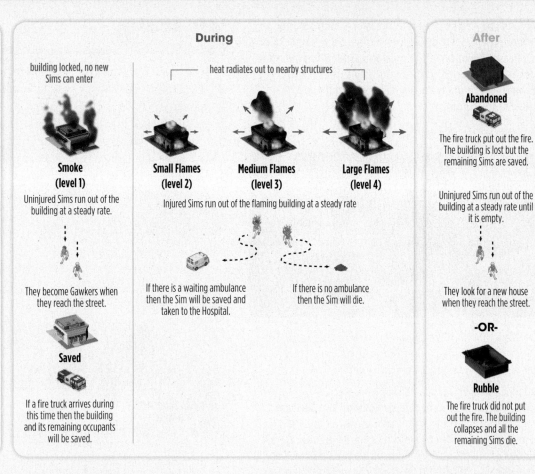

Before

No Fire
Sims safe inside.

During

building locked, no new
Sims can enter

**Smoke
(level 1)**
Uninjured Sims run out of the
building at a steady rate.

They become Gawkers when
they reach the street.

Saved

If a fire truck arrives during
this time then the building
and its remaining occupants
will be saved.

heat radiates out to nearby structures

**Small Flames
(level 2)**

**Medium Flames
(level 3)**

**Large Flames
(level 4)**

Injured Sims run out of the flaming building at a steady rate

If there is a waiting ambulance
then the Sim will be saved and
taken to the Hospital.

If there is no ambulance
then the Sim will die.

After

Abandoned

The fire truck put out the fire.
The building is lost but the
remaining Sims are saved.

Uninjured Sims run out of the
building at a steady rate until
it is empty.

They look for a new house
when they reach the street.

-OR-

Rubble

The fire truck did not put
out the fire. The building
collapses and all the
remaining Sims die.

cantly, reducing the risk of the fire spreading to other buildings. But when dealing with fires, every minute counts. So make sure your Fire Station is equipped with a Fire Alarm and that your Large Fire Station has a Fire Dispatch Tower—both modules reduce the response time. Secondly, ensure your roads are free of traffic, otherwise your vehicles may not make it to the fire before it spreads over wide area. If traffic is a problem in your city, consider adding a Fire Helipad to your Large Fire Station and attack the flames from the air, bypassing traffic altogether.

FIRE PREVENTION

In addition to reducing germs caused from ground pollution, collecting garbage significantly reduces a city's fire risk.

While you can rely on your fire trucks to extinguish fires, it's best if there are no fires in the first place. There are multiple steps you can take to reduce the risk of fires breaking out in your city. First, access the Waste Disposal menu and ensure all garbage cans are collected each day. Trash piling up in your streets significantly increases the chance of a fire breaking out, so address this issue by adding more garbage trucks to deal with the garbage problem. Next, access the Bulldoze menu and demolish any abandoned buildings or rubble—these eyesores also increase fire risk. Now open the Education menu and ensure that every kid in your city is enrolled in school. Educated Sims are far less likely to cause fires than uneducated Sims, so to prevent your Sims from doing stupid things, consider plopping a Grade School or Public Library to increase the education level of your population. Crime can also increase the risk of fire, particularly if you have an arsonist on the loose. Open the Police menu and consider expanding police services if there are multiple criminals operating freely within your city. As a final step to reduce fire risk, add at least one Fire Marshal Office module to your Large Fire Station. The fire marshal randomly inspects multiple buildings throughout the city on a daily basis. Buildings that have been visited by a fire marshal are completely immune to fires for several days. As you can see, there is not a one-step solution to preventing fires, but by addressing garbage, abandoned buildings, education, and crime and adding fire marshals, you can significantly reduce your city's risk for fires, allowing you to maintain a smaller and more cost-effective fire service.

EXPANSION OF SERVICE

The Fire Alarm and Fire Dispatch Tower reduce response time, helping your fire trucks reach fires in their early smoldering stage, before flames are even visible.

Like all city services, providing fire protection isn't cheap, so it's important to keep the size of your fire services in line with the current risk. Open the Fire menu and study the numbers in the info tab. Here you can see the number of buildings burned down each day as well as the numbers of fires and hazmat fires extinguished on a daily basis. Obviously, if any buildings have burned down, you have a problem. But why are buildings burning down? Is it because you don't have enough fire trucks? Or is it because the fire trucks couldn't reach the fire due to traffic? To uncover the answer, monitor your fire trucks as they respond to a fire. A fire truck can respond to one fire at a time, so if there's multiple fires and only one truck, consider adding a garage or two. The standard Fire Station is cheap and easily expandable, making it the most economical solution for fighting fires. If fires continue breaking out and your standard fire trucks aren't cutting it, consider building a Large Fire Station for increased response time and specialty vehicles like the hook & ladder truck, hazmat truck, and fire helicopter. But always take into account the hourly cost of operating each additional building and module. A top-of-the-line, fully equipped Large Fire Station can cost more than §3,000 to operate every hour!

⚠ CAUTION

If you have any mines or high density industrial buildings in your city, it's wise to invest in a Hazmat Garage, built at the Large Fire Station. These buildings have an increased risk for hazmat fires—toxic, green blazes resulting in sickness-causing air and ground pollution. If you don't have a hazmat truck, these fires will spread uncontrollably. All other fire vehicles are incapable of putting out a hazmat fire.

VOLUNTEERING FIRE RESOURCES

Sharing fire vehicles with the region is the right thing to do—plus you earn a §200 fee each time one of your vehicles extinguishes a fire in a neighboring city.

Just like garbage and recycling collection trucks, your fire service vehicles can be shared with neighboring cities in the region. Open the Region View, then access the Fire menu to begin allocation of vehicles to other cities. Don't worry, sharing fire trucks and vehicles does not reduce your own city's fire coverage—technically these vehicles can respond to fires simultaneously in both cities. Furthermore, any fires your vehicles extinguish in a neighboring city nets your city a small fee, appearing within the Recent Transactions window of the Budget panel. Don't have any fire services in your city? Then consider asking the mayor of a neighboring city for a little help. Since there is no down side to extending fire services to a nearby city, the mayor will probably be more than happy to oblige unless that city's fire resources are tied up assisting another city.

FIRE: POINTS TO REMEMBER

→ All buildings have a chance to catch on fire.

→ Buildings on terrain with lots of water have lower fire risk.

→ Buildings with educated Sims have lower fire risk.

→ Overflowing garbage and abandoned buildings are a fire risk.

→ Educated Sims are less likely to start fires.

→ The Fire Station and Large Fire Station increase land value.

→ Add fire trucks to put out more fires.

→ Hazmat trucks from the Large Fire Station must put out hazmat fires.

→ Industrial buildings have a greater chance to catch fire.

→ Fires have a chance to spread to surrounding buildings.

→ The fire marshal lowers the chance of fires.

→ Some criminals start fires.

→ Fire helicopters can avoid traffic on the way to put out a fire.

→ Cities can extend their fire coverage to their neighbors.

→ Any fire vehicle can be offered to any connected city.

→ The city receiving fire coverage gets free fire coverage.

→ The city providing fire coverage receives income for fires extinguished.

Health

Ambulances respond to stabilize injured Sims before transporting them to a Clinic or Hospital for treatment. Injured Sims will die if an ambulance is late or never responds.

You know that cough going around? Maybe you should do something about it. Don't take any health issue lightly. Untreated sickness can lead to injury, and untreated injuries lead to death. Injuries can result from long-term sickness or can happen suddenly, as the result of an accident or fire. When an injury occurs, make sure an ambulance is available, otherwise the injured Sim will die.

Beyond the personal tragedies, sickness and injures can have a ripple effect on the city's economy. Sick Sims stay home from work, reducing efficiency (profit) at their place of employment. And if Sims stay sick longer, they'll have no money to shop or pay their rent, potentially leading to eviction from their house. All of this can result in lower tax revenue. While it may seem cold and heartless, it's in your city's best financial interest to keep Sims healthy...and paying taxes. So build a Clinic or Hospital to treat sickness and injuries before the city's budget takes a hit.

Clinic

Cost: §20,000

Operational Cost: §400 per hour

Patient Rooms: 10

Waiting Room Capacity: 10

Prerequisites:

→ Town Hall

Description: Is there a cough going around or a series of unfortunate industrial accidents? This small Clinic can treat your sick and injured Sims.

The Clinic is your city's first line of defense in the persistent battle against sickness and injuries. In its stock state, the Clinic is equipped with one ambulance and can treat ten patients at a time. Such rudimentary health coverage should be more than sufficient for a small city of less than 5,000 Sims. But as your city grows, and sickness and injuries increase, expand the Clinic with additional Ambulance Bays and Patient Rooms. When expanded to capacity, the Clinic can treat up to 55 patients simultaneously and dispatch up to four ambulances. If a Clinic is busting at the seams, treating 40 patients or more, consider building a Hospital. Although Hospitals have a high initial cost, their operating cost is less than a fully expanded Clinic.

MODULES

Clinic Sign

Cost: §200

Operational Cost: None

Maximum Modules: 1

Description: Sick people don't have time to read the address...they need a sign!

Ambulance Bay

Cost: §10,000

Operational Cost: §200 per hour

Capacity: 4 injured Sims

Maximum Modules: 4

Description: Ambulances respond to injury emergencies throughout your city. Add an Ambulance Bay to add another ambulance and reduce your Clinic's response time.

Patient Rooms

Cost: §12,000

Operational Cost: §300 per hour

Patient Rooms: 15

Maximum Modules: 4

Description: Provides extra rooms for Sims on bedrest, allowing you to treat more patients at a time.

Hospital

Cost: §120,000

Operational Cost: §1,700 per hour

Patient Rooms: 50

Waiting Room Capacity: 40

Prerequisites:

→ City Hall

→ Department of Safety in the region

Description: Too many subdural hematomas? Then you need this major medical center. Treat many more sick and injured Sims in this large medical facility. Improve quality of care with additions to your Hospital.

The Hospital is the flagship of your city's health care system, greatly increasing coverage, recovery time, and survivability for all Sims. When expanded with the maximum number of Patient Rooms, this facility can treat 350 Sims simultaneously, allowing it to serve a metropolis as well as neighboring cities within the region. In its stock state, treatment offered by the Hospital is identical to treatment offered by a Clinic. But with the addition of the Diagnostic Lab and Surgical Center modules, you can significantly reduce recovery times from sickness and injuries, getting Sims back to work faster. The Emergency Center can even double the lifespan of injured Sims, allowing them to survive longer while waiting for an ambulance—this is essential if your city has traffic problems. Too many germs in your city? Build a Wellness Center to dispatch a germ-cleaning wellness van. But the cost of running a Hospital and its modules is enormous, so start small and expand the Hospital as more funds become available.

MODULES

Hospital Sign

Cost: §200

Operational Cost: None

Maximum Modules: 1

Description: It's kind of important to know where the Hospital is.

Ambulance Bay

Cost: §15,000

Operational Cost: §400 per hour

Number of Ambulances: 2

Capacity: 8 injured Sims

Maximum Modules: 4

Description: Dispatch paramedics to bring injured Sims to your Hospital for treatment. Additional Ambulance Bays reduce your Hospital's response time.

Patient Rooms

Cost: §40,000

Operational Cost: §1,400 per hour

Patient Rooms: 75

Maximum Modules: 4

Description: Additional patient rooms provide you enough capacity to care for the entire region!

Emergency Center

Cost: §40,000

Operational Cost: §400 per hour

Time Until Death: 2x previous time until death

Maximum Modules: 1

Description: Patient, calm emergency operators keep Sims with injuries on the line, helping them survive twice as long while waiting for an ambulance to arrive.

Wellness Center

Cost: §30,000

Operational Cost: §450 per hour

Wellness Vans: 1

Maximum Modules: 4

Description: Dispatches a wellness van to visit residences in your city. The wellness van helps Sims clean up, removing some of the germs that can cause sickness. Prevention is better than the cure!

Diagnostic Lab

Cost: §60,000

Operational Cost: §750 per hour

Sick Recovery Time: 1/2 the previous recovery time

Prerequisites:

➜ University in the region

➜ University with School of Science in the region

Maximum Modules: 1

Description: Advanced Science enables faster diagnoses for sick Sims. Sims recover from sickness twice as fast!

Surgical Center

Cost: §80,000

Operational Cost: §750 per hour

Injury Recovery Time: 1/2 the previous recovery time

Prerequisites:

➜ University in the region

➜ University with School of Medicine in the region

➜ Complete research project at University in the region

Maximum Modules: 1

Description: This top-notch Surgical Center attracts the most skilled surgical talent. The hotshot surgeons here will heal injured Sims twice as fast!

 TIP

Given the large number of modules associated with it, leave plenty of room around your Hospital for expansion. Consider devoting an entire city block to the Hospital and its modules.

Health Management

Clinics and Hospitals are well-equipped for treating sick and injured Sims. But how does sickness occur in the first place? Are there factors you can control to mitigate health risks in your city? And how do you know when it's time to expand your health care coverage? These are all important questions you should be asking yourself. In this section, we'll take a look at each issue, offering explanations and solutions while stressing the importance of keeping sky-rocketing health care costs low.

POLLUTION AND GERMS

In the Germs data map you can see buildings infested by germs due to ground or air pollution. Buildings adjacent or downwind from factories and other polluting facilities run the highest risk of being overrun by germs.

Wondering why all your Sims are getting sick? Sickness is caused by germs, and germs are generated by air and ground pollution. Access the Germs data map as well as the Air and Ground Pollution data maps. Using these data layers you can see the problem areas of your city where pollution is spreading germs. Uncollected garbage and sewage that seeps to the surface can lead to germ-causing ground pollution. Deal with any ground pollution issues first by ensuring garbage is being collected and that your sewage system is functioning normally. Addressing air pollution is much more problematic. The best way to do this is through smart zoning early on, ensuring your residential and commercial zones are not downwind from factories and buildings (like the Oil or Coal Power Plant) producing air pollution. As long as the wind carries air pollution away from your residential and commercial zones, you can avoid widespread sickness outbreaks. However, Sims working within those polluted zones are more vulnerable. So if running a city relying heavily on industrial zones or polluting city specialization, construct a Hospital with a Diagnostic Lab module to treat sickness and reduce recovery time.

 TIP

Injuries are most common in industrial buildings. If injuries are occurring frequently, add an Emergency Center to your Hospital to double the lifespan of injured Sims waiting for an ambulance. Also, consider constructing a Surgical Center module to reduce injury recovery time.

PREVENTATIVE HEALTH CARE

Uneducated Sims are more likely to get sick. Construct a Grade School or other education buildings to increase the population's education level.

As an esteemed mayor, you probably know it's wise to wash your hands before eating a meal. But such common sense practices aren't obvious to every Sim living in your city. Your city's education system can help spread the word, encouraging good hygiene and sanitation—educated Sims are less likely to become sick than uneducated Sims. So build a Public Library, Grade School, or any other education building to increase your population's education level. The current education level of your population can be seen in the Education menu's info tab. You also can click on any residence to see if the tenants are educated— the word "Educated" will appear at the bottom of each building's information window. In addition to educating your population, consider adding a Wellness Center to your Hospital. This module dispatches a wellness van that sanitizes areas of the city with high levels of germs. If you haven't addressed the root cause of the germs (pollution), the germs will return, however.

 CAUTION

If your city relies on mass transit to move large amounts of Sims to and from neighboring cities, you run the risk of a plague outbreak, putting a sudden strain on your health care system. Prepare for overflowing Clinics and Hospitals as a flood of sick and injured Sims seek treatment.

EXPANSION OF SERVICES

The Hospital is expensive but can simultaneously treat hundreds of Sims when expanded to full capacity. Click on the Hospital periodically to make sure there are plenty of Patient Rooms still available. If not, consider adding more.

Providing health care is a fundamental responsibility necessary to keep Sims happy, healthy, and productive. But it's also extremely expensive, putting a serious strain on the city's budget. It's important to keep costs low while still providing adequate coverage. To determine your city's current health care needs, click on your Clinic to see how many patients it's treating—if the Clinic is filled to capacity, consider expanding it. Also, pay attention to the info tab within the Health menu. This tab shows the number of deaths in the city per day as well as the number of injured and sick treated per day. Obviously, if Sims are dying you have a problem—perhaps you need more ambulances to respond to injuries. But you may also be suffering a deficiency in coverage if sick and injured Sims are going untreated. A single Clinic can serve the health care needs of a small city. But once your city grows to a population of 15,000-20,000, it may be time for a Hospital. Whether expanding Clinics or building a Hospital, make sure you can afford all new additions to your health care system, as each building and module has a high hourly operational cost. When you build a Hospital, shut down your old Clinics to save money drained from your budget on an hourly basis. The Clinics can be reopened later to alleviate capacity strains at your Hospital—this is often cheaper than adding new Patient Rooms.

 TIP

If traffic congestion is a problem in your city, you may be better off constructing multiple Clinics scattered throughout the city instead of one centrally located Hospital. This allows ambulances dispatched from Clinics to cover smaller sections of the city, decreasing response time while minimizing the risk of ambulances getting stuck in traffic jams.

VOLUNTEERING HEALTH RESOURCES

Volunteer health vehicles and earn a $100 fee each time one of your ambulances responds to an injury in a neighboring city.

As soon as you construct a Clinic or Hospital, you can share the ambulances associated with these buildings to provide health care in neighboring cities. The wellness van associated with the Wellness Center module can also be volunteered. Access the Region View, then open the Health menu to begin allocating health vehicles to neighboring cities, connected by the highway. As with fire trucks and other emergency vehicles, when volunteering ambulances and wellness vans your city loses no coverage—the same vehicle can serve both cities simultaneously. There's no down side to sharing your vehicles. In fact, your city receives a fee each time one of your ambulances or wellness vans responds to an emergency in the neighboring city—fees received are shown in the Budget panel's Recent Transactions window. If your city is new and has no health coverage yet, request ambulances from other mayors in the region. Your city pays nothing to receive coverage, but the responding city will generate extra income when responding to injuries in your city—it's a win-win situation for both parties!

Health: Points to Remember

→ Sickness is caused by germs.

→ Germs are created by pollution.

→ Sick Sims stay home from work and don't shop.

→ If sick Sims can't get to a Clinic or Hospital they might become injured.

→ Educated Sims get sick less often.

→ Kids don't get sick.

→ Injuries can happen at industrial buildings.

→ Ambulances must pick up injured Sims, otherwise they'll die.

→ The Clinic and Hospital increase land value.

→ Cities can extend their health coverage to their neighbors.

→ Any health vehicle can be offered to any connected city.

→ The city receiving health coverage gets free health coverage.

→ The city providing the health coverage receives income for the sick and injured Sims they treat.

Police

Buildings tagged with graffiti are the early signs of a growing crime problem. Expand police coverage before crime takes over the city.

Do you love the sound of police sirens echoing through the night air? Or maybe you're just tired of criminals setting fires, robbing shops, and embezzling funds from your treasury. In any case, your city needs a police force. No matter how perfect you think your city is, criminals will take up residence or visit from neighboring cities in the region. What the criminals do when they reach your city depends on your police presence. A robust police force can suppress crime, discouraging criminals from going through with their devious plans. But criminals are persistent, and will eventually find weaknesses in your police coverage. When this occurs, your police must respond to the crime and apprehend the criminal before the criminal can get away, otherwise a criminal will level up and unleash more severe crimes on your city. Is your city's police force up to the challenge?

Police Station

Cost: §30,000

Operational Cost: §400 per hour

Jail Cells: 10

Patrol Cars: 2

Patrol Rate: Every 60 minutes

Prerequisites:

→ Town Hall

Description: Patrol cars respond to crimes in progress and arrest the criminals—if they can catch them! Police bring arrested criminals to the station to be rehabilitated in jail cells. The Police Station suppresses crime nearby.

Building a Police Station is a good first step to suppressing crime in your city. The station comes with two patrol cars that conduct regular patrols and respond to crimes in progress. If a patrol car responds to a crime before a criminal can escape, the police officer within the patrol will apprehend the suspect and haul them off to the Police Station's jail, capable of holding 10 criminals at a time.

Add more Patrol Car Lots to increase the number of patrol cars available and expand the jail capacity with additional ground or top floor Jail Cells. Since patrol cars from the Police Station can only respond to crimes in progress, criminals have more time to get away, especially if your city is experiencing traffic congestion. Therefore the Police Station isn't the most effective tool for apprehending criminals, but its mere presence, and that of its patrol cars, may be enough to make criminals think twice before breaking the law.

MODULES

Police Station Sign

Cost: §200

Operational Cost: None

Maximum Modules: 1

Description: Criminals are a superstitious, cowardly lot. Strike fear into their hearts.

Police Station Flagpole

Cost: §20

Operational Cost: None

Maximum Modules: 1

Description: Every police station needs this to show their patriotism!

Patrol Car Lot

Cost: §10,000

Operational Cost: §225 per hour

Patrol Cars: 2

Patrol Rate: Every 60 minutes

Maximum Modules: 4

Description: Increase your police presence with extra patrol cars.

Jail Cells (Ground Floor)

Cost: §15,000

Operational Cost: §300 per hour

Jail Cells: 15

Maximum Modules: 4

Description: Meager accommodations for criminals. Criminals are rehabilitated after several days. Must be built on the ground.

Jail Cells (Top Floor)

Cost: §15,000

Operational Cost: §300 per hour

Jail Cells: 15

Maximum Modules: 4

Description: Meager accommodations for criminals. Criminals are rehabilitated after several days. Cannot be built directly on the ground.

Police Precinct

Cost: §95,000

Operational Cost: §1,700 per hour

Jail Cells: 50

Patrol Cars: 4

Patrol Rate: Every 30 minutes

Prerequisites:

→ City Hall

→ Department of Safety in the region

Description: If "Police State" were an amusement park, the Police Precinct would be the fun house. More than just a big police station, the precinct has more jail cells and more patrol cars, and can be outfitted with advanced crime-fighting modules.

When it comes to fighting crime, no facility is better equipped than the Police Precinct. While this building has the same suppression and incarceration capabilities as the smaller Police Station, the addition of new modules gives the Police Precinct the ability to hunt down criminals wherever they're hiding. When plopping this building, immediately add the Police Dispatch Tower. This module instantly routes patrolling units to crimes in progress, increasing the chances of catching criminals in the act. The Detective Wing gives police detectives the ability to analyze evidence and arrest criminals at large while they're at home—a must for identifying and arresting white collar tax evaders and embezzlers. Add a Police Helipad to track and arrest criminals from the air, ideal during hot pursuits when your patrol cars are stuck in traffic. You can also address crime before it takes root through the Crime Prevention Center, dispatching a crime prevention van to discourage kids from becoming criminals. The Police Precinct's capabilities and capacity can also be expanded, dispatching up to 28 patrols cars and jailing more than 300 criminals. What more could you want? Get out there and start rounding up criminals! They're certainly not going to turn themselves in.

MODULES

Police Precinct Sign

Cost: §200

Operational Cost: None

Maximum Modules: 1

Description: If you miss the search light and huge antenna, this helps you find the Police Precinct.

Patrol Car Lot

Cost: §15,000

Operational Cost: §600 per hour

Patrol Cars: 6

Patrol Rate: Every 30 minutes

Maximum Modules: 4

Description: Beef up your police force with more patrol cars. Getting more cops on the beat will help prevent more crimes and help arrest more criminals.

Jail Cells (Ground Floor)

Cost: §22,000

Operational Cost: §700 per hour

Jail Cells: 70

Maximum Modules: 4

Description: This top-of-the-line cell block has electric locking doors, security cameras, and room for more hardened criminals. Welcome to the future! Must be built on the ground.

Jail Cells (Top Floor)

Cost: §22,000

Operational Cost: §700 per hour

Jail Cells: 70

Maximum Modules: 4

Description: This top-of-the-line cell block has electric locking doors, security cameras, and room for more hardened criminals. Welcome to the future! Cannot be built directly on the ground.

Police Dispatch Tower

Cost: §10,000

Operational Cost: §525 per hour

Response Time: Instant!

Maximum Modules: 1

Description: The farther your signal goes, the better. Use the Dispatch Tower to help your patrol cars respond to crimes in progress instantly.

Detective Wing

Cost: §60,000

Operational Cost: §750 per hour

Detective Cars: 1

Prerequisites:

→ University in the region

→ University with School of Law in the region

→ Complete research project at University in the region

Maximum Modules: 4

Description: While patrol cars can arrest criminals committing crimes, you need detectives to investigate criminals at large. Detectives will park their detective car outside the homes of criminals at large and arrest them.

Crime Prevention Center

Cost: §30,000

Operational Cost: §400 per hour

Crime Prevention Vans: 1

Maximum Modules: 4

Description: Take a pro-active approach to crime fighting by sending officers to schools, parks, and more to teach kids the value of taking the fight out of crime.

Police Helipad

Cost: §20,000

Operational Cost: §750 per hour

Police Helicopter: 1

Prerequisites:

→ Municipal Airport in the city or International Airport in the region

Maximum Modules: 4

Description: We can keep our authoritative eye in the sky on these do-bad criminals.

Police Management

Apprehending and throwing criminals in jail is relatively simple. But unless you know how crime operates, and address its root causes, the fight against crime will never subside. New criminals will continually appear, potentially overburdening your police force and city's budget. But what can you do to prevent crime? In this section we'll take a look at the inner-workings of the crime system as well as offer some pro-active solutions to suppressing and reducing crime within your city and region.

UNDERSTANDING CRIME

So exactly how does crime work? The accompanying diagram illustrates the general flow of criminal activity within your city. Criminals start their day at home, like every other Sim. But instead of going to work, they'll look for a target based on their preferred criminal specialty—arsonists will look for buildings to set on fire, shoplifters will look for shops to steal from, and so on. But if their target is located in an area with a high police presence, they'll turn around and go home. In this sense, suppression through the placement of Police Stations and Police Precincts as well as frequent patrol car drive-bys can prevent crimes from even taking place.

But what if there isn't enough of a police presence to deter a crime? In that case, the crime is committed and the criminal begins traveling back home. Police have a limited amount of time to catch the criminal as the perp travels from the scene of the crime to home. If criminals reach

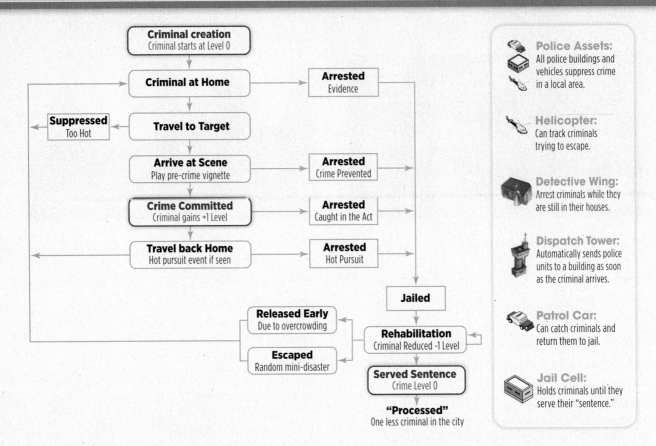

Police Assets:
All police buildings and vehicles suppress crime in a local area.

Helicopter:
Can track criminals trying to escape.

Detective Wing:
Arrest criminals while they are still in their houses.

Dispatch Tower:
Automatically sends police units to a building as soon as the criminal arrives.

Patrol Car:
Can catch criminals and return them to jail.

Jail Cell:
Holds criminals until they serve their "sentence."

their homes before the police can apprehend them, they get away with their crimes. However, if a Detective Wing is present at a Police Precinct, there's a chance the criminal can be caught at the target area, before the crime is even committed. Or if the criminal makes it home following a crime, a detective can use evidence gathered from the crime scene to identify and arrest the criminal at home. But with only one detective car per Detective Wing, a backlog of unsolved crimes can become overwhelming.

When a criminal is arrested, the criminal is put in the jail of a Police Station or Police Precinct. Criminals spend approximately 3-4 days in jail where they're rehabilitated. Once a criminal served the time, the criminal is essentially erased from the simulation—the criminal doesn't reenter society. However, if a criminal is released early, due to overflowing jails or escape, rehabilitation is interrupted and the criminal returns home, resuming the same criminal behavior. So make sure you have plenty of room in your jails, otherwise the revolving door brand of criminal justice will come back to bite you.

> **(i) NOTE**
>
> Criminal activity reduces the happiness of all law-abiding Sims and businesses. Suppressing crime, through patrols or the construction of a nearby Police Station or Police Precinct, increases the happiness of high wealth residential and commercial buildings.

CRIMINAL BEHAVIOR

Access the Crime map to identify high-crime neighborhoods. Criminals living in high and medium wealth buildings commit white collar crimes, including tax evasion and embezzlement.

Criminals aren't part of your normal worker, shopper, happiness-seeking population. They're a different element, attracted by opportunities to commit crimes. Your city is populated by criminals at regular intervals, and different types of buildings create criminals. For instance, arsonists are created at abandoned buildings. Petty theft and violent criminals are generated by residential buildings with no or low education. White collar criminals are created by medium and high wealth residential buildings with no money/jobs—they need to find some way to pay for that fancy mansion!

CRIMINALS

Level	Criminal	Description
ARSON		
1	Light Arsonist	Only targets abandoned buildings.
2	Heavy Arsonist	Targets any building.
PETTY THEFT/VIOLENT CRIME		
1	Shoplifter	Merchandise stolen from shops during business hours.
2	Robber	Shop is robbed while closed, usually at night.
3	Mugger	Targeted Sim is injured, requiring ambulance.
4	Murderer	Targeted Sim is killed.
WHITE COLLAR CRIME		
1	Tax Evader	Targeted building pays no taxes.
2	Embezzler	Buildings with operational costs are targeted. Hourly costs are doubled.

Every time a criminal gets away with a crime, the criminal is emboldened, and levels up. After successfully burning down an abandoned building, a light arsonist will become a heavy arsonist and target any building in the city. In the petty theft and violent crime category, criminals start out as shoplifters before leveling up to become robbers, muggers, and murderers. Educated white collar criminals begin as a tax evader before graduating to embezzler. As you can see, the longer criminals operate unchallenged, the more severe their crimes become. It's important to catch these criminals early on, before their crimes endanger the lives of the city's law-abiding citizens.

> ### ⓘ NOTE
>
> Casinos create large numbers of petty theft criminals, who begin as shoplifters before advancing into violent crimes. Plop a Police Station or Police Precinct close to casinos to catch these criminals before their crime spree turns deadly.

CRIME PREVENTION

The jig is up for these failed bank robbers—they're cornered with nowhere to hide. Perhaps if they had access to education they would have chosen a different lifestyle?

Police don't prevent the creation of criminals—they merely deal with them. The best way to discourage criminals from taking root in your city is through education. Sending kids to school not only gives them an education, but it also keeps them off the streets and out of trouble. For example, a low wealth residential building with kids and no educational opportunities or parks has a high chance of producing a criminal. A similar low wealth residential building with access to schools, parks, and other kid-friendly activities has a reduced chance of producing a criminal. Providing jobs is also a critical portion of your crime prevention strategy. Study the Population panel to make sure there are enough jobs to go around for each of the three wealth classes. If there's a shortage of jobs, criminals may appear. White collar criminals run amok in cities with medium and high wealth residential buildings, but few medium and high wealth jobs in the city or region to support them. You can further discourage the creation of criminals with the Crime Prevention Center module at the Police Precinct. This dispatches a crime prevention van, teaching kids the benefits of an education over a life of crime.

EXPANSION OF SERVICE

Open the Police menu to watch criminals move throughout the city, as indicated by colored icons. The presence of this Police Precinct and frequent patrols in the surrounding area help suppress crime, discouraging these criminals from breaking the law.

Just like fire and health services, establishing and maintaining a police presence isn't cheap, but it's a service vital to keeping the criminal element from running rampant. Start small and expand as demand for greater police coverage increases. Open the Police menu to review the data in the info tab. Here you can see the number of crimes committed per day as well as the number of criminals at large and in jail. If there are numerous criminals at large, it's time to expand the police force, preferably with the addition of a Detective Wing. You can also access the Crime map to see the types of crime committed throughout the city as well as high concentrations of criminals—if there's more orange (crime) than blue (police) on the map, consider building additional Police Stations or Police Precincts. Unfortunately, you only have a finite amount of resources in your fight against crime, determined by the treasury and city budget, so place your police buildings in high-crime neighborhoods to get the biggest bang for your buck. Even if you don't catch all the criminals living in each neighborhood, the police presence may discourage criminals from acting out on their sociopathic impulses.

> ⚠️ **CAUTION**
>
> In rare instances your city may encounter an undead outbreak, serving as a test for your police system. These nocturnal zombies roam the streets by night, infecting other Sims they encounter.

VOLUNTEERING POLICE RESOURCES

Do your neighboring cities have crime problems? Volunteer police vehicles to help prevent their criminals from spilling into your city.

Crime isn't contained within individual cities. Like air pollution, it can spill out into the region, as criminals travel to neighboring cities to commit their crimes. Even if your city is relatively crime-free, with few or no resident criminals, your city may still attract criminals from nearby cities with crime problems. Since crime is a regional problem, all mayors should cooperate to fight it by volunteering their police vehicles. Any time you build a Police Station or Police Precinct, you'll have patrol cars you can share with neighboring cities. Open the Region View, then access the Police menu to begin allocating your police vehicles to nearby cities. In addition to patrol cars, you can also volunteer detective cars, crime prevention vans, and police helicopters. As with fire and health vehicles, volunteering a police vehicle doesn't leave your city unprotected—each vehicle you volunteer can cover both cities simultaneously. As a bonus, your police vehicles also receive a fee for each criminal they catch in a neighboring city—these fees appear in the Budget panel's Recent Transactions window. Beyond earning fees, fighting crime in neighboring cities will help keep your city safe by removing criminals from the region.

Police: Points to Remember

→ Police Stations and patrol cars prevent crimes and arrest criminals.

→ Criminals start as uneducated kids.

→ A lack of jobs can lead to a rise in crime.

→ If criminals are successful they commit worse crimes.

→ Police take criminals to holding cells.

→ Once criminals serve their time they are rehabilitated and released.

→ If holding cells are full, criminals are released early.

→ Criminal activity is most common at night.

→ Criminals can travel from neighboring cities that have high crime.

→ The Detective Wing allows police to arrest criminals in their homes.

→ Criminals are attracted to casinos and commercial areas.

→ Police helicopters can track and arrest criminals in their homes.

→ The Police Station and Police Precinct increase land values.

→ Cities can extend their police coverage to their neighbors.

→ Any police vehicle can be offered to any connected city.

→ The city receiving police coverage gets free police coverage.

→ The city providing the police coverage receives income for criminals they catch.

Heroes & Villains Set

With the inclusion of the Heroes and Villains set, the evil Dr. Vu is on the loose, creating havoc in your city. Police have their hands full against this super villain as he solicits Sims to become his henchmen and carry out his dastardly deeds. Fortunately, your city has a crime-fighting protector: Maxis Man!

DR. VU

Dr. Vu has several doctorates in vaguely sinister sounding fields, such as mental conditioning, near field communications, and biochemical manipulation. He has turned his genius to creating a global empire for technological and (secretly) criminal domination. Dr. Vu uses his considerable wealth and company (VuCom) to subjugate others. The legitimate headquarters of his empire is Vu Tower, where he watches over his empire and creates his Cult of Vu. Used throughout the company's ads are the simple statement "Vu you."

Dr. Vu lives at Vu Tower. He leaves Vu Tower during the morning commute and travels to high tech industry buildings, giving them (and the city's treasury) small amounts of money. He only visits each business a maximum of once per day. If it's not time for the evening commute yet and he has visited all the high tech industry, he goes home early. Otherwise, he returns to Vu Tower during the evening commute.

Ordinary citizens that visit Vu Tower at night emerge as identical cult-like criminals of different levels. They all wear the same black turtlenecks that match Dr. Vu. These cult members spread around the city, committing a variety of crimes. Once converted to the

Cult of Vu, they live at Vu Tower, traveling to and from there during the normal commute. Once Maxis Man or the police arrest these henchmen, they leave the jail as normal citizens, with their criminal levels reset.

In addition to producing criminals, Vu Tower has several other functions. As a high tech icon, the building encourages the growth of high tech (tech level 3) industry in nearby industrial zones. Vu Tower also boosts the city's attraction rating, drawing tourists and local visitors, much like a landmark. By clicking on Vu Tower you can purchase modules like the VuMobile Garage or Vu Laboratory. Vu Laboratory allows you to dispatch the VuBot, a destructive robot that can only be stopped by Maxis Man in his Reticulator.

MAXIS MAN

Unbeknownst to most, Maxis Man is secretly earnest inventor Will Maxwell. Maxwell was a small businessman who sold his own inventions. Many of these worked great, but due to his own naivete and the predatory practices of companies like VuCom, his business failed. Realizing he wasn't cut out for business, Maxwell took all of the inventions he had created and set his sights to helping the people of the city himself.

You can send out Maxis Man at any time by clicking on Maxis Manor. Maxis Man serves as an extension of your health, fire, and police services—he can patrol for crime, treat injured Sims, and even put out fires. More importantly, Maxis Man can confront Dr. Vu and his evil VuBot. Each time Maxis Man patrols the city and performs heroic actions he earns Renown Points that allows him to level up and unlock new modules like the Turbo Machine Garage and Reticulator Landing Pad. The Reticulator is required to battle Dr. Vu (at VuTower) or the VuBot. If Maxis Man is successful, Dr. Vu is thrown in jail and Vu Tower creates no criminals. But don't expect Dr. Vu to linger in jail for long...

Parks

As your city increases in density, parks are even more critical, offering the masses a place to gather and gain happiness.

Everybody wants a park in their neighborhood. No, seriously. Everybody wants a park, and they won't hesitate to tell you at each opportunity. In addition to fulfilling the demands of a nature- and activity-starved public, parks are a great way to increase land value, encouraging the construction of higher wealth residential and commercial buildings. Sims like parks because it gives them another place to gain happiness, whether they have money or not. No shops? No worries, they can always get happiness from a park. Furthermore, parks give kids a place to release childhood energy and teenage angst, decreasing the chances they'll turn to a life of crime. Some parks can even attract tourists, benefiting nearby commercial buildings. So listen to the public—they know parks will make their lives better. It's high time you get the picture too.

Basic Parks (§)

These small parks offer a variety of outdoor activities for kids and adults. They're small, cheap, and have little to no impact on land value. Build these parks within walking distance of low wealth residential areas to offer Sims another way to gain happiness.

Blacktop Park

Cost: §100

Operational Cost: §10 per hour

Visitors per day: 12

Description: Just enough room for foursquare and hopscotch.

Swings Playground

Cost: §100

Operational Cost: §10 per hour

Visitors per day: 12

Description: Swing time! Higher!

Rides Playground

Cost: §100

Operational Cost: §10 per hour

Visitors per day: 12

Description: The perfect spot to drop the tykes off if you want to have them spun or bounced!

BBQ Pit

Cost: §100

Operational Cost: §10 per hour

Visitors per day: 12

Description: A handy spot where random Sims can put meat to fire surrounded by foliage. What could possibly go wrong?

BBQ Pavilion

Cost: §400

Operational Cost: §40 per hour

Visitors per day: 48

Description: Add a faint whiff of mesquite and lighter fluid to your park.

Water Park Playground

Cost: §400

Operational Cost: §40 per hour

Visitors per day: 48

Description: Kids will love splashing around in this fun, watery playground.

Small Field

Cost: §400

Operational Cost: §40 per hour

Visitors per day: 48

Description: Hope you like grass, because there's a bunch of it here!

Small Field with Parking

Cost: §400

Operational Cost: §40 per hour

Visitors per day: 48

Description: Not every open field of grass has convenient attached parking! Raises medium wealth land value.

Medium Field with Parking

Cost: §1,600

Operational Cost: §160 per hour

Visitors per day: 192

Description: Not quite enough space for a game of two-hand touch and too many trees to fly a kite. Just enjoy the nature! Raises medium wealth land value.

Large Field with Parking

Cost: §1,600

Operational Cost: §160 per hour

Visitors per day: 192

Description: Perfect for rounds of paintball or just massive games of hide and seek. Raises medium wealth land value.

Sports Parks (§§)

Feel like a quick pick-up game? Or maybe you just want to grind rails and work on your aerials. These sports parks encourage Sims of all ages to get out of the house and channel their inner athlete. Build these parks in neighborhoods where you want to encourage the growth of medium wealth buildings.

Public Tennis Court

Cost: §400

Operational Cost: §40 per hour

Visitors per day: 24

Description: Tennis, anyone? Sims will love playing tennis matches on your new court! Raises medium wealth land value.

Basketball Court

Cost: §400

Operational Cost: §40 per hour

Visitors per day: 24

Description: You've got outside tickets to watch ballers take the rock to the hole! Raises medium wealth land value.

Volleyball Court

Cost: §400

Operational Cost: §40 per hour

Visitors per day: 24

Description: Catch every service and spike with a volleyball court in your city! Raises medium wealth land value.

Medium Skate Park

Cost: §800

Operational Cost: §80 per hour

Visitors per day: 48

Description: Ample ramps and plentiful pipes fill this skate park to the brim! Raises medium wealth land value.

Large Skate Park

Cost: §1,600

Operational Cost: §160 per hour

Visitors per day: 96

Description: Put those empty swimming pools to rad use! Raises medium wealth land value.

Soccer Field

Cost: §10,000

Operational Cost: §600 per hour

Visitors per day: 180

Description: Sims will hit the field to play soccer. Raises medium wealth land value.

Baseball Field

Cost: §10,000

Operational Cost: §500 per hour

Visitors per day: 150

Description: Play ball! Kids who join a junior baseball team will be less likely to start shoplifting. Raises medium wealth land value.

Nature Parks (§§)

Who doesn't love the sound of birds chirping while taking a leisurely walk along a flower-lined path? These nature parks offer Sims a chance to escape the hustle and bustle of city life and relax in a quiet, serene environment. Plop these parks in neighborhoods where you want to encourage the construction of medium wealth buildings.

Pond

Cost: §200

Operational Cost: §20 per hour

Visitors per day: 12

Description: Ducks, mini-boat regattas, or just poking at lily pads; the options are nearly endless. Raises medium wealth land value.

Wavy Path Park

Cost: §400

Operational Cost: §40 per hour

Visitors per day: 24

Description: Craft your very own custom, easy-to-escape maze! Raises medium wealth land value.

Straight Path Park

Cost: §400

Operational Cost: §40 per hour

Visitors per day: 24

Description: Help your Sims walk the straight and narrow with this handy park. Raises medium wealth land value.

Colorful Path Park

Cost: §400

Operational Cost: §40 per hour

Visitors per day: 24

Description: The flowers help you not wander around in circles. Raises medium wealth land value.

Tall Tree Row

Cost: §100

Operational Cost: §10 per hour

Visitors per day: 24

Description: Add some green between your heavy-polluting buildings to at least make it seem like you're making an effort to be green.

Short Tree Row

Cost: §100

Operational Cost: §10 per hour

Visitors per day: 24

Description: Add some green between your heavy-polluting buildings to at least make it seem like you're making an effort to be green.

> ✅ **TIP**
>
> The Tall and Short Tree Row parks don't increase land value, but they can serve as an effective buffer, ideal for absorbing pollution from nearby industrial buildings.

Medium Path Park

Cost: §800

Operational Cost: §80 per hour

Visitors per day: 48

Description: This spacious park has ample paths for ambling and a lovely bed of colorful flowers. Raises medium wealth land value.

Tree-Lined Walkway

Cost: §800

Operational Cost: §80 per hour

Visitors per day: 48

Description: Beautiful trees and colorful flowers border this peaceful walkway. Raises medium wealth land value.

Wavy Tree-Lined Walkway

Cost: §800

Operational Cost: §80 per hour

Visitors per day: 48

Description: Parks Department officials maintain that the landscaping crew was not drunk when laying this walkway. Raises medium wealth land value.

Large Park Path

Cost: §3,200

Operational Cost: §320 per hour

Visitors per day: 192

Prerequisites:

→ City Hall

→ Department of Tourism in the region

Description: This well-manicured park has plenty of space for even the largest cities. Raises medium wealth land value.

City Park

Cost: §3,200

Operational Cost: §320 per hour

Visitors per day: 192

Prerequisites:

→ City Hall

→ Department of Tourism in the region

Description: Even big cities need a sunny patch of greenery. Raises medium wealth land value.

> ✓ **TIP**
>
> The City Park lures tourists from the region and beyond—don't be surprised if more tourists occupy this park than residents. Make sure adjacent roads and mass transit can accommodate the visitors. Tourists won't spend any money here, but they're likely to visit nearby shops, casinos, and hotels after leaving the park.

Community Park

Cost: §3,200

Operational Cost: §320 per hour

Visitors per day: 192

Prerequisites:

→ City Hall

→ Department of Tourism in the region

Description: Gathering place for local mime troupes by day and wannabe vampire gangs by night. Raises medium wealth land value.

Plant Forest

Cost: §50

Operational Cost: None

Description: Plant a small forest amongst your skyscrapers to give the gnomes somewhere to hide!

Clear Forest

Cost: §50

Operational Cost: None

Description: Clear cut forests to make way for your urban sprawl.

Plazas (§§§)

Even wealthy residents and office workers need a place to unwind after a long day of shoveling Simoleons into their bank accounts. These swanky plazas offer the perfect balance of trees, flowers, shrubs, and public art, helping even the most stressed Sims forget their troubles. Place plazas in areas where you want to encourage the construction of high wealth buildings.

Simple Walkway

Cost: §1,200

Operational Cost: §120 per hour

Visitors per day: 48

Description: This wide walkway has a scattering of trees and bushes for a touch of green in the middle of your city. Raises high wealth land value.

Double Walkway

Cost: §1,200

Operational Cost: §120 per hour

Visitors per day: 48

Description: This walkway is a bit wider than most, with shady tree coverage. Raises high wealth land value.

 TIP

If you want wealthy Sims, you're going to need parks.

Flower Plaza

Cost: §400

Operational Cost: §40 per hour

Visitors per day: 24

Description: For when you love flowers so much you need a park filled to the brim with them. Raises high wealth land value.

Small Sculpture Garden

Cost: §400

Operational Cost: §40 per hour

Visitors per day: 24

Description: The plaque at the base reads "Pointless Oval–Henri Less." Raises high wealth land value.

 TIP

Your city's homeless will congregate in parks, taking up valuable space.

Medium Sculpture Garden

Cost: §1,200

Operational Cost: §120 per hour

Visitors per day: 48

Description: The geometric sculpture at the center of this plaza is titled "Taxation Representation". What does it mean? What does it mean? Raises high wealth land value.

Large Sculpture Garden

Cost: §2,400

Operational Cost: §240 per hour

Visitors per day: 96

Description: Gaze upon "Man", a sculptural treatise on man's eternal struggle with nature...and himself. Raises high wealth land value.

Large Urban Sculpture Garden

Cost: §2,400

Operational Cost: §240 per hour

Visitors per day: 96

Description: This striking iron Gordian knot sculpture is brought to you by Simfinity. "Simfinity: engineering everything". Raises high wealth land value.

Urban Greenspace

Cost: §2,400

Operational Cost: §240 per hour

Visitors per day: 96

Description: Add a nice spot for overwhelmed office drones to soak up the sun on their lunch hour. Raises high wealth land value.

Tiered Urban Greenspace

Cost: §2,400

Operational Cost: §240 per hour

Visitors per day: 96

Description: It's almost like there's nature in the middle of your city! Raises high wealth land value.

Formal Parks (§§§)

A touch of water, in the form of fountains and reflecting pools, can make all the difference when searching for a soothing, stress-free environment. Or take in a live performance at the Amphitheater to escape the worries of the day. Place these parks in areas to encourage the creation of high wealth buildings.

Fountain Plaza

Cost: §400

Operational Cost: §40 per hour

Visitors per day: 24

Description: Flagstones. Fountain. Flowers. What else could you ask for? Raises high wealth land value.

Fenced Fountain Plaza

Cost: §400

Operational Cost: §40 per hour

Visitors per day: 24

Description: A gothic fence frames this small plaza filled to the brim with fountains. Raises high wealth land value.

Small Fountain Park

Cost: §1,200

Operational Cost: §120 per hour

Visitors per day: 48

Description: Beautiful shiny tiles and colorful flowers frame a simple fountain. Raises high wealth land value.

Reflecting Pool Park

Cost: §2,400

Operational Cost: §240 per hour

Visitors per day: 96

Description: Perfect for modern Narcissuses (Narcissi?). Raises high wealth land value.

Large Fountain Park

Cost: §2,400

Operational Cost: §240 per hour

Visitors per day: 96

Description: A massive fountain sits at the center of a dramatic plaza. Raises high wealth land value.

Amphitheater

Cost: §4,800

Operational Cost: §480 per hour

Visitors per day: 192

Prerequisites:

➜ City Hall

➜ Department of Tourism in the region

Description: High-falutin' smarty types gather here to watch plays and such. Raises high wealth land value.

Park Management

Plopping parks is easy enough, but it can also be costly for a city under tight budget constraints. Still, parks serve an important role within the community by raising land values and giving Sims a way to boost their happiness—and the happier Sims are, the greater your approval rating! But you do need to take care in which parks you plop and where you place them. It's also important to take into account the number of homeless Sims roaming about your city and their impact on your park system.

ALTERING LAND VALUE

The green radius around a park represents its range of influence, illustrating which areas will see an increase in land value.

Need to attract more medium or high wealth Sims to your city? The easiest way to encourage medium and high wealth Sims to move into your city is through the placement of parks. Most parks raise the surrounding land value, instantly encouraging higher wealth construction in adjoining residential and commercial zones. Sports and Nature parks are the best way to spur the growth of medium wealth buildings while Plazas and Formal Parks encourage high wealth buildings—most Basic Parks have no impact on land value. Before you plop a park, take note of the green radius around it, representing the range of its influence on land value. Usually the larger, expensive parks have a wider radius effect on surrounding land value than the smaller, cheap parks. So if the selected park doesn't have the intended impact, choose another one from the Parks menu to see its influence radius. Make a habit of building parks frequently, ensuring each residence in the city has at least one park within walking distance. Even if an area has natural high land value, the addition of a park gives Sims in the neighborhood another option for gaining happiness, particularly if there are no shops nearby.

⚠ CAUTION

Be careful when placing parks around low wealth neighborhoods. Anything other than Basic Parks will raise land value, causing low wealth buildings to be replaced by medium or high wealth buildings. Suddenly, those low wealth residents may have nowhere to go, and be forced to leave the city. When this happens, they also leave behind unfilled low wealth jobs, potentially leading to the failure of commercial and industrial buildings where they worked.

ADDITIONAL PARK BENEFITS

Zoom in on parks to watch your Sims enjoying a variety of outdoor activities. It looks like these Sims have organized a friendly match on a Soccer Field.

Parks are much more than a way to boost the land value of your city. They also give Sims a place to go to gain happiness. Even Sims without money can visit parks and gain happiness—this is a good way to keep unemployed Sims happy. Sims without access to shops catering to their wealth level can also visit parks as an alternative to shopping. When school isn't in session, parks also provide a place for kids to spend their time productively, reducing the chances of creating a criminal. Parks can also scrub away ground and air pollution. Plop parks over former Sewage Outflow Pipes or Garbage Dump Sites to slowly reduce ground pollution caused by these dirty utilities. Or build a wall of parks around industrial areas to help absorb some of the air pollution emitted by factories, power plants, and other polluting buildings. But like all city buildings, parks incur an hourly operational cost—keep tabs on the total expense of your park system within the Budget panel. Compared to fire, health, and police services, parks are dirt cheap. But your Sims will demand a lot of them, and those expenses can add up over time.

(City Specialization) (Mass Transit) (Tourism) (Great Works) (Disasters) (SimCity World) (Behind the Scenes) (Quick Reference)

✓ TIP

Some parks, like the City Park, Community Park, and Amphitheater, increase your city's attraction rating, drawing tourists. While this is a boon for local businesses, make sure your roads and mass transit system can handle the extra load. Otherwise, your streets (and the regional highway) may become clogged with taxi cabs as tourists crowd into your city.

HOMELESS SIMS

Each park has a finite capacity. If you have a large homeless population, they may occupy all the slots, preventing other visitors from enjoying the park.

When low wealth Sims run out of money, they're evicted from their residences. These homeless Sims then live in abandoned buildings, potentially even squatting in the same house they once lived in. With no money or job, homeless Sims spend most of the day foraging for food from uncollected garbage cans and loitering in parks. Despite their predicament, homeless Sims still gain happiness from being in a park. However, they also occupy a place in the park that other Sims can't use. Each park has a finite amount of space, as indicated by the number of visitors they can accommodate per day. Each homeless Sim occupies one of these slots. If the homeless situation becomes dire, you can have entire parks overrun by the homeless, preventing tax-paying residents from visiting parks to gain happiness. To clamp down on homeless Sims, make sure all garbage cans are collected and bulldoze abandoned buildings. With nowhere to sleep and nothing to eat, homeless Sims will eventually leave your city.

ⓘ NOTE

With the exception of taking up space in parks, homeless Sims are relatively harmless. However, their presence does reduce the happiness of high wealth commercial buildings and draws complaints from medium wealth commercial buildings. If you want to create a haven for the homeless, leave some garbage cans uncollected, don't bulldoze abandoned buildings, and build plenty of parks. Of course, the excess garbage can spread germs and increase the risk of fires. And abandoned buildings lower land value and encourage arson. But you'll be helping the homeless. Isn't that worth the risk?

Parks: Points to Remember

→ Parks increase land value around them.

→ Higher land value will attract higher wealth residential and commercial buildings.

→ Parks make Sims happy, even if they have no money.

→ Homeless fill up parks, preventing others from using them.

→ Both residents and tourists can visit parks.

→ Parks increase the attraction rating of a city.

CITY SERVICES ACHIEVEMENTS

Icon	Name	Criteria
	Bad Move, Creeps	Have your police capture their first criminal.
	A Burning Region of Fire	Have 50 fires extinguished in your region in a day.
	EMT ASAP	Pick up and treat 50 injured Sims in one day.
	Extraditions	Have your police capture 50 criminals in neighbors' cities.
	Godfather	Have 50 crimes in one month in a region of 5,000+ residents.
	High Tech Fire Fightin'	Add the HazMat Garage, the Fire Helipad, and the Fire Marshal Office to a Large Fire Station in your city.
	Laboratory Outbreak (Secret)	Add a Diagnostic Lab to a Hospital and have 15 Sims die in a day to gain access to the Zombie Attack disaster.
	Medical Miracle	Plop a Hospital and treat 200 sick Sims in a day.
	Only You Can Prevent City Fires	Put out more than 10 fires in a day.
	Redemption of the Sims	Rehabilitate 50 Criminals in a day.
	Revolving Doors	Have 25 criminals released from jail cells in one day due to overcrowding.
	You're on Fire!	Extinguish 1 Hazmat fire in your city in a day!

CHAT WITH THE DEVELOPERS

The City Services of *SimCity*

JOHN GIORDANO, GAMEPLAY SCRIPTER

Greetings fellow *SimCity* lovers! My name is John Giordano. I am a Gameplay Scripter. My role in the project has been focused on scripting mainly for the Fire, Power, and Waste Disposal systems. What I do is write code in the GlassBox Engine scripting language that determines how these systems will interact with the simulation. The work that I do involves a lot of logic. It's like a giant, crazy game of chess, only we have hundreds of thousands of game pieces and one hundred times more rules! In any case, I've been knee-deep in building this game with my scripting brethren here at Maxis. Needless to say, we are proud of what is shaping up to be a fantastic simulation game!

I am very proud to be working on this game because I am a huge *SimCity* fan in my own right. (I have all the Maxis manuals from *SimCity* classic onwards scattered on my desk.) I am glad to have worked on many of the building expansion options that you will have for city services. To give you an example, you can open any city service building in the building editor, and start modifying it in a number of interesting ways. For instance, I worked on a fire bell that you can add to the Fire Station that will halve the amount of time it takes for a fire truck to respond to fire. This is important, because you will find that in order to build a thriving city, you will have to expand services in ways like this. If you've got buildings that are at a high risk for fire, like industrial factories, you may decide to add a Fire Marshal Office to the Large Fire Station. When you do this, you'll see someone going from door to door, inspecting hazardous buildings, and reducing the risk of fire significantly!

Every service building you build will be a little bit different, with different functionalities. You might make a helicopter-only service town. You may invest in community outreach and prevent problems before they start.

The best part about our city services this time around is that everything is a real simulation. In past games, these systems would be statistical models that would add to a radius in which all nearby buildings would get an area of effect. In this *SimCity*, the simulation is that a house really catches on fire and the fire trucks really respond to it. There is no invisible simulation here; it's all raw and right in front of you.

Each city service building has a basic and more advanced type of building that you can put down. For instance, the police system has the classic Police Station that you start out with that can be expanded with more police cars, but if you're really steering your city towards safety, you will get offered a Police Precinct. This is a huge building with more police coverage and expansion options. My favorite so far is the Detective Wing. This guy will actually go throughout your city to start solving crimes, finding out where suspects live, and calling in backup to come take them down.

All these options can be shared with other cities in a region. For instance, if my neighboring city builds a Hospital with a Surgical Center, we can share those benefits together. In this case it would allow our injured Sims to heal much faster, making it easier to manage health in both of our cities. If I wanted, I could tell my neighboring city to add a Diagnostic Lab, which would help detect diseases and reduce sickness recovery time.

There's really much more gameplay that you will get out of these expandability options that past *SimCity* games didn't have. Every service building you build will be a little bit different, with different functionalities. You might make a helicopter-only service town. You may invest in community outreach and prevent problems before they start. There's so much more meat on the bone this time, and we can't wait to get you digging into this delicious *SimCity* experience as soon as possible!

Education

Have you been listening to the protestors gathered outside City Hall?

Sooner or later, medium and high wealth Sims will demand access to education. Providing an educational system will do a lot more for your city than simply appease a few exasperated parents. An educated population benefits the entire city, reducing crime, fire risk, pollution, garbage, and sickness. Educated Sims also recycle more and consume less power and water, essentials for promoting an environmentally friendly community. But don't pass the granola yet. Like utilities and city services, schools generate no income, meaning you'll need to find other ways to fund your educational system. But if you stay the course and gain access to a Community College or University, you can encourage the creation of clean and high tech industry, resulting in greater tax revenue and far less pollution. So look over the budget and work your fiscal magic to carve out enough funding for at least one school in your city. Do it for the children. They're the future.

Don't forget to go to **www.primagames.com** to access guide updates free of charge with your voucher code.

Education Buildings

Build a Grade School as soon as you can afford it. Your city's education level is shown in the Education menu's info tab, along with current enrollment.

The kids in your city have been idle far too long. It's time to send them to school...or at least a library. Open the Education menu and browse through the selection of buildings. Initially you can only select the Public Library and Grade School. But as school attendance increases (and a Department of Education exists in the region) you'll gradually gain access to the High School, Community College, and University. When it comes to attending a school, Sims aren't picky—they'll attend the school closest to their residence. It's not uncommon for kids to walk to a Community College or University instead of taking a bus to the nearest Grade School or High School. So don't feel like you need to provide one type of each school—that would be very expensive.

Public Library

Cost: §10,000

Operational Cost: §100 per hour

Capacity: 200 Sims

Prerequisites:

→ Town Hall

Description: There is no Sim as loyal as a book. Sims visit the Public Library when they can't afford to go shopping. As Sims visit the Public Library, your city will gradually become more educated.

Look at all these books! And any Sim can come here for free? What a deal! The Public Library is a cheap way to give your city's education level the slightest boost. It won't have the same impact as a Grade School or High School, but it at least gives Sims with no money a place to go and gain happiness, similar to a park. And unlike the Grade School or High School, the Public Library is open to all Sims, not just kids. It even increases the city's attraction rating by a small amount, potentially drawing more tourists. Plop the Public Library in a residential area and take note of nearby houses as they light up with green happy face icons. Who wouldn't want a library in their neighborhood?

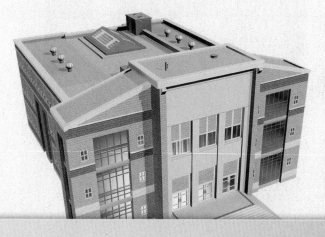

Grade School

Cost: §16,000

Operational Cost: §400 per hour

Desks: 150

Prerequisites:

→ Town Hall

Description: Educate your Sims and you'll have more skilled workers. Increases medium wealth residential land value.

Want to get kids off the streets? Then build a Grade School as soon as your city can afford it. Who knows, they might learn something too. This facility is the first step to creating a skilled, educated workforce, helping fill various jobs. But the amount of skilled workers produced by a Grade School is very small when compared to the High School or Community College. Still, educating kids has numerous benefits, including a reduction in crime by minimizing the chances of a criminal being created. Build the Grade School in a residential neighborhood—it will encourage the construction of medium wealth houses nearby. But not all kids live within walking distance, so provide buses and School Bus Stops to transport all kids in the city to the school. As enrollment increases, add additional Classrooms to increase the number of available desks, ensuring every kid in the city has the opportunity for an education.

MODULES

Grade School Sign

Cost: §200

Operational Cost: None

Maximum Modules: 1

Description: Shows students the current events of the week.

Flagpole

Cost: §100

Operational Cost: None

Maximum Modules: 1

Description: Just don't stick your tongue to it when it's snowing!

School Bus Lot

Cost: §3,000

Operational Cost: §100 per hour

Buses: 2

Bus Capacity: 20 Students

Maximum Modules: 4

Description: The School Bus Lot adds extra school buses that can be used to pick up more kids around the city.

Classrooms

Cost: §10,000

Operational Cost: §200 per hour

Desks: 200

Maximum Modules: 4

Description: Requires more teachers and staff, but lets you teach more students each day.

Top Floor Classrooms

Cost: §10,000

Operational Cost: §200 per hour

Desks: 200

Maximum Modules: 4

Description: Even more classrooms and education jobs, but these must go on the topmost floor of the school.

> ✓ **TIP**
>
>
>
> Building your population's education level takes a while, so add a Grade School as soon as you can afford it. The greater the education level, the fewer problems your city will face when it comes to crime, health, and fire.

School Bus Stop

Cost: §200

Operational Cost: §10 per hour

Bus Stop Capacity: 20 Students

Prerequisites:

→ Grade School or High School in city or region

Description: Your school buses will stop here to pick up kids and take them to school each day. Yes, even weekends.

Not everyone is lucky enough to live across the street from a school, so immediately after building a Grade School or High School, start placing these School Bus Stops along roads throughout your city. Select the School Bus Stop from the Education menu and notice how the roads closest to your schools are green, indicating areas within walking distance of the campus. Roads further from a school turn orange and red in color—these are areas where kids can't get to school without taking a bus. Add a School Bus Stop along these roads and notice how the red and orange colors turn green, indicating school bus service for the area, leading to a widespread outbreak of happiness of nearby residential buildings. Continue placing School Bus Stops along your road system until the roads adjacent to each residential building are green—there's no need to extend school bus service into industrial and commercial areas because kids don't live there. All School Bus Stops serve both Grade School and High School students. Every morning students will gather at each stop to await being picked up by a bus. After school, the students are dropped off at the same stop. If some students are left behind due to overcrowded buses, you'll need to increase your bus coverage by adding the School Bus Lot module to your Grade School or High School. If the info tab in the Education menu shows 100% enrollment, your schools and buses are getting the job done.

(i) NOTE

Building a High School in one city unlocks School Bus Stops in all connected cities. This allows students to travel throughout the region to get their education. Kids walk to these stops and buses come from the city with the High School to pick them up in the morning and drop them off in the afternoon.

High School

Cost: §60,000

Operational Cost: §1,000 per hour

Desks: 800

Prerequisites:

→ City Hall

→ Department of Education in region

→ Educate 500 students in a day

Description: High Schools help kids stay off the streets, keep them out of trouble, and educate them. Educated Sims recycle more, pollute less, and cause fewer fires.

Do the Sims in your city crave more education? Then consider building a High School...if you can afford it. The High School functions much like the Grade School, albeit with more desks and a higher price tag. In addition to educating local Sims within your city, the High School can also accept students from connected cities in the region— if your neighbors add School Bus Stops in their city, your buses will transport visiting students to your High School. Students attending the High School learn to consume less power and water. An increase in recycling also means less garbage in your city. While the High School comes with 800 desks, those spots can fill up fast, especially if busing kids in from other cities. Be ready to expand capacity with additional Classrooms. Or plop a Gymnasium to increase tourism and allow student athletes to compete in regional sports—local sports stories occasionally appear on the *SimCity* wire at the top of the HUD.

MODULES

High School Sign

Cost: §200

Operational Cost: None

Maximum Modules: 1

Description: Somehow this sign has managed to remain graffiti-free despite being surrounded by teenagers.

Flagpole

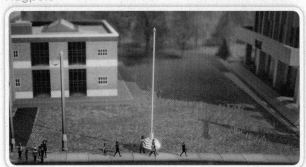

Cost: §100

Operational Cost: None

Maximum Modules: 1

Description: Show your pride—add a pole that totally holds a flag!

School Bus Lot

Cost: §10,000

Operational Cost: §100 per hour

Buses: 2

Bus Capacity: 60 Students

Maximum Modules: 4

Description: Adds a school bus to pick up students when used in conjunction with bus stops.

Classrooms

Cost: §17,000

Operational Cost: §500 per hour

Desks: 1,000

Maximum Modules: 4

Description: Educate even more sullen, sulky kids each day. You'll need more teachers and staff to handle the moody handfuls, of course.

Gymnasium

Cost: §10,000

Operational Cost: §250 per hour

Capacity: 500 Sims

Maximum Modules: 1

Description: Home to the triumph of the human spirit and misery of the nerds. Boosts tourist attraction in the city. Increases medium wealth residential land value.

 TIP

Running low on money? If you have a Grade School and a High School, consider shutting down the Grade School. Using the existing School Bus Stops, the former Grade School students can catch a ride to the High School for their education. The High School and its school buses have a higher capacity, making it more than capable of handling the extra students. But you may need to expand it with additional Classrooms and School Bus Lots to accommodate the new kids.

Community College

Cost: §42,000

Operational Cost: §500 per hour

Desks: 500

Prerequisites:

→ City Hall

→ Department of Education in region

→ Educate 800 students in a day

Description: Sure, it's not accredited, but it's a lot cheaper and smaller than a University. Adds to medium wealth residential land value. Increases tech level of nearby industrial buildings.

Do you have an interest in clean industry? Then build a Community College as soon as possible. This facility is the catalyst required to promote the appearance of tech level 2 buildings within industrial zones throughout the city and region. Why would you want clean industry? For one, these industrial buildings provide a lot of jobs, like factories. But unlike factories, they don't belch out heavy air pollution. Clean industrial buildings also produce more tax revenue than the factories associated with dirty industrial. Students attending a Community College are responsible for their own transportation. By default they will walk or drive to the campus, but they can also take mass transit. Given the regional appeal of a Community College, expect plenty of visiting students and work to accommodate them by placing bus or streetcar stops next to the campus. This will help cut down on commuter traffic around the Community College. As more and more students enroll, be ready to increase capacity with an Extension Wing module.

MODULES

College Sign

Cost: §200

Operational Cost: None

Maximum Modules: 1

Description: A large sturdy sign generously donated by the Spline Foundation.

Flagpole

Cost: §100

Operational Cost: None

Maximum Modules: 1

Description: Conforms to ANSI/NAAMM FP-1001-97 specifications for metallic flagpole safety.

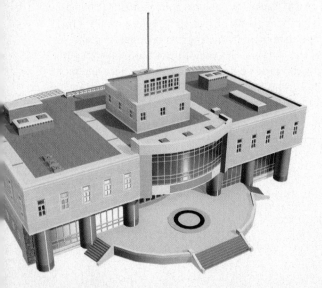

Extension Wing

Cost: §12,000

Operational Cost: §375 per hour

Desks: 750

Maximum Modules: 4

Description: Adds more classrooms and teaching jobs. Generously donated by Anon Y. Mous.

University

Cost: §88,000

Operational Cost: §1,600 per hour

Desks: 800

Prerequisites:

→ City Hall

→ Department of Education in region

→ Educate 1,200 students in a day

Description: The University provides the highest grade of education to your population. Research advanced technologies at the various schools of higher learning. Increases tech level of nearby industrial buildings.

The University is the pinnacle of the education system, producing the highest level of educated Sims. Build the University to trigger the creation of tech level 3 industrial buildings. High tech industrial buildings require a steady supply of workers with Community College and University educations, so it's important to keep enrollment high if you want to sustain these industrial businesses. Early on, construct a Dormitory to keep a large number of students on campus—this helps reduce traffic around the University while keeping desks filled without the need for creating residential units nearby. Like the City Hall, the University can also be upgraded based on the number of students it has educated. With each upgrade, a new school module can be added, increasing the number of desks as well as unlocking special perks, including modules for other buildings and research projects. There are ten different research projects that can be initiated at the University, unlocking new technologies for power plants, Great Works, the Hospital, and Police Precinct. The more students enrolled, the faster research projects are completed.

UNIVERSITY UPGRADES

Level	Students Educated	Unlock
1	1,600	School of choice.
2	2,600	School of choice.
3	3,600	School of choice.
4	4,600	School of choice.
5	5,600	School of choice.

MODULES

University Sign

Cost: §200

Operational Cost: None

Maximum Modules: 1

Description: Directs students to the University when they stumble back home late at night.

RESEARCH PROJECTS

Project	Cost	Prerequisite	Description
Concentrated Solar Array	§40,000	School of Science	Grants approval for the Concentrated Solar Array module for the Solar Power Plant.
Solar Farm Great Work	§100,000	School of Science	Grants approval for the Solar Farm Great Work for the region to build.
Vertical Turbine	§20,000	School of Engineering	Grants approval for the Vertical Turbine module for the Wind Power Plant.
Gen II Thermal Reactor	§75,000	School of Science	Grants approval for the Gen II Thermal Reactor module for the Nuclear Power Plant.
Fast Neutron Reactor	§130,000	Gen II Thermal Reactor Research	Grants approval for the Fast Neutron Reactor module for the Nuclear Power Plant.
Clean Coal Generator	§20,000	School of Engineering	Grants approval for the Clean Coal Generator module for the Coal Power Plant.
Clean Oil Generator	§27,000	School of Engineering	Grants approval for the Clean Oil Generator module for the Oil Power Plant.
Surgical Center	§80,000	School of Medicine	Grants approval for the Surgical Center module for the Hospital.
Detective Wing	§60,000	School of Law	Grants approval for the Detective Wing module for the Police Precinct.
Space Center Great Work	§120,000	School of Engineering	Grants approval for the Space Center Great Work for the region to build.

Pedestrian Path

Cost: Free

Operational Cost: None

Description: Pedestrian only pathway. Insert "pathway to education" metaphor here.

Dormitory

Cost: §40,000

Operational Cost: §500 per hour

Capacity: 500 Students

Maximum Modules: 3

Description: Adds additional students to your population without having to build additional housing.

School of Business

Cost: §40,000

Operational Cost: §1,000 per hour

Desks: 500

Maximum Modules: 1

Description: Get your students down to business! When attended by students, increases commercial profit across the region.

School of Engineering

Cost: §40,000

Operational Cost: §1,000 per hour

Desks: 500

Maximum Modules: 1

Description: This is where you put those nerds. When attended by students, increases low and medium wealth industrial profit across the region. Unlocks Hazmat Garage at Large Fire Station and access to Vertical Turbine, Clean Coal Generator, Clean Oil Generator, and Space Center research projects.

School of Law

Cost: §40,000

Operational Cost: §1,000 per hour

Desks: 500

Maximum Modules: 1

Description: Crack down on crime. When attended by students, lowers rehabilitation time of incarcerated criminals in the region. Unlocks Detective Wing research project.

School of Medicine

Cost: §40,000

Operational Cost: §1,000 per hour

Desks: 500

Maximum Modules: 1

Description: When attended by students, reduces the chance Sims in the region will get sick. Unlocks access to Surgical Center research project.

School of Science

Cost: §40,000

Operational Cost: §1,000 per hour

Desks: 500

Maximum Modules: 1

Description: Teach science, don't get blinded by it! When attended by students, increases high tech industrial profit in the region. Unlocks Diagnostic Lab at Hospital and access to Concentrated Solar Array, Solar Farm, and Gen II Thermal Reactor research projects.

Education Management

So what is your city's education level? What about tech level? In addition to showing your city's current enrollment, the info tab within the Education menu also shows your city's current education and tech level, as represented by grayed-out icons. These icons will slowly fill in as the city's education and tech levels increase. In this section we explain how these two levels operate and their correlation to education and industry. We also look at transportation considerations and the science projects offered by the University.

 TIP

Educated Sims are less likely to accidently start a fire or to get sick from germs.

Knowledge: Education Level

Access the Education data map to see education levels in your city.

Education level is a measure of how much education you currently have in the residential sections of your city. The graphical representation (in the Education menu's info tab) is an average of the individual residential buildings. The number of green graduate cap icons shown can be increased by sending more students to school. The education level only increases when students return from school to their houses, so Dormitory students and commuting students from the region do not contribute to this.

The benefits vary with the level of education in the building—the individual unit, not the average. At education level one, the house has a reduced chance of creating a blue collar criminal, helping keep your streets safe. Level two sees a reduction in power and water usage, putting less strain on these utilities. There are no additional benefits at level three, but at level four residential buildings see another reduction in power and water usage. At level five, residents install solar panels on their roof, greatly reducing the building's need for power.

Skill: Tech Level

Click on an industrial building to see its current tech level. High tech buildings won't show up until a University has been built in the region.

(i) NOTE

In addition to gaining perks from the various education levels, educated Sims are less likely to cause fires and get sick. They also recycle more, producing less garbage.

Tech level is essentially education for the industrial sections of your city. Higher tech levels provide opportunities for clean and high tech industry to be created. If a Community College and University are present in the region, you'll start to see clean (tech level 2) and high tech (tech level 3) industrial buildings when the appropriate levels of tech are reached. Higher tech buildings create more tax revenue, making them worth the effort and expense to promote higher education. The more students that are present in the Community College or University, the more tech education is produced. This type of education is only dependent on the number of students, not their origin, so local, commuting, and Dormitory students all contribute to this production.

The benefit of education on industry is very different than on residential. Instead of providing a bonus to the buildings, it allows higher tech (based on the type of higher education placed) to be created. While these higher tech industrial buildings produce more tax revenue, they also require tech education to remain in business. The education provided by the higher education schools (Community College and University) act as both catalyst for creation and as upkeep. So keep those higher education institutions filled to meet the demand of clean and high tech industrial buildings.

(i) NOTE

Looking to staff a Nuclear Power Plant with educated workers? Educated workers are present whenever the buildings have enough tech education. The only way to ensure this is by producing as much tech education as possible by keeping your higher education buildings (Community College or University) filled with students. The proximity of the power plant to the school also will have an effect, but this must be balanced with the fact that Sims don't want to live too close to a Nuclear Power Plant.

Transportation

Don't be surprised if your Community College and University draw heavy traffic. Rely on mass transit to help alleviate some of the congestion.

In a perfect city, every student could walk to the school of their choice, but it isn't feasible to construct a school in every neighborhood. When students can't reach a Grade School or High School on foot, they require a school bus to get to and from campus. Provide plenty of school buses and plop School Bus Stops throughout your city to encourage every kid in your city to get to school. Community Colleges and Universities function a little differently since neither have school buses. Instead, most students drive to school when they can't reach a campus on foot. Given the large number of desks offered by these schools, expect traffic problems around these institutions. Therefore, build the Community College and University next to an avenue to accommodate the traffic. Also, consider mass transit options such as buses and streetcars. Equipping the University with a Dormitory or two can also reduce traffic, keeping most students on campus and off the roads.

University Research Projects

Click on the University to see the progress toward completing the current research project. Not going fast enough? Bring in more students.

The University is a jewel to behold. But when you're not admiring the impressive architecture and well-kept grounds, put those eggheads to work on a research project. Click on the University to open its window, then select the Start Research Project button. This brings up an additional window

prompting you to choose from ten different projects. Each project has a different cost and prerequisite, often requiring the construction of an additional school at the University. For example, you need a School of Medicine before you can pursue the Surgical Center project. Once completed, each project unlocks a specific module or one of the Great Works, like the Solar Farm or Space Center. These completed research projects are shared throughout the region, giving every city access to the unlocked technology. But projects aren't completed instantly—it takes time to do all that research. The more students in the University, the faster the project is completed. So if a project is stalled or simply taking too long, consider adding a Dormitory and additional schools to increase the number of students on campus.

 TIP

Got a crime problem? Add a School of Law at the University and start the Detective Wing research project. This allows your Police Precinct to dispatch a detective car and catch criminals at home, before they can commit a new crime.

Education: Points to Remember

→ Kids will go to school if they can walk or ride a bus.
→ All schools benefit residents through education.
→ Educated houses consume less power and water.
→ Educated Sims are less likely to start fires.
→ Educated houses create fewer criminals.
→ Educated Sims get sick less often.
→ Colleges and Universities attract clean and high tech industry.

CITY SERVICES ACHIEVEMENTS		
Icon	**Name**	**Criteria**
	No Child Left Behind	Plop 20 School Bus Stops in one city.
	SimCity University!	Have a University with each School module.

City Specialization

Mayor, I have some bad news. The treasury is running a little low—maintaining all those city services and schools isn't cheap.

And I don't think the Sims can tolerate another tax increase. But now for some good news. We've identified a number of natural resources, just beneath the city. Consider building mines or an Oil Well to extract those resources, then export them though a Trade Depot to make a quick profit. Or take city specialization to great heights by processing resources through a Smelting Factory or Oil Refinery to produce even more valuable metal, alloy, plastic, or fuel. By exploring opportunities in the metals, petroleum, trading, and electronics businesses, you may get the city's budget back on track. And all those Sims bellyaching about no jobs? These specializations employ tons of workers of various wealth and education levels, potentially leading to a boost in tax revenue as more Sims move in and new shops open. It's too early to tell, but city specializations may be the economical antidote we've been looking for!

City Specialization Overview

Have you managed to pull some raw ore, coal, or crude oil from the ground? What are you going to do with it? Extracting resources is just the first step and will earn you no money. So before you start mining or drilling, it's important to understand how resources and resources move throughout your city and region.

In the accompanying example, a Coal Mine produces coal, which is stored in the mine's output lot. Trucks from the Coal Mine are then used to transport coal to a variety of possible locations—trucks automatically deliver coal to any input lots open to local deliveries. Coal can be sent to a Coal Power Plant to generate power for the city and region. It can also be sent to a Smelting Factory where it is combined with raw ore to create alloy, a valuable commodity in its own right, essential in electronics or constructing Great Works. The coal can also be gifted to neighboring cities or simply sold for a quick profit on the global market through a Trade Depot or Trade Port. When a Trade Depot or Trade Port is set to export, trucks, trains, or cargo ships arrive from the region to buy coal at the current market price. If no Coal Mine exists, it's still possible to supply the Smelting Factory and Coal Power Plant with coal from imports bought on the global market or gifted from a neighboring city.

Don't forget to go to www.primagames.com to access guide updates free of charge with your voucher code.

TRANSPORTING CARGO

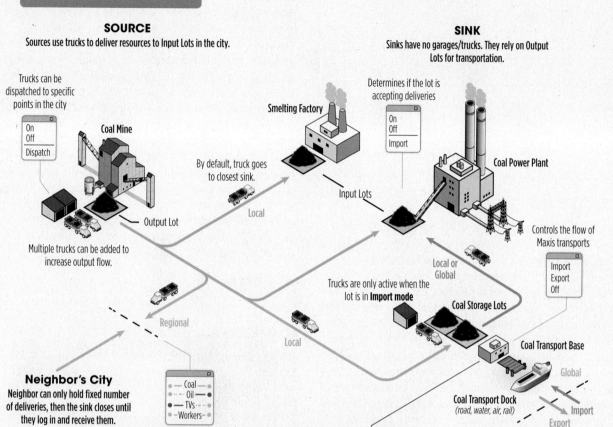

SOURCE

Sources use trucks to deliver resources to Input Lots in the city.

Trucks can be dispatched to specific points in the city

On
Off
Dispatch

Coal Mine

Output Lot

Multiple trucks can be added to increase output flow.

By default, truck goes to closest sink.

Local

Smelting Factory

Input Lots

SINK

Sinks have no garages/trucks. They rely on Output Lots for transportation.

Determines if the lot is accepting deliveries

On
Off
Import

Coal Power Plant

Controls the flow of Maxis transports

Import
Export
Off

Local or Global

Trucks are only active when the lot is in **Import mode**

Coal Storage Lots

Coal Transport Base

Local

Global

Coal Transport Dock
(road, water, air, rail)

Import
Export

Regional

Neighbor's City

Neighbor can only hold fixed number of deliveries, then the sink closes until they log in and receive them.

— Coal —
— Oil —
● TVs —
— Workers —

Both sides can control the resources that are allowed across the border.

Trade Depot / Trade Port
(Road, Rail, Water)
Can act as a source (Import mode) or a sink (Export mode), depending on player's needs. Can transfer cargo from one transportation network to another. (i.e., from trucks to boats)

Global Market
All Global Market vehicles are owned by Maxis.

Trucks are the key to moving resources throughout your city. Make sure your mines, Oil Wells, and other buildings have enough truck garages to accommodate all that cargo.

As you can see, it's a very fluid process with many options and moving pieces. But whatever your intentions, it's important to keep the supply chain moving. Any interruptions can bring the whole system to a halt, reducing profits. And

if your city is relying on those profits to cover its expenses, a financial collapse may be imminent. For best results, place the participating buildings as close to each other as possible. In this case it means placing the Coal Mine, Smelting Factory, Coal Power Plant, and Trade Depot or Trade Port within close proximity. This significantly reduces transportation time, minimizing the chances of trucks getting stuck or delayed in traffic on the opposite side of the city. With less travel time, trucks from the Coal Mine can make regular deliveries to the input lots of all participants in the supply chain.

(i) NOTE

For information on the Culture and Gambling specializations, flip ahead to the Tourism chapter to learn what it takes to attract visitors, sending them home with fond memories...and empty pockets.

Planning

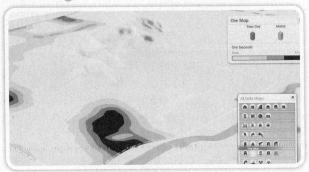

Access the data maps early on to identify resources beneath your city site. This makes it easier to plan the layout of your road system and supply chain.

The creation of an efficient city specialization supply chain should begin early on, preferably before you even connect a city to the highway. Use the data maps to locate your resources, and then determine where each building should go. While money is in short supply at these early stages, it costs nothing to plan ahead. If you intend to sell your resources on the global market, where will your Trade Depot go? Or if you have access to rail or water, plan to eventually build a Trade Port to move large amounts of cargo. Due to geography, some participants in the supply chain may need to be placed far apart. Figure out what kind of roads will be necessary to keep resources moving, preferably avoiding high-traffic areas in the process. Try to keep roads connecting supply chain participants as isolated from the rest of the city as possible. If these roads become clogged by commuters or tourists, everything may grind to a halt.

Specialization

With three sprawling Oil Wells and a nearby Oil Refinery, this is an oil town. Consider specializing in one city specialization, especially if you have multiple deposits or reservoirs of one natural resource.

Running any one of the city specializations requires a lot of your attention. Most buildings and their associated road networks occupy a large portion of your city, lowering land value and spreading air and ground pollution. When you have a city with numerous natural resources, consider

focusing on city specializations instead of taking a balanced RCI approach. Like industry, city specializations require workers to operate, so it's important to supply a work force by zoning some residential, which workers will require. Workers can also be imported from other cities, so make sure mass transit options are available to get commuters to work in a timely fashion. Importing workers from other cities allows your specialized city to focus solely on producing resources and making money—if virtually no Sims live in the city, you won't have to worry too much about commercial, industrial, or education. But you will still need to provide basic utilities and city services including power, water, sewage, waste disposal, fire, police, and health. City specialization isn't taxed, so these expenses must be offset through selling resources to the global market. But as long as your city specializations have a steady supply chain, income generated from selling resources should be more than enough for your city to pay its bills.

☑ TIP

Need help figuring out the various city specializations? Click on the Guide Me button within each city specialization menu to initiate a series of tutorial missions guiding you through the fundamentals of running each specialization.

City Specialization HQs

Divisions associated with each HQ do not have to be attached. Instead, these separate office buildings can be plopped within a radius around the HQ, even across the street.

Each city specialization comes with its own headquarters, or HQ. These towering office buildings aren't immediately available for construction—you earn them. Mine, drill, or sell the specified amount of resources to unlock the HQ associated with each specialization. HQs function much like the City Hall, utilizing a similar upgrade scheme—upgrades are often tied to production or sales. Once an upgrade is triggered, the HQ grows even taller, often dwarfing the highest skyscrapers in your city. More importantly, upgrades also give you access to new divisions, department-like buildings that can be built adjacent to the HQ. Each division grants access to new buildings, allowing you to expand your business. For example, you'll need a Refining Division at your Petroleum HQ before you can build an Oil Refinery. Once you've attained every division associated with an HQ, there's no stopping you—all buildings are unlocked and the sky's the limit. The HQs also allow you to compete with friends and other *SimCity* players in the leaderboards. Once you've plopped an HQ, the production of metals, oil, or other associated resources will be tracked on the leaderboards. Feel free to compete with your friends and see who can mine the most coal or generate the most plastic. A little friendly competition won't hurt, and you'll earn a small fortune in the process.

The Global Market

The massive storage lots available at the Trade Port make it ideal for importing, exporting, or simply storing large volumes of resources.

Don't feel like digging in the dirt to extract coal or raw ore? Have a phobia of Oil Well accidents? No worries. As long as you have the money, you can buy/import any commodity your city needs directly from the global market. Or if you need money, you can sell/export those same resources, securing a nice little profit for your city. The global market is accessed through Trade Depots and Trade Ports. These specialized facilities serve as warehouses, capable of storing all ten resources in the game: coal, raw ore, crude oil, metal, alloy, plastic, fuel, processors, TVs, and computers. These resources are stored in separate storage lots, each capable of importing or exporting. Or if you simply want to accumulate resources for use in local industry or a Great

Works project, you can simply use the Trade Depot or Trade Port as a storage facility, holding on to those goods until you're ready to use or sell them. When importing or exporting, the amount of money exchanged is based on the current market value of each commodity. Just like real-world stock markets and commodity exchanges, market values change throughout the day based on real-time supply and demand. For example, the plastic you imported an hour ago may be worth a lot more now, giving you the opportunity to export it for a profit. For more information on the global market and managing your Trade Depots and Trade Ports, advance to the Trading section within this chapter.

Gifting

Using the Gift menu in the Region View you can send Simoleons or any of the ten resources to a connected city in your region.

If you have some surplus Simoleons or resources, why not share them with your fellow mayors? They may need the extra help now. And who knows, they may even return the favor in the future. The sharing of Simoleons and resources is handled through the Gift menu in the Region View. Here you can select from any of the ten resources currently stored at any of your Trade Depots or Trade Ports and transfer them to another city in the region. Before a city can accept a gift, they must have a storage lot with enough capacity to contain the incoming goods. In some instances, a mayor may have to add a new storage lot to accept a shipment. Once the gift has been initiated, resources are exchanged between the two cities by either truck, train, or cargo ship. So don't panic if the incoming resources don't appear in your storage lots immediately—they're in transit. Gifting is important as cities begin to specialize. For example, if one city has a Coal Mine and a neighboring city has an Ore Mine, they can exchange their resources to create alloy at their respective Smelting Factories. Or if you're not in a giving mood, chat with local mayors to establish deals, exchanging a predetermined volume of resources for a set price. Gifting really enhances the sense of community encouraged by multi-city play. Sharing resources will only make your region stronger.

Depletion of Resources

There's only a one-year supply of crude oil left beneath this Oil Well. What happens when the oil runs out? Time to start planning for the future before this Oil Well runs dry.

Whether you're mining or drilling, the amount of raw ore, coal, or crude oil beneath your city should keep you in business for several years. But then what? These natural resources are finite, and if you play the same city for several years, there will come a point when these raw materials are depleted. Periodically click on your mines and Oil Wells to see exactly how many more years you can keep extracting resources from each deposit or reservoir. As supply dwindles, access your data maps to identify other deposits or reservoirs beneath your city and consider moving operations to a new location. If there's no more resources beneath your city, it's time to rethink your business strategy. By importing crude oil, raw ore, and coal from a Trade Depot or Trade Port, you can keep your Smelting Factory and Oil Refinery in business, while continually supplying any Coal or Oil Power Plants. Or perhaps you can get these raw materials from a neighboring city? In any case, plan ahead for this transitional phase to avoid a sudden disruption of supply. Shortly before you run out of resources, begin imports at a Trade Depot or Trade Port. This will lessen the likelihood of a supply interruption and your businesses and power plants will continue functioning without a hitch. Shut down and bulldoze your old mines and Oil Wells to save money and clear space for new construction. Maybe it's time to pursue high tech industry or the electronics specialization?

Mining: The Metals Specialization

The Advanced Coal Mine is unmatched when it comes to coal extraction. But you'll need plenty of workers to get this mine up and running. All those jobs can be a boon for the local economy!

Do you see those deposits of raw ore and coal beneath your city? Instead of building houses, shops, parks, and factories directly over those rich deposits, consider digging mines. Extracted ore and coal can be sold for a handsome profit on the global market, helping offset expenses incurred from running utilities and providing city services. Or if you're really serious, go all the way and process the coal and ore at a Smelting Factory to create metal and alloy, resources with an even higher value on the global market. Furthermore, metal and alloy can be supplied to Great Works projects. Or you can send alloy to Processor Factories to create processors used in electronics. The metals specialization is deep, with many income-generating possibilities. And it all begins by extracting minerals from the ground. Ready to start digging?

Coal Mine

Cost: §22,500

Operational Cost: §100 per hour

Production Rate: 24 tons/day

Prerequisites:

→ Provide working power

→ Provide working water

→ Coal under your city

→ Have seven industrial buildings

Description: It's time to get your hands dirty—dirty, filthy, and rich. Rip the earth's coal heart out for profit! Use your coal in a Coal Power Plant, or sell it to local industry or on the global market via a Trade Depot. Employ hordes of low wealth workers deep in your mine.

Do you have deep deposits of coal buried beneath your city? This could be the answer to your city's financial and power woes. Using coal supplied from a Coal Mine you can fuel a Coal Power Plant, cranking out enough power to electrify multiple connected cities in the region. Or you could send that coal to a Smelting Factory where it can be combined with raw ore to create alloy. But if you need to recoup costs now, simply send the coal to a Trade Depot or Trade Port and sell it on the global market for a quick and easy profit. To yield the most coal, plop the Coal Mine directly over a coal deposit. Additional Coal Shafts can branch off from the mine to increase the footprint and the mine's overall yield. Keep a close eye on the mine's 20 ton output lot—if it becomes full, the mine will shut down until trucks haul away some coal to make more room. If your output lot is near capacity, add more Coal Delivery Truck Garages. Additional trucks help ensure the output lot has plenty of room, delivering coal to input lots at Coal Power Plants, Smelting Factories, Trade Depots, or Trade Ports— the more trucks you have, the more frequent the deliveries.

MODULES

Coal Mine Sign

Cost: §200

Operational Cost: None

Maximum Modules: 1

Description: Coal is like the meat at the middle of the delicious sandwich of your city.

 TIP

If you extract all the coal from your city, it may be time to start another city or re-specialize.

Coal Delivery Truck Garage

Cost: §10,000

Operational Cost: §50 per hour

Truck Capacity: 2 tons

Maximum Modules: 4

Description: It's a dirty job haulin' coal, but somebody's gotta do it. Delivers coal from the mine to Coal Power Plants, Trade Depots, Trade Ports, or industry in your city.

Coal Shaft

Cost: §14,000

Operational Cost: §25 per hour

Production Rate: 24 tons/day

Maximum Modules: 4

Description: Extend your extraction operation with an additional Coal Shaft. Increase your Coal Mine's extraction rate and add more available jobs.

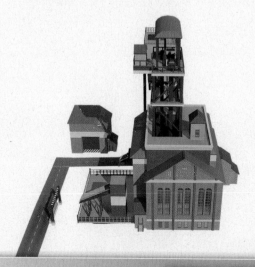

Ore Mine

Cost: §22,500

Operational Cost: §125 per hour

Production Rate: 24 tons/day

Prerequisites:

→ Provide working power

→ Provide working water

→ Ore deposits under your city

→ Have seven industrial buildings

Description: Are you easily fascinated by shiny things? Well, then look at this! Send workers beneath your city to extract raw ore. Sell raw ore to local industry or on the Global Market via a Trade Depot.

The Ore Mine functions identically to the Coal Mine, but is used to extract raw ore from beneath your city. Plop the mine directly over a raw ore deposit and add more Ore Shafts to expand the facility and increase its overall yield. As you expand the mine, make sure the trucks can keep up with all the ore being dumped in the mine's output lot. If the lot is near capacity, add more Ore Delivery Truck Garages to prevent the mine from being shut down due to an overflowing output lot. These trucks deliver raw ore to Trade Depots, Trade Ports, and Smelting Factories accepting local deliveries. Unlike coal, raw ore isn't very useful on its own. It can't fuel a power plant, but it can still be sold on the global market for some quick money. Ore shows its most potential when processed at a Smelting

Factory where it can be turned into metal or combined with coal to create alloy. Both metal and alloy are critical elements required in electronics and Great Works projects, or you can sell them on the global market for much more than raw ore. If you get into the ore specialization, set your sights on plopping a Smelting Factory as soon as possible.

MODULES

Ore Mine Sign

Cost: §200

Operational Cost: None

Maximum Modules: 1

Description: This sign warns against rock slides, sinkholes, and "surprise detonations".

Ore Delivery Truck Garage

Cost: §10,000

Operational Cost: §50 per hour

Truck Capacity: 2 tons

Maximum Modules: 4

Description: When you've got more ore than you know what to do with, get another Ore Delivery Truck and get that ore out to Trade Depots, Trade Ports, and industry faster to make money faster!

> ✓ **TIP**
>
> Send trucks with resources directly to neighboring cities to help with their industry!

Ore Shaft

Cost: §16,000

Operational Cost: §40 per hour

Production Rate: 24 tons/day

Maximum Modules: 4

Description: More ore! Increase your Ore Mine's extraction rate by adding another shaft. Sure, it'll add more maintenance cost, but you'll get more jobs and more ore! More!

Smelting Factory

Cost: §54,500

Operational Cost: §300 per hour

Production Rate: 24 tons/day

Prerequisites:

→ Mining HQ with Smelting Division

Description: Sure, raw ore is nice, but do you know what's really nice? Metal and alloy. Smelt raw ore into metal or add coal into the mix to smelt alloy. Sell metal or trade alloy to local industry or on the global market via a Trade Depot.

This is where the magic happens, producing metal from raw ore and smelting alloy from a mixture of ore and coal. Before you can build a Smelting Factory, you must first build a Metals HQ and upgrade it with a Smelting Division. Once granted access to the Smelting Factory, build it as close as possible to your existing mines to cut down on delivery times—you don't want those delivery trucks to get bogged down in traffic. In its stock state, the facility comes with one Metal Furnace, allowing

you to produce metal from raw ore. If you want to create alloy, add an Alloy Furnace and make sure you're accepting both raw ore and coal deliveries—you need both to create alloy! The Smelting Factory has both input and output lots, requiring periodic monitoring. The material storage lots are for incoming raw ore and coal, supplied by delivery trucks from mines or Trade Depots—if these lots run dry, consider adding more truck garages at your mines or Trade Depots. The product storage lots hold recently manufactured metal and alloy, waiting to be shipped out to Trade Depots, Trade Ports, Great Works sites, and Processor Factories. If the product storage lots become full, the factory will shut down, since it has nowhere to store its manufactured products. Add extra Smelting Delivery Truck Garages to ensure there's plenty of space in the product storage lots. If you've made enough money, consider stockpiling large amounts of metal and alloy at a Trade Port for use in Great Works projects—alloy is required in all Great Works and metal is necessary to construct the International Airport and Arcology.

MODULES

Smelting Factory Sign

Cost: §200

Operational Cost: None

Maximum Modules: 1

Description: Enhancing your Smelting Factory with a sign lends it that respectable, responsible look.

Smelting Delivery Truck Garage

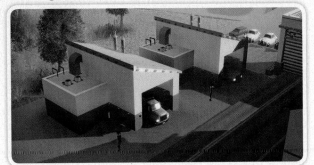

Cost: §10,000

Operational Cost: §50 per hour

Truck Capacity: 2 tons

Maximum Modules: 4

Description: Now that you've smelt it, deal it! This garage adds one Smelting Delivery Truck so you can get your metal and alloy to Trade Depots, Trade Ports, Processor Factories, and industry.

Metal Furnace

Cost: §21,000

Operational Cost: §50 per hour

Production Rate: 24 tons/day

Maximum Modules: 4

Description: Play with fire without getting burned! Melt raw ore and remove the impurities to create metal. Metal can be sold to local industry or the global market via a Trade Depot. Many Great Works require large amounts of metal.

Alloy Furnace

Cost: §36,000

Operational Cost: §150 per hour

Production Rate: 24 tons/day

Maximum Modules: 3

Description: When coal and ore really love each other, a baby alloy is born. Alloy can be sold to local industry or the global market via a Trade Depot. Alloy is used to create processors in Processor Factories. Many Great Works require large amounts of alloy.

> ### (i) NOTE
>
> You can still produce metal and alloy, even after you've depleted the coal and raw ore in your city. By importing raw ore and coal from the global market (through a Trade Depot or Trade Port) you can purchase the materials required to produce metal and alloy. While the price of raw ore and coal fluctuates, what you pay for these materials is usually much less than you can make by selling metal and alloy back to the global market, resulting in a nice profit.

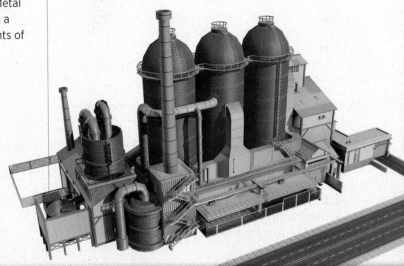

Metals HQ

Cost: §37,500

Operational Cost: §450 per hour

Prerequisites:

→ Mine 80 tons of coal OR raw ore in a day

Description: The Metals HQ is the bedrock of any coal or raw ore extraction city. Sell coal or raw ore to upgrade your HQ and gain advancements like the Smelting Factory, Advanced Coal Mine, or the Trade Port.

METALS HQ UPGRADES

Level	Name	Criteria	Unlock
1	Metals HQ	Mine 96 tons of coal or raw ore in a day.	One division of your choice.
2	Metals, Co.	Earn §350,000 in metals daily profit.	One division of your choice.
3	Metals, Inc.	Earn §350,000 in metals daily profit.	One division of your choice.
4	Metals Global	Earn §2,000,000 in metals daily profit.	One division of your choice.

Once you've extracted the requisite amount of coal or ore from beneath your city, you can plop a Metals HQ—be careful where you place it because you'll want to leave room for expansion. This fancy office building can be upgraded into a towering skyscraper by simply selling more and more raw ore, coal, metal, and alloy. With each upgrade the building grows taller and also allows you to build one of three divisions—like departments at City Hall, the choice is yours! If you want to produce metal and alloy soon, choose the Smelting Division first to unlock local access to the Smelting Factory. For your second upgrade, consider choosing the Commerce Division so you can build Trade Ports with Coal and Raw Ore Storage Lots throughout the region—yes, you only need one Commerce Division for the whole region! Select the Engineering Division last, as it only provides local access to the Advanced Coal Mine—unless you really, really want the Advanced Coal Mine.

MODULES

Corporate Sign

Cost: §200

Operational Cost: None

Maximum Modules: 1

Description: What's more metal than a metal sign on a metal building that houses a metals company?

Commerce Division

Cost: §20,000

Operational Cost: §400 per hour

Regional Access Granted: Trade Port, Coal and Raw Ore Storage Lots at the Trade Port

Maximum Modules: 1

Description: Tired of tripping over coal or raw ore? You need to get some of that out of town! Make major Simoleons on the global market!

Engineering Division

Cost: §20,000

Operational Cost: §400 per hour

Local Access Granted: Advanced Coal Mine

Maximum Modules: 1

Description: Leave behind the paltry output of the measly Coal Mine. The engineers at the Engineering Division have plans for a whole new Advanced Coal Mine!

Smelting Division

Cost: §20,000

Operational Cost: §400 per hour

Local Access Granted: Smelting Factory

Maximum Modules: 1

Description: Add smelting to your metals operation to make more profit and diversity! Use educated workers to research the Alloy Furnace project.

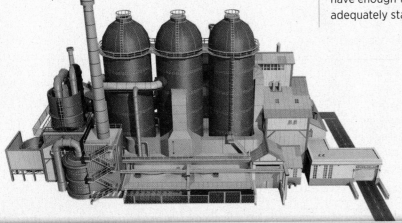

Advanced Coal Mine

Cost: §60,000

Operational Cost: §400 per hour

Production Rate: 96 tons/day

Prerequisites:

→ Mining HQ with Engineering Division

Description: Take advantage of recent metallurgical advancements and the repeal of certain environmental laws! Extract coal faster, from a larger area, with this powerful coal mine. This mine employs a massive number of workers and has a huge lot ready to be filled with coal.

Not enough coal? The Advanced Coal Mine has got you covered! This facility more than triples the daily coal output of the standard Coal Mine, making it the quickest and most efficient way to extract coal from beneath your city. But before you can build it, you must first plop a Metals HQ with a Engineering Division. Given the rapid extraction rate, the facility comes equipped with a much larger output lot, capable of holding 80 tons of coal. Still, it will be a chore for trucks to keep up with the rapid production, so be ready to plop additional Heavy Coal Delivery Truck Garages to prevent the output lot from reaching capacity—if the output lot is full, the mine is temporarily shut down. Adding more trucks is crucial, particularly if you increase production with Advanced Coal Shafts. These modules allow you to extend the mine's footprint, leading to increased production. But if you want the mine to operate at peak efficiency, you'll need to supply a small army of low wealth workers. Zone extra residential or make sure you have enough workers coming in from neighboring cities to adequately staff this behemoth.

MODULES

Coal Mine Sign

Cost: §200

Operational Cost: None

Maximum Modules: 1

Description: This sign is larger, but there just seems to be an even thicker coating of hardened coal.

Heavy Coal Delivery Truck Garages

Cost: §20,000

Operational Cost: §50 per hour

Truck Capacity: 2 tons

Maximum Modules: 10

Description: It takes a big truck to haul this much coal. This is where you keep that big truck.

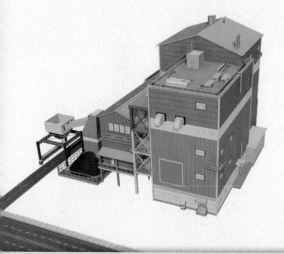

Advanced Coal Shaft

Cost: §50,000

Operational Cost: §250 per hour

Production Rate: 48 tons/day

Maximum Modules: 8

Description: Extract massive amounts of coal faster by adding another shaft to your Advanced Coal Mine.

Managing the Metals Specialization

Now that you're familiar with the various buildings associated with the metals specialization, it's time to put that knowledge to work. In this section we take a quick look at everything you need to do to get your business up and running. But don't overlook the risks associated with this specialization, otherwise your mines and workers may fall victim to rampant injuries and hazmat fires. Take all steps necessary to ensure this specialization is as safe as possible.

MEDDLING IN METAL

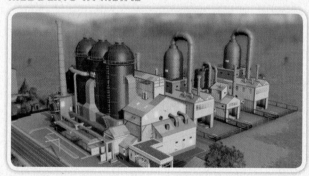

If you're serious about the metal specialization, build a Smelting Factory as soon as possible to begin producing metal and alloy.

So you want to start mining? Are you certain your city has deposits of raw ore and coal? One out of the two is fine, but if you really want to make a run at the metals specialization, it's best to choose a city site with both coal and raw ore. Once you've established your basic infrastructure, induing a Coal Power Plant, zone a few industrial areas—you need a minimum of seven industrial buildings to unlock the Coal and Ore Mines. Plop your mines directly over deposits, positioning them for optimal yield and expansion opportunities utilizing shaft modules. As your mines come to life and start producing coal and ore, sell the first few loads on the global market (through a Trade Depot) to earn some extra money. As soon as the Metals HQ is available, plop it to begin progress toward your first upgrade. Choose the Smelting Division first so you can unlock the Smelting Factory. Instead of selling your raw ore and coal on the global market, ship it to the Smelting Factory to create metal and alloy—then ship these new resources to a Trade Depot for export. With one Coal Mine, one Ore Mine, and one Smelting Factory active in your city, you're poised for greatness. But don't rest on your laurels. Look for opportunities to expand, both at your existing facilities and throughout the city. Are there more deposits to exploit? Then build more mines. If your one Smelting Factory can't keep up with the input, build a second one. Of course, as your metals business expands, so will pollution. So don't operate with blinders on—excessive mining and smelting takes its toll on the environment and may even lead to a low approval rating as Sims complain about the poor living conditions. But you'll be making lots of money!

NOTE

If you want to export coal, raw ore, metal, or alloy by cargo ship or train, you'll need a Trade Port, requiring access to the Trade HQ and its Metals Division.

MINE SAFETY

This Large Fire Station is a good start, but it'll need a Hazmat Garage to extinguish dangerous hazmat fires at your mines.

While the metals specialization is a profitable one, it's also very dangerous, particularly for the poor Sims hauling coal and raw ore out of the mines. To deal with the large number of injuries, it's strongly advised to invest in a Hospital equipped with a Surgical Center. The Surgical Center reduces the recovery time for injuries, helping injured miners get back to work quickly. If your ambulances are having trouble reaching your mines in time, consider adding an Emergency Center to increase the lifespan of injured workers as they wait for an ambulance. Mines also have a risk for hazmat fires. These toxic infernos can only be extinguished by a hazmat truck dispatched from a Large Fire Station equipped with a Hazmat Garage. Without access to a hazmat truck, your entire mining operation may go up in flames—miners lucky enough to escape the flames will probably fall sick due to the toxic fumes. Running a Hospital and Large Fire Station isn't cheap, but with the money you're making, you can easily afford it. Anyway, promoting a (relatively) safe and healthy work environment will result in greater yields, making you even more money.

Mining: Points to Remember

→ Build mines to extract coal and ore.

→ Extract coal or ore to use, gift, or sell on the global market.

→ Coal and ore can also be used to make metal and alloy, ideal for constructing Great Works.

→ Mines will stop producing if their output storage lot is full.

→ Use a Trade Depot or Trade Port to sell resources on the global market.

→ Local industry can ship resources to metals consumers.

→ Mining adds the risk of hazmat fires to your city.

→ Metals HQ unlocks more buildings through its divisions.

→ Metals HQ allows you to compete on leaderboards.

Drilling: The Petroleum Specialization

Plopping an Oil Well over an oil reservoir is the first step to getting your petroleum empire off the ground. Consider placing a Trade Depot nearby to export crude oil to the global market .

There's a good chance a sizable fortune is bubbling just beneath the surface of your city...and you may not even know about it. Activate the Oil data map to locate ancient deposits of crude oil, accumulated in elliptical pools called oil reservoirs. By plopping Oil Wells over these reservoirs you can pump crude oil to the surface and sell it for a profit on the global market. But oil is even more profitable when processed at an Oil Refinery to produce plastic and fuel, vital ingredients to Great Works. Or ship plastic to a Processor Factory to assist in the foundation of a burgeoning electronics specialization. There are multiple ways to generate income through the petroleum business, depositing fat wads of Simoleons into your city's treasury with each transaction. But don't get ahead of yourself. The buildings associated with this Specialization are expensive and occupy a lot of space—never mind the pollution. So consider taking out a loan and set aside a large portion of your city to pursue your dreams of making it big off all that beautiful black gold!

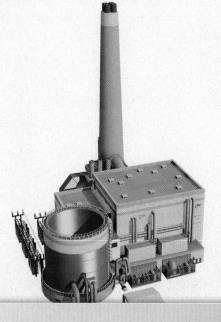

Oil Well

Cost: §37,500

Operational Cost: §150 per hour

Production Rate: 2,400 BPD

Prerequisites:

→ Provide working power

→ Provide working water

→ Oil under your city

→ Have seven industrial buildings

Description: What a better way to thank the dinosaurs for hooking you up with all that oil than to make Simoleons off them? Pump crude oil from reservoirs under your city. Run your city on crude oil with an Oil Power Plant! Sell barrels of your crude oil to local industry or on the global market via a Trade Depot. Thanks, dinos!

Building an Oil Well is the starting point for beginning your oil empire. Before placing an Oil Well, make sure you position it directly over a large oil reservoir—the Oil data map is automatically activated when an Oil Well is selected from the Drilling menu. Placing the Oil Well directly over a reservoir significantly increases its daily yield. However, some oil reservoirs are massive, extending far beyond the reach of your well. Instead of building multiple Oil Wells side by side, simply expand your existing well by extending its Service Road and building additional Oil Pumpjacks along it. The Service Road can expand a well's footprint over a massive area, usually allowing one well to completely occupy the area above a large oil reservoir. You can place up to eight additional Oil Pumpjacks along the Service Road, each one drawing more oil from the ground—the stock facility already comes with two Oil Pumpjacks. But the faster you pump oil, the quicker the output storage lot is filled. If the output storage lot reaches capacity, the Oil Well facility is temporarily shut down, so build additional Oil Delivery Truck Garages to provide more trucks. These trucks automatically deliver barrels of oil to local Trade Depots, Trade Ports, Oil Power Plants, and Oil Refineries.

If you're planning to sell crude oil on the global market, build a Trade Depot close to the Oil Well to cut down on transportation time between the two facilities.

MODULES

Oil Well Sign

Cost: §200

Operational Cost: None

Maximum Modules: 1

Description: The sign says: "No free samples. Beware: Attack Armadillos".

Service Road

Cost: Free

Operational Cost: None

Maximum Modules: N/A

Description: Provides infrastructure to allow transportation of crude oil from pumpjacks to the main Oil Well.

Oil Delivery Truck Garage

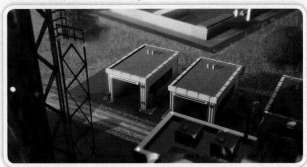

Cost: §10,000

Operational Cost: §50 per hour

Truck Capacity: 200 barrels

Maximum Modules: 4

Description: Provides an additional tanker truck to deliver crude oil to Oil Refineries, Oil Storage Lots, and Oil Power Plants.

Oil Pumpjack

Cost: §10,000

Operational Cost: §30 per hour

Production Rate: 1,200 BPD

Maximum Modules: 10

Description: Does running your Oil Well feel like sucking crude oil through a straw? Then get more straws! Add Oil Pumpjacks to your Oil Well to extend your reach and pump crude oil faster!

Petroleum HQ

Cost: §37,500

Operational Cost: §450 per hour

Prerequisites:

→ Build an Oil Well

→ Extract 80,000 barrels of crude oil in a day

Description: If you have crude oil in your veins and your heart pumps jet fuel, your city is ready for a Petroleum HQ. Sell crude oil on the global market via a Trade Depot to access petroleum improvements, including refineries, so you can produce fuel and plastic.

PETROLEUM HQ UPGRADES

Level	Name	Criteria	Unlock
1	Petroleum HQ	Extract 9,600 barrels of crude in a day.	One division of your choice.
2	Petroleum, Co.	Earn §200,000 in petroleum daily profit.	One division of your choice.
3	Petroleum, Inc.	Earn §2,000,000 in petroleum daily profit.	One division of your choice.

Once you get your oil specialization off to a good start, you'll eventually gain access to the Petroleum HQ, available in the Drilling menu. Like the Metals HQ, this fancy high-rise office building will likely dominate your city's skyline, drawing the envy of visiting mayors. Place this HQ in an area with plenty of room for expansion—you'll need space for the Refining and Commerce Divisions. By increasing profits from petroleum sales you can earn two upgrades for this HQ, gaining access to a division of your choice with each upgrade. Choose the Refining Division first to unlock access to the Oil Refinery, allowing you to produce fuel and plastic. The Commerce Division can come later, as you're probably not quite ready for a Trade Port yet. Plus, the extra income generated from fuel and plastic will earn you that final HQ upgrade rather quickly. In addition to gaining access to new buildings, the Petroleum HQ also allows you to compete in the leaderboards. Maximize oil production to climb to the top!

MODULES

Petroleum HQ Sign

Cost: §200

Operational Cost: None

Maximum Modules: 1

Description: "Dedicated to a clean environment!" the sign cheerfully claims.

Refining Division

Cost: §20,000

Operational Cost: §400 per hour

Local Access Granted: Oil Refinery

Maximum Modules: 1

Description: Petroleum is not only good for crude oil, you can refine the crude oil into fuel or plastic. Diversifying into other resources can help you weather the ups and downs of the global market.

Commerce Division

Cost: §20,000

Operational Cost: §400 per hour

Local Access Granted: Trade Port, Fuel and Computer Storage Lots at the Trade Port

Maximum Modules: 1

Description: Full of trade nerds who love watching the action of oil prices on the global market, the Commerce Division helps get your petroleum products to market.

Oil Refinery

Cost: §73,000

Operational Cost: §300 per hour

Production Rate: 24,000 BPD

Prerequisites:

→ Petroleum HQ with Refining Division

Description: Crude oil prices down? Then diversify! Take your crude oil and use it to create plastic to sell on the global market via a Trade Depot. Add a Fuel Distillation Unit to also create fuel to sell or use for Great Works!

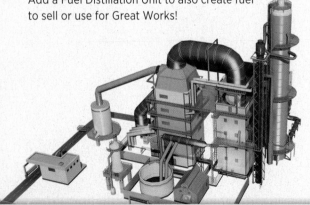

Take your oil specialization to the next level with an Oil Refinery. This facility inputs crude oil and produces fuel and plastic—both products are used in Great Works, and plastic is also essential for creating processors at Processor Factories associated with the electronics specialization. By default, the facility is equipped with one Fuel Distillation Unit, allowing you to create fuel immediately. If you want to create plastic, add a Plastic Polymerizer. As the refinery starts cranking out products, keep a close eye on the material and product storage lots—click on the Oil Refinery to open its window to see each lot's capacity. The material lot holds all incoming oil supplied by Oil Wells or Trade Depots. If there's a shortage, consider adding more truck garages at the Oil Wells or Trade Depots to increase input. Each product storage lot holds either fuel or plastic produced by the refinery. Shipping out these products are the responsibility of the delivery trucks at the refinery. Place additional Oil Refinery Delivery Truck Garages to keep plastic and fuel moving out and to prevent a halt in production due to full lots. With each additional Fuel Distillation Unit and Plastic Polymerizer added to the refinery, the plastic and fuel material storage lots double in capacity to accommodate the increased production. Still, it's important to keep an eye on these lots to make sure the delivery trucks are getting the job done. Send plastic and fuel to a Trade Port for export on the global market. Or simply use the Trade Port's massive storage lots to stockpile plastic and fuel for a future Great Works project—the Solar Farm requires plastic and the Space Center requires fuel.

MODULES

Oil Refinery Sign

Cost: §200

Operational Cost: None

Maximum Modules: 1

Description: The font on the sign seems pretty refined, but the sign's still kind of greasy.

Oil Refinery Delivery Truck Garage

Cost: §10,000

Operational Cost: §50 per hour

Truck Capacity: 2,000 barrels of processed oil

Maximum Modules: 4

Description: Adds a transport truck to move plastic and fuel to plastic and fuel consumers.

Fuel Distillation Unit

Cost: §46,000

Operational Cost: §150 per hour

Production Rate: 24,000 BPD

Maximum Modules: 3

Description: This is the answer to your hopes if you are selling fuel faster than you can make it. Create fuel faster with this fractional distillation unit!

Plastic Polymerizer

Cost: §30,000

Operational Cost: §50 per hour

Production Rate: 24,000 BPD

Maximum Modules: 4

Description: Plastic polymerizer. Sounds high tech, right? It is. In goes crude oil, out comes plastic. Science is amazing. Sell your plastic on the global market, or use it to create CPUs or for building Great Works.

Managing the Petroleum Specialization

Like all city specializations, there's a lot more to succeeding in the petroleum specialization than simply building Oil Wells and refineries. It's important to keep an eye on your input and output lots, ensuring oil, plastic, and fuel flow steadily between your facilities. Likewise, it's important to address the inherent risks associated with extracting and refining crude oil. Here's a few pointers to help get your petroleum specialization off the ground.

A CRAVING FOR CRUDE

The Oil Refinery shows you're serious about making it big in the petroleum specialization. This massive facility converts crude oil into fuel and plastic.

You can't become a cowboy-hat-wearing oil tycoon overnight. Like all things in *SimCity*, it's important to start small and expand as production and profits increase. Since you'll have a steady supply of oil, consider powering your city with an Oil Power Plant. This is a heavy polluter, but it can generate enough power to supply your city and several others. You'll also need to zone some industrial before the Oil Well is available. Begin your city specialization by plopping one Oil Well over a large oil reservoir. Use the Service Road to expand the Oil Well's footprint and add additional Oil Pumpjacks to increase production. Initially, ship all extracted crude oil to a nearby Trade Depot and export it to the global market to fill your city's treasury with a steady flow of Simoleons—make sure your Oil Power Plant is accepting local deliveries as well. Build the Petroleum HQ as soon as it's unlocked and add a Refining Division following its first upgrade. This allows you to build the Oil Refinery. At this point, direct oil shipments to the refinery so you can begin producing fuel and plastic—you'll need to add a Plastic Polymerizer to the refinery to make plastic. Transport these new products to the Trade Depot and sell them on the global market for an even bigger profit. Or contribute them to a Great Works site—plastic is also essential for making processors at the Processor Factory. As your oil specialization expands, so will the pollution generated by these dirty facilities. If you're relying on local workers, make sure your residential and commercial zones are far from your Oil Wells and Oil Refinery, otherwise you'll see an increase in health problems, not to mention complaints, leading to a downturn in your approval rating.

> **NOTE**
>
> If you want to export crude oil, plastic, or fuel by cargo ship or train, you'll need a Trade Port, requiring access to the Commerce Division at the Petroleum HQ.

OIL WELL OPTIMIZATION

Extend the Oil Well's Service Road and build additional Oil Pumpjacks to extract oil from a large area.

There's no need to build multiple Oil Wells when one will do. By extending a Oil Well's Service Road, you can expand the facility's footprint dramatically, ideal for extracting crude oil from even the largest oil reservoirs. Select the Service Road and connect it to the existing

Service Road at the edge of the base facility. Just like the Wind Power Plant or Garbage Dump, this Service Road can extend far beyond the Oil Well. Draw the Service Road directly through the center of the reservoir, and then position new Oil Pumpjacks on either side of the road. The Oil Well comes with two Oil Pumpjacks and you can place up to eight more along the Service Road, greatly increasing production. But as oil production increases, the output storage lot will fill up fast. Build additional Oil Delivery Truck Garages to haul away accumulating barrels of oil to a Trade Depot, Oil Power Plant, or Oil Refinery. The well can only store 20,000 barrels of oil regardless of how many Oil Pumpjacks you add. When storage reaches capacity, the Oil Well temporarily shuts down until more storage space is cleared, so keep those trucks moving to prevent a halt in production.

EMERGENCY RESPONSE

In addition to providing a Large Fire Station with a Hazmat Garage, build a Hospital to respond to injuries at your wells and refineries.

Like mines, Oil Wells and Oil Refineries are dangerous places to work. Make sure you have the appropriate facilities in place to respond to emergencies. A Hospital equipped with an Emergency Center and Surgical Center are recommended for responding to accidents resulting in injuries—consider building the Hospital close to your facilities to decrease ambulance response times. These facilities also have an elevated risk for hazmat fires. As soon as you can afford it, build a Large Fire Station and add a Hazmat Garage. Failure to address the risk of hazmat fires may result in your expensive facilities going up in smoke, killing and injuring multiple workers in the process. Hazmat fires also spread toxic pollution, potentially making nearby Sims sick, further impacting your city's health care system. So take the risk of injuries and hazmat fires seriously before they take a toll on your workers, facilities...and bottom line.

Drilling: Points to Remember

→ Build Oil Wells to extract oil.

→ Extract oil to use, gift, or sell on the global market.

→ Petroleum can be used to make other goods or used for Great Works.

→ These buildings will stop producing if their storage lot is full.

→ Use a Trade Depot or Trade Port to sell resources on the global market.

→ Local industry can ship freight to Petroleum buildings.

→ Drilling adds the risk of hazmat fires to your city.

→ Petroleum HQ unlocks more buildings through its divisions.

→ Petroleum HQ allows you to compete on leaderboards.

Trading

Build a Trade Depot early on. It's required to sell your resources on the global market. Just make sure you add the appropriate storage lot modules to hold your products.

Do you have a passion for buying low and selling high? Or perhaps you just need to sell off some of that coal you've been digging out of the ground? What you need is a Trade Depot to import and export your way to prosperity! Both the Trade Depot and its bigger brother, the Trade Port, give your city the ability to trade every commodity on the global market. If you're producing any sort of resource or product in your city you'll definitely want to export those goods for a quick profit. But why would you want to import something? Imagine you have a coal mining town with no raw ore. Simply import raw ore from the global market, send it to your Smelting Factory, and mix it with your mountains of coal to create that elusive alloy. Or hold on to that raw ore and wait for the price to go up before selling it back to the global market for profit. Regardless of what kind of city specialization you choose, you'll need to be familiar with the importing and exporting mechanics inherent to the trading specialization. And it all begins with a modest Trade Depot...

Trade Depot

Cost: §10,000

Operational Cost: §75 per hour

Global Market Delivery: Every 60 minutes

Description: Import, export, and store resources like coal and crude oil with this basic unit. Also accepts freight shipments for industry. Does not require power or water to function.

The Trade Depot is your city's portal to the global market, allowing you to import and export a variety of resources—this is how you make money from all those resources and products you've been accumulating. But before a Trade Depot can accept incoming goods, you must first add the appropriate storage lot. For example, if you're ready to import or export crude oil, add a Crude Oil Storage Lot. With the storage lot in place, the Trade Depot can then accept deliveries from local city specializations, local industry, the global market, or from other mayors in the region sending your city gifts. But space is limited, capping storage lots at four modules per Trade Depot, so only add the modules you really need. And if that's not enough space, simply build another Trade Depot—they're fairly inexpensive.

Once you have the storage lots you want, click on the Manage Global Market Deliveries button to set up desired interactions with the global market. Each commodity accepted by the Trade Depot is represented, allowing you to import (buy) or export (sell). If you import a commodity, a truck will arrive from the region to deliver the goods and your city will be charged the current market price upon delivery. If you export, a truck arrives from the region and hauls away the stored goods, instantly depositing Simoleons in your city's treasury. You can also simply store resources at your Trade Depot, when the Use Locally option is selected—this is the default setting. This allows local businesses (and power plants) to draw from the resources stored at the Trade Depot. As you can see, the Trade Depot is a very active hub and major player in your city's economy. Keep an eye on your city's Trade Depots to ensure all resources are flowing smoothly. Otherwise, consider adding more storage lots and trucks to smooth out any kinks in your supply chain.

MODULES

Trade Depot Sign

Cost: §200

Operational Cost: None

Maximum Modules: 1

Description: This sign has a complex list of directions to different storage lots.

Freight Truck Garage

Cost: §3,000

Operational Cost: §50 per hour

Import/Export Deliveries: 2 tons of goods per trip

Maximum Modules: 4

Description: Time to get that convoy movin'! Add a Freight Truck Garage to increase the rate at which you can send resources from the Trade Depot to manufacturers and consumers in your city.

Freight Shipping Warehouse

Cost: §2,000

Operational Cost: §15 per hour

Freight Capacity: 54 tons

Maximum Modules: 4

Description: This small warehouse accepts freight shipments from local industry. Industry that doesn't have a place to ship its freight may go out of business.

Coal Storage Lot

Cost: §2,000

Operational Cost: §15 per hour

Storage Capacity: 20 tons

Maximum Modules: 3

Description: Adds storage space for coal. Use the coal locally, or import it from the global market at low prices and export it at high prices.

Crude Oil Storage Lot

Cost: §2,000

Operational Cost: §15 per hour

Storage Capacity: 2,000 barrels

Maximum Modules: 4

Description: Adds storage space for crude oil. Use the crude oil locally, or import it from the global market at low prices and export it at high prices.

Raw Ore Storage Lot

Cost: §2,000

Operational Cost: §15 per hour

Storage Capacity: 20 tons

Maximum Modules: 4

Description: Adds storage space for raw ore. Use the raw ore locally, or import it from the global market at low prices and export it at high prices.

☑ TIP

A Trade Depot or Port is the only way to sell resources your city produces on the global market.

Metal Storage Lot

Cost: §2,000

Operational Cost: §15 per hour

Storage Capacity: 20 tons

Maximum Modules: 4

Prerequisites:

→ Metal Reclamation Line at Recycling Center

→ OR Metals HQ

→ OR Metals Division at Trade HQ

Description: Adds storage space for metal. Use the metal locally, or import it from the global market at low prices and export it at high prices.

Alloy Storage Lot

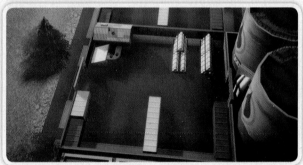

Cost: §2,000

Operational Cost: §15 per hour

Storage Capacity: 20 tons

Maximum Modules: 4

Prerequisites:

→ Alloy Reclamation Line at Recycling Center

→ OR Metals HQ

→ OR Metals Division at Trade HQ

Description: Adds storage space for alloy. Use the alloy locally, or import it from the global market at low prices and export it at high prices.

Fuel Storage Lot

Cost: §2,000

Operational Cost: §15 per hour

Storage Capacity: 2,000 barrels

Maximum Modules: 4

Prerequisites:

→ Petroleum HQ

→ OR Petroleum Division at Trade HQ

Description: Adds storage space for fuel. Use the fuel locally, or import it from the global market at low prices and export it at high prices.

Plastic Storage Lot

Cost: §2,000

Operational Cost: §15 per hour

Storage Capacity: 20 tons

Maximum Modules: 4

Description: Adds storage space for plastic. Use the plastic locally, or import it from the global market at low prices and export it at high prices.

Processors Storage Lot

Cost: §2,000

Operational Cost: §15 per hour

Storage Capacity: 200,000 crates

Maximum Modules: 4

Prerequisites:

→ Electronics HQ

→ OR Electronics Division at Trade HQ

Description: Adds storage space for processors. Use the processors locally, or import them from the global market at low prices and export them at high prices.

Computer Storage Lot

Cost: §2,000

Operational Cost: §15 per hour

Storage Capacity: 200,000 crates

Maximum Modules: 4

Prerequisites:

→ Electronics HQ

→ OR Electronics Division at Trade HQ

Description: Adds storage space for computers. Use the computers locally, or import them from the global market at low prices and export them at high prices.

TV Storage Lot

Cost: §2,000

Operational Cost: §15 per hour

Storage Capacity: 200,000 crates

Maximum Modules: 4

Prerequisites:

→ Electronics HQ

→ OR Electronics Division at Trade HQ

Description: Adds storage space for TVs. Use the TVs locally, or import them from the global market at low prices and export them at high prices.

Trade HQ

Cost: §37,500

Operational Cost: §450 per hour

Prerequisites:

→ Town Hall

→ Plop three different storage lots

→ Trade §72,000 in global market resources in a day

Description: Amass a fortune as an import/export master! Buy from the global market at low prices and sell when you can make the most Simoleons! Make profit from the global market to expand your trading actions. Upgrades available based on daily profit goals.

TRADE HQ UPGRADES

Level	Name	Criteria	Unlock
1	Trading HQ	Trade §72,000 in resources on the global market.	One division of your choice.
2	Trading, Co.	Earn §250,000 in trade daily profit.	One division of your choice.
3	Trading, Inc.	Earn §2,000,000 in trade daily profit.	One division of your choice.
4	Trading Global	Earn §4,000,000 in trade daily profit.	One division of your choice.

Like the other HQs, this shimmering skyscraper adds a sense of awe to your skyline, sure to catch the eye of mayors in neighboring cities. But when building this HQ, make sure you allow plenty of room for expansion so you can add up to three divisions. As with the other HQs, upgrades are awarded for reaching specific daily profit goals. With each upgrade earned, the HQ grows taller and one trade division of your choice is made available type of specialization your city is. If you're big into mining, choose the Metals Division. Or select the Petroleum Division if you've got a big oil city underway. The Electronics Division is only necessary for cities smart enough to produce processors, TVs, and computers. Each division unlocks access to the Trade Port as well as several associated storage lot modules associated with the Trade Port. The Trade Port is ideal for importing and exporting massive amounts of resources by train or cargo ship. But even if you don't have access to water or rail, the storage lots at the Trade Port are massive, perfect for stockpiling enormous volumes of resources—consider holding on to these goods until the market price turns in your favor, then sell them on the global market for a huge profit!

MODULES

Trade HQ Sign

Cost: §200

Operational Cost: None

Maximum Modules: 1

Description: This well-polished sign seems like it is pretty expensive.

Electronics Division

Cost: §20,000

Operational Cost: §400 per hour

Local Access Granted: Plastic, Alloy, Processor, TV, and Computer Storage Lots at the Trade Port

Maximum Modules: 1

Description: Expand your trading options to electronics and all the resources needed to build them!

Metals Division

Cost: §20,000

Operational Cost: §400 per hour

Local Access Granted: Coal, Raw Ore, Metal, and Alloy Storage Lots at the Trade Port

Maximum Modules: 1

Description: Expand your trading options to metal resource extraction!

Petroleum Division

Cost: §20,000

Operational Cost: §400 per hour

Local Access Granted: Crude Oil, Fuel, and Plastic Storage Lots at the Trade Port

Maximum Modules: 1

Description: Expand your trading options to petroleum resource extraction and the goods it can be refined into!

Trade Port

Cost: §60,000

Operational Cost: §225 per hour

Global Market Delivery: Every 60 minutes

Prerequisites:

➜ Trade HQ

➜ OR Commerce Division at Petroleum HQ

➜ OR Commerce Division at Metals HQ

➜ OR Commerce Division at Electronics HQ

Description: Allows importing, exporting, and storage of commodity resources or freight. Larger storage lots allow for ten times the capacity of the Trade Depot. Rail and cargo ship connections allow import and export via rail or water. Requires water and power to function.

Want to import and export large volumes of resources by train or cargo ship? Then you need a Trade Port as soon as you can afford it. But first, you need to unlock it. The Trade Port becomes available once you build the Trade HQ or after adding a Commerce Division to the Petroleum, Metals, or Electronics HQ. When possible, build the Trade Port within close proximity to rails or a waterway. This allows you to place a Freight Rail Terminal or Cargo Ship Dock—these are separate modules and don't necessarily need to connect to the Trade Port. Leave plenty of expansion space around your Trade Port for various storage lots—you can add a total of six to each Trade Port. While these storage lots look identical to those offered by the Trade Depot, they hold nearly ten times more product. But before you can add certain storage lots, you must first build the proper division associated with the commodity. For example, if you want to add the Coal Storage Lot, you'll need a Metals HQ with a Commerce Division or a Metals Division at your Trade HQ—there are at least two possibilities to unlock access to most storage lots at the Trade Port. Beyond the larger storage lots and its access to train and cargo ships, the Trade Port functions identically to the Trade Depot. If you don't have access to water or rail, you can still use the Trade Port's massive capacity to store large amounts of resources—imports and exports are carried by trucks, just like the Trade Depot. Given the large capacity of the storage lots, the Trade Depot is ideal for stockpiling construction materials for Great Works. Or simply buy low and sell high to accrue profits by trading on the global market. Whatever your intent, the Trade Port is an integral part of succeeding in any of the commodity-based city specializations.

MODULES

Trade Depot Sign

Cost: §200
Operational Cost: None
Maximum Modules: 1
Description: This sign seems to have accumulated a thick layer of road grime.

Heavy Rail Tracks

Cost: §6
Operational Cost: None
Maximum Modules: N/A
Description: Tracks to connect the Passenger Train Station to the rail network or to connect up to a Freight Train Terminal at a Trade Port.

Delivery Truck Garage

Cost: §3,000
Operational Cost: §50 per hour
Import/Export Deliveries: 2 tons of goods per trip
Maximum Modules: 4
Description: Adds a truck to move one resource type from your Trade Port to consumers in your city. Trucks frequently pick up from the Trade Port.

Freight Rail Terminal

Cost: §70,000

Operational Cost: §400 per hour

Global Market Delivery: Every 360 minutes

Maximum Modules: 1

Description: Allows import and export of resources via freight train. Each storage lot at the Trade Port adds another freight car to the freight train. Trains arrive every few hours.

Cargo Ship Dock

Cost: §100,000

Operational Cost: §400 per hour

Global Market Delivery: Every 180 minutes

Maximum Modules: 1

Description: Allows import and export of resources via high-capacity cargo ships. Cargo ships only carry one resource at a time, but in massive amounts. Cargo ships arrive several times a day.

Freight Shipping Warehouse

Cost: §20,000

Operational Cost: §150 per hour

Storage Capacity: 100 tons

Maximum Modules: 6

Description: This high-capacity warehouse accepts freight shipments from local industry. Industry that doesn't have a place to ship its freight may go out of business.

Coal Storage Lot

Cost: §20,000

Operational Cost: §150 per hour

Storage Capacity: 100 tons

Maximum Modules: 6

Prerequisites:

→ Metals HQ with Commerce Division

→ OR Trade HQ with Metals Division

Description: Adds a large amount of storage for coal. Use the coal locally, or import it from the global market at low prices and export it at high prices.

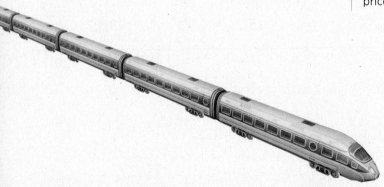

Crude Oil Storage Lot

Cost: §20,000

Operational Cost: §150 per hour

Storage Capacity: 10,000 barrels

Maximum Modules: 6

Prerequisites:

→ Petroleum HQ with Commerce Division

→ OR Trade HQ with Petroleum Division

Description: Adds a large amount of storage for crude oil. Use the crude oil locally, or import it from the global market at low prices and export it at high prices.

Metal Storage Lot

Cost: §20,000

Operational Cost: §150 per hour

Storage Capacity: 100 tons

Maximum Modules: 6

Prerequisites:

→ Metals HQ with Commerce Division

→ OR Trade HQ with Metals Division

Description: Adds a large amount of storage for metal. Use the metal locally, or import it from the global market at low prices and export it at high prices.

Raw Ore Storage Lot

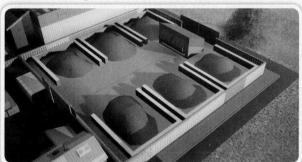

Cost: §20,000

Operational Cost: §150 per hour

Storage Capacity: 100 tons

Maximum Modules: 6

Prerequisites:

→ Metals HQ with Commerce Division

→ OR Trade HQ with Metals Division

Description: Adds a large amount of storage for raw ore. Use the raw ore locally, or import it from the global market at low prices and export it at high prices.

Alloy Storage Lot

Cost: §20,000

Operational Cost: §150 per hour

Storage Capacity: 100 tons

Maximum Modules: 6

Prerequisites:

→ Metals HQ with Commerce Division

→ OR Trade HQ with Metals Division

→ OR Electronics HQ with Commerce Division

Description: Adds a large amount of storage for alloy. Use the alloy locally, or import it from the global market at low prices and export it at high prices.

Fuel Storage Lot

Cost: §20,000

Operational Cost: §150 per hour

Storage Capacity: 10,000 barrels

Maximum Modules: 6

Prerequisites:

→ Petroleum HQ with Commerce Division

→ OR Trade HQ with Petroleum Division

Description: Adds a large amount of storage for fuel. Use the fuel locally, or import it from the global market at low prices and export it at high prices.

Plastic Storage Lot

Cost: §20,000

Operational Cost: §150 per hour

Storage Capacity: 100 tons

Maximum Modules: 6

Prerequisites:

→ Petroleum HQ with Commerce Division

→ OR Trade HQ with Petroleum Division

Description: Adds a large amount of storage for plastic. Use the plastic locally, or import it from the global market at low prices and export it at high prices.

 TIP

A smooth supply chain is key if you want to top the Electronics leaderboards.

Processors Storage Lot

Cost: §20,000

Operational Cost: §150 per hour

Storage Capacity: 1,000,000 crates

Maximum Modules: 6

Prerequisites:

→ Electronics HQ with Commerce Division

→ OR Trade HQ with Electronics Division

Description: Adds a large amount of storage for processors. Use the processors locally, or import them from the global market at low prices and export them at high prices.

Computer Storage Lot

Cost: §20,000

Operational Cost: §150 per hour

Storage Capacity: 1,000,000 crates

Maximum Modules: 6

Prerequisites:

→ Electronics HQ with Commerce Division

→ OR Trade HQ with Electronics Division

Description: Adds a large amount of storage for computers. Use the computers locally, or import them from the global market at low prices and export them at high prices.

TV Storage Lot

Cost: §20,000

Operational Cost: §150 per hour

Storage Capacity: 100 tons

Maximum Modules: 6

Prerequisites:

→ Electronics HQ with Commerce Division

→ OR Trade HQ with Electronics Division

Description: Adds a large amount of storage for TVs. Use the TVs locally, or import them from the global market at low prices and export them at high prices.

⚠ CAUTION

Be cautious when stockpiling large volumes of resources at a Trade Port. If a fire breaks out, you run the risk of losing everything warehoused within the various storage lots—potentially worth millions on the global market! If you're paranoid, build a Fire Station next to your Trade Port to minimize risk.

Managing the Trade Specialization

If you want to succeed in any of the city specializations, you'll eventually need to dabble with the importing and exporting of resources through a Trade Depot or Trade Port. The trade specialization is deeply intertwined with mining, drilling, and electronics, making it even more important to know the ins and outs of the global market. It's equally important to manage the various storage lots, ensuring your businesses have access to the resources they need in order to prevent any snags in your supply chain.

TIP

Global market prices on resources change every hour. Buy low and sell high to profit!

PLAYING THE MARKET

If you have a lot of Simoleons to play with, run your import/export business out of a Trade Port. The large storage lots allow you to move high volumes of resources for even bigger profits.

Unlike most of the city specializations, you can jump into the trade game right away by establishing a Trade Depot—you don't even need water or power! But what you do with the Trade Depot is entirely up to you. Want to play the global market by buying low and selling high? Then consider importing resources like crude oil, alloy, or plastic. The market value of each commodity fluctuates based on current supply and demand, taking into account every player accessing the global market in *SimCity*. If a commodity becomes scarce, its price goes up. But if players are flooding the market with one particular product, the price will plummet. Prices are updated approximately every 60 real-world minutes. You can check the current price of each commodity by clicking on any Trade Depot or Trade Port and selecting the Manage Global Market Deliveries button. If those resources you imported have gone up in price, consider exporting them now to secure a quick and easy profit. Otherwise, hold on to them until the price is more favorable.

TRUCKS, TRAINS, AND CARGO SHIPS

The Freight Rail Terminal and Cargo Ship Dock don't have to be directly attached to the Trade Port, so leave some breathing room around your Trade Port to accommodate more storage lots.

In addition to playing the market, the Trade Depot is essential for exporting resources extracted and produced in your city. If you have a mine or Oil Well, get that coal, raw ore, or crude oil to a Trade Depot and begin exporting to the global market to generate extra income for your city. As you make more money on the market, you'll gain access to the Trade HQ and Trade Port. The Trade Port is simply a bigger and badder version of the Trade Depot, allowing you to store and import/export massive volumes of resources. The Trade Port also offers access to trains and cargo ships through the addition of a Freight Rail Terminal or Cargo Ship Dock. As you move up from trucks, to trains, to cargo ships, the capacity of each vessel increases by a magnitude of ten. So if a truck can carry 2 tons, each train car can hold 20 tons, and each cargo ship can hold 200 tons. Whenever possible, try to export resources by cargo ship, especially if your storage lots are near capacity. However, be careful when importing resources through a Trade Port equipped with a Cargo Ship Dock—you might end up with a whole lot more stuff than you can handle...or afford. For this reason, it's more feasible to manage imports through a Trade Depot.

IMPORT/EXPORT FUNDAMENTALS

Play it safe when importing resources. The relatively small storage lots at the Trade Depot make it easier to manage product arriving from the global market when your treasury is low—incoming shipments stop when the lot is full.

Are your city's output lots overflowing with resources? Or maybe local industry requires resources your city can't produce? To manage imports and exports, click on a Trade Depot or Trade Port and select the Manage Global Market Deliveries button. This opens a new window allowing you to select from different resources based on which storage lots are present—each commodity is represented by an icon in the tabs at the top of the window. Click on a tab and then choose whether to import or export the selected commodity. If you choose to import, your city will pay the current market rate to have the selected commodity delivered—new deliveries arrive at different intervals based on the mode of transportation. If you choose to export, product within the selected storage lot will be sold to the global market at the current market rate—a truck, train, or cargo ship will arrive from the region and haul off the products, depositing a payment

in your treasury, appearing in the Recent Transactions window of the Budget Panel. In addition to importing or exporting, you can also choose to use the selected commodity locally—in this case, the Trade Depot or Trade Port simply serves as a storage warehouse for excess product consumed by local industry. This comes in handy if the output lots at your mines or Oil Wells are overflowing—these storage lots serve as a backup, allowing you to store product until you're ready to sell it or ship it to another building like the Smelting Factory or Oil Refinery. The massive storage lots at the Trade Port are perfect for hoarding materials necessary to construct Great Works.

LOCAL INDUSTRY AND FREIGHT

See all those crates in that Freight Shipping Warehouse? Each crate contains goods produced by local industry.

If you have multiple factories in your city, always add at least one Freight Shipping Warehouse module at a Trade Depot or Trade Port. This module serves as an overflow warehouse for freight produced at local factories. If industry has no shops to send their freight to, they'll go out of business. In this sense, the warehouse serves as a safety net, accepting surplus freight when there aren't enough shops in your city to accept it. From the warehouse, the freight is then shipped out to commercial shops or sold on the global market—build additional Freight Truck Garages to add more trucks, helping deliver freight to consumers at a faster rate. Supplying local factories with one of these warehouses greatly increases their chances of survival, allowing them to ship large amounts of freight throughout the city and region regardless of their access to shops. Freight shipped from the Trade Depot or Trade Port to shops or the global market earns your city no money directly. However, as the factories producing the freight become more profitable, they pay more in taxes, boosting your city's income through increased tax revenue.

Trading: Points to Remember

→ Storage lots allow you to import resources or make money by exporting them.

→ Import resources like coal to fuel your power plant.

→ Click on a Trade Depot or Trade Port to see the global market controls.

→ Trucks, trains, and cargo ships will automatically pick up resources when selling to the global market.

→ Prices for resources fluctuate based on how many are bought or sold.

→ Local industry can ship freight to Trade Depots or Trade Ports with a Freight Shipping Warehouse.

→ Trucks in Trade Depots and Trade Ports help deliver freight and resources to your local businesses.

→ Increase your output by adding more storage lots.

Electronics

You can begin dabbling in the electronics specialization before you even build a Processor Factory. The Electronics Division at the Trade HQ allows you to import and export processors, TVs, and computers from a Trade Depot.

Surely all those Sims graduating from the Community College and University are looking for better jobs than those offered by your dirty factories and mines. (Not that there's anything wrong with working in a factory or mine.) Maximize the potential of your city's exceptional brainpower by pursuing the lucrative electronics specialization. By utilizing two basic resources—alloy and plastic—you can foster a high tech empire through the production of processors, TVs, and computers. But fair warning, the electronics specialization isn't cheap and it can't be initiated early on. Instead, you must slowly mold your city into a gadget-producing powerhouse, establishing higher institutions of learning to assemble an educated workforce. It's equally important to secure a steady supply chain, ensuring your city has access to plentiful volumes of alloy and plastic. These can be generated locally, imported from the global market, or gifted by neighboring cities. If you think your city is up for the challenge, set your sights on the electronics biz and become the envy of all mayors in the region.

Processor Factory

Cost: §160,000

Operational Cost: §700 per hour

Production Rate: 360,000 crates/day

Prerequisites:

→ Provide working power

→ Provide working water

→ Have five clean industrial buildings

Description: These days, it seems there are processors in everything. Those should be your processors! Use alloy and plastic to create processors to sell on the global market via a Trade Depot. You can import alloy and plastic from the global market if you need to. Educated workers will increase the factory's efficiency.

If you've managed to nurture a city where education is a priority, you stand a good chance of gaining access to the Processor Factory. To unlock this facility you need a minimum of five clean industrial (tech level 2) buildings in your city. The only way to encourage the appearance of these buildings is through an educated workforce produced by a Community College or University. But having an educated workforce is much more than a prerequisite—it's an absolute necessity to run a successful Processor Factory. So even after you have five clean industrial buildings, keep investing in higher education to supply this factory with more skilled workers. Next, you need access to plastic and alloy to create processors. If you have a Smelting Factory and Oil Refinery in your city, supplying the Processor Factory with enough raw material should be no problem. However, if you're missing one or both of these elements, you'll need to either import it from the global market (significantly adding to production costs), receive it from another city as a gift, or acquire it through recycling. Once the facility is up and running, invest in additional Processor Assembly Line modules to increase production. Just make sure you have enough trucks to move out all those processors the factory is cranking out. If the product storage lot reaches capacity, the factory will temporarily shut down. To avoid interruptions, add more Delivery Truck Garages and ship these processors out to Trade Depots for export onto the global market. Or, consider storing all these processors at a Trade Port, using its massive Processors Storage Lot to warehouse up to 1,000,000 crates. Eventually you can use these processors to supply the Consumer Electronics Factory, producing computers and TVs. But you'll need to sell off some of those processors if you want to unlock the Consumer Electronics Division at the Electronics HQ, necessary to unlock the Consumer Electronics Factory.

MODULES

Processor Factory Sign

Cost: §200

Operational Cost: None

Maximum Modules: 1

Description: This way, the future!

Delivery Truck Garage

Cost: §10,000

Operational Cost: §50 per hour

Truck Capacity: 20,000 crates

Maximum Modules: 4

Description: Within this garage are trucks that deliver your processors around town to the industry that uses them, Trade Depots, and Trade Ports. Under the hood of those trucks...you guessed it: more processors.

Processor Assembly Line

Cost: §50,000

Operational Cost: §350 per hour

Production Rate: 360,000 processors/day

Maximum Modules: 4

Description: At the digital computing heart of all technology lies the humble processor! Amass even more processors in your factory with this additional assembly line.

 TIP

Instead of selling off all those processors or shipping them to a Consumer Electronics Factory, store some at a Trade Port for use in the Solar Farm Great Works project.

Electronics HQ

Cost: §37,500

Operational Cost: §450 per hour

Prerequisites:

→ Manufacture 500,000 processors in a day

Description: Embrace technology and prepare for our eventual robot overlords! Crank out processors to upgrade and improve your HQ. Research new technological innovations in consumer electronics. Upgrades available based on electronics daily profit.

ELECTRONICS HQ UPGRADES

Level	Name	Criteria	Unlock
1	Electronics HQ	Manufacture 7,200 crates of processors in a day.	One division of your choice.
2	Electronics, Co.	Earn §1,500,000 in electronics daily profit.	One division of your choice.
3	Electronics, Inc.	Earn §5,000,000 in electronics daily profit.	One division of your choice.

As your Processor Factory ramps up production with additional Processor Assembly Lines, you'll eventually unlock access to the Electronics HQ. This is another modern, glass-skinned office building, making a classy high tech addition to your city's skyline. Like the other city specialization HQs, this building can be upgraded by reaching specific sales goals—this means you're going to need to sell off some of those processors at the Trade Depot or Trade Port. With each upgrade, the HQ becomes taller and you gain access to one division of your choice. There are only two divisions available at the Electronics HQ: the Consumer Electronics Division and the Commerce Division. Which division you build first depends on your situation. If you have ample supply of plastic and alloy within your city, go for the Consumer Electronics Division so you can build a Consumer Electronics Factory and begin cranking out TVs and computers. However, if you have no local access to plastic or alloy, consider choosing the Commerce Division first. This division unlocks the Plastic and Alloy Storage Lots

at the Trade Port, ideal for importing large volumes of all the materials you need. But when possible, avoid importing alloy or plastic—it's much cheaper to produce it yourself at your own Smelting Factory and Oil Refinery.

MODULES

Electronics HQ Sign

Cost: §200

Operational Cost: None

Maximum Modules: 1

Description: The address is given as "1337 Haxorz Ave.", which doesn't seem correct...

Consumer Electronics Division

Cost: §20,000

Operational Cost: §400 per hour

Local Access Granted: Consumer Electronics Factory

Maximum Modules: 1

Description: Put your processors to practical use! The Consumer Electronics Division wants your processors in consumers' homes, inside of TVs and computers.

Commerce Division

Cost: §20,000

Operational Cost: §400 per hour

Local Access Granted: Processor, Alloy, and Plastic Storage Lots at the Trade Port

Maximum Modules: 1

Description: What use are all those processors if you can't get them to market? The Commerce Division seeks to solve this problem.

Consumer Electronics Factory

Cost: §360,000

Operational Cost: §1,200 per hour

Production Rate: 360,000 crates/day

Prerequisites:

→ Consumer Electronics Division at Electronics HQ

Description: Take your very useful, high tech processors and put them in TVs, so Sims can fall asleep watching videos of people getting hit in the gut. Sell your TVs for profit on the global market via a Trade Depot. Educated workers will increase the factory's efficiency.

Immediately after building a Consumer Electronics Division at your Electronics HQ, you gain access to the Consumer Electronics Factory. This is the single most expensive building in the game, so make sure you're ready for it before you decide to plop it. Otherwise, it will sit idle, draining your treasury while producing nothing. First off, make sure you have an adequate supply of educated workers in your city produced by a Community College or University. Next, ensure you have

a surplus supply of plastic and alloy, taking into account the materials consumed by the Processor Factory. If you have the workforce and raw materials in place, plop the factory and start making TVs from processors and plastic. The facility comes equipped with one TV Assembly Line—you can add up to two more to ramp up production. Or, if you have access to surplus alloy and processors, plop a Computer Assembly to begin outputting computers. Click on the factory to monitor its material and product storage lots—you want to keep the material lots full and the product lots empty. If the TV and computer product lots reach capacity, the factory will temporarily shut down. To prevent this, add more Delivery Truck Garages to ship TVs and computers out of the factory at a steady rate. Transport TVs and computers to a Trade Port where you can either sell them on the global market or stockpile them for a Great Works project—you need TVs for the Arcology and computers for the Space Center.

MODULES

Consumer Electronics Factory Sign

Cost: §200

Operational Cost: None

Maximum Modules: 1

Description: Shows the way to the Consumer Electronics Factory. Mostly for delivery trucks. It's frowned upon for consumers to visit the factory themselves.

Delivery Truck Garage

Cost: §10,000

Operational Cost: §50 per hour

Truck Capacity: 20,000 crates

Maximum Modules: 4

Description: This well-padded truck delivers your TVs and computers to Trade Depots, Trade Ports, or Great Works.

TV Assembly Line

Cost: §100,000

Operational Cost: §750 per hour

Production Rate: 360,000 crates/day

Maximum Modules: 3

Description: How will people watch Action Team 5 on SimNews 5 at 11 without TVs? Create TVs from processors and plastic to sell on the global market. You can import plastic or processors from the global market if you need to.

Computer Assembly Line

Cost: §200,000

Operational Cost: §850 per hour

Production Rate: 360,000 crates/day

Maximum Modules: 3

Description: Sims around the world are desperate to play *SimCity*! Use processors and alloy to create computers to sell on the global market via a Trade Depot. You can import alloy or processors from the global market if you need to.

Managing the Electronics Specialization

Of all the city specializations, electronics is by far the most difficult and expensive to get underway, requiring long-term planning and multi-stage development with a heavy emphasis on education. Furthermore, gaining access to the required materials (plastic and alloy) can lead to a cumbersome and costly supply chain. But if you're willing to put in the time and effort, producing processors, TVs, and computers is very profitable, more than offsetting all the expenses your city has incurred by investing in education and supporting industries.

Education First

The Community College is the gateway to the electronics specialization, providing access to clean industry as well as a steady supply of skilled workers.

No matter how bad you want to start cranking out processors, TVs, and computers, you can't just jump into the electronics business from the start. Instead, you need to focus on building a city with a strong emphasis on education. Without a large educated workforce, your Processor and Consumer Electronics Factories will be worthless. Start off with a relatively balanced RCI city to ensure you have an adequate tax base to afford the various education buildings. Schools generate no income, making them a huge drain on your city's budget. If taxes aren't enough, consider turning to other city specializations such as metals or petroleum to help offset the expenses—alloy and plastic produced by these businesses will come in handy later too!

You'll need at least five clean industrial buildings before you can build the Processor Factory. Build a Community College and zone industrial around it to promote the growth of clean industry.

When you've unlocked the Community College, place it in an open area of your city or make room by bulldozing buildings. As students begin enrolling, zone industrial close to the Community College. Initially, dirty (tech level 1) factories will appear. However, as the education level increases, new clean (tech level 2) factories will appear, attracted by all the educated Sims flowing out of the nearby Community College—yes, proximity makes a difference. Once you have at least five clean industrial buildings, you can begin your electronics business with the Processor Factory. But never let up on education. If you can afford it, consider placing a University near your Processor and Consumer Electronics Factories to create even more highly educated workers. Once the University is up and running, consider bulldozing your Community College to save money. One University can supply your electronics buildings with all the educated workers they need. Now you can finally shift your attention to producing processors, TVs, and computers for export or use in a regional Great Works project.

Self-Sufficient Supply Chain

Consider spreading your city specializations across two or three connected cities and use gifting to supply your electronics city with the plastic and alloy it needs to produce processors, TVs, and computers.

Acquiring the plastic and alloy required to produce electronic products can be rather problematic, especially if you've selected a city site with no natural deposits of raw ore, coal, or crude oil. Sure, you can purchase alloy and plastic directly from the global market, but doing so is very expensive and may even be cost prohibitive depending on the current market prices. Therefore, if you're really intent on pursuing success in the electronics business, do your best to supply your own plastic and alloy—even producing one of these ingredients can make a big difference in your profit margins.

Planning for an electronics business should begin at the very start, before you even choose a city site. Look for a city site with an ample supply of raw ore, coal, and crude oil. City sites with all three natural resources may be difficult to find in an already crowded region, so consider creating a new game in a new region, giving you the first pick. Alternatively, spread production across two or three cities and then gift alloy and plastic to the city where you intend to start your electronics business—as long as you're the mayor of each city, you can easily manage the flow of resources free of charge. This is preferable to cramming metals, petroleum, and the electronics businesses into one city, while still trying to fulfill the education needs of your Processor and Consumer Electronics Factories. The pollution inherent to the metals and petroleum businesses aren't necessarily the best fit for your smarty pants education city anyway.

TIP

Don't forget about recycling. It's possible to get small amounts of plastic and alloy from a Recycling Center. Depending on output, the plastic and alloy produced may be enough to supply one Processor Factory. But you'll probably need to supplement the supply with imports from the global market, especially if you want to expand production and build a Consumer Electronics Factory.

Electronics: Points to Remember

→ Electronics factories convert simple resources into complex electronics.

→ Electronics can be sold to the global market or used in Great Works.

→ A Trade Depot or Trade Port is the only way to sell electronics.

→ Electronics require various materials (plastic, alloy, processors) to operate.

→ It's cheaper to create your own materials than to purchase them.

→ Local industry can ship resources to electronics factories.

CITY SPECIALIZATION ACHIEVEMENTS

Icon	Name	Criteria
	A Lot of Lots	Place 6 unique storage lot types on any Trade Depot or Trade Port.
	All Oiled Up	Pump 10,000 barrels of crude oil in a day.
	Blast Furnace	Smelt a total of 100 tons of metal.
	Dug Too Greedily and Too Deep (Secret)	Mine 100 tons of coal or raw ore in your city to gain access to the Earthquake disaster.
	Electrical Magic	Assemble 4,000 crates of processors in a day.
	King Coal	Extract a total of 100 tons of coal.

CITY SPECIALIZATION ACHIEVEMENTS

Icon	Name	Criteria
	Moving Pictures	Assemble 100 crates of TVs in one day in a single city.
	Refined Tastes	Refine 40 barrels of fuel and 40 crates of plastic in a single city in one hour.
	To Be, Ore Not To Be	Extract a total of 100 tons of raw ore.
	Specialist First Class	Select "Guide Me" for any city specialization.
	Trading Empire	Ship 250,000 Global Market export shipments.
	You Mean Business!	Plop every City Specialization HQ in the game.

CHAT WITH THE DEVELOPERS

How I Mayor: Trade City

JOHN SCOTT CLARKE, SOFTWARE ENGINEER

DAY ONE

My name is John Scott Clarke and I am a Software Engineer and JavaScript developer for the *SimCity* team. I thought it would be fun to share some thoughts about a city in a region I've been playing with my six-year-old daughter after work. It's been fun to play the game with her, though her sense of city design tends to leave out important things like building industries and commerce to create jobs and allow freight to be sold for profit. I'm happy she even wants to play, so I am not going to bore her trying to explain those needs. Instead, I decided that after she went to sleep I would just build a neighboring city that would be a heavy industry with no cares to pollution or its residents. That will help balance out her utopia of parks and trees which resulted in a glut of high-wealth houses and shops.

Unfortunately, the best spot for an industrial city on the region map was now taken by my daughter's city, so I settled with a neighboring spot with some coal and decided I would just trade for everything else I needed. There is also another neighboring city I have been using to test out various things, so it will also benefit nicely from an industrial city nearby.

First thing first, find the coal deposits using the Coal data map (they appear as black marks on the ground) and make sure I have major roads leading up to them for the coal mines. It's too early to start mining just yet; I have to build a town of some sort first so that I have workers, power, and water to support a mine. Workers also need shops, and shops need freight from industry, so I need to get all that rolling before I can plop a mine.

DAY TWO

Now that I have the Simoleons and infrastructure to support a mine, I go ahead and plop it. Too bad for those shops across the street—hope they don't mind the pollution! (Muahahahahah!!) The mine will start operating as soon as workers arrive, so I need to find something to do with all the coal the mine will produce. I could plop a Coal Power Plant, but I don't want to start paying for that just yet, so I decide to plop a Trade Depot instead. The Trade Depot gives me extra space to store coal and lets me trade it on the global market for additional income outside of taxes. I will be able to import and export other resources at the trade lot, too, but for now, all I care about is coal.

With the Trade Depot placed and trading on the global market, I turn my focus back to the Coal Mine and bump up the output on that by adding extra Coal Shafts. This will help to unlock the Metals Headquarters faster and boost income a bit via trade. I want the HQ so I can then unlock the Smelting Factory, which lets me create alloy and metal from coal and ore. Metals sell at higher prices than just coal, so it should be worth it to get a Smelting Factory up and running.

DAY THREE

While I wait for unlocks, I take the time to build more residential, commercial, and industrial to boost income from taxes while also adding new workers. Health is always a big problem in industry-based cities, so I place a Clinic as my first way to combat all the germs that the pollution is spreading. It's not going to solve my city's health problem, but since it's expandable with buildings (like the option to add more Ambulance Bays or Patient Rooms as needed) it does at least give me a way to relieve the pressure to help keep my residential zones from going completely abandoned.

DAY FOUR

Now I have the Metal and Trade HQs unlocked and placed. This will let me place my Smelting Factory and a Trade Port, which is an upgraded version of the Trade Depot. The Trade Port lets me import and export resources via both rail and water instead of just roads, which is going to allow me to

make a lot more money. I also set up both a bus system and a Passenger Train Station to help get commuting workers in and out of the city faster.

DAY FIVE

My industrial city is up and running. Its budget is suffering because I had to import ore to keep my Smelting Factories running (I sadly don't have any to mine in my own city), but otherwise the city is humming along nicely with some help from its neighbors. In turn, it's providing jobs and freight, as well as water, sewage, and garbage services to its neighbors. All those neighbors have also worked together to build one of our Great Works! Pretty impressive.

> First thing first, find the coal deposits using the Coal data map (they appear as black marks on the ground) and make sure I have major roads leading up to them for the coal mines. It's too early to start mining just yet; I have to build a town of some sort first so that I have workers, power, and water to support a mine.

Mass Transit

All the honking you hear outside isn't a show of support, Mayor.

Those blaring horns are the sound of frustrated motorists stuck in traffic jams. The road network has been adequately upgraded, yet gridlock is still a common occurrence, particularly during the morning and evening commutes. If we don't do something fast, the traffic problems could lead to complete paralysis, preventing Sims from getting to work and emergency vehicles from responding to fires, injuries, and crimes. It's time to turn to buses, streetcars, trains, boats, and planes to encourage alternative modes of transportation. Mass transit systems aren't cheap, but as the city increases in density, it's essential to keep Sims, freight, resources, and emergency vehicles moving. The more mass transit alternatives we provide, the fewer cars on the roads, significantly decreasing the likelihood of traffic jams. Let's start by providing buses first, then later we can expand our mass transit network to accommodate the city's growing population as well as the influx of commuters and tourists.

Don't forget to go to **www.primagames.com** to access guide updates free of charge with your voucher code.

Buses

The Bus Terminal dispatches high-capacity municipal buses ideal for transporting Sims throughout the city and region.

Is your city ready for mass transit? Buses are the most cost-effective method to transport Sims around your city and the connected region. Start with a Shuttle Bus Depot and a few Bus Stops, then expand service as necessary to increase ridership and promote a congestion-free city. While buses remove cars from the roads, the buses also rely on roads to get around. In extreme cases, buses may add to the very congestion you're trying to avoid. As your city increases in density, look for other transportation alternatives such as streetcars, otherwise your buses will get caught in traffic, leading to long waits at each Bus Stop, and making your bus network a less appealing option for Sims. Long waits and overcrowded buses can lead Sims to skipping work, potentially having a ripple effect on the city economy. So monitor the info tab within the Mass Transit menu to keep an eye on wait times and daily ridership. This information can help identify problems with your bus network. Add more buses to your system over time to decrease wait times and increase ridership.

Shuttle Bus Depot

Cost: Ş20,000

Operational Cost: Ş300 per hour

Buses: 3

Bus Capacity: 40 Sims

Prerequisites:

→ Town Hall

Description: Help your Sims get around the city! Shuttle buses stop here for low and medium wealth Sims.

At the first sign of congestion, plop a Shuttle Bus Depot and several Bus Stops to get some cars off the roads. The small shuttle buses dispatched from this depot can carry 40 Sims each—half the capacity of municipal buses from the Bus Terminal. Shuttle buses are local too, restricted to transporting Sims within the city limits. Still, the Shuttle Bus Depot is much more affordable, providing your city with the most economical approach to mass transit. As ridership increases, add additional Shuttle Bus Lot modules. In addition to increasing ridership, dispatching more shuttle buses will reduce the wait time at stops, ensuring Sims get where they need to go in a timely manner. The Shuttle Bus Depot itself does not function as a Bus Stop, so it doesn't really matter where you plop it. Consider placing it in a low-traffic area to prevent backups as all those shuttle buses enter and exit. When expanded to capacity, one depot can dispatch a total of 24 buses, carrying a total of 960 Sims at any given time. If wait times at Bus Stops are still long, consider adding an additional Shuttle Bus Depot or a Bus Terminal to accommodate more riders.

MODULES

Shuttle Bus Lot

Cost: Ş7,000

Operational Cost: Ş100 per hour

Buses: 3

Bus Capacity: 40 Sims

Maximum Modules: 8

Description: Expand your shuttle service! Provides parking for three shuttle buses.

Bus Stop

Cost: Ş200

Operational Cost: Ş10 per hour

Bus Stop Capacity: 125 Sims

Prerequisites:

→ Shuttle Bus Depot

→ OR Bus Terminal in region

Description: Wait for it...buses stop here for low and medium wealth Sims.

These stops function similar to the School Bus Stops available in the Education menu. However, the buses that stop here are only dispatched from a Shuttle Bus Depot or Bus Terminal—school buses from the Grade School or High School will simply drive past these stops. Bus Stops are available whenever you have a Shuttle Bus Depot or Bus Terminal—the Bus Terminal can be in your city or within a connected city in the region. Just as you did with your School Bus Stops, place these stops at regular intervals throughout your city. With each stop placed, the nearby street turns green, indicating the stop is within walking distance (approximately 400 meters or a five-minute walk) of the highlighted area. Place another stop where the green color in the road begins to fade, expanding bus service to a new area. Continue placing Bus Stops all over the city until most of your road network is green. But don't go overboard. Focus your Bus Stops in the most heavily populated areas. There's no need to place Bus Stops in wealthy neighborhoods, because wealthy Sims don't ride buses. But make sure all low and medium wealth buildings and job-generating buildings are near a Bus Stop. As ridership catches on, fewer and fewer cars will clog your streets. This is most noticeable during the morning and evening rush hour commutes.

Park and Ride

Cost: §400

Operational Cost: §30 per hour

Bus Stop Capacity: 80 Sims

Prerequisites:

→ Shuttle Bus Depot

→ OR Bus Terminal in region

Description: Municipal and shuttle buses stop here for low and medium wealth Sims. Commuters can park in the back before taking the bus.

The Park and Ride is essentially a Bus Stop with an attached parking lot. These come in handy when dealing with commuters traveling in and out of your city, transferring Sims from their cars onto buses. If you have Sims coming into your city for work or to shop, consider placing a few Park and Rides near your highway connection. This helps intercept cars early on before they clog your roads. The commuters leave their cars behind and then hop on a bus to reach their desired destination. If dealing with commuters leaving your city or traveling great distances within your city, consider placing Park and Rides within residential neighborhoods. This gives local Sims a chance to leave their car behind and board a bus to reach their job within the city or in a neighboring city. Like the Bus Stops, the Park and Ride serves buses from the Shuttle Bus Depot as well as from the Bus Terminal. Even if you have no buses dispatched from your city, you can still build a Park and Ride as long as a Bus Terminal exists in the

region. Watch as these large buses enter from the highway and make stops at each of your Bus Stops and Park and Rides. In such cases, you can let your neighbors incur the bulk of the mass transit expenses while you simply supply Bus Stops and Park and Rides for their buses to service.

Bus Terminal

Cost: §45,000

Operational Cost: §750 per hour

Buses: 3

Bus Capacity: 80 Sims

Prerequisites:

→ City Hall

→ Department of Transportation in region

Description: A terminal for larger municipal and regional buses. Low and medium wealth Sims can drive here before taking the bus. Municipal buses can pick up and drop off Sims inside the city as well as at neighboring cities with Bus Stops. Regional buses can drop off and pick up tourists here.

The Bus Terminal dispatches large 80-passenger municipal buses throughout the city and region, providing a significant improvement over the Shuttle Bus Depot when it comes to capacity and range. The Bus Terminal also offers a large parking garage, allowing commuters to park their car and take a bus to their destination—just like the Park and Ride. As a result, the Bus Terminal draws plenty of traffic as cars enter and exit the parking garage. Therefore, build the Bus Terminal along a Medium or High Density Avenue that isn't already impacted by traffic—the constant activity around the Bus Terminal can lead to sluggish traffic flow, potentially leading to the sort of gridlock you're trying to avoid. If you already have a number of existing Bus Stops and Park and Rides plopped throughout your city, there's no need to add extras—the municipal buses use the same stops as your shuttle buses. If you have any tourist attractions in your city, such as a casino or landmark, consider building the Bus Terminal nearby. Municipal buses from the region stop at the Bus Terminal to load and unload tourists, making it a cheap and efficient transportation hub when attempting to supplement your city's economy through tourism. As long as the Bus Terminal is close to an attraction, tourists can disembark and walk to nearby casinos, landmarks, parks, and shops. But a Bus Terminal alone won't solve all the congestion problems associated with tourism.

MODULES

Bus Terminal Sign

Cost: §200

Operational Cost: None

Maximum Modules: 1

Description: No, it's not a stop. You actually have to go inside!

Municipal Bus Garage

Cost: §15,000

Operational Cost: §250 per hour

Buses: 3

Bus Capacity: 80 Sims

Maximum Modules: 8

Description: Expand your bus fleet!

Streetcars

Buses: Points to Remember

→ Buses help solve traffic problems within the city by reducing the number of cars on the road.

→ Shuttle and municipal buses use the same Bus Stops.

→ Only low and medium wealth Sims use buses.

→ Municipal Buses also help bring more Sims in from outside your city—both commuters and tourists.

→ Buses provide a way for homeless to leave the city.

→ The Bus Terminal will transport Sims between cities.

→ Sims will walk 400 meters to a Bus Stop.

→ Commercial buildings like Bus Stops.

ⓘ NOTE

No vehicles in *SimCity*—including all cars, trucks, buses, trains, boats, and planes—generate pollution. Managing traffic flow in a dense city is challenging enough without having to worry about smog!

The Streetcar Depot must be placed next to a High Density Streetcar Avenue. Streetcar Stops can be added to the avenue's median.

Streetcars are the quintessential image that comes to mind when most Sims think of mass transit. These train-like vehicles travel along tracks embedded in avenues, carrying up to 200 Sims per streetcar. To start an efficient streetcar system you'll need a sizable network of High Density Streetcar Avenues as well as a Streetcar Depot. Sims board and disembark from streetcars at Streetcar Stops, placed along the median of the avenues. Once your streetcar system is up and running, monitor its efficiency within the info tab of the Mass Transit menu. Here you can see average wait times at stops as well as daily ridership. Try to keep wait times below 20 minutes to provide a reliable service Sims actually want to use. To decrease wait times at stops, add more streetcars through the construction of additional Streetcar Garages at the Streetcar Depot. Since stops have to be placed on High Density Streetcar Avenues, the efficiency of the system is also tied to the layout of these avenues. Unless you have a road network consisting entirely of High Density Streetcar Avenues, you'll need to carefully plan out the flow of traffic and look for opportunities to extend streetcar service into high density neighborhoods.

Streetcar Depot

Cost: §30,000

Operational Cost: §375 per hour

Streetcars: 3

Streetcar Capacity: 200 Sims

Prerequisites:

→ Town Hall

Description: Ding! Ding! This station provides the basis of a streetcar system in your city. Includes three streetcars, but you'll need to add Streetcar Stops for it to have anywhere to go. Must be placed on a High Density Streetcar Avenue.

If you want to see streetcars zipping up and down your avenues, you'll need a Streetcar Depot. This building houses and dispatches streetcars throughout your city. Before placing this depot, upgrade an existing avenue to a High Density Streetcar Avenue using the Road Selector tool in the Roads menu. Don't just upgrade any avenue. Look for areas of congestion where the addition of streetcars can help alleviate gridlock. Once you've upgraded at least one long stretch of the avenue, build the Streetcar Depot next to it—this depot must be adjacent to a High Density Streetcar Avenue so the streetcars can access the tracks running down the median. The stock Streetcar Depot comes with three streetcars, capable of transporting

200 Sims each. You can add more streetcars by building additional Streetcar Garage modules, each capable of housing and servicing two extra streetcars. In all, one Streetcar Depot can dispatch a total of 15 streetcars, capable of transporting as many as 3,000 Sims at any given time. If your streetcars are still filled to capacity, consider adding another Streetcar Depot to increase ridership and reduce wait times at stops.

MODULES

Streetcar Sign

Cost: §200

Operational Cost: None

Maximum Modules: 1

Description: It's a sign of things to come. Ha ha...what?

Streetcar Garage

Cost: §3,000

Operational Cost: §300 per hour

Streetcars: 6

Streetcar Capacity: 200 Sims

Maximum Modules: 1

Description: Is streetcar desire out of control in your city? Add another Streetcar Garage to prevent passengers from being left waiting at stops.

Streetcar Stop

Cost: §500

Operational Cost: §30 per hour

Streetcar Stop Capacity: 200 Sims

Prerequisites:

→ Streetcar Depot

Description: The best place for Sims to stop in the middle of the road! Placed on a High Density Streetcar Avenue, this stop allows Sims to get on and off streetcars.

These stops give Sims a place to wait for the next streetcar. Each streetcar in your system stops here to pick up and drop off Sims. You can plop these stops along the median of any High Density Streetcar Avenue connected to a Streetcar Depot. Just like Bus Stops, when you place a Streetcar Stop, the avenue is highlighted in green, with the green area representing the walking distance to the stop. Any Sim within this green area can easily walk to the stop before seeking another form of transportation. Add more Streetcar Stops to expand this green highlighted area, ensuring each Sim along the avenue is never too far away from a stop. Ideally it's best to provide streetcar coverage along the entire length of your High Density Streetcar Avenue. However, if money is tight, don't bother placing stops in high wealth neighborhoods—high wealth Sims do not ride streetcars. As ridership increases, these stops will become crowded and the wait times will increase. But instead of placing additional stops, build additional Streetcar Garages at the Streetcar Depot. This will increase the frequency in which streetcars arrive at each stop, increasing ridership and decreasing wait times.

 TIP

Streetcars give low and medium wealth Sims a traffic-easing way to get around your city.

High Density Streetcar Avenue

Cost: §12

Operational Cost: None

Number of Lanes: 6

Maximum Density Supported: High

Description: This wide six-lane road supports high density zones with traffic lights at intersections. Streetcar tracks running down the center provide support for Streetcar Stops.

This is the same avenue available in the Roads menu, included here for greater ease when creating your streetcar network. The avenue performs identically to the High Density Avenue, but the addition of streetcar tracks down the center median allows more Sims to share the road. Before you can take advantage of streetcars you must first construct a Streetcar Depot adjacent to this avenue. Streetcar stops can then be constructed along the avenue's median, giving Sims a place to board and disembark from the streetcar. As ridership increases, fewer and fewer cars appear on the avenue, reducing congestion.

Streetcar Tracks

Cost: §3

Operational Cost: None

Description: Two tracks for streetcars to travel along, useful for connecting sections of your city that do not share roads. Does not support Streetcar Stops.

These Streetcar Tracks are ideal for connecting two High Density Streetcar Avenues that never intersect. Just like roads, simply draw a line of tracks between the two avenues to make the connection. These tracks allow the streetcars to move along corridors not filled with cars, trucks, and other vehicles. However, streetcars still have to obey basic traffic rules when intersecting other roads, causing them to stop at intersections. When possible, set these tracks in areas where they don't intersect other roads, even if it means extending the tracks through undeveloped areas of your city. Your entire system will be much more efficient if the streetcars can avoid intersections. However, there's one down side to these tracks—you can't place Streetcar Stops on them. So even if the streetcar is traveling through a particular neighborhood, residents can't make use of it unless there's a stop located on a High Density Avenue.

> ✓ **TIP**
>
> Sims will walk approximately 200 meters when transferring from one form of mass transit to the next, so make sure you have Bus and Streetcar Stops near each of your major transportation hubs, like the Passenger Train Station, Ferry Terminal, and Municipal Airport. This allows Sims to hop off a train, ferry, or plane and immediately get on a bus or streetcar.

Streetcars: Points to Remember

→ Like buses, streetcars help alleviate traffic by giving low and medium wealth Sims new ways to get around your city.

→ Streetcars can carry more Sims than buses and have fewer issues with local traffic due to the dedicated streetcar tracks.

→ There are special avenues that streetcars run along. Streetcar Stops can only be added to these avenues.

→ You can also run dedicated Streetcar Tracks, but these do not support stops. Use these to connect separate avenues with Streetcar Tracks.

> ✓ **TIP**
>
> Streetcar Stops have to be placed on High Density Streetcar Avenues, not Streetcar Tracks.

Trains

Each train can carry as many as 400 Sims, so don't be surprised if a large crowd emerges from a Passenger Train Station.

While buses and streetcars are ideal for transportation within the city, trains address regional transit concerns by moving vast numbers of Sims between connected cities. To take advantage of trains, your city must have an existing rail line, usually located on the perimeter of the city site. Build a Passenger Train Station directly on the main rail line, or draw the rail system deeper into your city with the addition of Heavy Rail Tracks, creating a rail hub right next to your city's busiest attractions and shops. The Passenger

Train Station is only useful for commuters if neighboring cities also have a train station of their own. If not, the Passenger Train Station is worthless, requiring commuters to rely on other forms of transportation to reach their job in a neighboring city. Don't be surprised if floods of tourists arrive at your city's Passenger Train Station, looking for fun and excitement. For this reason, always make sure there's plenty to do around your Passenger Train Station—zoning commercial or plopping a casino or landmark nearby will keep those tourists busy!

> ⓘ **NOTE**
>
> The trains that arrive at a Passenger Train Station only carry passengers. If you want to ship resources and freight, build a Trade Depot and place a Freight Rail Terminal along a rail line. This will attract cargo trains, ideal for importing and exporting large volumes of resources and freight.

Passenger Train Station

Cost: §40,000

Operational Cost: §375 per hour

Train Capacity: 400 Sims

Prerequisites:

→ City Hall in region

→ Department of Transportation in region

Description: All aboard! Build this station along rail tracks to service trains from the region. Passenger trains bring commuters and shoppers from cities connected by train, plus low and medium wealth tourists from the region.

If your city has a rail connection, plop a Passenger Train Station along the tracks to serve as an alternative mode of transportation for commuters and tourists flowing in and out of your city. This station can be placed directly on the existing rail line running through your city, or you can branch off the main rail line using Heavy Rail Tracks, directing incoming trains to any point in your city. This is helpful when you want to plop a Passenger Train Station in a more central location, allowing riders to disembark and walk to nearby shops, attractions, and jobs. Once connected to the rail line, then you must connect the station to your road network. The road attached to the Passenger Train Station has two connection points—connect both ends to encourage better traffic flow in and out of the station's parking lot. If you have other forms of mass transit in your city, build a Bus Stop and Streetcar Stop in front of the train station to provide multiple forms of transportation to and from this central hub. Up to 400 Sims can arrive in your city per train, so you need to provide an efficient way to transport these Sims throughout the city. And if your city is drawing tourists from the station, make sure there's enough shops, parks, and other attractions nearby to hold their attention. It's best to keep tourists busy within walking distance of the station to prevent them from clogging the roads or your buses and streetcars.

MODULES

Train Station Sign

Cost: §200

Operational Cost: None

Maximum Modules: 1

Description: Danger, train crossing!

Heavy Rail Tracks

Cost: §6

Operational Cost: None

Prerequisites:

→ City Hall in region

→ Department of Transportation in region

Description: Tracks to connect the Passenger Train Station to the rail network or to connect up to a Freight Rail Terminal at a Trade Port.

In most cities with rail service, the tracks run along the perimeter of the city site, far from key attractions, shops, and industry. Therefore, placing a Passenger Train Station along these perimeter locations doesn't always make the most sense. Instead, use Heavy Rail Tracks to branch off the main rail line, drawing trains deeper into your city to service both the Passenger Rail Station and the Freight Rail Terminal at Trade Ports. Simply extend these tracks from the main rail line the same way you would draw a road. These rail tracks can intersect existing roads, but traffic only stops when a train is rolling through town—trains yield to no vehicles, moving directly from the main rail line to their destination without interruption. Once a train has reached its destination, it automatically switches directions and returns to the main rail line—there's no need to construct a circuit or loop circling back to the main line.

> **(i) NOTE**
>
> When attempting to construct tracks over steep terrain, remember that trains can only climb a 10-degree grade. Streetcars, on the other hand, can pull a maximum 35-degree grade.

Trains: Points to Remember

→ Trains carry both low and medium wealth commuter Sims between cities with Passenger Train Stations.

→ Trains run less frequently, but carry more passengers.

→ Trains allow factories to ship freight outside the city.

→ Trains will ship resources in and out of the global market through a Trade Port.

→ Through Trade Ports, trains can ship resources between cities.

→ Trains can also bring in passengers from the International Airport Great Work if connected.

Boats

The Ferry Terminal already comes equipped with one Passenger Ferry Dock, but no activity will occur at this dock until another Ferry Terminal is active in the city or region.

Boats take regional transportation to the next level, allowing massive ferries and cruise ships to dock at your city. Ferries are ideal for moving large volumes of workers between cities in the region connected by the same waterway. With the addition of a Cruise Ship Dock at a Ferry Terminal, medium and high wealth tourists will flood into your city looking for places to spend their Simoleons. But before plopping a Ferry Terminal, put some thought into how you want to develop the waterfront, as space is usually limited. Will the waterfront be used strictly for industrial imports and exports through a Trade Port equipped with a Cargo Ship Dock? Maybe you just want to use it as a commuter transportation hub, ferrying workers between cities? Or will the waterfront be a commercial center with numerous shops and attractions to lure medium and high wealth tourists arriving by cruise ships? Whatever your decision, making the most of your waterfront will take a lot of money, so consider leaving

> **(i) NOTE**
>
> Ferry Terminals can't be placed along a shoreline that is too steep (cliffs) or where water is not deep enough for boats to travel.

these areas undeveloped until you can properly invest in the infrastructure. By that time you'll have a better idea of how the waterfront should be utilized.

> **(i) NOTE**
>
> The boats that arrive at a Ferry Terminal only carry passengers. If you want to ship resources and freight, build a Trade Depot and place a Cargo Ship Dock along your waterfront. This will attract cargo ships, ideal for importing and exporting large volumes of resources and freight.

Ferry Terminal

Cost: §31,000

Operational Cost: §575 per hour

Ferry Capacity: 1,000 Sims

Prerequisites:

→ City Hall in region

→ Department of Transportation in region

Description: When placed along a shoreline, the Ferry Terminal provides a dock for commuters to travel by passenger ferry. Improve it by adding Cruise Ship Docks or additional Passenger Ferry Docks.

Is your city nestled along a picturesque shoreline or river? Then consider making use of that waterway to transport commuters and attract tourists by plopping a Ferry Terminal. The Ferry Terminal's location is restricted by your access to a natural waterfront. Place it directly on a waterfront location of your choice, then connect the terminal to your road network. Like the Passenger Train Station, the terminal has two road connections running directly in front of the facility. Connect both ends of the road to offer easy access to the terminal's parking lot. Initially the Ferry Terminal comes with one Passenger Ferry Dock, but can be expanded with one extra dock, including a Cruise Ship Dock—each terminal supports a maximum of two docks. If intending to use the Ferry Terminal as a hub for commuters, make sure a neighboring city also has a Ferry Terminal, otherwise the Passenger Ferry Dock will go unused. But if you're the only city in the region with a Ferry Terminal, you can still make use the of Cruise Ship Dock module. This allows medium and high wealth tourists to enter your city. Just make sure there's plenty for these picky tourists to do once they reach your city—zone high-end commercial around the Ferry Terminal and consider plopping a casino or landmark to boost the city's attraction rating. But don't expect all visitors to stay near the terminal. Place Bus and Streetcar Stops nearby to give visiting Sims a way to get around your city. These stops are also helpful for local Sims who want to reach the terminal without using a car.

MODULES

Ferry Terminal Sign

Cost: §200
Operational Cost: None
Maximum Modules: 1
Description: Caution: Very large boats.

 TIP

Trains and ferries are often used to move Sims between neighboring cities in the region. However, they can also be used to transport Sims within a city. If your city is divided by a river, use ferries to move Sims across the waterway, with Ferry Terminals on each riverbank, or place multiple Passenger Train Stations throughout the city and rapidly transport Sims across town.

Passenger Ferry Dock

Cost: §6,000
Operational Cost: §200 per hour
Ferry Capacity: 1,000 Sims
Maximum Modules: 2
Description: Dock for a passenger ferry to bring low and medium wealth workers from other cities in the region connected by water.

Cruise Ship Dock

Cost: §10,000
Operational Cost: §375 per hour
Ferry Capacity: 2,000 Sims
Maximum Modules: 2
Description: Anyone for a game of shuffleboard? Allows cruise ships to dock, bringing medium and high wealth tourists in from the region.

Boats: Points to Remember

- Ferries deliver large amounts of medium and high wealth Sims, both commuters and tourists.
- Ferries arrive less frequently than planes or trains, but carry many more Sims.
- The Ferry Terminal must be placed along a shoreline.
- Ferries can only send commuters between cities equipped with Ferry Terminals.
- Tourists from the region can always arrive at your Ferry Terminal.

Planes

Those Sims living in the apartment building next to the Municipal Airport probably won't be too happy with the frequent air traffic, but local industry will love that Cargo Terminal.

What self-respecting city would be complete without its own airport? The addition of a Municipal Airport opens your city to new opportunities, drawing medium and high wealth commuters and tourists while offering local industry the chance to export their freight by air. Helicopters associated with the Police Precinct, Large Fire Station, and Mayor's Mansion also require a Municipal Airport to operate, extending city services into the skies. Although the planes operating out of an airport carry fewer passengers and tourists than trains, ferries, and cruise ships, planes arrive with greater frequency, particularly as you expand the facility with additional Runways. This keeps the commuters and tourists flowing in and out of your city at a steady rate. But remember, if relying on a Municipal Airport as a commuter hub, make sure other cities in the region also have their own airports, otherwise medium and high wealth workers must rely on other forms of transportation to commute to and from work.

 TIP

Residents do not like living next to the Municipal Airport.

Municipal Airport

Cost: §85,000

Operational Cost: §500 per hour

Terminal Capacity: 200 Sims

Prerequisites:

→ City Hall in region

→ Department of Transportation in region

Description: Fly medium wealth tourists to your city on small passenger planes. Upgrade the airport for high wealth tourists and greater capacity or to ship cargo. Residents do not want to live near an airport, but airports boost the happiness of nearby factories.

Sims have a love/hate relationship with the Municipal Airport—nobody wants to live next to it, but they appreciate its ability to bring in tourists and export freight. If you're interested in air transportation, be prepared to set aside a large parcel of land to accommodate this sprawling facility—particularly if you plan to add more Runway modules. When possible, keep it far away from residential and commercial areas. Instead, consider placing it among your industrial zones. Factories love having an airport in the city because it allows them to export freight by air with the addition of a Cargo Terminal module—this works just like the Freight Shipping Warehouse at the Trade Depot and Trade Port. If your city has plenty of factories, make sure you place a Cargo Terminal early on to boost industrial profits. If you're more interested in attracting medium and high wealth tourists, build a Passenger Terminal and watch as commercial and private jets fly into your city to sample the local shops and attractions. As air traffic increases, so will the wait time for incoming and outgoing passengers. The addition of a new Runway or two allows the airport to accommodate more aircraft, resulting in fewer delays and less frustration on the ground. As with any mass transit hub, build Bus and Streetcar Stops next to the Municipal Airport—at least the medium wealth tourists will enjoy the opportunity to travel into your city by other means than cars or taxis.

MODULES

Municipal Airport Sign

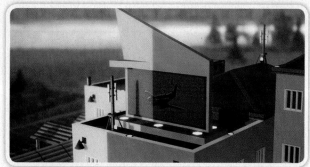

Cost: §200

Operational Cost: None

Maximum Modules: 1

Description: Has a very long list of items not allowed on board.

Cargo Terminal

Cost: §8,000

Operational Cost: §300 per hour

Maximum Modules: 4

Description: Send your city's industrial freight shipments out on cargo planes.

Passenger Terminal

Cost: §8,500

Operational Cost: §350 per hour

Maximum Modules: 4

Description: Increase your airport's capacity from rinky-dink to something more respectable. Allows private jet flights of high wealth tourists and large passenger planes filled with medium wealth tourists.

Runway

Cost: §15,000

Operational Cost: §250 per hour

Terminal Capacity: 200 Sims

Maximum Modules: 4

Description: Add an additional runway to increase the frequency of flights carrying passengers or cargo.

Planes: Points to Remember

→ Planes deliver small amounts of medium and high wealth commuters and tourists at a high frequency.

→ Add a Cargo Terminal to a Municipal Airport to ship industrial freight, making your local industry much happier.

→ You need a Municipal Airport in your city to get access to emergency services helicopters.

Mass Transit Management

Creating an efficient mass transit system can be challenging and expensive. To avoid costly modifications to your city later on, plan for mass transit at the outset. While buses can use existing roads, streetcars require avenues—it's easier to build all the avenues your city will need early on than to add them later. Make note of access to rail and waterways and determine the best way to incorporate a Passenger Train Station and Ferry Terminal into your master plan. If you feel air travel is important, set aside land for a Municipal Airport far from residential and commercial areas. Here's a few more pointers to take under consideration while establishing your mass transit network.

Gradual Expansion

Gridlock has taken hold along this avenue. Upgrade it to a High Density Streetcar Avenue and build a Streetcar Depot nearby to alleviate congestion along this thoroughfare.

None of the mass transit solutions are cheap, so it's wise to take a gradual approach, meeting demand as it arises. It's wise to begin with buses—they're relatively cheap and you can adjust their service areas with the addition of Bus Stops. But even your bus network will eventually become overburdened, requiring you to either fill your streets with more buses or turn to other forms of transportation. Choose streetcars next and upgrade your existing avenues to High Density Streetcar Avenues. Streetcars carry many more Sims than buses, but they're limited to traveling along avenues. As a result, it may be time to replace some of those old, congested streets with avenues so they can support streetcars. This means bulldozing the streets, along with any adjoining buildings, before laying down a new avenue. If your city is seeing a large number of commuters and tourists flowing in and out of your city, rely on trains, boats, and planes to encourage mass transit throughout the region. But neighboring cities must buy into mass transit too for this to work effectively. Communicate with other mayors in the region to ensure they have the proper infrastructure in place to accept or send commuters traveling by train,

boat, or plane. If not, your Passenger Train Station, Ferry Terminal, and Municipal Airport will be little more than tourist hubs while commuters continue to enter and exit the city via car or municipal bus, doing little to address traffic jams in your city.

Overlapping Networks

Give Sims as many transportation options as your city can afford. The University is a high-traffic destination, so place both Bus and Streetcar Stops next to it.

Put some thought into how each Sim gets around your city and construct a network of overlapping mass transit options to help all Sims reach their desired destination, whether it's in the city or region. To better understand the flow of commuters, it's helpful to click on a Sim and follow that Sim throughout a daily commute. Did the Sim drive to work? If so, why? Sims usually only drive to places they can't reach on foot or by mass transit. If any low or medium wealth Sim is driving a car, view it as a potential failure of your mass transit system and work to correct the problem. Is there a Bus or Streetcar Stop near their residence and job? Or maybe the buses and streetcars servicing nearby stops were full? If this is the case, expand service with additional stops, buses, and streetcars. In the case of regional commuters or tourists, you need to plan for local transportation options at regional hubs like the Bus Terminal, Passenger Train Station, Ferry Terminal, and Municipal Airport. Once commuters and tourists are in your city, how will they get around? Place Bus and Streetcar Stops near each of these hubs to give commuters and tourists a way to transfer from one form of mass transit to another. Overall, mass transit is all about providing Sims with multiple options to reach their destination. Each layer of mass transit you apply gives them a more compelling reason to leave their car at home.

Wealth and Mass Transit

The high wealth Sims living in these mansions won't use mass transit. To save money, don't bother placing Bus or Streetcar Stops here.

Unfortunately, you can't get everyone to utilize your clean, efficient mass transit system. High wealth Sims turn their noses up at buses, streetcars, trains, and ferries—but they will travel by private jet and cruise ships when arriving in your city as tourists. When it comes to getting around your city, high wealth Sims drive almost everywhere—they'll walk too, but only if their destination is within 400 meters of their current location. Keep this in mind when zoning residential in areas with high land value. There's no need to extend bus or streetcar services to such exclusive neighborhoods because the residents won't use them. Even when it comes to commuting, high wealth Sims would rather drive to a neighboring city than mix with lower wealth Sims on municipal buses, trains, or ferries. Fortunately, high wealth Sims usually only make up a fraction of your city's total population. As long as your low and medium wealth Sims use mass transit, your road network should be able to handle the minimal traffic generated by high wealth Sims driving around in their fancy cars.

Tourism

Use a Passenger Train Station as the regional transportation hub for tourist districts like this one. This will cut down on the number of taxis clogging your city's road network and highway connection.

Think twice before building a casino or landmark. Tourism is the ultimate test of your mass transit network. If you draw tourists into your city before a robust network is established, you run the risk of crippling your road system as entertainment-hungry and shop-starved tourists clog streets and avenues, arriving by car and taxi from the highway. To minimize tourists arriving from the highway, center tourist districts around a regional transportation hub such as a Bus Terminal, Passenger Train Station, Ferry Terminal, or Municipal Airport. All of these buildings are capable of bringing in large numbers of low and medium wealth tourists, supplying nearby shops, hotels, casinos, and landmarks with plenty of customers. The Municipal Airport's Passenger Terminal and the Cruise Ship Dock at the Ferry Terminal attract high wealth tourists, ideal for filling glitzy high-end casinos and luxury shops. By keeping all tourist activity centered around a regional transportation hub, you can minimize the need for additional mass transit as tourists can easily walk to nearby attractions. This also cuts down on cars and taxis arriving from the highway, allowing the self-contained tourist district to thrive on its own without impacting traffic in other areas of the city. Still, extend bus and streetcar service to your tourist district so local Sims can get to work at the attractions serving the tourists.

MASS TRANSIT ACHIEVEMENTS		
Icon	Name	Criteria
	A Streetcar Named SimCity	Have 1,000 Sims travel by streetcar in a day.
	All Aboard!	Have 1,000 Sims take the train in a day.
	Cruisin' Along	Have 2,000 Sims take a cruise in a day.
	Llamahound	Have a municipal bus from a neighbor make 100 trips into your city within a year.
	What Goes Up Must Come Down (Secret)	Have 200 tourists arrive on flights at the Municipal Airport in a day to gain access to the Meteor Strike disaster.

CHAT WITH THE DEVELOPERS

Owning the Streets of *SimCity*

GUILLAUME PIERRE, LEAD GAMEPLAY SCRIPTER

Hello *SimCity* fans! I'm Guillaume Pierre, Lead Gameplay Scripter on *SimCity*. My team and I build the game's simulation using the GlassBox Engine. Here I'm going to talk about something dear to my and transportation geeks' hearts: mass transit!

When left unchecked, cars will quickly take over city streets, resulting in massive traffic jams and the economic loop coming to a stop. Your Sims won't be able to get to work on time, robbers will get away as police cars get stuck, and trash will mount as garbage trucks can't make their rounds anymore! To solve your traffic problem in *SimCity*, we're providing a variety of public transportation options, starting with the shuttle buses and going all the way to the heavy rail trains and beyond.

Shuttle buses are the cheapest and easiest mass transit system to set up. These small buses carry a limited number of passengers and are appropriate for smaller cities. To set

some up, you just need to place a Shuttle Bus Depot, plop some stops on the sidewalks of your residential, business, and factory districts, and Sims will start riding the shuttle. At some point, you may invest in the larger municipal buses by building a Bus Terminal, and Sims will queue up at the same stops as they did before to ride them. You can also plop some Park and Ride stops that Sims will drive to and park their cars at before taking the bus.

In this *SimCity*, we're also introducing streetcars, which ride on a dedicated track in the middle of avenues, and carry more Sims than the shuttle or municipal buses. You can also connect two separate parts of town with rail tracks placed by themselves, without car lanes or sidewalks.

Some of the biggest vehicles going through your cities are trains, which come from the region and bring in tourists and neighbors into your city, more so than could ever drive in from the regional highway. Your Sims may even ride

> To solve your traffic problem in *SimCity,* we're providing a variety of public transportation options, starting with the shuttle buses and going all the way to the heavy rail trains and beyond.

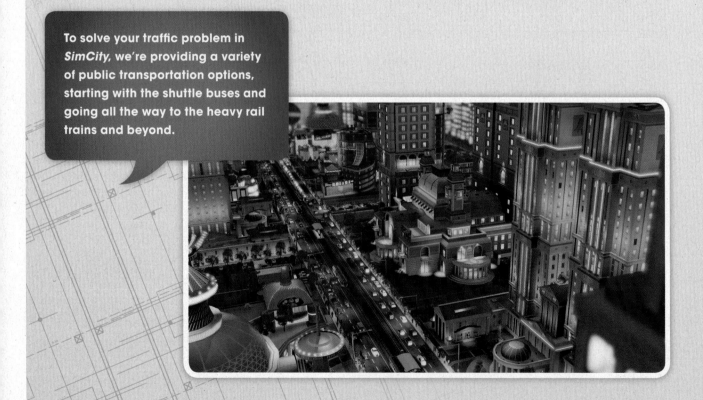

the train between two stations on opposite sides of town, or use them to go to neighboring cities. Rail is by far my favorite mode of transit; it really makes the city feels like a model train set.

Much like in real life, people will only walk so far to take public transportation, so when placing public transportation stops, we show you that distance as a green bar directly on the sidewalks via a data layer. As a result, you can easily tell which neighborhoods are accessible, and which ones Sims will have to drive out of. Each stop is responsible for figuring out what kind of destination exists near it, be it a work place, a home, or even another stop that may lead Sims to their eventual destination. Your Sims may very well start their journey aboard a local shuttle bus, then transfer to a streetcar, and eventually to a train in order to work at the factory town next door.

You evaluate the performance of their systems by checking:

1. How many people are waiting to be picked up.
2. How long they have to wait on average.
3. How many passengers are currently riding in vehicles.
4. How many have been dropped off that day.

Each stop has similar information available, so it's possible to really drill down on the data and make decisions on whether to add more vehicles or turn off infrequently used stops.

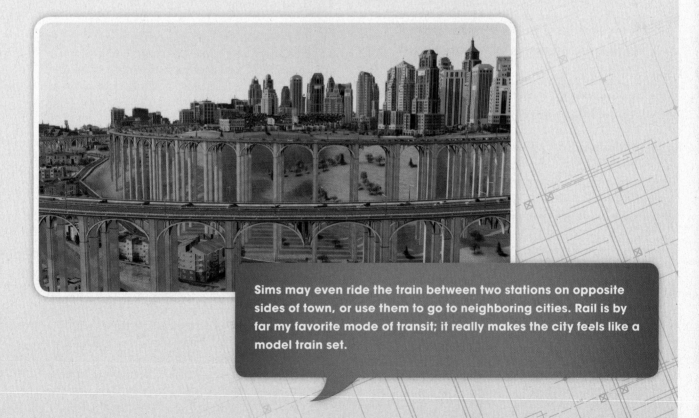

Sims may even ride the train between two stations on opposite sides of town, or use them to go to neighboring cities. Rail is by far my favorite mode of transit; it really makes the city feels like a model train set.

Tourism

Now that you have a mass transit system running, why not put it to the test?

Anyway, after all that work, it's time to have some fun—the Sims will surely appreciate more entertainment options. Build a casino, stadium, or landmark and watch as tourists rush into your city, eager to spend their money at local attractions and shops. As more and more tourists flood into the city, prepare for an increase in congestion along the highway and at regional transportation hubs. If you're relying on casinos to draw in tourists, be ready to counter a rise in crime too. But as long as you address traffic and crime problems before they get out of hand, you'll be well on your way to nurturing a successful tourist industry. Now, where did I put my camera?

Don't forget to go to **www.primagames.com** to access guide updates free of charge with your voucher code.

Tourist Flow

To better understand how tourism works, study the accompanying diagram illustrating how tourists flow in and out of your city. Every city has an attraction rating for each wealth class. This rating is based on commercial buildings, parks, and certain buildings such as casinos, stadiums, and landmarks. The higher the attraction rating, the more tourists. Not every tourist that wants to visit your city can make it there, so you need to provide sufficient transportation infrastructure to get them into your city. This is why mass transit is so important. Low wealth tourists enter your city by train, bus, car, or taxi. Medium wealth tourists arrive the same way, but also have the option of taking a cruise ship. High wealth tourists only arrive by cruise ship or plane.

Once in your city, tourists will look for places to spend their money. At first, low and medium wealth tourists are the most common. But as you upgrade attractions, you may lure some high wealth tourists as well. Each day a tourist attempts to spend money at shops or buildings catering to their class. Low wealth tourists will seek out low wealth establishments to spend their money while medium and high wealth tourists look for class-appropriate establishments to spend their Simoleons. This is why it's important to provide a wide mix of shops and attractions in your tourist districts, so there's something for everyone.

TOURISTS FROM REGION

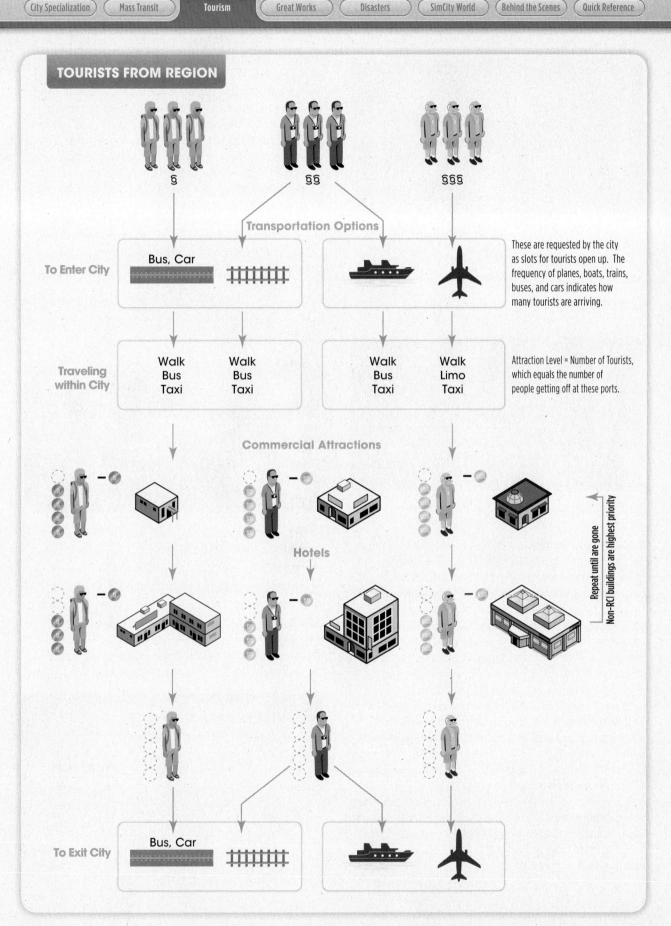

To Enter City

Bus, Car

These are requested by the city as slots for tourists open up. The frequency of planes, boats, trains, buses, and cars indicates how many tourists are arriving.

Transportation Options

Traveling within City

| Walk Bus Taxi | Walk Bus Taxi | Walk Bus Taxi | Walk Limo Taxi |

Attraction Level = Number of Tourists, which equals the number of people getting off at these ports.

Commercial Attractions

Hotels

Repeat until are gone
Non-RCI buildings are highest priority

To Exit City

Bus, Car

Casinos are a great way to lure tourists into your city. Just be ready to deal with an increase in crime.

After successfully spending money at a shop or other attraction, tourists look for a hotel to rest. Like shops, tourists will only stay at a hotel serving their class. If you have casinos in your city, you can attach hotel room modules, each catering to a different class of tourist. Hotels will also spring up in commercial zones near attractions. Use parks to adjust the land value to encourage the appearance of medium and high wealth hotels. If there are no hotels or no vacancies at hotels, the tourists will leave your city, with Simoleons still jingling in their pockets, so provide as many hotels as necessary to keep tourists in your city as long as possible. The goal is to keep tourists in your city until they've depleted all their money, at which point they will leave choosing from class-appropriate transportation options.

Gambling

A bit kitschy perhaps, but the Sci-Fi Casino is a hit with low and medium wealth tourists, as indicated by all those taxi cabs.

Nothing draws tourists into your city faster than a casino. Tourists love the thrill of wagering their Simoleons on games they have little chance of winning. But casinos offer more than just slot machines and blackjack tables—they also provide lodging and entertainment. Hotel rooms attached to casinos keep tourists in your city overnight, increasing the chance they'll spend money at the casino or a nearby shop the next day. Entertainment venues draw more tourists into the casino as well as increase your city's overall attraction rating, leading to even larger crowds of tourists rushing into your city. But casinos have some serious drawbacks too, namely crime and congestion. It's important to establish a comprehensive mass transit system to keep traffic flowing and a robust police presence to prevent throngs of criminals from running amok. These critical pieces of infrastructure aren't cheap, and should not be considered as an afterthought. Instead, if you're serious about getting into the gambling business, you need to start small, attracting tourists only when your city is ready to accommodate large numbers of visitors and confront an influx of devious criminals.

Gambling House

Cost: §15,000

Operational Cost: §260 per hour

Prerequisites:

→ Working water and power

→ 21 commercial buildings

Description: Tourists will wheel their oxygen tanks to this simple casino to blow their hard-earned Simoleons. Maximize profits with Gambling House improvements. Criminals turn up at casinos like bad pennies.

CAPACITY AND INCOME		
Wealth	**Tourist Capacity**	**Hourly Income**
Low	100	§10 per gambler
Medium	50	§14 per gambler
High	—	—

The Gambling House is your average entry-level casino catering to low and medium wealth tourists. But before building it, work out any kinks in your road network because the Gambling Hall will draw tons of tourists. To reduce congestion, consider plopping this casino next to a Bus Terminal, allowing tourists to enter your city by municipal bus and walk to the Gambling House and its modules. Also, don't turn a blind eye to the criminal element generated here. If you don't have a Police Station or Police Precinct nearby, set one close to the Gambling House to suppress crime in the area. Be sure to zone plenty of commercial nearby to ensure tourists have plenty of places to spend their money, even if they can't get in the casino—low wealth motels will spring up from commercial zones around the Gambling House, giving tourists a place to spend the night.

It may be necessary to build a few Gambling Halls to accommodate all the tourists. Pay close attention to the modules you attach, because each caters to a specific tourist. Consider building two separate Gambling Houses, one that caters to low wealth and another for medium wealth tourists. In your low wealth Gambling House, plop Cheap Rooms, Nickel Slots, and a Comedy Club. For your medium wealth Gambling House choose Nice Rooms, Blackjack Tables, and a Lounge. The modules attracting medium wealth tourists have a smaller capacity, but generate more money per tourist than the low wealth modules.

MODULES

Casino Marquees

Cost: §1,000

Operational Cost: §50 per hour

Maximum Tourists per day: 25

Maximum Modules: 1

Description: Like moths to a flame, tourists will flit on in to your casino. Increases casino tourist attraction with one of these marquees.

Cheap Rooms

Cost: §3,500

Operational Cost: §115 per hour

Low Wealth Rooms: 60

Maximum Modules: 4

Description: No-frills lodging for less than discerning tourists. Tourists will stay in lodging to spend any remaining Simoleons in the casino the next day.

Nice Rooms

Cost: §4,000

Operational Cost: §135 per hour

Medium Wealth Rooms: 30

Maximum Modules: 4

Description: These rooms aren't great, but at least they're "nice". Tourists will stay in lodging to spend any remaining Simoleons in the casino the next day.

Nickel Slots

Cost: §4,500

Operational Cost: §40 per hour

Low Wealth Gambler Capacity: 45

Maximum Modules: 4

Description: It's just a nickel at a time. How fast could that add up?

Blackjack Tables

Cost: §5,500

Operational Cost: §75 per hour

Medium Wealth Gambler Capacity: 30

Maximum Modules: 4

Description: Your casino won't bust if you get enough tourists into the casino. Try for at least 21...

Comedy Club

Cost: §4,000

Operational Cost: §75 per hour

Low Wealth Gambler Capacity: 45

Maximum Tourists per day: 25

Maximum Modules: 4

Description: The Laughs Per Minute (LPM) are low, but any distraction from how much money Sims are losing at the slots is welcome.

 TIP

Casinos, cultural buildings, parks, and shops provide tourist attraction.

Lounge

Cost: §4,000

Operational Cost: §225 per hour

Medium Wealth Gambler Capacity: 45

Maximum Tourists per day: 25

Maximum Modules: 4

Description: Now Featuring! Fernando and Don! Magic Motion! Tony T.! Weak drinks and lounge acts serve as a tourism draw.

Gambling HQ

Cost: §37,500

Operational Cost: §450 per hour

Prerequisites:

→ Working water and power

→ §50,000 casino revenue in a day

Description: The lights! The glitz! The glamor! Rake in the Simoleons from your casinos—just look out for criminal activity. Use the success of your casinos to gain improvements to your casinos' entertainment, lodging, or gaming. Upgrades available based on casino daily profits.

GAMBLING HQ UPGRADES

Level	Name	Criteria	Unlock
1	Gambling HQ	Earn §50,000 in a day from gambling.	One division of your choice.
2	Gambling, Co.	Earn §100,000 casino daily profit.	One division of your choice.
3	Gambling, Inc.	Earn §400,000 casino daily profit.	One division of your choice.
4	Gambling Global	Earn §1,000,000 casino daily profit.	One division of your choice.

After running a successful Gambling House or two, you'll be rewarded with access to the Gambling HQ. This HQ is required before you can build any of the other casinos in the Gambling menu. Just be sure to leave enough space around the HQ to accommodate its three divisions. As your casinos generate more profit, the HQ can be upgraded, causing the building to expand skyward. With each upgrade awarded, you can place a division of your choice nearby. Which division you choose largely depends on your current needs and goals. The Entertainment Division is required to set a variety of non-gambling venues used to attract more tourists into the city and casinos—so if business is slumping, put on a show to bring the crowds back in. The Gaming Division gives your casinos access to more gambling modules (poker, craps, and roulette), ideal for boosting business from medium and high wealth tourists. If you don't have enough hotels in your city, tourists will go home, taking their Simoleons with them. The Lodging Division helps address this problem by allowing the construction of hotel rooms at each casino, catering to medium and high wealth tourists. If you're serious about gambling, you'll eventually want all of these divisions. But for starters, the Lodging Division makes the most sense, with the aim of keeping tourists in your city as long as possible. Lodging offered at casinos also helps surrounding shops—the longer a tourist stays in your city, the more likely they'll visit surrounding commercial buildings, boosting the buildings' profits and the city's tax revenue.

MODULES

Gambling HQ Sign

Cost: §200

Operational Cost: None

Maximum Modules: 1

Description: Assure the city that this is a totally legitimate business establishment.

Entertainment Division

Cost: §20,000

Operational Cost: §400 per hour

Local Access Granted: Celebrity Stage, Disco Club, and Exclusive Club

Maximum Modules: 1

Description: Tourists are more attracted to casinos that provide entertainment.

Gaming Division

Cost: §20,000

Operational Cost: §400 per hour

Local Access Granted: Poker Parlor, Craps Parlor, and Roulette House

Maximum Modules: 1

Description: Enables new gaming modules that favor the house even more, providing more income per gambler.

Lodging Division

Cost: §20,000

Operational Cost: §400 per hour

Local Access Granted: Tower Rooms, Classy Rooms, Penthouse, and Penthouse Suite

Maximum Modules: 1

Description: With lodging in the casino, your gamblers can stay until they spend all their hard-earned money.

Sleek Casino

Cost: §140,000

Operational Cost: §1,500 per hour

Prerequisites:

→ Gambling HQ

Description: Glass and steel highlight the sweeping lines of this modern casino. Attracts medium wealth tourists.

CAPACITY AND INCOME		
Wealth	**Tourist Capacity**	**Hourly Income**
Low	100	§10 per gambler
Medium	200	§20 per gambler
High	100	§40 per gambler

The Sleek Casino offers plenty of lodging and gambling options for tourists of each economic strata. But you'll need to keep this casino packed with tourists to overcome its staggering hourly operational cost—so don't plop it until you have a thriving tourist industry underway. In its stock state, the casino can accommodate a total of 400 tourists, offering enough to do for visitors of every class. However, you'll need to add a Lodging Division at the Gambling HQ to provide rooms for these tourists to stick around. With a Lodging Division in place you can build the ground and tower-based Sleek Rooms, as well as a Penthouse for high wealth visitors. Gambling options can be expanded too with the Gambling Division, increasing low and medium wealth capacity with the Poker Parlor and Craps Parlor modules. As with any casino or landmark, make sure your mass transit system is up to the challenge. For best results, build the Sleek Casino within walking distance of a Passenger Train Station or Ferry Terminal. Provide bus and streetcar stops as well to provide tourists multiple transportation options. Oh, and don't forget the criminals. A Police Precinct will help suppress and, when necessary, arrest the endless flow of criminals produced by this casino.

MODULES

Flashy Casino Sign

Cost: §4,000

Operational Cost: §100 per hour

Maximum Tourists per day: 50

Maximum Modules: 1

Description: With this flashy sign on top of your casino, Sims from all over will seek your Sleek Casino!

Casino Marquee

Cost: §5,000

Operational Cost: §1,000 per hour

Maximum Tourists per day: 100

Maximum Modules: 1

Description: Don't be a square! Get this sleek, modern marquee sign and show the world you have style!

Sleek Rooms (Ground Floor)

Cost: §7,000

Operational Cost: §560 per hour

Low Wealth Rooms: 120

Maximum Modules: 4

Prerequisites:

→ Lodging Division at Gambling HQ

Description: Entice your gambling tourists to stay in your Sleek Casino. These rooms are close to the ground for quick access to the casino. Tourists will stay in lodging to spend any remaining Simoleons in the casino the next day.

> **ⓘ NOTE**
>
> If tourists can't find lodging in a casino, hotels will appear in nearby commercial zones, giving visitors the option to stay in your city overnight.

Sleek Rooms (Tower)

Cost: §9,000

Operational Cost: §560 per hour

Medium Wealth Rooms: 60

Maximum Modules: 4

Prerequisites:

→ Lodging Division at Gambling HQ

Description: Trap, er, host your gamblers in this shiny tower. Tourists will stay in lodging to spend any remaining Simoleons in the casino the next day.

Penthouse

Cost: §9,000

Operational Cost: §850 per hour

High Wealth Rooms: 40

Maximum Modules: 4

Prerequisites:

→ Lodging Division at Gambling HQ

Description: This exclusive penthouse suite is a block of rooms that can only be built on top of other rooms.

Poker Parlor

Cost: §10,000

Operational Cost: §675 per hour

Low Wealth Gambler Capacity: 180

Maximum Modules: 4

Prerequisites:

→ Gaming Division at Gambling HQ

Description: If you can get a full house to play in your poker games, you'll be flush with cash!

Craps Parlor

Cost: §15,000

Operational Cost: §900 per hour

Medium Wealth Gambler Capacity: 120

Maximum Modules: 4

Prerequisites:

→ Gaming Division at Gambling HQ

Description: Roll the hard six! Craps is a cheap game to maintain and makes your casino even more money.

> **✓ TIP**
>
> If tourists don't spend all their Simoleons in one day, they'll stay at nearby hotels.

Sci-Fi Casino

Cost: §120,000

Operational Cost: §1,125 per hour

Prerequisites:

→ Gambling HQ

Description: Take me to your dealer! Land your shuttlecraft at the rear docking bay of this medium wealth sci-fi-themed casino. Watch out for unsavory characters around the casino.

CAPACITY AND INCOME		
Wealth	**Tourist Capacity**	**Hourly Income**
Low	200	§10 per gambler
Medium	200	§20 per gambler
High	—	—

It may not be the lavish high-roller casino you're hoping for, but the Sci-Fi Casino is a step in the right direction. Consider adding it to your tourism district soon after building the Gambling HQ. Like the Gambling House, this casino only serves low and medium wealth tourists. Since those tourist are most likely already wandering around your city, this casino is the perfect fit. It's also much cheaper to run than the Sleek and Elegant Casinos. With the Lodging Division in place at the Gambling HQ, you can add a number of sci-fi-themed hotel rooms—medium wealth tourists get the Penthouse here! The Sci-Fi Casino also offers a few attractions for non-gamblers, helping draw more tourists. Build the Entertainment Division at the Gambling HQ to gain access to the Disco Club and Celebrity Stage. These modules will help pack the casino floor and hotel rooms with more tourists, boosting the casino's profits in the process. As with any tourist attraction, don't build the Sci-Fi Casino until you have the proper infrastructure in place, including mass transit and a robust police force. For best results, plop it between a Passenger Train Station and Police Precinct. This will help the casino draw plenty of foot traffic from the train station while the police presence suppresses crime.

MODULES

Holo Sign

Cost: §3,000

Operational Cost: §100 per hour

Maximum Tourists per day: 50

Maximum Modules: 1

Description: Draw earthlings to your Sci-Fi Casino with this holographic sign!

Casino Marquee

Cost: §3,000

Operational Cost: §100 per hour

Maximum Tourists per day: 50

Maximum Modules: 1

Description: Attract gambling humans to your Sci-Fi Casino with this imposing sign.

Rocket Rooms (Ground Floor)

Cost: §7,000

Operational Cost: §340 per hour

Low Wealth Rooms: 120

Maximum Modules: 4

Prerequisites:

→ Lodging Division at Gambling HQ

Description: This casino hotel launchpad features an umbilical tube to allow easy reentry to your Sci-Fi Casino.

Rocket Rooms (Tower)

Cost: §7,000

Operational Cost: §340 per hour

Low Wealth Rooms: 120

Maximum Modules: 4

Prerequisites:

→ Lodging Division at Gambling HQ

Description: Extend your hotel tower rocket and achieve maximum lodger capacity!

 TIP

If you're going to build a high-wealth casino, make sure that you can attract high-wealth tourists!

Penthouse

Cost: §10,000

Operational Cost: §500 per hour

Medium Wealth Rooms: 60

Maximum Modules: 4

Prerequisites:

→ Lodging Division at Gambling HQ

Description: This penthouse allows rich Sims to live like they are the captain of their very own rocket ship.

Disco Club

Cost: §45,000

Operational Cost: §375 per hour

Low Wealth Gambler Capacity: 180

Maximum Tourists per Day: 50

Maximum Modules: 4

Prerequisites:

→ Entertainment Division at Gambling HQ

Description: Thought disco was dead? Well not any more! Disco has hustled from its grave with a high-grade disco fever and is jive-talkin' in your casino!

Celebrity Stage

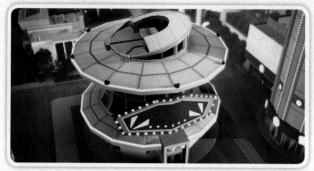

Cost: §15,000

Operational Cost: §1,125 per hour

Medium Wealth Gambler Capacity: 120

Maximum Tourists per day: 50

Maximum Modules: 4

Prerequisites:

→ Entertainment Division at Gambling HQ

Description: The Celebrity Stage attracts only the finest B- and C-grade celebrities. Remember that one guy, from that show? Check out his new one-man show! And that one gal, with the song? She's got a new one!

Elegant Casino

Cost: §300,000

Operational Cost: §3,000 per hour

Prerequisites:

→ Gambling HQ

Description: This stylish casino is evocative of a quaint Italian villa that caters solely to the nouveau riche. This expensive casino is only for the most discerning of cities. You'll need to entice high wealth tourists to meet the demanding maintenance costs.

CAPACITY AND INCOME

Wealth	Tourist Capacity	Hourly Income
Low	—	—
Medium	100	§28 per gambler
High	300	§56 per gambler

Tourists aren't the only ones taking a financial risk at the Elegant Casino—if your city isn't ready, you may be gambling away your city's treasury with this high-price resort. While the initial costs are high, the hourly operating costs for this casino are outrageous, potentially making this facility cost-prohibitive. The success of this casino hinges entirely on your city's ability to attract a steady flow of high wealth tourists. For best results, build this casino within walking distance of a Ferry Terminal equipped with a Cruise Ship Dock. Cruise ships bring in the largest amount of high wealth tourists. A Municipal Airport can also bring in the tourists necessary keep the casino busy, but supplying transportation between the airport and casino can be problematic because high wealth tourists don't travel by bus or streetcar—instead they'll take a limo. Plus, you don't want to plop a high-end casino within walking distance of a noisy airport. For these reasons, the cruise ship option is the most ideal, assuming your city has a waterfront. Ensure a robust police presence as well by building a Police Precinct nearby. If crime gets out of control, the casino will suffer, potentially leading to its downfall, taking the city's economy with it.

There are numerous modules that can be added, but make sure the casino is filled to capacity (and profitable) before applying any of them. A Lodging Division at the Gambling HQ will give the casino access to a number of hotel rooms catering to the medium and high wealth visitors. Increase the number of high wealth gamblers on the casino floor with the addition of the Roulette House module—you'll need the Gaming Division first. Or draw in celebrities and high rollers alike with the Exclusive Club module, requiring the Entertainment Division.

While the Elegant Casino is operational, constantly monitor its capacity and profitability by clicking on it. If there's not enough tourists, the casino will lose large sums of money every hour, costing your city thousands. If the casino isn't pulling a profit within a couple of days, shut it down and address transportation issues preventing medium and high wealth tourists from reaching the casino. Perhaps your city's attraction rating isn't high enough to draw the required number of high wealth tourists? If that's the case, consider placing landmarks such as the Sydney Opera House to serve as an additional draw. Also, don't forget to surround the casino with plenty of high wealth shops—use Plaza and Formal Parks to boost commercial land values.

MODULES

Decorative Sign

Cost: §6,000

Operational Cost: §500 per hour

Maximum Tourists per day: 100

Maximum Modules: 1

Description: This elegantly understated sign in a fan motif is for the sophisticated casino mogul.

Casino Marquee

Cost: §6,000

Operational Cost: §500 per hour

Maximum Tourists per day: 100

Maximum Modules: 1

Description: It's an exclusive casino, but drivers for the wealthy will still need to know where the place is. With this sign, they can see it from miles away!

Classy Rooms (Ground)

Cost: §10,000

Operational Cost: §565 per hour

Medium Wealth Rooms: 60

Maximum Modules: 8

Prerequisites:

➔ Lodging Division at Gambling HQ

Description: The literal base of your Elegant Casino's classy hotel tower! Tourists will stay in lodging to spend any remaining Simoleons in the casino the next day.

Classy Rooms (Tower)

Cost: §10,000

Operational Cost: §565 per hour

Medium Wealth Rooms: 60

Maximum Modules: 8

Prerequisites:

➔ Lodging Division at Gambling HQ

Description: Use this tower of Classy Rooms to create a hotel-casino. Tourists will stay in lodging to spend any remaining Simoleons in the casino the next day.

Penthouse Suite

Cost: §20,000

Operational Cost: §845 per hour

High Wealth Rooms: 40

Maximum Modules: 8

Prerequisites:

→ Lodging Division at Gambling HQ

Description: The most exclusive lodging in the most exclusive casino. No, you can't see a list of who stayed here before.

Exclusive Club

Cost: §40,000

Operational Cost: §1,500 per hour

High Wealth Gambler Capacity: 60

Maximum Tourists per day: 100

Maximum Modules: 8

Prerequisites:

→ Entertainment Division at Gambling HQ

Description: Casino patrons will be drawn to your casino to chill with celebrities and superstar athletes. Just please, no autographs!

Roulette House

Cost: §50,000

Operational Cost: §1,875 per hour

High Wealth Gambler Capacity: 80

Maximum Modules: 8

Prerequisites:

→ Gaming Division at Gambling HQ

Description: Remember what Lesley Snypes said, "Always bet on black. No, wait, red!" High wealth tourists love to watch that wheel go 'round and 'round with the hope they won't lose their money.

Gambling: Points to Remember

→ Casinos create revenue for your city.

→ The higher your city's attraction rating, the more Sims will visit your casinos.

→ Each casino appeals to a different wealth class of Sims.

→ Add modules to each casino to expand its capacity and appeal.

→ Criminals are drawn to casinos.

 TIP

Tourists will gamble at your casinos. The more attractive the casino, the more gamblers!

Culture

How about some Shakespeare? The Globe Theater may look a bit out of place among your flashy casinos, but it's yet another way to draw tourists into you city.

Let's face it. If you're not interested in gambling, there's not much to do or see in your city. It's time to change that by selecting one of the buildings in the Culture menu. Adding an Expo Center, Pro Stadium, or landmark to your city is just what you need to draw large numbers of tourists. But don't get ahead of yourself. Prematurely constructing one of these attractions can put a major strain on your transportation system, potentially leading to citywide paralysis as swarms of cars and taxi cabs descend from the regional highway, leading to gridlock. For this reason, it's essential to provide a comprehensive mass transit system to accommodate large crowds. Once you've handled the transportation system, consider zoning commercial nearby to encourage the creation of shops and hotels, giving tourists something to do after attending an event or visiting a landmark. The more shops and hotels in the area, the longer tourists are likely to stay in your city, spending their hard-earned Simoleons in the process.

Expo Center

Cost: §150,000

Operational Cost: §300 per hour

Maximum Event Payout: §156,000

Capacity: 3,000 Sims

Prerequisites:

→ Town Hall

Description: Invest in an Expo Center to turn your small town into a tourist destination! Schedule exciting events like football games and rock concerts, then prepare your city for tons of screaming fans!

EXPO CENTER EVENTS				
Event	Event Cost	Max. Payout	Attracts	Description
Motocross	§15,000	§66,000	Low wealth residents and tourists	Ooh! Make that jump! I loves me some mud!
Sports Event	§30,000	§111,000	Low/medium wealth residents and tourists	Yeah, go local sports team! Woo!
Rock Concert	§45,000	§156,000	Low/medium wealth residents and tourists	Needs more pyrotechnics... and cowbell. Definitely more cowbell.

This arena serves as a popular entertainment hub, attracting low/medium wealth residents and tourists. Like most attractions, build it within walking distance of a regional transportation hub such as the Passenger Train Station or Bus Terminal to accommodate large numbers of attendees. Supplement it with Bus and Streetcar Stops nearby. Events held at the Expo Center must be scheduled by clicking on the building and selecting the Schedule Event option. This brings up the Event Scheduler window, allowing you to choose from three possible events: Motocross, Sports Event, and Rock Concert. Each event costs a different amount to schedule. You'll only get your money back if enough local Sims and tourists attend the event. In this sense, running an event is a bit of a gamble, with your transportation system being a major factor in determining whether the event will be profitable. Expect traffic to increase around the arena a few hours before the start of the event—all events start at 8 PM. After the event starts, click on the Expo Center to see attendance levels and the payout. The payout increases as more and more Sims enter the Expo Center. You will only earn the maximum payout if the Expo Center is filled to its 3,000 Sim capacity. New events can be scheduled every day, but if you don't have enough money to schedule an event, consider shutting down the Expo Center to save money.

MODULES

Expo Center Sign

Cost: §3,000

Operational Cost: §50 per hour

Maximum Tourists per day: 50

Maximum Modules: 1

Description: With an Expo Center, you have to let people know where to go.

Pro Stadium

Cost: §225,000

Operational Cost: §600 per hour

Maximum Event Payout: §600,000

Capacity: 15,000 Sims

Prerequisites:

→ City Hall in region

→ Department of Tourism in region

Description: The Pro Stadium's generous size means even more tourists and huge profits around each event. Prepare your city's mass transit system for an onslaught of screaming fans! Unfortunately, their tickets are all fully refundable, so if they can't make it to the event in time, you'll miss out on the Simoleons.

PRO STADIUM EVENTS

Event	Event Cost	Max. Payout	Attracts	Description
Monster Truck Rally	§150,000	§300,000	Low/medium wealth residents and tourists	Low wealth Sims will love to watch Truck-inator devour lesser vehicles!
World Championship	§225,000	§450,000	Medium/high wealth residents and tourists	Um, it's pronounced "foot-bawl". Please.
Legends of Rock	§300,000	§600,000	Medium/high wealth residents and tourists	What's that? I can't hear you! Yeah, I got this T-shirt at the Legends of Rock show!

The Pro Stadium is a massive 15,000-seat arena capable of drawing huge crowds and piles of Simoleons. Like the Expo Center, don't fool around when it comes to providing mass transit around this facility. Build a Passenger Train Station as close to the stadium as possible so incoming tourists can walk to events. Also, make sure the stadium has adequate coverage by shuttle buses, municipal buses, and streetcars—build at least one Bus Stop and one Streetcar Stop within walking distance of the stadium. Events at the Pro Stadium function similarly to events held at the Expo Center. However, events here have a much higher initial cost to schedule, but the potential payouts are also much larger—the Legends of Rock event can bring in as much as §600,000 in one evening! For best results, schedule events in the early morning or right after an evening's event has concluded. This will give Sims and tourists plenty of time to make it to the stadium prior to the start of an event. Making money off events at the Pro Stadium is a true test of your city and region's transportation system—even in a large city, filling all 15,000 seats is no easy task. Make sure nearby cities have access to regional transit hubs like the Bus Terminal, Passenger Train Station, Ferry Terminal, or Municipal Airport to increase attendance. If neighboring mayors can't afford these additions, consider gifting them the Simoleons necessary to build these hubs in their cities—don't worry, you'll make all that money back over time. If times are tough, and your city doesn't have the funds necessary to schedule an event, consider shutting down the Pro Stadium to save some money. An empty event-less stadium only drains your city's treasury. You can always reopen it once the economy recovers.

MODULES

Pro Stadium Sign

Cost: §3,000

Operational Cost: §100 per hour

Low wealth tourists per day: 12,000

Medium wealth tourists per day: 12,000

High wealth tourists per day: 12,000

Maximum Modules: 1

Description: With a Pro Stadium, it's all about branding.

Landmarks

Prerequisites:

→ City Hall in region

→ Department of Tourism in region

Ready to add some international flair to your city? Landmarks are tourist magnets, drawing tons of camera-toting visitors from the region and beyond. There are several landmarks to choose from, shown in the accompanying table, each with a real-world counterpart. Each landmark has a huge attraction rating, mostly for low and medium wealth tourists—build the Sydney Opera House if you want to draw high wealth tourists. But before building any landmark, make sure your city's road and mass transit networks can handle the sudden deluge of visitors, otherwise a flood of cars and taxi cabs are likely to clog your city's streets, backing up onto the regional highway. As with the Expo Center and Pro Stadium, provide a mix of overlapping mass transit options around each landmark. First of all, make sure the landmark is within walking distance of a regional transportation hub like the Bus Terminal, Passenger Train Station, Ferry Terminal, or Municipal Airport. Add more mass transit alternatives by building at least one Bus Stop and Streetcar Stop nearby. Once you've attracted tourists, provide enough shops, hotels, and other attractions to keep them in the city as long as possible. Otherwise they'll leave after staring at your landmark for a few hours. The landmark is simply a magnet to draw tourists into your city. It's up to you to figure out ways to keep them in town until they've spent all their money.

 NOTE

The Globe Theater as well as the Oslo and Sydney Opera Houses function much like the Expo Center and Pro Stadium, allowing you to schedule events. Each landmark can bring in as much as §189,000 for each daily event. The Empire State Building, Tokyo Tower, and Willis Tower function as commercial office buildings.

Culture: Points to Remember

→ Cultural buildings increase the attraction of your city, which will draw more tourists.

→ Commercial buildings also increase attraction.

→ Tourists will shop and spend money in your commercial buildings.

→ Tourists from different wealth classes will use different transportation.

→ Some landmarks also provide happiness, like parks or shops.

→ The Expo Center and Pro Stadium hold events on a set schedule. Click on these buildings to schedule events.

→ The Expo Center and Pro Stadium require payment up front to schedule an event.

→ The Expo Center and Pro Stadium make more money for higher attendance.

→ You can only place three landmarks per city, so choose wisely.

✓ **TIP**

Be sure to check the description of each landmark to see the benefits it provides.

LANDMARKS

Image	Name	Origin	Cost	Hourly Cost	Max. Daily Tourist Visits	Description
	Arc de Triomphe	Paris, France	§330,000	§1,755	2,400	Perfect for the Francophiles, lend your city a touch of Gallic class!
	Cinquantenaire Arch	Brussels, Belgium	§25,000	§610	2,400	This imposing arcade celebrates your city's independence! Watch as tourists are drawn to take photos of the famous landmark.
	Dutch Windmill	The Netherlands	§25,000	§610	600	The Netherlands are famous for their beautiful pastoral windmills.
	Edifício Copan	São Paulo, Brazil	§25,000	§612	150	This wavy residential building adds a flowing sense of movement to even the densest urban cityscape.
	Empire State Building	New York City, USA	§750,000	§4,050	504	It's not the tallest building in the world (anymore), but this impressive building can be said to be the core of the Big Apple.
	Giralda	Seville, Spain	§25,000	§610	2,400	This bell tower is a former minaret for the Cathedral of Seville.
	Globe Theatre	London, England	§48,000	§1,000	1,557	All the world's a stage and now you can bring yet another replica of The Globe Theatre to your city!
	Kölner Dom	Cologne, Germany	§25,000	§610	2,400	Towering spires crown this famous gothic church from Cologne.
	Leaning Tower of Pisa	Pisa, Italy	§330,000	§1,755	600	Tilting 3.99 degrees, Sims will be hard pressed to walk in a straight line after visiting this famous tower.
	Oslo Opera House	Oslo, Norway	§150,000	§2,000	1,364	This angular modern opera house hosts opera and ballet performances.

LANDMARKS

Image	Name	Origin	Cost	Hourly Cost	Max. Daily Tourist Visits	Description
	Rundetårn	Copenhagen, Denmark	§160,000	§1,755	480	The "Round Tower" of Copenhagen is a historical monument and a public astronomical observatory.
	Statue of Liberty	New York City, USA	§750,000	§4,050	5,000	Where else can you stand in a lady's head? This giant statue is undeniable proof that France loves the United States. Add it to your city!
	St. Basil's Cathedral	Moscow, Russia	§160,000	§1,755	2,400	The official name of this Red Square cathedral is far too long to get into.
	Stockholm City Hall	Stockholm, Sweden	§25,000	§575	100	Don't be jealous that your City Hall's not as cool as Stockholm's. Now you can have it in your city as well.
	Sydney Opera House	Sydney, Australia	§200,000	§2,000	2,679	Add the distinctive silhouette of the Sydney Opera House to your city and watch droves of wealthy tourists flock to your city!
	Tokyo Tower	Tokyo, Japan	§25,000	§575	2,400	This tall lattice tower broadcasts J-dramas and anime to all the homes in your city.
	Washington Monument	Washington DC, USA	§25,000	§575	2,400	One of the most recognizable obelisks in the world, the Washington Monument stands erect at 169.294 meters.
	Willis Tower	Chicago, USA	§160,000	§1,755	504	This 108-story-tall building is the tallest building in the United States.
	Zamek Królewski w Warszawie	Warsaw, Poland	§330,000	§1,755	2,400	The Royal Castle of Warsaw is the historical home to the royal family of Poland.

Tourism Management

Establishing a successful and profitable tourist industry requires careful planning, patience, and constant monitoring of various moving pieces, so don't delve into the tourist trade until your city is ready for it, emphasizing mass transit and police coverage. As your tourist districts thrive, expand to keep the flow of tourists coming into your city. Despite the challenges, creating a city specializing in tourism is fun and rewarding. But it's never boring—there's always something to do. Here's a few pointers to help get your tourist city up and running.

Mass Transit Fundamentals

Build a Passenger Train Station across the street from a casino and revel in the sight of tourist pedestrian traffic.

The importance of mass transit cannot be overstated when it comes to accommodating tourists. Before you even think of luring tourists into you city with a casino or landmark, establish a network of overlapping mass transit options. There are two important questions to ask yourself: how will tourists from the region get into your city? Once there, how will they get around? The regional question is the most important to address as it can prevent the highway (and your road network) from becoming a parking lot. The Passenger Train Station is one of the most efficient ways to bring in low and medium wealth tourists—plop it within walking distance of your planned tourist district. If your city has a waterfront, consider using the Ferry Terminal's Cruise Ship Dock module to draw large numbers of medium and high wealth tourists. The Municipal Airport is another option for importing large numbers of medium and high wealth tourists. Ideally, it's best to place your casinos and landmarks within walking distance of these regional transportation hubs, cutting down on the need for taxis, buses, or streetcars. However, if such a layout isn't possible, provide Bus and Streetcar Stops at each hub to facilitate transportation to your city's attractions. Remember, Sims will only walk 200 meters when attempting to transfer from one mass transit system to another, so place those stops right next to your Passenger Train Station, Ferry Terminal, or Municipal Airport.

> **(i) NOTE**
>
> If you're on a budget, the Bus Terminal can bring low and medium wealth tourists into your city. But buses also add to the congestion of your road network. When possible, rely on trains, boats, and planes to transport tourists into your city.

Crime Suppression

This Police Precinct should be enough to handle the criminals pouring out of the nearby casinos.

Casinos don't attract criminals—they create them. The simulation produces one blue collar criminal at each casino at regular intervals, leading to a massive crime outbreak if your city isn't prepared. Open the Crime data map and notice the criminal activity around every casino. When it comes to battling crime around casinos, spare no expense. The Police Precinct isn't cheap, but is well-equipped to deal with the escalation in crime, particularly if you're planning to build more than one casino. The mere presence of a nearby Police Precinct is usually enough to suppress crime around the nearby casinos. But criminals may wander to other parts of your city, away from the police presence, to commit their crimes. Be ready to expand coverage with additional Patrol Car Lots and the Police Dispatch Tower. If you can afford it, the Police Helipad can make a big difference too. Additional Police Stations posted throughout the city may be necessary as well to supplement your police force. As your police force rounds up criminals, they'll need a place to put them. Consider adding additional Jail Cells to prevent early releases due to overcrowding. If crime is overtaking your city, consider shutting down your casinos until the police can make a dent. The revenue lost from the casinos may be painful, but it may be the only way to make headway in the city's fight against crime.

Casino Income

Open the Budget panel to see how much income your casinos are bringing in—look under the city specialization line in the ledger.

Casinos are a city specialization, similar to the metals, petroleum, trading, and electronics businesses. As a result, all expenses associated with casinos show up under the ledger's city specialization line in the Budget panel. But unlike the other city specializations, casinos generate profit on an hourly basis. So instead of showing up in the recent transactions window, all profits appear in the ledger, just like tax revenue. This creates a unique situation within the ledger where you can see both the (red) expenses and (green) income generated by city specialization. This makes it easy to get a quick overview of how well your casinos are doing collectively. If for some reason expenses exceed income, click on the individual casinos in your city to see which ones aren't profitable. A unprofitable casino can be a major drain on your city's revenue as well as an indicator of a deficiency in your city's attraction rating or mass transit system. If these issues cannot be identified and addressed in a timely fashion, shut down any unprofitable casinos until you can iron out the wrinkles. But keep in mind, it may take a few days for a casino to begin generating a profit. So be patient, particularly when beginning your casino empire.

Commercial Zones and Hotels

Cheap motels, like these, will appear in commercial zones near tourist attractions, giving visitors a place to spend the night.

Whether plopping casinos, stadiums, or landmarks, don't forget to zone commercial nearby. Tourist attractions can generate some revenue of their own, but their main purpose is to lure tourists into your city. Commercial buildings benefit greatly from tourism, resulting in higher profits for their business and increased tax revenue for the city. Hotels appear in commercial zones after a number of tourists fail in an attempt to find lodging vacancies in your city; simple supply and demand at work. Hotels serve an important role in your tourist industry, giving visitors a place to spend the night so they can resume their spending spree the next day. After spending money at a nearby attraction or shop, a tourist will seek out a nearby hotel to spend the night—and spend more Simoleons in the process. As long as there are enough hotel vacancies and appropriate wealth level shops or attractions to visit, a tourist will stay in your city until they've spent all their money. In addition to staying at hotels in commercial zones, tourists can also find overnight accommodations at casinos equipped with hotel room modules. But hotels aren't the only commercial buildings tourists will visit, so make sure there's enough shops in the area too, preferably within walking distance of key attractions. The steadier the flow of tourists, the more profit generated by your commercial zones.

> ✓ **TIP**
>
> Utilize mass transit to bring large quantities of tourists to your casinos!

TOURISM ACHIEVEMENTS

Icon	Name	Criteria
	Main Attraction	Have 300 low wealth tourists leave your city satisfied in one day.
	Penny Slots	Generate §200,000 in total revenue from casinos.
	Sunday! Sunday! Sunday!	Run a successful stadium event in your city.
	Sin City	Place one of each type of casino in a single city.

CHAT WITH THE DEVELOPERS

The Circulatory System of *SimCity*

TYLER THOMPSON, GAMEPLAY PRODUCER

Hi everyone! I'm Tyler Thompson, the Gameplay Producer here at Maxis, and I've really enjoyed helping the team make the new *SimCity* into a great game.

The new *SimCity's* simulation is driven by Sims, road networks, and traffic. I enjoy explaining it with a biological metaphor. The roads are the city's arteries and veins. The Sims circulate through those roads. They help keep the city alive by going to work, making factories run, keeping stores open, taking home money, going shopping with money, etc. Power, water, and sewage also flow under the roads. Almost every building relies on a vehicle to be effective: garbage trucks, police patrol cars, coal delivery trucks, school buses, taxis, and more. The result is a city where the streets are filled with a variety of vehicles and pedestrians, streaming from place to place and keeping the simulation alive.

Traffic jams strangle like a heart attack. Several times, I have looked up from decorating a casino to see dreaded lines of red tail lights. The consequences are pretty dire. Ambulances don't get to injured Sims before they die. Police don't make it to the bank in time to stop a robbery. The Coal Power Plant shuts down from lack of workers. Homes and factories are starting to become abandoned at the edges of the city. In a panic, I start demolishing troublesome intersections, replacing roads, and adding new avenues across town. I also apply some civic "blood thinner". I create a mass transit system featuring shuttle buses, large municipal buses, streetcars, and trains. This usually clears the major arteries and gets things flowing again.

Combine this circulatory system with our curvy road tool, and it means that you can make functional, organically shaped cities. We've made face-shaped cities,

concentric rings, guitar-shaped cities, and on and on. Often, the city's topography encourages curves. Riverside towns can have a snaking boardwalk. Mountainside cities bend around the base. Lakeside cities with a high-wealth district hug the waterfront. Yeah, I love to play optimized grids, but this game is frequently tempting me to throw away the ruler and start painting roads with a brush.

These curvy, organic cities can be effective because the simulation isn't about distances—it's about flow. When you start to understand this, it totally changes how you lay things out. When I place a Fire Station, I usually try to find a place that is central, well connected but not near heavy traffic. When I create a central avenue, I often limit the number of intersections with it so that cars don't wait for light after light. I sprinkle commercial sectors at the ends of residential roads to encourage pedestrian traffic. As the city grows, I watch for the long line of red brake lights and plop down bus stops like crazy.

Many times, I find myself just sitting back and watching the flow.

> **The roads are the city's arteries and veins. The Sims circulate through those roads. They help keep the city alive.**

Great Works

Mayor, now that the city is a smashing success, perhaps it's time to expand your vision and enhance your legacy with the construction of a Great Works project?

The Arcology, International Airport, Solar Farm, and Space Center benefit all connected cities in different ways. But it's inadvisable to undertake a Great Works project on your own. That's where your phenomenal diplomatic leadership skills come in. Reach out to other mayors in the region and form a coalition of cities with one common goal. By contributing resources and workers these cities can collaborate on a mutually beneficial Great Works project, serving as a beacon of progress throughout the region.

Don't forget to go to **www.primagames.com** to access guide updates free of charge with your voucher code.

Arcology

Cost: §1,000,000
Operational Cost: §300 per hour
Benefits:
→ Workers
→ Shoppers
→ Students
Construction Resources:
→ 2,800 tons of Metal
→ 1,000 tons of Alloy
→ 60,000 crates of TVs
Prerequisites:
→ City in the region with 58,000 residents

Description: Building this towering pinnacle of human architecture requires skilled workers and resources. This dense ecosystem contains everything necessary to sustain a massive community. Sims live here but many of them will commute to cities in the region to work, go to school, or shop.

Have a shortage of workers or shoppers? Don't like wasting space on residential zones? Then perhaps the Arcology is a good fit for your region. This structure functions like a massive futuristic apartment building, providing cities in the region with a practically endless supply of workers, shoppers, and students. These Sims travel to the connected cities in the region and fill vacant jobs, shop in commercial zones, and attend schools. This allows you to create bustling industrial and commercial cities without worrying about residential—at the end of the day, everybody goes home to the Arcology.

When it comes to producing metal and alloy, don't overlook the contributions of a Recycling Center. Every little bit helps.

When starting a game in a new region, the Arcology is likely the first Great Works project to be unlocked, only requiring a city with 58,000 residents. And as long as your region has a robust metals and electronics business underway, supplying the construction resources shouldn't be too difficult. Cities with access to both raw ore and coal can produce the metal and alloy required by building a Smelting Factory. The TVs required will need to be produced at a Consumer Electronics Factory supplied with a steady flow of plastic and processors—consider importing the plastic while getting the processors from an existing Processor Factory. Alternatively, all metal, alloy, and TVs can simply be purchased on the global market. This is easiest solution, particularly if the connected cities lack the raw materials necessary to complete construction. However, those TVs are really expensive!

International Airport

Cost: §1,000,000

Operational Cost: §300 per hour

Benefits:

→ Tourists

→ Accepts Freight

Construction Resources:

→ 2,500 tons of Metal

→ 1,500 tons of Alloy

→ 250,000 barrels of Crude Oil

Prerequisites:

→ Municipal Airport in the region

→ 100 tourists arrive at Municipal Airport in the region

Description: Construction of the International Airport requires resources and workers from cities in the region. Once opened, the International Airport brings flights of tourists into the region and ships freight on cargo planes.

If one or more cities in your region rely on tourism, the International Airport is a worthwhile project, serving as a major hub for incoming medium and high wealth tourists and outgoing freight. This facility is similar to the Municipal Airport, but functions on a regional scale, serving all connected cities. Beyond the obvious benefits, the International Airport also frees up space in cities currently relying on planes to bring in tourists. Individual cities no longer have to devote a huge portion of their city to a cumbersome Municipal Airport, allowing for the construction of more casinos, hotels, and landmarks. Getting rid of that noisy Municipal Airport is likely to make nearby residential neighborhoods happy as well.

If your city has vast oil reservoirs beneath the surface, supplying crude oil from an Oil Well should be no problem.

Before you can even select the International Airport as a Great Works project, at least one city in the region must have a Municipal Airport—a cumulative 100 tourists must also have arrived through Municipal Airports throughout the region. Once these prerequisites are met, the International Airport can be selected at any Great Works site in the region. Like all projects, this one needs plenty of alloy as well as metal and crude oil. A robust mining city with access to large deposits of raw ore and coal can supply the alloy and metal from a Smelting Factory. Meanwhile, an oil city should start setting aside thousands of barrels of crude oil. If two mining cities and two oil cities combine their resources, the construction materials will come together much faster, or you can augment production by purchasing resources on the global market. Although market values fluctuate, metal, alloy, and crude oil are relatively cheap to import.

Solar Farm

Cost: §500,000

Operational Cost: §300 per hour

Benefits:

→ Power

Construction Resources:

→ 150,000 crates of Plastic

→ 600 tons of Alloy

→ 45,000 crates of Processors

Prerequisites:

→ University with School of Science in the region

→ Complete Solar Farm research project at University in the region

Description: This dazzling solar array requires advanced resources and workers from participating cities in the region. Cities connected to the Solar Farm can purchase large amounts of power at a discounted cost.

Tired of those frequent power outages? Running out of space for power plants of your own? Of all the Great Works projects, the Solar Farm is perhaps the most practical, supplying all connected cities with unlimited clean, cheap power. Once constructed, connected cities can purchase power directly from the Solar Farm, similar to purchasing power from neighboring cities. But since this is a shared resource, all cities get a significant discount—after all, they built it! In addition to being cheap and dependable, the Solar Farm frees cities from the pollution/meltdown concerns associated with the Coal, Oil, and Nuclear Power Plants. If all connected cities buy power from the Solar Farm, you also don't have to worry about power plant-generated air pollution drifting in from a neighboring city, helping make the region a much healthier place for all Sims.

Add all four Processor Assembly Line modules to your Processor Factory to increase the production of processors needed at the Solar Farm site.

Like any worthwhile endeavor, building a Solar Farm isn't easy—you'll need access to three separate city specializations as well as a University. For best results, divide the gathering of construction resources among a minimum of three specialized cities. An oil city is responsible for producing plastic at an Oil Refinery while a mining city cranks out alloy from a Smelting Factory. Meanwhile, emphasize education in a third city with the construction of a University and electronics business. A University with a School of Science is required to complete the Solar Farm research project. Plus, the University can supply plenty of skilled workers for the Processor Factory. When it comes to producing processors, instead of buying plastic and alloy from the global market, import it from the oil and mining cities as gifts—this cuts down on production costs significantly. Ramping up production across all three city specializations may take a while, particularly for the education/electronics city. The gathering of resources and construction only adds to the timeline. But if your region has the patience and long-term vision, the Solar Farm is definitely worth the wait.

Space Center

Cost: §1,000,000

Operational Cost: §300 per hour

Benefits:

→ Tourists

→ Education

Construction Resources:

→ 170,000 barrels of Fuel

→ 1,400 tons of Alloy

→ 40,000 crates of Computers

Prerequisites:

→ University with School of Engineering in the region

→ Complete Space Center research project at University in the region

Description: This sprawling compound requires high tech resources from cities in the region. With the Space Center constructed, mayors in the region will reap the benefits of a more skilled workforce, resulting in more high tech industry. Mayors can schedule rocket launches, which draw tourists to the surrounding cities.

Reach for the stars with this dazzling monument to your region's commitment to higher education and mastery of extracting and refining natural resources. The Space Center has two primary benefits to the region, serving both as a tourist attraction and a higher learning institution, much like a University. Rocket launches are scheduled similarly to events at the Expo Center or Pro Stadium, drawing in tons of tourists to the connected cities eager to witness the launch—upgrade your mass transit network to accommodate the crowds. An increase in tourism boosts the profits of your city's commercial buildings, not to mention those of casinos and other profit-generating attractions. The Space Center also emits skill level to all connected cities, leading to the development of high tech (tech level 3) industry whether a city has a University or not. So if you want to get rid of all those polluting factories in the region while reaping the high profits of high tech, the Space Center is the Great Works project for you.

The Space Center requires lots of fuel. Maximize production at Oil Refineries by adding more Fuel Distillation Units.

Like the Solar Farm, achieving the benefits of a Space Center requires a great deal of effort and multi-city collaboration. Only attempt this project when you have a minimum of three cities with specializations in petroleum, metals, and electronics. Rely on the oil city to extract and refine crude oil into fuel with an Oil Refinery. Elsewhere, a mining city with deposits of raw ore and coal can create alloy at a Smelting Factory. At least one city should pursue higher education, building a University as well as an electronics business—the two work well together. Skilled workers from the University are perfect for staffing the Processor and Consumer Electronics Factories, required for producing all those computers. The University is also required to complete the Space Center research project—without it, the Space Center won't be available at a Great Works site.

Build a University in your electronics city to supply your Processor Factory and Consumer Electronics Factory with a steady supply of skilled workers needed to make all those computers.

Of all the resources required, supplying the computers is the most time consuming, largely due to the long-term process of ramping up a mature and profitable electronics business. Speed up the process by building out all Processor Assembly Line modules at the Processor Factory while supplying the facility with a skilled workforce from the University—use plastic and alloy gifted by the oil and metal cities to create processors. At the earliest opportunity, plop a Consumer Electronics Division at your Electronics HQ so you can construct the Consumer Electronics Factory. Don't even bother producing TVs at this factory. Instead, build out all Computer Assembly Line modules to increase production of computers, shipping them straight to the Space Center site from the nearest Trade Depot or Trade Port. Little by little the computers will arrive at the Space Center, eventually allowing construction to commence.

Before long, Sims will enjoy the sight of rockets streaming skyward, entertaining tourists and inspiring a high tech future for the region.

Great Works Management

Ready to start your Great Works project? Well, hold on just a second. Great Works are long-term projects, requiring careful multi-city planning, coordination, and patience. Since you're working together with other mayors, it's crucial to decide on a mutually beneficial Great Works project appropriate for all participants. You must also take into account the financial and logistical hurdles you'll face when producing or buying the required resources for each potential project. Like all things in *SimCity*, a little planning and asking yourself the right questions can go a long way. So before you get started, here's some advice to help get your grand vision off the ground.

Great Works Selection

Discuss Great Works projects with the other mayors and make sure everyone can contribute something to the construction process. Don't try to go it alone.

Have you figured out which of the four Great Works your region will focus its efforts on? Before settling on a Great Works project, consult with all the mayors connected to the intended Great Works site. The Great Works project only benefits and can be constructed by cities connected to the site with the highway, so there's no need to have a meeting with every single mayor in the region—just those connected to the site and your city. Usually, each Great Works site is connected to at least three cities. When playing in a region connected to different players, it's important to get feedback from everyone before making a decision. After all, you'll probably be relying on these other mayors to donate resources to the site, so it's important everyone buys into the concept and is eager to play a role in the construction process. While discussing the options with the other mayors, take into account the resources required to build each Great Works project and whether your region has ample resources to meet those demands. When a decision has been made, any of the mayors connected to a Great Works site can initiate the project, assuming all prerequisites have been met. It costs §1,000,000 to submit the application for the project, and this must be paid by one mayor. However, other mayors can contribute their own money to the pot by gifting Simoleons to the mayor responsible for submitting the application—if everyone kicks in §250,000 it's not such a steep financial commitment. Once the §1,000,000 has been paid, there is a slight delay while the application is approved. Take this time to ramp up production of resources within your cities so you're ready to start delivering construction materials to the site.

City Specializations

Every Great Works project requires alloy. Turn to the metals business and a city site with both raw ore and coal to begin producing this universal construction material at a Smelting Factory.

Due to the enormous amount of resources required to construct each Great Works project, it's a good idea to gear your cities toward producing only one or two types of construction materials. But such specializations should begin early on, not after submitting a Great Works application. If you have raw ore and coal beneath your city, it's best to pursue the metals business and begin producing metal and alloy from a Smelting Factory. If your city has large oil reservoirs, pump that crude oil out of the ground and process it into plastic and fuel at an Oil Refinery. Both the Space Center and Solar Farm require the completion of a research project at a University. If your city already has a University, pursue the electronics business using a Processor Factory and Consumer Electronics Factory to crank out processors, computers, or TVs—the University ensures these factories have a steady supply of skilled workers, helping boost production. With each connected city specializing in one city specialization, it reduces the amount of time required to gather the necessary construction materials to build each Great Works project.

Construction

Choose which resources to donate to the Great Works site and watch as trucks deliver the required materials.

Once the application for the Great Works project has been approved, each city can begin shipping materials to the site. But first, go to the Great Works site and sign up to contribute to the project by clicking the on/off toggle button beneath the appropriate resource—only contribute if you have the ability to produce one of the three resources. Once you've signed up to donate a particular resource, the Great Works site will begin drawing material from your city's Trade Depots and Trade Ports. If you've been exporting these resources, open the Manage Global Market Deliveries window at each Trade Depot and Trade Port and choose Use Locally for each resource you're donating to the Great Works site. This ensures all produced materials stay put until they can be transported to the Great Works site. For best results, conduct all transfers from a Trade Port. These facilities are capable of storing vast quantities of materials, ideal for supplying the Great Works site. Add more Delivery Truck Garage modules to the Trade Port to increase the flow of materials to the site—all materials are transported by truck along the regional highway. Little by little, construction resources begin trickling in at the Great Works site, as indicated by the green vertical meters in the Great Works Construction window. Even if all cities are prepared, the gathering of resources takes a long time. Instead of watching the trucks flow into the site from the various cities, turn your attention to your city and ensure the supply chains for each business are operating at peak efficiency—don't forget to deal with other problems in your city as well.

The Trade Port is essential to supplying the Great Works site with the required construction materials. Keep a close eye on your city's supply chain to ensure frequent deliveries.

When all the required material has been gathered at the Great Works site, construction can begin. During this phase, each city needs to supply workers to the site—a Great Works project won't build itself. Make sure your cities have plenty of residential neighborhoods zoned to accommodate the large number of workers required at the Great Works site. This could be a specialization in itself, with one residential city contributing the bulk of the workers. Like gathering resources, constructing the Great Works project takes a long time. Although it can be fun watching the gradual process, don't get too distracted. While gawking at the Great Works site your city continues functioning,

and there may be problems arising you should be paying attention to. Don't worry, the Great Works project will soon be complete, benefiting all connected cities. It's a long and arduous task, but in the end, the effort is worth it.

⚠ CAUTION

As you begin contributing resources to a Great Works site, make sure your city's economy can handle it. If you were relying on selling those resources on the global market to generate income, donating those resources can cause a sudden drop in revenue. Make sure your city has alternative streams of income before sending all your resources to a Great Works site. A bankrupt city won't help anyone.

Great Works: Points to Remember

→ Great Works can be initiated by any city once the requirements have been met.

→ Cities must be connected to a Great Works site to benefit from it.

→ Great works can provide power, jobs, tourism, and economic boosts to a city.

GREAT WORKS ACHIEVEMENTS

Icon	Name	Criteria
	We Are Not Alone (Secret)	Ship any resource to a Space Center Great Work to gain access to the UFO Encounter disaster.

CHAT WITH THE DEVELOPERS

Specializing *SimCity*

STONE LIBRANDE, LEAD DESIGNER

Hello again! This is Stone Librande, the Lead Designer of *SimCity*. One of the great things about working on this game is seeing the incredible progress the team has made. Every day I'm treated to another exciting new addition to the game: a new glass and steel skyscraper, a group of skateboarding Sims in a park, or the sight of the moon reflecting on the water as the sun goes down. It is truly inspiring to be working here with the talented team at Maxis.

One feature of the game that I have been concentrating on is the area of city specialization. *SimCity* allows a single player—or a group of players if you choose to play with other aspiring city builders—to connect up multiple cities in a larger region and share services and resources. This means that you don't need to put a power plant (or a Water Treatment Plant, or a Fire Station, or a school...) in every city in the region. Instead, you can focus on the types of buildings that make your city special and then have other cities supply the additional things you need. For example, you could make a completely suburban city with only houses and parks. Support it with a neighboring industrial city and your Sims will commute down the highway each morning on their way to work and then return back again at night.

You can also start up a city specialization (or two, or more) in your city. City specializations are new to *SimCity* and offer a unique way to play. In essence, they let you take on the role of a business mogul in addition to your typical role as the Mayor. There are five city specializations in the game: metals, petroleum, electronics, trade, and gambling. Each city specialization has a corresponding leaderboard, which makes it easy to see how you compare to other players operating that same business. Your rank is determined by the total amount of profit you have made during the last twelve game months. This encourages smart play, since you need to optimize your profits each month over the year; simply grinding away for long periods of time isn't an effective strategy to get to the top.

Three of these city specialization types revolve around manufacturing. The first two, Metals and Petroleum, rely on extracting resources from the ground and processing them into more valuable resources. If you want to get involved in these specialties, make sure to inspect the region to find where the coal, ore, and oil deposits are before you claim your city. As you advance your metals business, you can dig up larger quantities of coal and ore. You can make even more money if you start a Smelting Factory to convert your minerals into metals and alloy. If you opt for a petroleum specialization, you can drill for oil and then use a refinery to convert it into fuel and plastics. The third type of manufacturing, Electronics, doesn't need to dig up its resources; it converts shipments of metal, alloys, and plastic into processors, TVs, and computers. These high tech resources have the highest profit margins, but you will need a substantial investment in education and transportation infrastructure if you want to keep your factories humming.

Finally, there is the Gambling city specialization. This one is my personal favorite. It is a great choice for players that want to focus on tourists instead of markets. Your goal with a gambling city is to attract as many tourists as possible, which requires building airports, docks for cruise ships, train stations, and buses. But getting tourists into your city is only half the battle. You need to keep them there by building hotels and other entertainment options. Watching a bustling neon-filled casino city come to life at night is mesmerizing.

No matter how you choose to specialize your city, it is important to remember that it is your choice. Feel free to mix and match traditional *SimCity* buildings (schools, parks, Police Stations, etc.) with city specializations. Decide your proportion of residential, commercial, and industrial by zoning. Make a simple town with trailer parks or maximize your density with skyscrapers. Supply the region with power and water or buy it from someone else. There is no right way or wrong way to play. Discovering the benefits and drawbacks of the multitude of combinations is one of the hallmarks of *SimCity*!

The Trade specialization is all about buying low and selling high. It typically means your city will have many trucks, freight trains, and cargo ships moving goods into and out of your city. The key to a successful city is to import when the global market price is low and export when the price is high. Around the office, a lot of us tend to specialize our cities around one form of manufacturing plus a little bit of trade. This helps us get our metals, petroleum, or electronics resources to the market more efficiently.

> One feature of the game that I have been concentrating on is the area of city specialization. *SimCity* allows a single player—or a group of players if you choose to play with other aspiring city builders—to connect up multiple cities in a larger region and share services and resources.

Disasters

Mayor, the city is off to a great start. But what if a disaster strikes?

Are there enough fire trucks to extinguish all the fires? Are there enough ambulances to treat every injured Sim? The city is prone to a number of random (and not so random) disasters, each with its own potential for widespread devastation. But disasters aren't the end of the world. Instead, they provide the city a second chance to come back healthier and stronger than ever. If there's one time the city needs a strong leader, it's in the aftermath of a disaster. Do you have what it takes to lead the city through its darkest days?

> Don't forget to go to **www.primagames.com** to access guide updates free of charge with your voucher code.

Major Disasters

Build a city, then knock it down! This fire-breathing lizard cuts a linear path of destruction through your city until it finds the nearest Garbage Dump.

There are a total of six major disasters in the Disasters menu. However, none of the disasters are immediately available—they must be unlocked by completing achievements. Once unlocked, a disaster can either be triggered manually, by selecting it from the Disasters menu, or can occur randomly, as determined by the simulation and certain geographical features—earthquakes are most common in mountainous cities while tornadoes are more likely to occur in open plains. Although they're responsible for leveling buildings, each disaster has at least one beneficial perk. Here's a quick look at all of the disasters available, as well as some advice for using these disasters to your city's advantage.

> **(i) NOTE**
>
> Random disasters are disabled when playing in Sandbox mode, but you can still create destruction on your own by choosing an unlocked disaster from the Disasters menu.

Earthquake

Description: Randomly destroys buildings within a large radius.

Did you feel that? The violent shaking of an earthquake will definitely get your attention as buildings crumble into piles of rubble and numerous fires breakout across the city. Once the shaking stops, make sure you have enough fire coverage to contend with all the blazes popping up around the earthquake's epicenter. An earthquake won't destroy every building, but the spread of fires could lead to a secondary disaster even more destructive than all that shaking. When triggering an earthquake of your own, be prepared for the widespread destruction to follow, ensuring any buildings you wish to spare are outside the affected area, marked in red. Earthquakes can also occur randomly, particularly in mountainous areas.

> **🔓 UNLOCK**
>
> **DUG TOO GREEDILY AND TOO DEEP**
>
> Mine 100 tons of coal or raw ore in your city to gain access to the Earthquake disaster!

Big Lizard

Description: Destroys all buildings within a linear path.

What could be cooler than a giant fire-breathing lizard stomping through your city? This red dragon-like reptile tunnels out of the ground beneath your city and begins marching, in a linear path, directly toward the nearest Garbage Dump. Along the way the big lizard destroys every building in its path, occasionally stopping to roar and ignite nearby buildings with fire. The big lizard concludes its visit to your city by consuming garbage at your Garbage Dump before eventually returning to its subterranean lair. Triggering a Big Lizard attack can be a useful way to clear a path through some unwanted buildings—it's certainly more entertaining than bulldozing. When choosing a point for the big lizard to enter your city, take into account the proximity to the nearest Garbage Dump, because your new friend will make a beeline for that lovely collection of garbage, destroying every building along the way.

> **🔓 UNLOCK**
>
> **WHAT'S COOKING?**
>
> Burn 100 tons of garbage in an Incinerator at the Garbage Dump to gain access to the Big Lizard disaster.

Meteor Strike

Description: Randomly destroys buildings within a large radius, sometimes creating a circle of ground pollution or radiation.

This spectacular disaster is better than any fireworks show. Watch as swarms of meteorites descend on your city, crashing into buildings and starting fires. When triggering this disaster on your own, place the wide red radius over a targeted area of your city and kick back and watch the destruction. Regardless of how this disaster is triggered you'll need good fire coverage to put out all those fires. Meteors also have a chance of leaving behind ground pollution and radiation, potentially making the site unlivable.

🔓 UNLOCK

WHAT GOES UP MUST COME DOWN

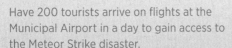

Have 200 tourists arrive on flights at the Municipal Airport in a day to gain access to the Meteor Strike disaster.

Tornado

Description: Randomly destroys buildings in a wandering path.

The tornado is likely the first disaster you'll unlock, rewarded after placing 24 turbine module at a Wind Power Plant. Consider giving the tornado a whirl before your city gets too beautiful. While you can choose the starting position of a tornado, there's no way to control where it goes once it touches down in your city. The tornado wanders randomly throughout your city, destroying every building in its path. Given its unpredictable nature, the tornado isn't the most precise disaster if you're looking to clear some space in a specific area. Like all disasters, tornadoes have a chance of appearing on their own—if your city is set in an open plain, there's a greater chance of a tornado appearing.

🔓 UNLOCK

BLOWIN' IN THE WIND

Have 24 Wind Turbines at Wind Power Plants in your city to gain access to the Tornado disaster.

Other Disasters

In addition to the five major disasters available in the Disasters menu, there are also two other disasters to watch out for. You cannot trigger these disasters directly. Instead, they occur randomly based on certain conditions.

Nuclear Meltdown: If a Nuclear Power Plant is staffed by uneducated workers, there's an increased chance of a nuclear meltdown, spreading radioactive ground pollution over a wide radius around the power plant. Radiation dissipates over time, but a large portion of your city will remain unlivable until then.

Plague: A reliance on mass transit can lead to the outbreak of a plague, putting serious strain on your Clinics and Hospitals as sick Sims seek treatment. Untreated sick Sims will become injured. If there aren't enough ambulances to go around, these injured Sims will die.

UFO Encounter

Description: Randomly destroys a building, abducts Sims, or steals resources from storage lots.

Who are they? Where do they come from? It's unclear what these otherworldly visitors want from your city. The objective of each visit is random. Sometimes a UFO appears overhead and annihilates a random building. Other times UFOs only abduct Sims or steal resources from one of your storage lots. But despite their mischievous behavior, visitations by a UFO produce a burst of skill similar to a University, encouraging the creation of high tech (tech level 3) buildings in industrial zones. When abducting Sims, the UFO also has a high chance of targeting criminals in jails at your Police Station or Police Precinct. So if you're facing an overcrowding jail situation, it may be time for a visit from a UFO. But it's impossible to tell what will happen when the UFO appears over your city—it may very well blow away your entire Police Precinct!

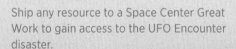

🔓 UNLOCK

WE ARE NOT ALONE...

Ship any resource to a Space Center Great Work to gain access to the UFO Encounter disaster.

⚠ CAUTION

Remember, there are no saved games to revert back to. So think twice before unleashing a disaster on your city—the damage is irreversible.

Zombie Attack

Description: Zombies roam the streets at night and feast on the brains of unsuspecting Sims.

Beware of green glowing zombies emerging from the Hospital at night. These nocturnal brain-eating ghouls feed on the brains of innocent Sims, leading to the creation of more zombies with each encounter. Your police force will have their hands full trying to contain this outbreak. Fortunately, when the sun rises, all zombies crumble, bringing an end to this terror. Unlike the other major disasters, zombie attacks do not damage any buildings. But the nightly death toll is reported in the morning, tallying the number of unfortunate Sims who met a gruesome fate.

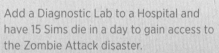

🔓 UNLOCK

LABORATORY OUTBREAK

Add a Diagnostic Lab to a Hospital and have 15 Sims die in a day to gain access to the Zombie Attack disaster.

Disaster Management

For the most part, disasters are bad for your city. Sure, they all have their perks, but the widespread random destruction usually isn't worth any benefit. However, maybe your city needs an overhaul? And disasters are much more efficient for leveling large swaths of your city than a bulldozer. Plus, they're fun to watch. Whether you trigger a disaster yourself or one randomly occurs, it's important to be prepared for the aftermath by planning ahead and fostering relationships with neighboring cities to assist in disaster relief.

Triggering Disasters

Some disasters, like the earthquake and meteor, have a wide impact radius, dishing out destruction over a large area.

So you still want to unleash a disaster on your city? First, you must complete the secret achievements associated with each disaster. Once a disaster is unlocked, it appears within the Disaster menu. Simply select the desired disaster from the menu and then choose where in your city you want the disaster to begin. The cursor becomes a transparent glowing red circle, showing you where the disaster will be centered. For radius-based disasters like the earthquake and meteor, this red circle is large, indicating the area that will be affected—this is a good way to target specific areas of your city you wish to demolish. For the unpredictable disasters like the tornado or UFO, you can choose an area where the disaster will first appear. But for the tornado, you have no idea where it will travel, potentially carving a destructive path through areas you never intended to destroy. And as for the UFO, you can give it an approximate appearance site, but there's no telling what it will do when it arrives—it may destroy a building, abduct Sims, or simply steal resources from a nearby storage lot. The big lizard is a bit more predictable, traveling in a straight line from the starting point to the nearest Garbage Dump, clearing a path along the way. But no disaster allows the control of a bulldozer, so don't expect scalpel-like precision when it comes to demolishing parts of your city. Be prepared to tolerate unforeseen collateral damage.

> **⚠ CAUTION**
>
> Avoid triggering disasters near a Trade Depot or Trade Port. The destruction of storage lots at these facilities can mean the loss of precious resources worth hundreds of thousands.

Emergency Response

You'll need some help putting out all those fires. Ask neighboring cities to volunteer fire trucks and other emergency vehicles.

The occurrence of a random disaster can be completely demoralizing. But there's no time to shed a tear for Sims and buildings lost in the destruction. Chances are buildings are burning and injured Sims are scattered about requiring urgent treatment. It's time to jump into action and salvage what's left of your tattered city. Any untouched Fire Stations and Large Fire Stations will immediately jump into action, dispatching trucks to fires. Clinics and Hospitals will do the same, sending out ambulances to gather injured Sims. But your city's emergency services may not be enough. If you haven't already, reach out to neighboring cities and request ambulances and fire trucks to assist in the aftermath of a disaster. Your fellow mayors should be more than happy to help—plus they earn fees for each fire they extinguish and each injured Sim they treat. In the chance your entire emergency infrastructure has been destroyed, you'll need to rely solely on assistance from other cities to stop the spread of fires. For this reason, it's a good idea to plan ahead, long before a disaster strikes. Volunteer your emergency vehicles to other cities and other mayors are likely to do the same. All volunteered emergency vehicles automatically respond when needed, providing some comfort in knowing that you're not in this alone.

Cleanup

Look at all that rubble! Bulldoze those rubble piles as soon as possible. New construction can't begin until the rubble is gone.

Once the smoke clears and all fires have been extinguished, it's time to think about rebuilding. Sometimes disasters provide a fresh start, allowing you to improve your city by better meeting the demands of the surviving residents. But before you can start drafting new plans, you need to deal with all those unsightly piles of rubble where buildings once stood. Rubble reduces land value, so it's important to get rid of it as soon as possible—pause the game and then go to work with the bulldozer. While you're at it, you may also want to bulldoze any unwanted roads, as a disaster only destroys buildings. With the rubble cleared, do a quick triage of your city's infrastructure. Address the loss of any utilities, replacing power plants and water sources first, followed by sewage and waste disposal. Next, repair damage to any facilities associated with city special-

izations and their supply lines, especially if your economy depends on exports. The rebuilding of city services such as Hospitals, Police Stations, and Fire Stations can wait as long as other cities volunteer emergency vehicles to provide coverage. Rebuilding isn't cheap, so consider taking out loans. Neighboring cities may also assist in disaster relief by gifting Simoleons. Once your city's infrastructure is restored, turn your attention to rebuilding the demolished parts of your city. Here's your second chance to make the city better than ever!

DISASTER ACHIEVEMENTS

Icon	Name	Description
	Blowin' in the Wind	Have 24 Wind Turbines at Wind Power Plants in your city to gain access to the Tornado disaster.
	Dug Too Greedily and Too Deep	Mine 100 tons of coal or raw ore in your city to gain access to the Earthquake disaster.
	Laboratory Outbreak	Add a Diagnostic Lab to a Hospital and have 15 Sims die in a day to gain access to the Zombie Attack disaster.
	We Are Not Alone	Ship any resource to a Space Center Great Work to gain access to the UFO Encounter disaster.
	What Goes Up Must Come Down	Have 200 tourists arrive on flights at the Municipal Airport in a day to gain access to the Meteor Strike disaster.
	What's Cookin'?	Burn 100 tons of garbage in an Incinerator at the Garbage Dump to gain access to the Big Lizard disaster.

CHAT WITH THE DEVELOPERS

Build and Destroy: Detailing Disasters

ALEX PECK, DEVELOPMENT DIRECTOR

Hi everyone! I'm Alex Peck, a development director on *SimCity*. The first time I saw the original *SimCity* at a friend's house, I was so intrigued by it that I snuck away from his dinner party to get some more time on his computer. Ten years later, I was privileged to work on *SimCity 4* and *SimCity 4 Rush Hour*, and now ten years after that I'm here at Maxis working on a new take on the series.

SimCity is a game that really satisfies our creative urges. But it's always had a darker side in the form of disasters. Random disasters are good at shaking up a city and keeping things from becoming too static. And user-controlled disasters are for the player who likes to kick over his own sandcastles—you know who you are.

Our first prototype disaster in the new *SimCity* was the meteor shower. It started out as just a single meteorite smacking into a residential suburb, but upon seeing it in action, we immediately decided to dial it up to see what would happen. We added some tension by having most of the meteors burn up before they hit the ground—we call these "fizzlers"—but an unpredictable amount of larger, damaging meteorites may appear during the sequence.

While we were creating this, out of sheer curiosity I checked to see how often meteorites actually cause damage, and it seems rather rare. Wikipedia only notes a few human injuries, a dog in Egypt, and one extremely unfortunate cow. Guess the solar system that *SimCity* is located in must have far more debris than our own!

UFOs in particular resulted in a fun brainstorming session. Rather than simply wantonly raining destruction from above, we thought UFOs should have a bit of a mysterious flavor to them. They will enter your city with various agendas to carry out, perhaps simply leaving if they can't find what they are looking for. What are the aliens going to do with that poor Sim they abducted? I leave it to your imagination.

For this incarnation of the game we also decided to add some physics to the mix, resulting in buildings that shatter into pieces and fall to the ground. This paid off when someone said "Can the UFO cut a building in half?" and our physics programmer Robert Perry said, "Sure!" (Check out Robert's discussion on physics next.)

Whether it's an earthquake, a meteor shower, a tornado, or even the simple demolition tool, we have provided a number of tools to cater to your darker side.

> The first time I saw the original *SimCity* at a friend's house, I was so intrigued by it that I snuck away from his dinner party to get some more time on his computer. Ten years later, I was privileged to work on *SimCity 4* and *SimCity 4 Rush Hour*, and now ten years after that I'm here at Maxis working on a new take on the series.

CHAT WITH THE DEVELOPERS

Shaking it Up: *SimCity*'s Physics

ROBERT PERRY, PHYSICS ENGINEER

Hey everyone! I'm Robert Perry and I'm the engineer in charge of physics for *SimCity*. The two things I enjoy most are building things and solving problems. *SimCity* is a fun way for me to do both.

When we use the phrase, "what you see is what we sim," we really mean it. With that said, why should physics get left out? Physics provides another tool to simulate what happens in a city. We've coupled physics with the GlassBox engine to create an even deeper simulation. Every building in *SimCity* is simulated in the physics engine. Buildings are attached to the ground with a physics model that simulates the forces that act on that building. When a module is stacked on a building, the building reacts. If multiple modules are stacked on a building, they all react. If an object strikes a building, the building reacts—modules included.

Disasters are where the physics system is put to best use. Disasters are able to affect the game physics in a variety of ways. A small meteorite will set a building rocking; a large one will reduce it to a pile of rubble on the blackened, scorched ground. Physics is a great simulation tool and it adds depth and nuance to the game, but there are some things we don't solve using physics. One example is vehicles. The transport team has done a great job with the vehicles and there's not a lot the physics would add there. Vehicles turn, merge, and navigate with detailed behavior. At the scale the vehicles operate at the physics system wouldn't add enough benefit to justify the cost in performance.

> **Disasters are where the physics system is put to best use. Disasters are able to affect the game physics in a variety of ways. A small meteorite will set a building rocking; a large one will reduce it to a pile of rubble on the blackened, scorched ground.**

When we've hit instances where physics alone isn't the best solution, we've been able to team up with the artists to create integrated solutions. Simulating a tornado is far beyond the scope of *SimCity*. We use a hybrid approach with the tornado that allows an artist to create a particle system to drive physics bodies. The tornado sucks up buildings and vehicles, drives them up and through its funnel with an animated particle system, and seamlessly releases them to the physics system. The final result is that tornados will chew through your city and fling buildings and vehicles like a giant blender that has been released in your city.

Earthquakes, in particular, make for good use of physics, as triggering this particular disaster will shake buildings to the ground (as one would expect). And UFOs, besides abducting Sims and stealing resources, will slice buildings in two with a laser. Typical alien behavior.

What I've talked about here is just a small taste of what to expect in the new *SimCity*. As you know, disasters have always been a big part of *SimCity* and they're better than ever. Make no mistake, buildings will crumble, debris will fly, and stuff will explode. This *SimCity* is a simulation with great depth and detail. Physics allows us to layer on more detail and ultimately bring more fun to *SimCity*. I'm looking forward to hearing what everyone thinks of the disasters.

SimCity World

Now that you have a good grasp on what it takes to be a successful Mayor, look to *SimCity* World for a deeper and more rewarding experience.

Did your friend just pass you on the Crime leaderboard? Then get busy filling your city with criminals to reclaim your position. Or perhaps you're ready to take on a challenge, requiring you to work with other mayors in your region to complete a specific goal in a short span of time? Did you just buy some alloy this morning? Check its current price on the global market—if the price has gone up, consider exporting that alloy to net an easy profit. The ever-changing dynamics offered by *SimCity* World ensure there's always new ways to interact with the game and the community, creating a fresh gameplay experience no matter how long you've been sitting in the Mayor's chair.

> Don't forget to go to **www.primagames.com** to access guide updates free of charge with your voucher code.

CityLog

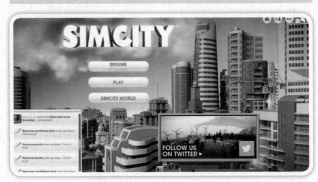

Access the CityLog feed directly from the main menu. This is a great way to receive updates of recent activity while you were away from the game.

CityLog is the pipeline to your fellow mayors, feeding you messages and updates from the *SimCity* community. A popup appears whenever you have a new message. Click on the CityLog button in the lower left corner to view the latest message feed. The CityLog lists your friends' latest activities, including whenever they start a new region, their achievements, notable rankings, and invitations to play in their region. The CityLog also displays challenge updates, announcing the start of a challenge and the eventual winner. Click any of these messages to be taken to view details of the message or update.

Achievements

In the Achievements window, the grayed-out entries represent achievements you haven't earned yet. Time to get to work!

Want to work toward a specific goal? Then turn to the game's numerous achievements. For the most part, *SimCity* is an open world gaming experience, allowing you to define and complete your own goals. Achievements are optional tasks with clearly defined criteria. For example, the Medical Miracle achievement requires you to treat 200 Sims at a Hospital within a day. Achievements sometimes require

you to play the game in counterintuitive ways that may not benefit your city or its residents. For Medical Miracle, it may be helpful to pollute your water source to produce the 200 sick Sims required to complete the achievement. Other achievements are more easy to attain and occur naturally through gameplay by accumulating resources—you get the King Coal achievement for extracting 100,000 tons of coal. Playing to earn achievements adds an addictive element to the game, allowing for a more focused gameplay experience. There's also a competitive factor, since all achievements earned are shared on the CityLog, updating your friends on your latest successes.

> **ⓘ NOTE**
>
> For a list of achievements, flip to the Quick Reference chapter in the back of the guide.

SimCity World Interface

From the game's main menu, click on the *SimCity* World button to open a window giving you access to the leaderboards, challenges, and global market. Use the information here to guide your gameplay and interact with friends and the community in new ways.

Leaderboards

The leaderboards are a fun way to see how your cities and regions stack up against the competition.

Select the Leaderboards tab to view how your cities and regions rank. There are a total of 15 leaderboards, allowing you to compete with friends or the worldwide *SimCity* community. The leaderboards are broken up into two sections. The first ten leaderboards appear under the Stats tab, giving you breakdowns of the current leaders in population, Simoleons, wealth, approval rating, education, crime, health, sickness, pollution, and green regions. The second set of leaderboards appears under the

Headquarters tab and reveals the current city specialization leaders including metals, petroleum, trade, electronics, and gambling. Use the buttons at the bottom of the screen to filter the leaderboards based on just your friends, your own top regions, or the global *SimCity* community—even if you can't place on the global leaderboards, try to at least beat your friends!

Challenges

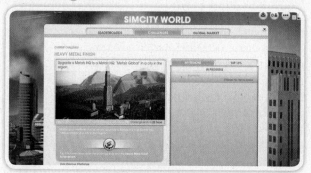

The Challenges tab shows the current challenge available to all players. But the clock is ticking—better get started!

Choose the Challenges tab to view the current community challenge. Challenges add a competitive and goal-oriented element to a game that otherwise has no defined victory conditions. Take on these challenges to earn unique achievements, not to mention bragging rights. But completing challenges often requires the cooperation of your fellow mayors in the region. For instance, the Black

Gold challenge requires your region to sell 2,000,000 barrels of crude oil. But it's not that simple. You must complete the challenge goal in the fastest time possible. The top 10% fastest regions will win the exclusive challenge achievement. Replay the challenge in different regions throughout the challenge period to see if you can improve your time. As a result, achievements awarded from challenges are super exclusive, instantly showing off your astute mayoral skills to friends and the community.

(i) NOTE

New challenges are released on a regular basis. Flip to the Quick Reference chapter in the back of the guide for a preview of the first few challenges available shortly after the game's launch.

Global Market

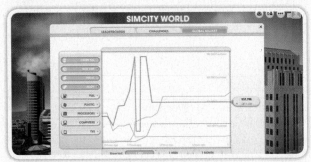

Keep tabs on the fluctuating prices in the global market and look for opportunities score some extra income for your city by importing and exporting out of a Trade Depot or Trade Port.

Ready to buy low and sell high? Access the Global Market tab to view the prices of all resources in the game. You can filter the chart to view data just for the last day, the last week, or the last month—prices shown are for a single truckload of each resource. Use the information here to determine what resources to focus on exporting and what you can expect to pay if you need to import any resources. Prices on the global market are driven by real-time supply and demand. So if players begin dumping tons of coal onto the market, the price for coal will drop. Likewise, if a resource like plastic becomes scarce as demand increases, the market price for plastic will rise. By playing the global market you can carve out a nice profit for your city through the trade business, importing and exporting resources from a Trade Depot or Trade Port.

(i) NOTE

Global market prices are updated approximately every hour, so keep checking back frequently to identify potential profit-making opportunities.

Online Resources

SIMCITY OFFICIAL WEBSITE

www.simcity.com

Make this your first stop for all things *SimCity,* including all the latest news, media, and community updates. Also, don't forget to check out the forums, frequented by developers and some of the most knowledgeable players around the world.

SIMCITY BLOG

www.simcity.com/blog

Head over to the *SimCity* Blog for more information directly from the game's designers, including plenty of gameplay tips as well as an insider look at the game's development.

SIMCITYEDU

www.simcityedu.org

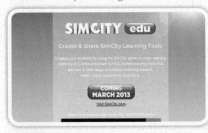

*SimCity*EDU serves as a resource for classroom teachers who have a strong interest in utilizing digital platforms as a learning tool to drive student interest in STEM (Science, Technology, Engineering, and Mathematics) subjects.

SIMTROPOLIS

www.simtropolis.com

Simtropolis is a *SimCity* fan site with a very active and passionate community. Come here to find friends by participating in the forums or learn more about *SimCity* by browsing through the extensive omnibus or wiki.

CHAT WITH THE DEVELOPERS

Popping the Bubble: Exploring *SimCity* World

MEGHAN MCDOWELL, PRODUCER

Hi everyone! My name is Meghan McDowell and I'm a producer on *SimCity*. I've worked at Maxis for eight years and I'm really pleased to be part of the new *SimCity*. Part of my role here at the studio is to shape the *SimCity* World feature.

SimCity World is a collection of features that enhance a player's game experience by connecting them with one another. Through challenges, leaderboards, and the global market, *SimCity* World lets mayors shape their cities' stories in different ways, connect and engage with each other, and contribute to a global *SimCity* community. We built the *SimCity* World features as a way to surface that interconnected world to the player and show them how their gameplay can be complemented by being a part of it.

Part of our way of doing that is through CityLog, the tool that allows players to connect, notify, and act on events in *SimCity*. CityLog does a lot of things. It allows you to see if your friends have founded new cities in regions that you can join. Or it tells you that your friends have passed you on a leaderboard. If there's a challenge going on in a region, it shows you your progress. It even messages any global market changes you may want to take advantage of. Lastly, it lets you know about any achievements your friends are earning in case you want to strive to achieve the same ones. All of the messages you see in CityLog have an action you can take. You don't have to act, but if you are looking for new and interesting ways to play (or just want to keep tabs on what your friends are doing), CityLog can help keep you up to date.

> I've worked at Maxis for eight years and I'm really pleased to be part of the new *SimCity*. Part of my role here at the studio is to shape the *SimCity* World feature.

One of the new ways to play is through our regular challenges. Challenges are competitive, where regions compete against each other and vie to win exclusive rewards. Challenges are completely optional, but are a great way to prove to the world what kind of Mayor you are. They take strategy and coordination to succeed at. You can work alone, with your region, or with the entire community to complete them.

To coincide with challenges we also have leaderboards. There are many different types of leaderboards in the game and they encourage you to compete or simply to see how you compare to the rest of the mayors in *SimCity*. They range from traditional leaderboards like biggest population, more deviant boards like biggest polluters, and competitive leaderboards like most profitable casino city. You can compare yourself to the global *SimCity* community or to your friends. Right now, I'm gunning for the top of the Crime leaderboards in the studio. I'm quite the lawless Mayor!

The global market makes up the last piece of *SimCity* World, and it is here where goods and resources can be bought and sold. The market fluctuates depending on how our players are playing. Players can affect the global market by how they play. So if oil prices are up, players may decide to invest in oil drilling in their city so that they can profit from it by selling the goods to other players.

Before I go, I just wanted to say I'm having a lot of fun playing *SimCity* and every day something fun, unexpected, and amazing goes on in the game. I'm excited for all of you to get your hands on it. See you on the leaderboard!

Behind the Scenes

Maxis: A Closer Look

The **SimCity** development team at the Maxis studio in Emeryville, California.

Maxis, originally founded in 1987 and now an Electronic Arts label with studios in Emeryville, Redwood Shores, and Salt Lake City, has created some of the world's most popular franchises including *SimCity*, *Spore*, and *The Sims*—one of the best selling franchises in gaming history. Maxis games exemplify deep simulations that encourage player-driven creativity.

Soon after entering the office, visitors are greeted by a familiar logo set against the backdrop of a massive cityscape, clearly a nod to the **SimCity** *franchise.*

These simulations, often referred to as "god games," allow players to create the environments and stories of the games themselves. Will Wright, co-founder of Maxis, says that what players really like about games like *SimCity* and *The Sims* is exploring what he calls "possibility space."

"I believe both games (*SimCity* and *The Sims*) deliver an experience that is uniquely Maxis," says Lucy Bradshaw, Senior Vice President of Maxis. "We take real world systems, deconstruct them, and then put them back together again in a fashion that invites our players to tinker, experiment, explore, and master these systems—from urban planning to family dynamics. Through play and experimentation, you begin to understand how the game system works, and as you begin to master that system, you get to decide how you want to play."

Lead Designer Stone Librande lays out a prototype city consisting of tiny papercraft buildings.

Many members of the Maxis team have been playing *SimCity* since its first release in the late 1980s. Key staff—Lucy Bradshaw, Ocean Quigley, Stone Librande, and others—have been with the company for more than a decade. Despite the long hours and bug fixes involved in the final push to the launch of *SimCity*, the delight in the game is palpable. One team member has developed an elaborate story about a resident criminal he is keeping tabs on. Another finds that his prize city has suffered a nuclear meltdown (see Developer Cities in the Getting Started chapter). When a game can still offer discovery, surprise, and sometimes heartbreak to the people who have been living and breathing its development for months and months, you know you have a good thing going.

*When creating the new **SimCity**, the team drew inspiration from many sources. The office is filled with numerous artifacts from this process, including tiny city models as well as walls covered with reference photography.*

The games developed at Maxis are built to be fun, and they are. They also give players glimpses into systems and theories that shape the world we live in. The team at Maxis brings a wealth of information and experience to the development of games like *SimCity*. Wandering around the studio, one finds mechanical engineers, artists, philosophers, psychologists, musicians, and, yes, computer programmers. The assumptions underlying the structure of the games they create are not arbitrary, but are based on the real world. The folks at Maxis believe these games are more than just entertainment; they also invite us to think critically and creatively. We not only learn how the game works—we also learn about how the world works.

*Here a few team members enjoy a quick lunch break before getting back to work, helping make this the best **SimCity** yet!*

SimCity Legacy: The Whole Story

Production on the first **SimCity** *began in 1985. The working name for the game in development was Micropolis.*

The official launch date of the first *SimCity* game to be on the shelves was in 1989, but its true history began four years earlier.

It all started when the then-unknown game developer Will Wright was working on a game called *Raid on Bungeling Bay*. The game was a fly 'em, shoot 'em up game, where the player controlled a helicopter loaded with missiles and machine guns. The helicopter flew out on missions to destroy island archipelagoes. In the development of the game, Wright found he was having more fun developing the islands than he was destroying them. And so the seed was sown. Why not create a game about constructing cities instead of destroying them?

After pitching the idea to game publishers with no success, Wright decided to develop the game himself. Designed for the Commodore 64, the first *SimCity* hit the shelves in 1985, where it pretty much stayed. Fortunately, Wright met Jeff Braun, a man who was able to make things happen, and the two formed the Maxis Company in 1987.

SimCity

1989: Maxis publishes **SimCity** *for the PC and Mac, and Broderbund agrees to distribute it.*

In 1989, Maxis launched *SimCity* for the PC and Mac. Broderbund agreed to distribute it. The game was not an immediate success. Sales were so slow that Wright and Braun handled tech support for the game themselves answering phones from Braun's apartment. Word-of-mouth reports of the game spread in the next few months, and people began to take notice. *Newsweek* magazine published a full-page story on the game, and sales took off. Interest in this new genre of realistic, open-ended, non-violent games was not limited to gamers. The CIA, Department of Defense, and others expressed interest in different kinds of simulations. Educators of all stripes started using *SimCity* as a classroom tool.

From 1990–1993, Maxis released three new simulation games. More than just variations on a theme, each of these games highlighted different aspects of real-life interactions and processes. *SimEarth* is a game based

SimCity Timeline

1985: *MICROPOLIS*

Platform: Commodore 64

Game designer Will Wright begins working on what will become *SimCity* under the working title *Micropolis*.

1989: *SIMCITY*

Platform: Amiga, Macintosh, PC, and Commodore 64

SimCity is published in North America. Later in 1989, the game is later released for the Atari ST.

1991: *SIMCITY*

Platform: Super NES

SimCity is released for Nintendo's Super NES platform in North America and Japan. The SNES version features seasonal graphics, bonus scenarios, and a wacky city advisor named Dr. Wright.

1993: *SIMCITY 2000*

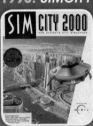

Platform: Macintosh

SimCity 2000, the sequel to *SimCity*, is released for the Macintosh operating system. The game features different land elevations, underground layers, new facilities, a variety of power plants, neighboring cities, more elaborate budget and finance controls, and disaster scenarios.

on James Lovelock's Gaia theory of planetary evolution. *SimAnt* pits different ant colonies against each other, until the victorious colony has amassed the power to invade the human dwelling. *SimFarm* brings in the idea of commodities and markets, and challenges the player to develop and manage a farm that weathers fluctuations in crop prices and the weather.

SimCity 2000

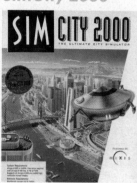

*Released in January 1994, **SimCity 2000** became the top selling game in the world and remained in the number one spot for half a year.*

In 1994, *SimCity 2000*, the sequel to *SimCity*, was released for the Macintosh operating system. The game featured different land elevations, underground layers, new facilities, a variety of power plants, neighboring cities, more elaborate budget and finance controls, and disaster scenarios. It was a hit. In the first four months of its release, *SimCity 2000* sold more than 300,000 copies. Another new aspect of the game, which has been incorporated into every version since, was the ability to rotate the view of your city, so players can see their creations from all angles. Many of the new features in the game were the direct result of player feedback to the development team, another tradition that became a standard component of Maxis game titles.

In 1995 Maxis went public, and in 1996 committed to the release of four new titles. It was a stretch, but four new games were shipped that year: *SimCopter*, *SimTunes*, *SimPark*, and *Full Tilt! Pinball*. Maxis was a hot commodity.

In 1997, the studio was purchased by EA. Former Electronic Arts CEO Larry Probst offered this anecdote about the acquisition and Wright's latest project.

"We were really fortunate because Maxis had *SimCity* and when we started the due diligence we asked, 'What's going on with Will Wright?' Their response was, 'He's working offsite with six or seven people on an architectural design tool.' It turned out he was in an office literally next door to where EA was located."

After seeking out Wright, the acquisition would become a no-brainer. "They started talking and kicking around some creative ideas and that was the beginning of *The Sims*. We ended up acquiring Maxis, hiring Will, getting *The Sims*, and the rest is history," recalls Probst.

1995: *SIMCITY 2000*

Platform: PC, Super NES, Saturn

SimCity 2000 is released for Super NES, Saturn, and Windows. It is later released for PlayStation, N64, and Game Boy Advance.

1999: *SIMCITY 3000*

Platform: PC, Macintosh, and Linux

SimCity 3000 is the first *SimCity* game published by Electronic Arts. *SimCity 3000* expands upon city management and business deals.

2003: *SIMCITY 4*

Platform: PC and Mac OS X

SimCity 4 is released, featuring a 3D graphics engine, day and night cycles, and three modes: God Mode, Mayor Mode, and My Sim Mode.

2007: *SIMCITY SOCIETIES*

Platform: PC

SimCity Societies is developed by Tilted Mill Entertainment and published by Electronic Arts for the PC. The game focuses less on city planning and more on citizens and societal values.

SimCity 3000

*In **SimCity 3000**, players could add architecture and engineering to their skill sets. The new architecture tool allowed you to design your own buildings, then watch them come alive as part of the cityscape.*

In 1999, *SimCity 3000*, the third installment in the *SimCity* series, was released for Windows, Macintosh, and Linux. It was the first *SimCity* game published by Electronic Arts. *SimCity 3000* expanded upon city management and business deals as well as featured new advisors and petitioners, news tickers, real world landmarks, and a live music score.

The upgraded version of *SimCity 3000*, *SimCity 3000 Unlimited*, offered improvements and allowed the player to create its cities with European and Asian style buildings, layouts, and landmarks. *SimCity 3000* also allowed for negotiating business deals with (simulated) mayors of neighboring cities. The economics of city functioning became more fine-tuned, as did the graphics of the terrain and landscape (green grass, different types of trees).

The early years of the new millennium heralded in a new variant on *SimCity*. In February 2000, Maxis/EA released *The Sims*. Now, the inhabitants of *SimCity* had up close and personal lives of their own. The game was a hit, and in the next three years, ten different versions of *The Sims* hit the shelves.

SimCity 4

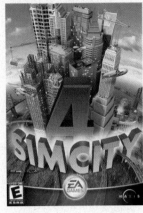

SimCity 4, the fourth generation, ships for Windows and Mac OS X platforms in 2003.

And then there was night. *SimCity 4*, released in 2003, introduced day and night cycles to the game. Adding more realism to the concept of time, the game simulated urban decay and gentrification as conditions change in a neighborhood. Cities also came in regions, where players could develop smaller districts of a large metropolitan area. And you could still be chief city architect.

With the My Sim mode of the game, *SimCity 4* could be used in conjunction with *The Sims*. Your favorite Sims could be imported into a city for use in the My Sim mode. Players could also import city layouts created in *SimCity 4* into *The Sims 2,* giving you the power to design your own neighborhoods. Later in the year, Maxis released *Rush Hour: SimCity 4*, an expansion pack with enhanced transportation and architecture options.

It's been ten years since the last chapter of *SimCity*. Of course, things weren't quiet during that time. *SimCity* was released for other platforms. *Spore*, the game of evolution, was released. And, as always, there was more Sims activity. Perhaps you've waited all those ten years for this next chapter in the *SimCity* story, or perhaps this is your first introduction to the game. Either way, we think the wait was worth it.

2008: *SIMCITY CREATOR*

Platform: Wii and Nintendo DS

SimCity Creator is released featuring advanced zones, sophisticated transportation, customizable buildings based on several themes, and the option to take overhead 3D tours of the city by helicopter or airplane.

2011: *SIMCITY DELUXE*

Platform: iOS and Android

SimCity Deluxe is released as an app for iPad and Android.

2013: *SIMCITY*

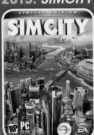

Platform: PC and Mac

Maxis releases the new *SimCity*, giving players the power to change the world once again.

CHAT WITH THE DEVELOPERS

SimCity Image Filters

OCEAN QUIGLEY, CREATIVE DIRECTOR

Hi—Ocean Quigley here to tell you about some of the final touches I've added to *SimCity*.

A big part of what makes a game look beautiful is the way that all of the colors work together. Usually, an artist does what's called "color grading" to make everything look just right. You've probably seen examples of it in movies – think of the sepia tones of *O Brother, Where Art Thou?* or the vivid greens and reds of *Amélie* or the teal and orange palette of pretty much any Michael Bay movie ever. In fact, it's kind of startling to look at movie footage before it's been color graded—it looks OK, but nothing like it does when it's finished.

Instagram and Hipstamatic, among many others, have turned that process into filters that you can apply to your snapshots. And what filter you choose makes a big impact on how the photo makes you feel. Different people respond to different filters, and people have their favorites (and ones that they hate).

For *SimCity*, rather than choose for you, I figured it was best to let you make up your own mind. So I've come up with a bunch of different filters that give different sensibilities to the game. You can use whichever ones you like. Here's the first batch. Take a look:

The Film Noir filter does a filtered black and white transform.

This is Soft. It's Kip Katsarelis's favorite filter. It bleaches and mutes the colors just a little bit, making the city look more realistic. I think that a lot of people are going to wind up playing with this one.

Starting with the default view, without any filter.

Warmer is Guillaume Pierre's favorite filter. It pushes the palette into a brownish range and is modeled on your standard FPS colors.

This is the Juicy filter. It's a bit darker in mid-tones and adds a warm saturation to the scene.

Cooler is Scott Nagy's favorite filter. It gives the game a cool, mid-century Kodachrome feel.

Neutral is basically the same as having no filter, just with a little bit more contrast. Faded washes out the colors, and adds a little silvering to everything. Green Tones is modeled on 1970s-era movies. Platinum is kind of a silly one, but I liked it. It's evocative of Hollywood glamour photography from the golden age of cinema. Teal and Orange is your typical Hollywood blockbuster palette. It brings out the contrast in the game. Orange and Gray washes out all the colors except orange.

The Neutral filter just punches the contrast a little bit and adds vignetting.

This is the Faded filter, which washes out greens and blues.

Green Tones is inspired by mid-1970s movie film stock.

Here's the Platinum filter, for that 1930s glamour look, complete with a little solarization.

And the Hollywood favorite, Teal and Orange. I like it a lot, despite its cliched reputation.

Orange and Gray takes all of the colors that aren't red/orange and makes them gray. Pretty simple.

Bleached emulates a bleach bypass technique, like you see in fashion photography. Sepia Toned makes the game feel like it's all old-timey. Black and Red is a super-high-contrast palette, inspired by a movie that sounded a lot like *SimCity*. Desaturated is another hardcore FPS-style palette, with most of the colors stripped out. And Vintage is inspired by cross-processed film. It looks like the 1970s to me.

Desaturated pulls out most of the color, for people who don't like bright colors in their video games.

Bleached applies a bleach-bypass-style filter. It's a technique you see in a lot of fashion photography.

And Vivid is for people who do.

The Sepia Toned filter, which makes everything look kind of old fashioned.

Here's the Vintage filter, which looks like cross-processed film. It's got a 1970s vibe, I think.

Switching to the Black and Red filter, which gives the city a more menacing quality.

In addition to filters that stylize the game with different color treatments, there are more functional ones. These filters apply various transforms to make the game more playable to people who are color blind. There are a few other graphics options to make the game look the way that you want it to. You can turn the tilt-shift effect up or down. And you can turn on the ultra lighting effects to get in-camera lens flare and blooming when you look at bright light sources. It makes the camera relate to lighting in a more realistic way.

> *SimCity* is a game with a tremendous amount of player creativity. I wanted to extend those options to the way that you look at the game itself. Thanks!

CHAT WITH THE DEVELOPERS

SimCity's Art of Building

MIKE KHOURY, ART DIRECTOR

Hi everyone! I'm Mike Khoury and I'm an Art Director on *SimCity*. I joined life at Maxis way back on the *SimCity 4: Rush Hour* expansion. I began work on the new *SimCity* pretty early on with Creative Director Ocean Quigley, and helped build out the style and look for the game. I prototyped the first Sim and made the first production building with our toolset back when we were first starting out.

We've come a long way since then. I currently art direct the player-placed buildings in our game. Basically, buildings that service your city, like fire stations, schools, and bus stations. These buildings span from simple buildings, to complex industrial facilities, and even famous landmarks. Our modular buildings span function across residential, commercial, or industrial types of architecture. And the modules themselves provide both gameplay benefits as well changes to the actual building. For instance, you can attach extra classrooms to a school to house more students or you can place a fire alarm on top of a Fire Station to decrease firefighter response times.

One of the best parts of working on this game, as a science geek, is all the research and knowledge you accumulate by having to make all these varied systems and objects. On the "buildings team" as we call it, we are always working closely with engineers, designers, and scripters to design and make buildings that are modular and have function to how they are assembled. The challenge with these buildings is to make them still look believable and realistic and fit within our game scale, even though they are put together in parts and can be assembled in different ways. As a designer of modular buildings, the challenge is to make a language of parts that are interesting and work well together, rather than a single final product.

My schooling and background is in industrial design, so I have a passion and a knack for designing such objects and systems. I also was the Lead Artist responsible for the creature, building, and vehicle editors in *Spore*. The challenges *Spore* presented for making the editable parts are similar to the challenges these modular buildings are currently giving us.

Now that you understand what we're creating, let's talk about the process we use to make one of the modular buildings and the family of buildings it belongs to. Let's look at coal. Several buildings span that category in our game: Coal Mines (which extract the raw resource and can also refine it), Coal Power Plants (which use the coal to power cities), and coal storage and shipping lots (which store the coal and allow for building an empire of trade). As I mentioned earlier, basic research is the foundation of creating one of our buildings because we want to try to stay faithful to the simulation and to the core of *SimCity* style, which is grounded in contemporary reality.

The design team usually boils down the basic functionality they need out of the buildings in a design document, including how game agents like Sims and vehicles interact with it. We start by researching those basic functioning buildings online and in books. In the case of coal, I even had a chance to visit a remote gold mining ghost town in California, which was awesome. We then meet about that idea as a group and look at our visual research, and talk about how this would work and feel like in the game.

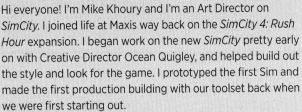

My schooling and background is in industrial design, so I have a passion and a knack for designing such objects and systems. I also was the Lead Artist responsible for the creature, building, and vehicle editors in *Spore*.

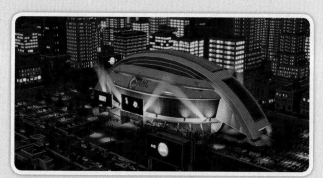

Once we have gathered a bunch of research and feel confident as a team that we have the basic idea nailed down, a concept artist will go off and sketch the building out in small, loose sketches. Although the sketches are loose, they need to follow a convention of scale to work in the game.

All our modular buildings adhere strictly to a unit-based system of measurement, so everything needs to be built to specific increments of size to be able to "snap" to other parts properly. The combinatory nature of these types of interactions for even three or four modules interacting with each other can get quite complex quickly when you take into account things like alignment, usage of space, and look/feel/scale of objects, as well as trying to not make everything look like it's made of similar homogenous boxy shapes.

Once the concept artist comes back with sketches, we decide to go with a direction and move into white-box (i.e., basic untextured) modeling phase. In this stage we are roughly modeling the forms and masses in 3D software, adhering to our system of units for size, and assign what we call snapping properties to the different modules depending on how we want them to attach or snap to each other. Once we have assigned the specific snap properties to the module, we try it out in game as a white-box and evaluate scale, form, and basic snap behavior and usability. Design and scripting can now work with this basic white-box for a while, assigning different behaviors and attributes to it to make the building work and do its job.

It becomes apparent quickly if a module is too big or small or doesn't allow for enough flexibility to accommodate gameplay. We then adjust this white-box according to feedback and put it through the review process. Once we have a good white-box and it passes the tests, we start the detailed color concept phase. Our concept artists use the original loose sketch, the accumulated visual research, and the white-box geometry as a blank canvas to paint in the lighting, textures, and detail in a 2D rendering that make the building look finished. When we have an approved color concept, we take the white-box model and begin to fully detail and texture the model, using proprietary in-house tools to match the 2D color concept as closely as possible in our game engine.

This then becomes our first take at a building. Other art teams like VFX, lot designers, lighting artists, and animators then take turns at this final model to give it polish and life. Of course in reality this doesn't happen sequentially, and often one artist is working in a preliminary stage and updating their work when the building is finalized later. The white-box model becomes a great branching point where a lot of different hands can get to a model, and still allow for art to continue to polish and make it look final over time.

Well I hope this was a good read for you and provided some insight into how we craft our content in house.

CHAT WITH THE DEVELOPERS

The Sound and Music of *SimCity*

KENT JOLLY, AUDIO DIRECTOR

Hello, I'm Kent Jolly, the audio director for *SimCity*. I've been with Maxis since 1998. The first big game that I worked on was *SimCity* 3000 as a sound designer, and from there I went on to work on *The Sims*, *SimCity 4*, and *Spore*. It's really cool to be working on *SimCity* again after such a long time. There is so much more we can do now than we could have done before. I'm going to talk a little bit about how we've implemented traffic sound effects in this game.

One of my favorite aspects of *SimCity*, and especially this new *SimCity*, is the challenge of creating a great traffic and city ambience. The reason I'm singling out the traffic is because it's amazing how different it is this time around. Because of the GlassBox engine, the traffic is no longer a representation of congestion or road type, it's actually showing you where people in your city are going. People are on their way to work, going out of town, going to the shop, going home, and more. That means that cars don't just disappear because there isn't "traffic" there, and it means that you don't see trucks in an industrial area just because it's an industrial area, you see all of this happening in your city because it's really moving resources from a manufacturing plant to a commercial store and so on. So, how does that affect audio?

In previous *SimCity* games we simply counted the number of cars and then played sounds randomly in that general area to replicate the simulation. If it was a residential area then you got "residential" car sounds, and if it was an industrial area you heard more truck sounds. In this *SimCity* the cars are actually tracked individually! We wait for a car to hit a stop light and then when it leaves the intersection we can play a sound of a car pulling away—and not just any car sound, the right car sound! We can also track the car as it moves and play a sound as it drives past.

We also change the sound based on the simulation speed of the game. As the cars go faster and faster, we adjust the audio to match what you see, but it remains true to the actual traffic.

I've worked on the *SimCity* franchise since *SimCity* 3000, and there has always been great music. Obviously, the new *SimCity* is no exception. Our composer Chris Tilton (who has worked on popular TV shows like *Fringe*) has done an amazing job, delivering not only great compositions, but compositions recorded with interactivity in mind.

The music in *SimCity* works a lot like the previous ones in the sense that there are full-length tunes that are chosen to play back at random, like a jukebox. The difference is that in this version the "jukebox" is a little more intelligent. Rather than just picking a tune to play, we look at the population of the city and pick a tune that is suited to the size of the city. As your city grows, so does the playlist of music, and you get tunes that feel "bigger" and more dramatic as your cities grow larger.

In addition to the playlist changing based on city size, the music changes based on your zoom level and whether or not you are viewing the game normally, are in Region View, or are using the building editor (the in-game editor that allows you to customize certain buildings). We did this by splitting the music up into several "stems" that can work in conjunction with each other, but also can stand on their own. So, when you go into a "light" data layer (where we showcase small visual elements like power/water traveling to buildings), we add percussion. When you go into a "heavy" data layer (where we show off more data-focused charts and graphs), we play up the electric guitar, drop other elements completely, and process the percussion with effects. When you are zoomed out, we use the orchestra, but when you zoom in it gets replaced with guitar.

So that's the music design in a nutshell. It was a blast to put this together, and a real treat to go to Warner Brothers and sit in on the recording sessions with Chris Tilton. I hope you enjoy the music in *SimCity* as much as I do!

CHAT WITH THE DEVELOPERS

The Sounds of Nonsense: Recording Simlish

KADET KUHNE, AUDIO SPECIALIST

Hi there! I'm Kadet Kuhne and I want to share a glimpse of the casting, recording, and implementation process for *SimCity*. I was hired on to the sound team at Maxis as a Voice Director and Sound Designer, and it has been a blast and truly an honor to work with such a talented team of artists on this awesome iteration of *SimCity*.

Working under the direction of Audio Director Kent Jolly and Designer Shawn Stone, our goal was to record a vast array of voices according to various archetypes covering residential, commercial, and industrial domains. These include residents, professionals, business persons, government employees, foremen, blue collar workers, industry barons, high tech bosses, and police and fire department workers, just to name a few. To start our recording session, I sent our character wish list along with audio samples, written Simlish examples, and audition instructions to EA's internal service that sends out casting calls to voice talent agencies. Within days, I received plenty of options to sift through.

One fascinating aspect of casting for *SimCity* was listening to hundreds of auditions in Simlish (the fictional, needs-based Sims language originally developed through experimentation with fractured Ukrainian, French, Latin, Finnish, English, Fijian, and Tagalog) while, at the same time, seeking nuanced performances according to character type, age, occupation, and emotion. Unique from previous incarnations of Simlish, our aim was to also include accents exemplifying various countries, though by no means representative of all. The timbre of the voices of the talent along with notable acting and recording experience was substantial enough to successfully illustrate the characters I was seeking to cast with my final candidates.

Recording at EA in Redwood City was a highlight of the process. With two rounds of sessions covering multiple days along with Engineers Miik Dinko and Christopher Davidson and the diverse stream of talent, there was no shortage of determined focus and humorous outtakes. For each character we recorded four emotional deliveries—happy, neutral, angry, and sad—at three different lengths covering a range of one- to six-second sound bites. In *SimCity*, the Sims are viewed from an aerial perspective, so the greatest challenge for the talent was projecting their voices loudly while simultaneously conveying the intended emotion and accent or tone of their character. We captured thousands of takes for the missions they send you on. We also recorded plenty of wild sounds for use in the game that cover events like Sims arriving at home, PA announcements at work, and reactionary screams for when disasters strike.

After selecting and editing the best takes, the files were mastered and given a touch of reverb and equalization to set the spatial signature of a cityscape. Then I uploaded each character into "random containers" for each mood and length. When a player clicks on a character's speech bubble in game, the appropriate group of samples is chosen by the software to match the text, and different takes are heard each time, which increases gameplay variety. There are also female and male versions for every role that gets called up at random by the code—transportation chiefs, auto foremen, coal barons, doctors, teachers, bus drivers, city advisors, police chiefs, and so many more populate the vast world of *SimCity*.

After months of playing *SimCity* through many stages of development, it is such a thrill to see the characters come to life with their unique and expressive voices. The directives and opinions of the Sims given to players in the text-based speech bubbles are now effectively personalized with the emotive tonality of the characters speaking. Plus, there are tons of opportunities to hear these characters move about your city that we are loading in daily, such as greeting you upon clicking on them as they walk down the street or hearing them call out a goodbye to their co-workers after a long day at the factory. Listen carefully because your city is filled with distinct voices from various walks of life!

Quick Reference

Looking for more information?

For ease of reference and comparison, details on all buildings, missions, challenges, and achievements have been compiled here. However, some of this information may change over time. *SimCity* is a constantly evolving game, with the development team making occasional tweaks and updates to ensure a fun and balanced gameplay experience for all. As information and data changes in the game, we'll continue to update this guide at www.primagames.com. As the owner of this guide, you have access to our updated eGuide—go to www.primagames.com and enter the provided voucher code to gain access to the eGuide. Here you can find the same information in the print guide as well as new content pertaining to recent updates. Check back frequently for updated stats, challenges, achievements, and more.

CITY BUILDINGS

Image	Name	Description	Prerequisites	Max. Modules	Cost	Hourly Cost
		UTILITIES: POWER				
	Wind Power Plant	Harness the green energy of the wind by building a sprawling wind farm. Power Production Rate: 3 MW in 10 mph winds. Air Pollution Output: None.	None	N/A	§8,000	§80
	Service Road	Allows workers to get out to the windmills. Has underground lines for power transmission. Extend the Service Road to fit more turbines if you need to!	None	N/A	Free	None
	Wind Power Sign	Put down a sign so all the pizza delivery drivers stop going past you.	Wind Power Plant	1	§200	None
	Small Horizontal Turbine	The small horizontal-axis wind turbine produces a small amount of electricity. Must be plopped along a Service Road. Power Production Rate: 3 MW in 10 mph winds.	Wind Power Plant	24	§5,000	§40
	Large Horizontal Turbine	The large horizontal-axis wind turbine produces a moderate amount of electricity. Must be plopped along a Service Road. Power Production Rate: 5.1 MW in 10 mph winds.	Wind Power Plant	20	§10,000	§60

CITY BUILDINGS

Image	Name	Description	Prerequisites	Max. Modules	Cost	Hourly Cost
	Vertical Turbine	It looks crazy! It also produces huge amounts of power. Service Roads only please! Power Production Rate: 15 MW in 10 mph winds.	University with School of Engineering in region, complete research project at University in region	1	§20,000	§170
	Coal Power Plant	Imports coal directly from the global market to generate enough power for even a large city. It also creates pollution. A lot of pollution. Power Production Rate: 75 MW. Coal Burn Rate: 4.32 tons/day. Air Pollution Output: High.	None	N/A	§17,000	§450
	Coal Power Plant Sign	Someone has smeared "Clean Coal, my foot!" onto this sign.	Coal Power Plant	1	§200	None
	Dirty Coal Generator	For when all other considerations are secondary to cost. Requires a decent amount of coal to operate and pollutes a lot. Power Production Rate: 75 MW. Coal Burn Rate: 4.32 tons/day. Air Pollution Output: High.	Coal Power Plant	3	§5,000	§425
	Advanced Coal Generator	Costs more but produces less pollution as well as making decent levels of power. Y'know, for when you care about the environment a tiny bit. Power Production Rate: 75 MW. Coal Burn Rate: 8.64 tons/day. Air Pollution Output: Medium.	Coal Power Plant	3	§15,000	§375
	Clean Coal Generator	This is as "clean" as it's going to get, Bub. This is coal, after all. Power Production Rate: 75 MW. Coal Burn Rate: 5.76 tons/day. Air Pollution Output: Low.	University with School of Engineering in region, complete research project at University in region	1	§20,000	§600
	Oil Power Plant	Everything runs on oil, right? Imports crude oil directly from the global market. Converts crude oil into power...and pollution. Power Production Rate: 150 MW. Oil Burn Rate: 864k barrels/day. Air Pollution Output: High.	None	N/A	§27,500	§856
	Oil Power Plant Sign	This *cough* sign says *cough* "Dedicated to the Environment" *cough**cough*.	Oil Power Plant	1	§200	None
	Conventional Oil Generator	Crude oil is used to convert water into steam to produce power. Power Production Rate: 150 MW. Oil Burn Rate: 360k barrels/day. Air Pollution Output: High.	Oil Power Plant	4	§7,500	§756
	Combustion Turbine Generator	Crude oil is burned under pressure to produce power. Power Production Rate: 150 MW. Oil Burn Rate: 120k barrels/day. Air Pollution Output: Medium.	Oil Power Plant	3	§20,000	§1,185

CITY BUILDINGS

Image	Name	Description	Prerequisites	Max. Modules	Cost	Hourly Cost
	Clean Oil Generator	After crude oil is used in a combustion turbine generator, excess exhaust is used to convert water into steam. Power Production Rate: 150 MW. Oil Burn Rate: 240k barrels/day. Air Pollution Output: Low.	Oil Power Plant, University with Engineering Department, complete research project at University in region	3	§27,000	§1,295
	Solar Power Plant	Collect the power of the sun itself to give your city clean energy. By day, solar panels absorb power. At night, they use power stored in batteries. Power Production Rate: 4 MW during peak hours. Air Pollution Output: None.	None	N/A	§33,000	§145
	Solar Power Sign	They'll see the sign. It'll open their eyes. They'll see the sign.	Solar Power Plant	1	§200	None
	Fixed Solar Array	Bulky but cheap, these panels are the bread and butter of solar power. Power Production Rate: 4 MW during peak hours. Air Pollution Output: None.	Solar Power Plant	16	§16,000	§105
	Concentrated Solar Array	These futuristic dishes are small, efficient, and expensive. They pack much more power than the basic panel and take up much less space!	Solar Power Plant, University with School of Science, Complete Research Project at University	16	§40,000	§320
	Nuclear Power Plant	Educated Sims and large amounts of water can create free, albeit radioactive, power. Careful! If this power plant is staffed with unskilled workers, it may emit variable amounts of radiation. Power Production Rate: 300 MW. Air Pollution Output: None.	City Hall, Department of Utilities	N/A	§145,000	§1,300
	Nuclear Power Plant Sign	When headless fish start showing up in the daily catch, this will show people where to go.	Nuclear Power Plant	1	§200	None
	Gen I Thermal Reactor	This standard reactor requires more water for coolant, but adds jobs and produces power that's almost problem free. Almost. Power Production Rate: 300 MW. Air Pollution Output: None.	Nuclear Power Plant, University with Science Department	3	§45,000	§1,200
	Gen II Thermal Reactor	This mid-sized generator uses slightly more water and skilled workers, but produces slightly more power. Power Production Rate: 400 MW. Air Pollution Output: None.	Nuclear Power Plant, University with School of Science, Complete Research Project at University	3	§75,000	§2,300
	Fast Neutron Reactor	Uses more water and skilled workers, but produces more power and three-eyed llamas. Power Production Rate: 600 MW. Air Pollution Output: None.	Nuclear Power Plant, Complete Gen II Thermal Reactor Research Project at University	3	§130,000	§3,200

CITY BUILDINGS

Image	Name	Description	Prerequisites	Max. Modules	Cost	Hourly Cost
UTILITIES: WATER						
	Water Tower	Pumps a decent amount of water from the water table to your city. Beware of ground pollution, which can carry sickness-transmitting germs. Average Water Pump Rate: 6 kgal/hr.	None	N/A	§3,500	§100
	Water Pumping Station	Thirsty? Quench it with this large, expandable water production facility. With all the extra water, you could make a bit of extra income selling water to neighboring cities. Average Water Pump Rate: 80 kgal/hr.	City Hall, Department of Utilities	N/A	§24,000	§400
	Basic Water Pump	If there's still water in the water table, add another Basic Water Pump to extract more to meet your city's needs or to sell to the region. Average Water Pump Rate: 80 kgal/hr.	Water Pumping Station	6 (one comes with base)	§30,000	§200
	Filtration Pump	Everyone needs water, but if your ground is polluted, you don't want to drink germs! This filters out most contaminants as it pumps, sending mostly clean water to your city. Average Water Filter Rate 80 kgal/hr.	Water Pumping Station	6 (one comes with base)	§60,000	§400
UTILITIES: SEWAGE						
	Sewage Outflow Pipe	Converts sewage into ground pollution. Better in a spot you pick than backing up into John and Jane Q. Public's backyard! Max Sewage Flow Rate: 11.7 kgal/hr. Ground Pollution Output: 120,000 ppm/hr.	None	N/A	§3,500	§100
	Sewage Treatment Plant	What kind of civilized city dumps their waste in a field?! Clean that sewage before disposing of it with this Sewage Treatment Plant. If you don't want a sewage spill, be mindful of its capacity! Max Sewage Treatment Rate: 700 kgal/hr. Max Sewage Flow Rate: 300 kgal/hr. Ground Pollution Output: None.	City Hall, Department of Utilities	N/A	§64,000	§400
	Sewage Treatment Tank	Ew! Holds even more sewage water! Increase your Sewage Treatment Plant's capacity so it doesn't overflow with human waste. Max Sewage Treatment Rate: 700 kgal/hr. Ground Pollution Output: None.	Sewage Treatment Plant	7 (one comes with base)	§40,000	§200
GOVERNMENT						
	Town Hall	This allows you to do business deals, manage systems, and start negotiating with neighboring cities. Automatic upgrade to City Hall.	Connection to region, RCI, working water and power	N/A	Free	§200
	City Hall	This allows you to do business deals, manage systems, and start negotiating with neighboring cities.	Town Hall, population of 1,000	7 upgrades based on population levels	Free	§200

CITY BUILDINGS

Image	Name	Description	Prerequisites	Max. Modules	Cost	Hourly Cost
	City Hall Sign	What's the name of this town anyway?	City Hall	1	§200	None
	Department of Education	If you believe the children are our future, then you need a Department of Education! With this City Hall department, you can add High Schools and your very own University! Regional Access Granted: High School and University.	City Hall Upgrade	1	§15,000	§500
	Department of Finance	Embrace your inner CPA! The Department of Finance grants the ability to tax wealth levels independently. Regional Access Granted: Tax Rate Control per Zone and Wealth.	City Hall Upgrade	1	§15,000	§500
	Department of Safety	Maslow put safety at the second level of his hierarchy of needs pyramid. Give your Sims a sturdy foundation. Protect your populace with improved fire, health, and police city services. Regional Access Granted: Hospital, Large Fire Station, and Police Precinct.	City Hall Upgrade	1	§15,000	§500
	Department of Tourism	Turn your city into a tourist trap with the Department of Tourism. Tourist attractions like parks, stadiums, and landmarks will draw Sims to your city, ready to spend cash! Regional Access Granted: Landmarks, Pro Stadium, and Large Parks.	City Hall Upgrade	1	§15,000	§500
	Department of Transportation	Address commuter or tourist traffic. The Department of Transportation will enable advanced transit options like streetcars, passenger rail, and even a municipal airport! Regional Access Granted: Passenger Train Station, Bus Terminal, Municipal Airport, and Ferry Dock.	City Hall Upgrade	1	§15,000	§500
	Department of Utilities	Clean up your city, starting at the City Hall! The Department of Utilities gives you the ability to plop advanced sewage, water treatment, and recycling buildings. Regional Access Granted: Water Treatment Plant, Sewage Treatment Plant, and Recycling Center.	City Hall Upgrade	1	§15,000	§500
	Simcopter One	For mayors who like to make a big entrance.	City Hall, Airport in city or region	1	§6,000	None
	Mayor's House	For the neighborly, lend-a-cup-of-sugar, mow-their-front-lawn kind of mayor. Raises medium wealth land value.	Town Hall, Population of 10,000, 70% Approval Rating	1	§15,000	§100

CITY BUILDINGS

Image	Name	Description	Prerequisites	Max. Modules	Cost	Hourly Cost
	Mayor's Mansion	Keep your Sims happy for long enough and you can move in! Sims all over the city will celebrate when you move into the city! As you run your city well, your Sims will even give you gifts to add to your Mayor's Mansion. Raises high wealth land value.	Town Hall, Population of 40,000, 75% Approval Rating	1	§30,000	§100
	Flag of the City	How can you not be proud when looking at your own city's flag? You know what it took to build this place!	Maintain an approval rating of 75% or more	1	§200	None
	Mayor's BBQ Pit Patio	As Mayor, you have a lot at stake, but there's never a bad time to cook a great steak!	Maintain an approval rating of 75% or more	1	§1,000	§10
	Circular Fountain	If you look into the water long enough, you'll see your future. Nah, kidding. It's only water.	Maintain an approval rating of 75% or more	1	§1,000	§10
	Mayor's Statue	Mayor, the whole city is proud of you. Proud, like... an eagle. Definitely not a peacock. Definitely not.	Maintain an approval rating of 80% or more	1	§1,000	None
	Balcony	Look upon your domain from here. Just be careful, it's the first place all the tomatoes get tossed!	Maintain an approval rating of 80% or more, four upgrades of Mayor's Mansion	1	§1,000	§10
	Guest House	It's a known fact: visiting dignitaries, roaming rock stars, and famous movie stars love to hang out with cool mayors. Serves as lodging for one high wealth tourist.	Maintain an approval rating of 80% or more, four upgrades of Mayor's Mansion	1	§1,000	§10
	Guard Post	Make your mansion look even more menacing, Mayor. Maybe those protesters will think twice about bothering you. Or not.	Maintain an approval rating of 80% or more, four upgrades of Mayor's Mansion	1	§1,000	§10
	Sports Car Garage	Complete with your new smokin' hot car! It's okay, break the speed limit...you're the Mayor!	Maintain an approval rating of 80% or more, four upgrades of Mayor's Mansion	1	§1,000	§10
	Extension Wing	What's better than having a giant mansion all to yourself? MORE giant mansion all to yourself!	Maintain an approval rating of 85% or more, eight upgrades of Mayor's Mansion	1	§1,000	§10
	Limo Garage	You're Mayor. Why should you have to drive yourself? Have your driver bring the car around and travel in style.	Maintain an approval rating of 85% or more, eight upgrades of Mayor's Mansion	1	§1,000	§10

CITY BUILDINGS

Image	Name	Description	Prerequisites	Max. Modules	Cost	Hourly Cost
	Greenhouse	You know how to grow a city, Mayor...but can you grow your garden? Just keep those pesky ants away...	Maintain an approval rating of 85% or more, eight upgrades of Mayor's Mansion	1	§1,000	§10
	Tennis Court	Play tennis with your Mayor friends and keep fit so you can quickly jump into action when disasters strike!	Maintain an approval rating of 85% or more, eight upgrades of Mayor's Mansion	1	§1,000	§10
	Swimming Pool	The life of a Mayor is never easy. That's why you need at least 18 hours a day of relaxing pool time. You're only human!	Maintain an approval rating of 90% or more, twelve upgrades of Mayor's Mansion	1	§1,000	§10
	Lookout Tower	Gaze down upon your city from the relative safety of your house's Lookout Tower!	Maintain an approval rating of 90% or more, twelve upgrades of Mayor's Mansion	1	§1,000	§10
	Party Wing	Sometimes a Mayor just has to let loose! Throw your raging parties here with only the city's elite Sims!	Maintain an approval rating of 90% or more, twelve upgrades of Mayor's Mansion	1	§1,000	§10
	Simcopter One	Real Mayors fly to work! Never be late to City Hall ever again!	Maintain an approval rating of 90% or more, twelve upgrades of Mayor's Mansion	1	§6,000	None

UTILITIES: WASTE DISPOSAL

Image	Name	Description	Prerequisites	Max. Modules	Cost	Hourly Cost
	Garbage Dump	Sims hate piles of garbage in front of their homes, so dump it all here! Add more garbage trucks to have garbage collected faster. Waste Capacity: 40 tons. Ground Pollution Output: 7,000 ppm/hr.	Town Hall	N/A	§9,000	§300
	Service Road	Dirt road for garbage trucks to take to dump garbage in Dump Zones...and it smells nasty. Add more Service Roads to give you room to place more Dump Zones.	Garbage Dump	N/A	Free	None
	Garbage Truck Garage	Add another garbage truck to your dump to speed up garbage collection. Vehicle Capacity: 1.5 tons. Garbage Trucks: 2.	Garbage Dump	8 (one comes with base)	§5,000	§100
	Dump Zone	Designate more space for garbage dumping. Just avoid people's backyards okay? Waste Capacity: 40 tons. Ground Pollution Output: 3,500 ppm/hr.	Garbage Dump	8 (one comes with base)	Free	None
	Garbage Incinerator	Burn the garbage away! Air pollution? Nah, nobody cares about that. Garbage Burn Rate: 6 tons/hr. Air Pollution Output: High.	Garbage Dump	4	§25,000	§300

CITY BUILDINGS

Image	Name	Description	Prerequisites	Max. Modules	Cost	Hourly Cost
	Recycling Center	Educated Sims will want to recycle. Used alloy, metal, and plastic can be collected and brought here to be reclaimed, to be used or sold on the global market via a Trade Depot. Does not replace the Garbage Dump. Waste Capacity: 20 tons.	City Hall, Department of Utilities	N/A	§111,000	§700
	Recycling Collection Truck Garage	Increase your recycling collection rate with an additional truck for collecting raw recycled alloy, metal, or plastic. Vehicle Capacity: 4.5 tons.	Recycling Center	8 (one comes with base)	§3,000	§100
	Reclamation Delivery Truck Garage	Houses a recycling delivery truck for delivering plastics, metals, or alloys that have been reclaimed to businesses that need them. Vehicle Capacity: 1 ton.	Recycling Center	4 (one comes with base)	§3,000	§100
	Alloy Reclamation Line	Converts reclaimed alloy into usable alloy that your delivery trucks can deliver to Great Works projects, Trade Depots, Trade Ports, or local industry. Recycling Production Rate: 0.1 tons/hr.	Recycling Center	4	§25,000	§400
	Metal Reclamation Line	Converts reclaimed metal into usable metal that your delivery trucks can deliver to Great Works projects, Trade Depots, Trade Ports, or local industry. Recycling Production Rate: 0.1 tons/hr.	Recycling Center	4	§25,000	§400
	Plastic Reclamation Line	Converts reclaimed plastic into usable plastic that your delivery trucks can deliver to Great Works projects, Trade Depots, Trade Ports, or local industry. Recycling Production Rate: 0.1 tons/hr.	Recycling Center	4 (one comes with base)	§25,000	§400

CITY SERVICES: FIRE

Image	Name	Description	Prerequisites	Max. Modules	Cost	Hourly Cost
	Fire Station	Stop the spread of fire across your city! Improve coverage by adding more fire trucks. Response Time: 12 minutes.	Town Hall	N/A	§20,000	§400
	Fire Station Flagpole	Wouldn't be a Fire Station without a flagpole, right? Hopefully the pole doesn't confuse any of the firefighters into sliding down it....	Fire Station	1	§100	None
	Fire Station Sign	It's nice to have a sign, for when you're running around in a panic looking for the Fire Station.	Fire Station	1	§200	None
	Fire Alarm	Wake those sleepy firefighters from dreams of Dalmatians jumping over fences. Fire trucks are dispatched twice as fast!	Fire Station	1	§3,000	§75
	Fire Station Garage	Attach this garage to your Fire Station and gain an additional fire truck. And maybe your firemen can start a garage band during their time off?	Fire Station	4	§15,000	§200

CITY BUILDINGS

Image	Name	Description	Prerequisites	Max. Modules	Cost	Hourly Cost
	Large Fire Station	This Fire Station is hot stuff! Go all out with better trucks, larger fire coverage, the addition of hazmat for those stubborn industrial fires, and a fire helicopter! That's right, we said helicopter. Response Time: 6 minutes.	City Hall, Department of Safety	N/A	§85,000	§1,700
	Fire Station Flagpole	Wouldn't be a Fire Station without a flagpole, right? Hopefully the pole doesn't confuse any of the firefighters into sliding down it....	Large Fire Station	1	§100	None
	Large Fire Station Sign	It should be pretty obvious from the sirens where the Large Fire Station is, but the sign makes it more official.	Large Fire Station	1	§200	None
	Fire Dispatch Tower	This state-of-the-art dispatch tower communicates over satellite. Speeds up response time of all your fire vehicles! Fire trucks are dispatched twice as fast!	Large Fire Station	1	§10,000	§525
	Large Fire Station Garage	With all the capabilities of a regular fire truck, the hook and ladder that comes with this one extends its coverage by quite a bit.	Large Fire Station	4 (one comes with base)	§15,000	§400
	Fire Marshal Office	The fire marshal drives around the city, visiting homes, factories, and shops. Places the fire marshal visits are immune to fire for several days. This suppresses the risk of fire within your city!	Large Fire Station	4	§20,000	§500
	Hazmat Garage	This hazmat truck puts out heavy industrial fires caused by hazardous materials. Without it, hazmat fires will burn unchecked!	Large Fire Station, University with School of Engineering, Complete Research Project at University	4	§40,000	§250
	Fire Helipad	Put out fires in a blink of a helicopter blade! Make sure you have enough Water Towers. This one uses a lot of water!	Large Fire Station, Airport in city or region	4	§60,000	§1,400

CITY SERVICES: HEALTH

Image	Name	Description	Prerequisites	Max. Modules	Cost	Hourly Cost
	Clinic	Is there a cough going around or a series of unfortunate industrial accidents? This small Clinic can treat your sick and injured Sims. Patient Rooms: 10. Waiting Room Capacity: 10.	Town Hall	N/A	§20,000	§400
	Clinic Sign	Sick people don't have time to read the address... they need a sign!	Clinic	1	§200	None

CITY BUILDINGS

Image	Name	Description	Prerequisites	Max. Modules	Cost	Hourly Cost
	Ambulance Bay	Ambulances respond to injury emergencies throughout your city. Add an Ambulance Bay to add another ambulance and reduce your Clinic's response time. Capacity: 4 injured Sims.	Clinic	4	§10,000	§200
	Patient Rooms	Provides extra rooms for Sims on bedrest, allowing you to treat more patients at a time. Patient Rooms: 15.	Clinic	4	§12,000	§300
	Hospital	Too many subdural hematomas? Then you need this major medical center. Treat many more sick and injured Sims in this large medical facility. Improve quality of care with additions to your Hospital. Patient Rooms: 50. Waiting Room Capacity: 40.	City Hall, Department of Safety	N/A	§120,000	§1,700
	Hospital Sign	It's kind of important to know where the Hospital is.	Hospital	1	§200	None
	Ambulance Bay	Dispatch paramedics to bring injured Sims to your Hospital for treatment. Additional Ambulance Bays reduce your Hospital's response time. Capacity: 8 injured Sims. Number of Ambulances: 2.	Hospital	4	§15,000	§400
	Wellness Center	Dispatches a wellness van to visit residences in your city. The wellness van helps Sims clean up, removing some of the germs that can cause sickness. Prevention is better than the cure! Wellness Vans: 1.	Hospital	4	§30,000	§450
	Patient Rooms	Additional Patient Rooms provide you enough capacity to care for the entire region! Patient Rooms: 75.	Hospital	4	§40,000	§1,400
	Emergency Center	Patient, calm emergency operators keep Sims with injuries on the line, helping them survive twice as long while waiting for an ambulance to arrive. Time Until Death: 2x previous time until death.	Hospital	1	§40,000	§400
	Diagnostic Lab	Advanced science enables faster diagnoses for sick Sims. Sims recover from sickness twice as fast! Sick Recovery Time: 1/2 the previous recovery time.	Hospital, University with Medical School	1	§60,000	§750
	Surgical Center	This top-notch Surgical Center attracts the most skilled surgical talent. The hotshot surgeons here will heal injured Sims twice as fast! Injury Recovery Time: 1/2 the previous recovery time.	Hospital, University with Medical School, Complete Research Project at University	1	§80,000	§750

CITY BUILDINGS

Image	Name	Description	Prerequisites	Max. Modules	Cost	Hourly Cost
CITY SERVICES: POLICE						
	Police Station	Patrol cars respond to crimes in progress and arrest the criminals, if they can catch them! Police bring arrested criminals to the station to be rehabilitated in jail cells. The Police Station suppresses crime nearby. Jail Cells: 10. Patrol Cars: 2. Patrol Rate: Every 60 minutes.	Town Hall	N/A	§30,000	§400
	Police Station Flagpole	Every police station needs this to show their patriotism!	Police Station	1	§20	None
	Police Station Sign	Criminals are a superstitious, cowardly lot. Strike fear into their hearts.	Police Station	1	§200	None
	Patrol Car Lot	Increase your police presence with extra patrol cars. Patrol Cars: 2. Patrol Rate: Every 60 minutes.	Police Station	4	§10,000	§225
	Jail Cells (Ground Floor)	Meager accommodations for criminals. Criminals are rehabilitated after several days. Must be plopped on the ground. Jail Cells: 15.	Police Station	4	§15,000	§300
	Jail Cells (Top Floor)	Meager accommodations for criminals. Criminals are rehabilitated after several days. Cannot be plopped directly on the ground. Jail Cells: 15.	Police Station	4	§15,000	§300
	Police Precinct	If "Police State" were an amusement park, the Police Precinct would be the fun house. More than just a big police station, the precinct has more jail cells, more patrol cars, and can be outfitted with advanced crime-fighting modules. Jail Cells: 50. Patrol Cars: 4. Patrol Rate: Every 30 minutes.	City Hall, Department of Safety	N/A	§95,000	§1,700
	Police Precinct Sign	If you miss the search light and huge antenna, this helps you find the Police Precinct.	Police Precinct	1	§200	None
	Police Dispatch Tower	The farther your signal goes, the better. Use the Police Dispatch Tower to help your patrol cars respond to crimes in progress instantly. Response Time: Instant!	Police Precinct	1	§10,000	§525
	Patrol Car Lot	Beef up your police force with more patrol cars! Getting more cops on the beat will help prevent more crimes and arrest more criminals. Patrol Cars: 6. Patrol Rate: Every 30 minutes.	Police Precinct	4	§15,000	§600

CITY BUILDINGS

Image	Name	Description	Prerequisites	Max. Modules	Cost	Hourly Cost
	Jail Cells (Ground Floor)	This top-of-the-line cell block has electric locking doors, security cameras, and room for more hardened criminals. Welcome to the future! Must be plopped on the ground. Jail Cells: 70.	Police Precinct	4	§22,000	§700
	Jail Cells (Top Floor)	This top-of-the-line cell block has electric locking doors, security cameras, and room for more hardened criminals. Welcome to the future! Cannot be plopped directly on the ground. Jail Cells: 70.	Police Precinct	4	§22,000	§700
	Crime Prevention Center	Take a pro-active approach to crime fighting by sending officers to schools, parks, and more to teach kids the value of taking the fight out of crime.	Police Precinct	4	§30,000	§400
	Detective Wing	While patrol cars can arrest criminals committing crimes, you need detectives to investigate criminals at large. Detectives will park their surveillance car outside the homes of criminals at large and arrest them.	Police Precinct, University with Law School, Complete Research Project at University	4	§60,000	§750
	Police Helipad	We can keep our authoritative eye in the sky on these do-bad criminals. Holds one helicopter.	Police Precinct, Airport in city or region	4	§20,000	§750

CITY SERVICES: EDUCATION

Image	Name	Description	Prerequisites	Max. Modules	Cost	Hourly Cost
	Grade School	Educate your Sims and you'll have more skilled workers. Increases medium wealth residential land value. Desks: 150.	Town Hall	N/A	§16,000	§400
	Flagpole	Just don't stick your tongue to it when it's snowing!!!	Grade School	1	§100	None
	Grade School Sign	Shows students the current events of the week.	Grade School	1	§200	None
	School Bus Lot	The School Bus Lot adds extra school buses that can be used to pick up more kids around the city. Bus Capacity: 20 kids. Number of Buses: 2 buses.	Grade School	5 (one comes with base)	§3,000	§100
	Classrooms	Requires more teachers and staff, but lets you teach more students each day. Capacity: 200 students.	Grade School	4	§10,000	§200
	Top Floor Classrooms	Even more classrooms and education jobs, but these must go on the topmost floor of the school. Capacity: 200 students.	Grade School	4	§10,000	§200

CITY BUILDINGS

Image	Name	Description	Prerequisites	Max. Modules	Cost	Hourly Cost
	School Bus Stop	Your school buses will stop here to pick up kids and take them to school each day. Yes, even weekends. Bus Stop Capacity: 20 kids.	Grade School or High School	N/A	§200	§10
	High School	High Schools help kids stay off the streets, keep them out of trouble, and educate them. Educated Sims recycle, pollute less, and cause fewer fires. Desks: 800.	City Hall, Department of Education	N/A	§60,000	§1,000
	Flagpole	Show your pride. Add a pole that totally holds a flag!	High School	1	§100	None
	High School Sign	Somehow this sign has managed to remain graffiti free despite being surrounded by teenagers.	High School	1	§200	None
	School Bus Lot	Adds a school bus to pick up students when used in conjunction with bus stops. Bus Capacity: 60 kids. Number of Buses: 2.	High School	4	§10,000	§100
	Gymnasium	Home to the triumph of the human spirit and misery of the nerds. Boosts tourist attraction in the city. Increases medium wealth residential land value. Capacity: 500.	High School	1	§10,000	§250
	Classrooms	Educate even more sullen, sulky kids each day. You'll need more teachers and staff to handle the moody handfuls, of course. Capacity: 1,000 students.	High School	4	§17,000	§500
	Public Library	There is no Sim as loyal as a book. Sims visit the Public Library when they can't afford to go shopping. As Sims visit the Public Library, your city will gradually become more educated. Capacity: 200.	Town Hall	N/A	§10,000	§100
	Community College	Sure, it's not accredited, but it's a lot cheaper and smaller than a University. Adds to medium wealth residential land value. Desks: 500. Increases tech level of nearby industrial buildings.	Educate 800 students in a day	N/A	§42,000	§500
	Flagpole	Conforms to ANSI/NAAMM FP-1001-97 specifications for metallic flagpole safety.	Community College	1	§100	None
	College Sign	A large sturdy sign generously donated by the Spline Foundation.	Community College	1	§200	None

CITY BUILDINGS

Image	Name	Description	Prerequisites	Max. Modules	Cost	Hourly Cost
	Extension Wing	Adds more classrooms and teaching jobs. Generously donated by Anon Y. Mous. Capacity: 750 desks.	Community College	4	§12,000	§375
	University	The University provides the highest grade of education to your population. Research advanced technologies at the various schools of higher learning. Desks: 800. Increases tech level of nearby industrial buildings.	City Hall, Department of Education	N/A	§88,000	§1,600
	Pedestrian Path	Pedestrian only pathway. Insert "pathway to education" metaphor here.	University	N/A	Free	None
	University Sign	Directs students to the University when they stumble back home late at night.	University	1	§200	None
	Dormitory	Adds additional students to your population without having to build additional housing. Capacity: 500 students.	University	3	§40,000	§500
	School of Business	Get your students down to business! When attended by students, increases commercial profit across the region. Capacity: 500 students.	Pick one new Department with each University upgrade.	1	§40,000	§1,000
	School of Engineering	This is where you put those nerds. When attended by students, increases low and medium wealth industrial profit across the region. Capacity: 500 students.	Pick one new Department with each University upgrade.	1	§40,000	§1,000
	School of Law	Crack down on crime. When attended by students, lowers rehabilitation time of incarcerated criminals in the region. Capacity: 500 students.	Pick one new Department with each University upgrade.	1	§40,000	§1,000
	School of Medicine	When attended by students, reduces the chance Sims in the region will get sick. Capacity: 500 students.	Pick one new Department with each University upgrade.	1	§40,000	§1,000
	School of Science	Teach science, don't get blinded by it. When attended by students, increases high tech industrial profit in the region. Capacity: 500 students.	Pick one new Department with each University upgrade.	1	§40,000	§1,000

CITY BUILDINGS

Image	Name	Description	Prerequisites	Max. Modules	Cost	Hourly Cost
	MASS TRANSIT: BUSES					
	Shuttle Bus Depot	Help your Sims get around the city! Shuttle buses stop here for low and medium wealth Sims. Number of Buses: 3. Bus Capacity: 40 Sims.	Town Hall	N/A	§20,000	§300
	Shuttle Bus Lot	Expand your shuttle service! More shuttle buses means your shuttle bus system can support more passengers. Number of Buses: 3. Bus Capacity: 40 Sims.	Shuttle Bus Depot	8 (one comes with base)	§7,000	§100
	Bus Stop	Wait for it...buses stop here for low and medium wealth Sims. Requires a Bus Terminal in the region or a Shuttle Bus Depot. Bus Stop Capacity: 125 Sims.	Bus Terminal in region or Shuttle Bus Depot	N/A	§200	§10
	Park and Ride	Municipal and shuttle buses stop here for low and medium wealth Sims. Commuters can park in the back before taking the bus. Requires a Bus Terminal in the region or a Shuttle Bus Depot. Bus Stop Capacity: 80 Sims.	Shuttle Bus Depot or Bus Terminal in region	N/A	§400	§30
	Bus Terminal	A terminal for larger municipal and regional buses. Low and medium wealth Sims can drive here before taking the bus. Municipal buses can pick up and drop off Sims inside the city as well as at neighboring cities with Bus Stops. Regional buses can drop off and pick up tourists here. Number of buses: 3. Bus Capacity: 80 Sims.	City Hall, Department of Transportation	N/A	§45,000	§750
	Bus Terminal Sign	No, it's not a stop. You actually have to go inside!	Bus Terminal	1	§200	None
	Municipal Bus Garage	Expand your bus fleet! Number of Buses: 3. Bus Capacity: 80 Sims.	Bus Terminal	8 (one comes with base)	§15,000	§250
	MASS TRANSIT: STREETCARS					
	Streetcar Depot	Ding! Ding! This station provides the basis of a streetcar system in your city. Includes three streetcars, but you'll need to add Streetcar Stops for it to have anywhere to go. Must be plopped on a High Density Streetcar Avenue. Number of Streetcars: 3. Streetcar Capacity: 200 Sims.	Town Hall	N/A	§30,000	§375
	Streetcar Sign	It's a sign of things to come. Ha ha...what?	Streetcar Depot	1	§200	None

CITY BUILDINGS

Image	Name	Description	Prerequisites	Max. Modules	Cost	Hourly Cost
	Streetcar Garage	Is streetcar desire out of control in your city? Add another streetcar to prevent passengers from being left waiting at stops. Number of Streetcars: 2. Streetcar Capacity: 200 Sims.	Streetcar Depot	6	§3,000	§300
	Streetcar Stop	The best place for Sims to stop in the middle of the road! Placed on a High Density Streetcar Avenue, this stop allows Sims to get on and off streetcars. Streetcar Capacity: 200 Sims.	Streetcar Depot	N/A	§500	§30
	High Density Streetcar Avenue	This wide six-lane road supports high density zones with traffic lights at intersections. Streetcar tracks running down the center provide support for Streetcar Stops. Number of lanes: 6. Maximum Density Supported: High.	None	N/A	§12	N/A
	Streetcar Tracks	Two tracks for streetcars to travel along, useful for connecting sections of your city that do not share roads. Does not support Streetcar Stops.	None	N/A	§3	None

MASS TRANSIT: TRAINS

Image	Name	Description	Prerequisites	Max. Modules	Cost	Hourly Cost
	Passenger Train Station	All aboard! Plop this station along rail tracks to service trains from the region. Passenger trains bring commuters and shoppers from cities connected by train plus low and medium wealth tourists from the region. Train Capacity: 400 Sims.	City Hall, Department of Transportation	N/A	§40,000	§375
	Train Station Sign	Danger, train crossing!	Train Station	1	§200	None
	Heavy Rail Tracks	Tracks to connect the Passenger Train Station to the rail network or to connect up to a Freight Rail Terminal at a Trade Port.	None	N/A	§6	None

MASS TRANSIT: BOATS

Image	Name	Description	Prerequisites	Max. Modules	Cost	Hourly Cost
	Ferry Terminal	When plopped along a shoreline, the Ferry Terminal provides a dock for commuters to travel by passenger ferry. Improve by adding Cruise Ship Docks or additional Passenger Ferry Docks. Ferry Capacity: 1,000 Sims.	City Hall, Department of Transportation	N/A	§31,000	§575
	Ferry Terminal Sign	Caution: very large boats.	Ferry Terminal	1	§200	None
	Passenger Ferry Dock	Dock for a passenger ferry to bring low and medium wealth workers from other cities in the region connected by water. Ferry Capacity: 1,000 Sims.	Ferry Terminal	1 (comes with base)	§6,000	§200

CITY BUILDINGS

Image	Name	Description	Prerequisites	Max. Modules	Cost	Hourly Cost
	Cruise Ship Dock	Anyone for a game of shuffleboard? Allows cruise ships to dock, bringing medium and high wealth tourists in from the region. Cruise Ship Capacity: 2,000 Sims.	Ferry Terminal	1	§10,000	§375
MASS TRANSIT: PLANES						
	Municipal Airport	Fly medium wealth tourists to your city on small passenger planes. Upgrade the airport for high wealth tourists and greater capacity or to ship cargo. Residents do not want to live near an airport, but airports boost the happiness of nearby factories. Terminal Capacity: 200.	City Hall, Department of Transportation	N/A	§85,000	§500
	Municipal Airport Sign	Has a very long list of items not allowed on board.	Municipal Airport	1	§200	None
	Cargo Terminal	Send your city's industrial freight shipments out on cargo planes.	Municipal Airport	4	§8,000	§300
	Passenger Terminal	Increase your airport's capacity from rinky-dink to something more respectable. Allows private jet flights of high wealth tourists and large passenger planes filled with medium wealth tourists.	Municipal Airport	4	§8,500	§350
	Runway	Add an additional runway to increase the frequency of flights carrying passengers or cargo. Terminal Capacity: 200.	Municipal Airport	4 (one comes with base)	§15,000	§250
PARKS: BASIC PARKS						
	Blacktop Park	Just enough room for foursquare and hopscotch. Visitors per day: 12.	None	15	§100	§10
	Swings Playground	Swing time! Higher! Visitors per day: 12.	None	15	§100	§10
	Rides Playground	The perfect spot to drop the tykes off if you want to have them spun or bounced! Visitors per day: 12.	None	15	§100	§10
	BBQ Pit	A handy spot where random Sims can put meat to fire surrounded by foliage. What could possibly go wrong? Visitors per day: 12.	None	15	§100	§10

CITY BUILDINGS

Image	Name	Description	Prerequisites	Max. Modules	Cost	Hourly Cost
	BBQ Pavilion	Add a faint whiff of mesquite and lighter fluid to your park. Visitors per day: 48.	Town Hall	15	§400	§40
	Water Park Playground	Kids will love splashing around in this fun, watery playground. Visitors per day: 48.	Town Hall	15	§400	§40
	Small Field	Hope you like grass, because there's a bunch of it here! Visitors per day: 48.	Town Hall	15	§400	§40
	Small Field with Parking	Not every open field of grass has convenient attached parking! Raises medium wealth land value. Visitors per day: 48.	Town Hall	15	§400	§40
	Medium Field with Parking	Not quite enough space for a game of two-hand touch and too many trees to fly a kite. Just enjoy the nature! Raises medium wealth land value. Visitors per day: 192.	Town Hall	15	§1,600	§160
	Large Field with Parking	Perfect for rounds of paintball or just massive games of hide and seek. Raises medium wealth land value. Visitors per day: 192.	Town Hall	15	§1,600	§160

PARKS: SPORTS PARKS

Image	Name	Description	Prerequisites	Max. Modules	Cost	Hourly Cost
	Public Tennis Court	Tennis, anyone? Sims will love playing tennis matches on your new court! Raises medium wealth land value. Visitors per day: 24.	None	15	§400	§40
	Basketball Court	You've got outside tickets to watch ballers take the rock to the hole! Raises medium wealth land value. Visitors per day: 24.	None	15	§400	§40
	Volleyball Court	Catch every service and spike with a volleyball court in your city! Raises medium wealth land value. Visitors per day: 24.	None	15	§400	§40
	Medium Skate Park	Ample ramps and plentiful pipes fill this skate park to the brim! Raises medium wealth land value. Visitors per day: 48.	Town Hall	15	§800	§80
	Large Skate Park	Put those empty swimming pools to rad use! Raises medium wealth land value. Visitors per day: 96.	Town Hall	15	§1,600	§160

CITY BUILDINGS

Image	Name	Description	Prerequisites	Max. Modules	Cost	Hourly Cost
	Soccer Field	Sims will hit the field to play soccer. Raises medium wealth land value. Visitors per day: 180.	Town Hall	15	§10,000	§600
	Baseball Field	Play ball! Kids who join a junior baseball team will be less likely to start shoplifting. Raises medium wealth land value. Visitors per day: 150.	Town Hall	15	§10,000	§500

PARKS: NATURE PARKS

Image	Name	Description	Prerequisites	Max. Modules	Cost	Hourly Cost
	Pond	Ducks, mini-boat regattas, or just poking at lily pads; the options are nearly endless. Raises medium wealth land value. Visitors per day: 12.	None	15	§200	§20
	Wavy Path Park	Craft your very own custom, easy-to-escape maze! Raises medium wealth land value. Visitors per day: 24.	None	15	§400	§40
	Straight Path Park	Help your Sims walk the straight and narrow with this handy park. Raises medium wealth land value. Visitors per day: 24.	None	15	§400	§40
	Colorful Path Park	The flowers help you not wander around in circles. Raises medium wealth land value. Visitors per day: 24.	None	15	§400	§40
	Tall Tree Row	Add some green between your heavy-polluting buildings to at least make it seem like you're making an effort to be green. Visitors per day: 24.	None	N/A	§100	§10
	Short Tree Row	Add some green between your heavy-polluting buildings to at least make it seem like you're making an effort to be green. Visitors per day: 24.	None	N/A	§100	§10
	Medium Path Park	This spacious park has ample paths for ambling and a lovely bed of colorful flowers. Raises medium wealth land value. Visitors per day: 48.	Town Hall	15	§800	§80
	Tree-Lined Walkway	Beautiful trees and colorful flowers border this peaceful walkway. Raises medium wealth land value. Visitors per day: 48.	Town Hall	15	§800	§80
	Wavy Tree-Lined Walkway	Parks Department officials maintain that the landscaping crew was not drunk when laying this walkway. Raises medium wealth land value. Visitors per day: 48.	Town Hall	15	§800	§80

CITY BUILDINGS

Image	Name	Description	Prerequisites	Max. Modules	Cost	Hourly Cost
	Large Path Park	This well-manicured park has plenty of space for even the largest cities. Raises medium wealth land value. Visitors per day: 192.	Department of Tourism	15	§3,200	§320
	City Park	Even big cities need a sunny patch of greenery. Raises medium wealth land value. Visitors per day: 192.	Department of Tourism	15	§3,200	§320
	Community Park	Gathering place for local mime troupes by day and wannabe vampire gangs by night. Raises medium wealth land value. Visitors per day: 192.	Department of Tourism	15	§3,200	§320
	Plant Forest	Plant a small forest amongst your skyscrapers to give the gnomes somewhere to hide!	None	N/A	§50	None
	Clear Forest	Clear cut forests to make way for your urban sprawl.	None	N/A	§50	None

PARKS: PLAZAS

Image	Name	Description	Prerequisites	Max. Modules	Cost	Hourly Cost
	Flower Plaza	For when you love flowers so much you need a park filled to the brim with them. Raises high wealth land value. Visitors per day: 24.	None	15	§400	§40
	Double Walkway	This walkway is a bit wider than most, with shady tree coverage. Raises high wealth land value. Visitors per day: 48.	Town Hall	15	§1,200	§120
	Small Sculpture Garden	The plaque at the base reads "Pointless Oval-Henri Less". Raises high wealth land value. Visitors per day: 24.	None	15	§400	§40
	Simple Walkway	This wide walkway has a scattering of trees and bushes for a touch of green in the middle of your city. Raises high wealth land value. Visitors per day: 48.	Town Hall	15	§1,200	§120
	Medium Sculpture Garden	The geometric sculpture of at the center of this plaza is titled "Taxation Representation". What does it mean? What does it mean? Raises high wealth land value. Visitors per day: 48.	Town Hall	15	§1,200	§120
	Large Sculpture Garden	Gaze upon "Man", a sculptural treatise on man's eternal struggle with nature...and himself. Raises high wealth land value. Visitors per day: 96.	Town Hall	15	§2,400	§240

CITY BUILDINGS

Image	Name	Description	Prerequisites	Max. Modules	Cost	Hourly Cost
	Large Urban Sculpture Garden	This striking iron Gordian knot sculpture is brought to you by Simfinity. "Simfinity: engineering everything". Raises high wealth land value. Visitors per day: 96.	Town Hall	15	§2,400	§240
	Urban Greenspace	Add a nice spot for overwhelmed office drones to soak up the sun on their lunch hour. Raises high wealth land value. Visitors per day: 96.	Town Hall	15	§2,400	§240
	Tiered Urban Greenspace	It's almost like there's nature in the middle of your city! Raises high wealth land value. Visitors per day: 96.	Town Hall	15	§2,400	§240

PARKS: FORMAL PARKS

Image	Name	Description	Prerequisites	Max. Modules	Cost	Hourly Cost
	Fountain Plaza	Flagstones. Fountain. Flowers. What else could you ask for? Raises high wealth land value. Visitors per day: 24.	None	15	§400	§40
	Fenced Fountain Plaza	A gothic fence frames this small plaza filled to the brim with fountains. Raises high wealth land value. Visitors per day: 24.	None	15	§400	§40
	Small Fountain Park	Beautiful shiny tiles and colorful flowers frame a simple fountain. Raises high wealth land value. Visitors per day: 48.	Town Hall	15	§1,200	§120
	Reflecting Pool Park	Perfect for modern Narcissuses (Narcissi?). Raises high wealth land value. Visitors per day: 96.	Town Hall	15	§2,400	§240
	Large Fountain Park	A massive fountain sits at the center of a dramatic plaza. Raises high wealth land value. Visitors per day: 96.	Town Hall	15	§2,400	§240
	Amphitheater	High-falutin' smarty-types gather here to watch plays and such. Raises high wealth land value. Visitors per day: 192.	Department of Tourism	15	§4,800	§480

CITY SPECIALIZATION BUILDINGS

Image	Name	Description	Prerequisites	Max. Modules	Cost	Hourly Cost
			MINING			
	Coal Mine	It's time to get your hands dirty. Dirty, filthy, and rich. Rip the earth's coal heart out for profit! Use your coal in a Coal Power Plant, or sell it to local industry or on the global market via a Trade Depot. Employ hordes of low wealth workers deep in your mine. Production Rate: 24 tons/day.	Coal deposits in city limits, working power and water service, and seven industrial buildings.	N/A	§22,500	§100
	Coal Mine Sign	Coal is like the meat at the middle of the delicious sandwich of your city.	Coal Mine	1	§200	None
	Coal Delivery Truck Garage	It's a dirty job haulin' coal, but somebody's gotta do it. Delivers coal from the mine to Coal Power Plants, Trade Depots, Trade Ports, or industry in your city. Truck Capacity: 2 tons of coal.	Coal Mine	4 (one comes with base)	§10,000	§50
	Coal Shaft	Extend your extraction operation with an additional Coal Shaft. Increase your Coal Mine's extraction rate and add more available jobs. Production Rate: 24 tons/day.	Coal Mine	4	§14,000	§25
	Ore Mine	Are you easily fascinated by shiny things? Well, then look at this! Send workers beneath your city to extract raw ore. Sell raw ore to local industry or on the global market via a Trade Depot. Production Rate: 24 tons/day.	Ore deposits in city limits, working water and power service, and seven industrial buildings.	N/A	§22,500	§125
	Ore Mine Sign	This sign warns against rock slides, sinkholes, and "surprise detonations".	Ore Mine	1	§200	None
	Ore Delivery Truck Garage	When you've got more ore than you know what to do with, get another Ore Delivery Truck and get that ore out to Trade Depots, Trade Ports, and industry faster to make money faster! Truck Capacity: 2 tons of ore.	Ore Mine	4 (one comes with base)	§10,000	§50
	Ore Shaft	More ore! Increase your Ore Mine's extraction rate by adding another shaft. It'll add more maintenance cost, sure, but you'll get more jobs and more ore! More! Production Rate: 24 tons/day.	Ore Mine	4	§16,000	§40
	Smelting Factory	Sure, raw ore is nice, but do you know what's really nice? Metal and alloy. Smelt raw ore into metal or add coal into the mix to smelt alloy. Sell metal or trade alloy to local industry or on the global market via a Trade Depot. Production Rate: 24 tons/day.	Mining HQ with Smelting Division	N/A	§54,500	§300
	Smelting Factory Sign	Enhancing your Smelting Factory with a sign lends it that respectable, responsible look.	Smelting Factory	1	§200	None

CITY SPECIALIZATION BUILDINGS

Image	Name	Description	Prerequisites	Max. Modules	Cost	Hourly Cost
	Smelting Delivery Truck Garage	Now that you've smelt it, deal it! This garage adds one Smelting Delivery Truck so you can get your metal and alloy to Trade Depots, Trade Ports, Processor Factories, and industry. Truck Capacity: 2 tons of processed metals.	Smelting Factory	4 (one comes with base)	§10,000	§50
	Metal Furnace	Play with fire without getting burned! Melt raw ore and remove the impurities to create metal. Metal can be sold to local industry or the global market via a Trade Depot. Many Great Works require large amounts of metal. Production Rate: 24 tons/day.	Smelting Factory	4 (one comes with base)	§21,000	§50
	Alloy Furnace	When coal and ore really love each other, a baby alloy is born. Alloy can be sold to local industry or the global market via a Trade Depot. Alloy is used to create processors in Processor Factories. Many Great Works require large amounts of alloy. Production Rate: 24 tons/day.	Smelting Factory	3	§36,000	§150
	Metals HQ	The Metals HQ is the bedrock of any coal or raw ore extraction city. Sell coal or raw ore to upgrade your HQ and gain advancements like the Smelting Factory, Advanced Coal Mine, or Trade Port. Upgrades available based on daily profit goals for metal trading.	Mine 96 tons of coal or raw ore in a day	N/A	§37,500	§450
	Corporate Sign	What's more metal than a metal sign on a metal building that houses a metals company?	Metals HQ	1	§200	None
	Commerce Division	Tired of tripping over coal or raw ore? You need to get some of that out of town! Make major Simoleons on the global market! Regional Access Granted: Trade Port, Coal and Raw Ore Storage Lots at the Trade Port.	Metals HQ	1	§20,000	§400
	Engineering Division	Leave behind the paltry output of the measly Coal Mine. The engineers at the Engineering Division have plans for a whole new Advanced Coal Mine! Local Access Granted: Advanced Coal Mine.	Metals HQ	1	§20,000	§400
	Smelting Division	Add smelting to your metals operation to make more profit and diversity! Use educated workers to research the Alloy Furnace project. Local Access Granted: Smelting Factory.	Metals HQ	1	§20,000	§400
	Advanced Coal Mine	Take advantage of recent metallurgical advancements and the repeal of certain environmental laws! Extract coal faster, from a larger area, with this powerful coal mine. This mine employs a massive number of workers and has a huge lot ready to be filled with coal. Production Rate: 96 tons/day.	Mining HQ with Engineering Division	1	§60,000	§400
	Coal Mine Sign	This sign is larger, but there just seems to be an even thicker coating of hardened coal.	Advanced Coal Mine	1	§200	None

CITY SPECIALIZATION BUILDINGS

Image	Name	Description	Prerequisites	Max. Modules	Cost	Hourly Cost
	Heavy Coal Delivery Truck	It takes a big truck to haul this much coal. This is where you keep that big truck. Truck Capacity: 2 tons of coal.	Advanced Coal Mine	10 (one comes with base)	§20,000	§50
	Advanced Coal Shaft	Extract massive amounts of coal faster by adding another shaft to your Advanced Coal Mine. Production Rate: 48 tons/day.	Advanced Coal Mine	8	§50,000	§250

		DRILLING				
	Oil Well	What better way to thank the dinosaurs for hooking you up with all that oil than to make Simoleons off them? Pump crude oil from reservoirs under your city. Run your city on crude oil with an Oil Power Plant! Sell barrels of your crude oil to local industry or on the global market via a Trade Depot. Thanks, dinos! Production Rate: 2,400 barrels/day.	Oil deposits in city limits, working water and power service, and seven industrial buildings	N/A	§37,500	§150
	Service Road	Provides infrastructure to allow transportation of crude oil from pumpjacks to the main Oil Well.	Oil Well	N/A	Free	N/A
	Oil Well Sign	The sign says: "No free samples. Beware: Attack Armadillos".	Oil Well	1	§200	N/A
	Oil Delivery Truck Garage	Provides an additional tanker truck to deliver crude oil to Oil Refineries, Crude Oil Storage Lots, and Oil Power Plants. Truck Capacity: 200 barrels of oil.	Oil Well	4 (one comes with base)	§10,000	§50
	Oil Pumpjack	Does running your Oil Well feel like sucking crude oil through a straw? Then get more straws! Add Oil Pumpjacks to your Oil Well to extend your reach and pump crude oil faster! Production Rate: 1,200 barrels/day.	Oil Well	10 (two come with base)	§10,000	§30
	Petroleum HQ	If you have crude oil in your veins and your heart pumps jet fuel, your city is ready for a Petroleum Headquarters. Sell crude oil on the global market via a Trade Depot to access petroleum improvements, including refineries so you can produce fuel and plastic.	Extract 9,600 barrels of crude in a day	N/A	§37,500	§450
	Petroleum HQ Sign	"Dedicated to a clean environment!" the sign cheerfully claims.	Petroleum HQ	1	§200	None
	Refining Division	Petroleum is not only good for crude oil, you can refine the crude oil into fuel or plastic. Diversifying into other resources can help you weather the ups and downs of the global market. Local Access Granted: Oil Refinery.	Petroleum HQ	1	§20,000	§400

CITY SPECIALIZATION BUILDINGS

Image	Name	Description	Prerequisites	Max. Modules	Cost	Hourly Cost
	Commerce Division	Full of trade nerds who love watching the action of oil prices on the global market, the Commerce Division helps get your petroleum products to market. Local Access Granted: Trade Port, TV and Computer Storage Lots at the Trade Port.	Petroleum HQ	1	§20,000	§400
	Oil Refinery	Crude oil prices down? Then diversify! Take your crude oil and use it to create plastic to sell on the global market via a Trade Depot. Add a Fuel Distillation Unit to also create fuel to sell or use for a Great Works project!	Drilling HQ with Refining Division	1	§73,000	§300
	Oil Refinery Sign	The font on this sign seems pretty refined, but the sign's still kind of greasy.	Oil Refinery	1	§200	None
	Oil Refinery Delivery Truck Garage	Adds a transport truck to move plastic and fuel to plastic and fuel consumers. Fuel Truck Capacity: 200 barrels of fuel. Plastic Truck Capacity: 5 tons of plastic.	Oil Refinery	4 (one comes with base)	§10,000	§50
	Plastic Polymerizer	Plastic polymerizer. Sounds high tech, right? It is. In goes crude oil, out comes plastic. Science is amazing. Sell your plastic on the global market via a Trade Depot, or use it to create processors or for building Great Works. Production Rate: 24,000 crates/day.	Oil Refinery	4 (one comes with base)	§30,000	§50
	Fuel Distillation Unit	This is the answer to your hopes if you are selling fuel faster than you can make it. Create even more fuel with this fractional distillation unit! Production Rate: 2,400 barrels/day.	Oil Refinery	3	§46,000	§150

TRADING

Image	Name	Description	Prerequisites	Max. Modules	Cost	Hourly Cost
	Trade Depot	Import, export, and store resources like coal and crude oil with this basic unit. Also accepts freight shipments for industry. Does not require power or water to function. Global Market Delivery: Every 60 minutes.	Road for placement	N/A	§10,000	§75
	Trade Depot Sign	This sign has a complex list of directions to different storage lots.	Trade Depot	1	§200	None
	Freight Truck Garage	Time to get that convoy movin'! Add a Freight Truck Garage to increase the rate at which you can send resources from the Trade Depot to manufacturers and consumers in your city. Import/Export Deliveries: 2 tons of goods per trip.	Trade Depot	4 (one comes with base)	§3,000	§50
	Freight Shipping Warehouse	This small warehouse accepts freight shipments from local industry. Industry that doesn't have a place to ship its freight may go out of business. Freight Capacity: 54 tons.	Trade Depot	4 (one comes with base)	§2,000	§15

CITY SPECIALIZATION BUILDINGS

Image	Name	Description	Prerequisites	Max. Modules	Cost	Hourly Cost
	Coal Storage Lot	Adds storage space for coal. Use the coal locally, or import it from the global market at low prices and export it at high prices. Storage Capacity: 20 tons.	Trade Depot	4	§2,000	§15
	Crude Oil Storage Lot	Adds storage space for crude oil. Use the crude oil locally, or import it from the global market at low prices and export it at high prices. Storage Capacity: 2,000 barrels.	Trade Depot	4	§2,000	§15
	Raw Ore Storage Lot	Adds storage space for raw ore. Use the raw ore locally, or import it from the global market at low prices and export it at high prices. Storage Capacity: 20 tons.	Trade Depot	4	§2,000	§15
	Metal Storage Lot	Adds storage space for metal. Use the metal locally, or import it from the global market at low prices and export it at high prices. Storage Capacity: 20 tons.	Trade Depot, Metal Reclamation Line at Recycling Center OR Metals HQ OR Metals Division at Trade HQ	4	§2,000	§15
	Alloy Storage Lot	Adds storage space for alloy. Use the alloy locally, or import it from the global market at low prices and export it at high prices. Storage Capacity: 20 tons.	Trade Depot, Alloy Reclamation Line at Recycling Center OR Metals HQ OR Metals Division at Trade HQ	4	§2,000	§15
	Fuel Storage Lot	Adds storage space for fuel. Use the fuel locally, or import it from the global market at low prices and export it at high prices. Storage Capacity: 2,000 barrels.	Trade Depot, Petroleum HQ OR Petroleum Division at Trade HQ	4	§2,000	§15
	Plastic Storage Lot	Adds storage space for plastic. Use the plastic locally, or import it from the global market at low prices and export it at high prices. Storage Capacity: 20 tons.	Trade Depot	4	§2,000	§15
	Processors Storage Lot	Adds storage space for processors. Use the processors locally, or import them from the global market at low prices and export them at high prices. Storage Capacity: 200,000 crates.	Trade Depot	4	§2,000	§15
	Computer Storage Lot	Adds storage space for computers. Use the computers locally, or import them from the global market at low prices and export them at high prices. Storage Capacity: 200,000 crates.	Trade Depot	4	§2,000	§15
	TV Storage Lot	Adds storage space for TVs. Use the TVs locally, or import them from the global market at low prices and export them at high prices. Storage Capacity: 200,000 crates.	Trade Depot	4	§2,000	§15

CITY SPECIALIZATION BUILDINGS

Image	Name	Description	Prerequisites	Max. Modules	Cost	Hourly Cost
	Trade Port	Allows importing, exporting, and storage of commodity resources or freight. Larger storage lots allow for ten times the capacity of the Trade Depot. Rail and cargo ship connections allow import and export via rail or water. Requires water and power to function. Global Market Delivery: Every 60 minutes.	Trade HQ	N/A	§60,000	§225
	Heavy Rail Tracks	Tracks to connect the Passenger Train Station to the rail network or to connect up to a Freight Train Terminal at a Trade Port.	Trade Port	N/A	§6	None
	Trade Port Sign	This sign seems to have accumulated a thick layer of road grime.	Trade Port	1	§200	None
	Delivery Truck Garage	Adds a truck to move one resource type from your Trade Port to consumers in your city. Trucks frequently pick up from the Trade Port. Import/Export Deliveries: 2 tons of goods per trip.	Trade Port	4 (one comes with base)	§3,000	§50
	Freight Rail Terminal	Allows import and export of resources via freight train. Each storage lot at the Trade Port adds another freight car to the freight train. Trains arrive every few hours. Global Market Delivery: Every 360 minutes.	Trade Port	1	§70,000	§400
	Cargo Ship Dock	Allows import and export of resources via high-capacity cargo ships. Cargo ships only carry one resource at a time, but in massive amounts. Cargo ships arrive several times a day. Global Market Delivery: Every 180 minutes.	Trade Port	1	§100,000	§400
	Coal Storage Lot	Adds a large amount of storage for coal. Use the coal locally, or import it from the global market at low prices and export it at high prices. Storage Capacity: 100 tons.	Trade Port, Metals HQ with Commercial Division OR Trade HQ with Metals Division	6	§20,000	§150
	Freight Shipping Warehouse	This high-capacity warehouse accepts freight shipments from local industry. Industry that doesn't have a place to ship its freight may go out of business. Freight Capacity: 108 tons.	Trade Port	6 (one comes with base)	§20,000	§150
	Crude Oil Storage Lot	Adds a large amount of storage for crude oil. Use the crude oil locally, or import it from the global market at low prices and export it at high prices. Storage Capacity: 10,000 barrels.	Trade Port, Petroleum HQ with Commercial Division OR Trade HQ with Petroleum Division	6	§20,000	§150
	Raw Ore Storage Lot	Adds a large amount of storage for raw ore. Use the raw ore locally, or import it from the global market at low prices and export it at high prices. Storage Capacity: 100 tons.	Trade Port, Metals HQ with Commercial Division OR Trade HQ with Metals Division	6	§20,000	§150

CITY SPECIALIZATION BUILDINGS

Image	Name	Description	Prerequisites	Max. Modules	Cost	Hourly Cost
	Metal Storage Lot	Adds a large amount of storage for metal. Use the metal locally, or import it from the global market at low prices and export it at high prices. Storage Capacity: 100 tons.	Trade Port, Metals HQ with Commercial Division OR Trade HQ with Metals Division	6	§20,000	§150
	Alloy Storage Lot	Adds a large amount of storage for alloy. Use the alloy locally, or import it from the global market at low prices and export it at high prices. Storage Capacity: 100 tons.	Trade Port, Metals HQ with Commercial Division OR Trade HQ with Metals Division OR Electronics HQ with Commercial Division	6	§20,000	§150
	Fuel Storage Lot	Adds a large amount of storage for fuel. Use the fuel locally, or import it from the global market at low prices and export it at high prices. Storage Capacity: 10,000 barrels.	Trade Port, Petroleum HQ with Commercial Division OR Trade HQ with Petroleum Division	6	§20,000	§150
	Plastic Storage Lot	Adds a large amount of storage for plastic. Use the plastic locally, or import it from the global market at low prices and export it at high prices. Storage Capacity: 100 tons.	Trade Port, Petroleum HQ with Commercial Division OR Trade HQ with Petroleum Division	6	§20,000	§150
	Processors Storage Lot	Adds a large amount of storage for processors. Use the processors locally, or import them from the global market at low prices and export them at high prices. Storage Capacity: 1,000,000 crates.	Trade Port, Electronics HQ with Commercial Division OR Trade HQ with Electronics Division	6	§20,000	§150
	Computer Storage Lot	Adds a large amount of storage for computers. Use the computers locally, or import them from the global market at low prices and export them at high prices. Storage Capacity: 1,000,000 crates.	Trade Port, Electronics HQ with Commercial Division OR Trade HQ with Electronics Division	6	§20,000	§150
	TV Storage Lot	Adds a large amount of storage for TVs. Use the TVs locally, or import them from the global market at low prices and export them at high prices. Storage Capacity: 100 tons.	Trade Port, Electronics HQ with Commercial Division OR Trade HQ with Electronics Division	6	§20,000	§150
	Trade HQ	Amass a fortune as an import/export master! Buy from the global market at low prices and sell when you can make the most Simoleons! Make profit from the global market to expand your trading actions. Upgrades available based on Trade Daily Profit goals.	Trade §72,000 in resources on the global market. Plop three different storage lots.	N/A	§37,500	§450
	Trade HQ Sign	This well-polished sign seems like it is pretty expensive.	Trade HQ	1	§200	None
	Electronics Division	Expand your trading options to electronics and all the resources needed to build them! Local Access Granted: Trade Port, and Plastic, Alloy, Processors, TV, and Computer Storage Lots at the Trade Port.	One Division is available with each Trade HQ upgrade, in any order	1	§20,000	§400

CITY SPECIALIZATION BUILDINGS

Image	Name	Description	Prerequisites	Max. Modules	Cost	Hourly Cost
	Metals Division	Expand your trading options to metals resource extraction! Local Access Granted: Trade Port, and Coal, Raw Ore, Metal, and Alloy Storage Lots at the Trade Port.	One Division is available with each Trade HQ upgrade, in any order	1	§20,000	§400
	Petroleum Division	Expand your trading options to petroleum resource extraction and the goods it can be refined into! Local Access Granted: Trade Port, and Crude Oil, Fuel, and Plastic Storage Lots at the Trade Port.	One Division is available with each Trade HQ upgrade, in any order	1	§20,000	§400

ELECTRONICS

Image	Name	Description	Prerequisites	Max. Modules	Cost	Hourly Cost
	Processor Factory	These days, it seems there are processors in everything. Those should be your processors! Use alloy and plastic to create processors to sell on the global market via a Trade Depot. You can import alloy and plastic from the global market if you need to. Educated workers will increase the factory's efficiency. Production Rate: 360,000 crates/day.	Working water and power service and five clean industrial buildings	N/A	§160,000	§700
	Processor Factory Sign	This way, the future!	Processor Factory	1	§200	None
	Delivery Truck Garage	Within this garage are trucks that deliver your processors around town to the industry that uses them, Trade Depots, and Trade Ports. Under the hood of those trucks...you guessed it: more processors. Truck Capacity: 20,000 crates of electronics.	Processor Factory	4 (one comes with base)	§10,000	§50
	Processor Assembly Line	At the digital computing heart of all technology lies the humble processor! Amass even more processors in your factory with this additional assembly line. Production Rate: 360,000 processors/day.	Processor Factory	4 (one comes with base)	§50,000	§350
	Electronics HQ	Embrace technology and prepare for our eventual robot overlords! Crank out processors to upgrade and improve your HQ. Research new technological innovations in consumer electronics. Upgrades available based on Electronics Daily Profit.	Manufacture 7,200 crates of processors in a day	N/A	§37,500	§450
	Electronics HQ Sign	The address is given as "1337 Haxorz Ave.", which doesn't seem correct...	Electronics HQ	1	§200	None
	Consumer Electronics Division	Put your processors to practical use! The Consumer Electronics Division wants your processors in consumers' homes, inside of TVs and computers. Local Access Granted: Consumer Electronics Factory.	One Division is available with each Electronics HQ upgrade, in any order	1	§20,000	§400
	Commerce Division	What use are all those processors if you can't get them to market? The Commerce Division seeks to solve this problem. Local Access Granted: Trade Port, and Processors, Alloy, and Plastic Storage Lots at the Trade Port.	One Division is available with each Electronics HQ upgrade, in any order	1	§20,000	§400

CITY SPECIALIZATION BUILDINGS

Image	Name	Description	Prerequisites	Max. Modules	Cost	Hourly Cost
	Consumer Electronics Factory	Take your very useful, high-tech processors and put them in TVs, so Sims can fall asleep watching videos of people getting hit in the gut. Sell your TVs for profit on the global market via a Trade Depot. Educated workers will increase the factory's efficiency. Production Rate: 360,000 crates/day.	Electronics HQ	4	§360,000	§1,200
	Consumer Electronics Factory Sign	Shows the way to the Consumer Electronics Factory. Mostly for delivery trucks. It's frowned upon for consumers to visit the factory themselves.	Consumer Electronics Factory	1	§200	None
	Delivery Truck Garage	This well-padded truck delivers your TVs and computers to Trade Depots, Trade Ports, or Great Works.	Consumer Electronics Factory	4 (one comes with base)	§10,000	§50
	TV Assembly Line	How will people watch Action Team 5 on SimNews 5 at 11 without TVs? Create TVs from processors and plastic to sell on the global market. You can import plastic or processors from the global market if you need to. Production Rate: 360,000 crates/day.	Consumer Electronics Factory	3	§100,000	§750
	Computer Assembly Line	Sims around the world are desperate to play SimCity! Use processors and alloy to create computers to sell on the global market via a Trade Depot. You can import alloy or processors from the global market if you need to. Production Rate: 360,000 crates/day.	Consumer Electronics Factory	3	§200,000	§850
		CULTURE				
	Expo Center	Invest in an Expo Center to turn your small town into a tourist destination! Schedule exciting events like football games and rock concerts, then prepare your city for tons of screaming fans! Maximum Profit: §189,000. Maximum Attendance: 3,000.	Town Hall	N/A	§150,000	§300
	Expo Center Sign	With an Expo Center, you have to let people know where to go. Maximum Tourists per Day: 50.	Expo Center	1	§3,000	§50
	Pro Stadium	The Pro Stadium's generous size means even more tourists and huge profits around each event! Prepare your city's mass transit system for an onslaught of screaming fans! Unfortunately, their tickets are all fully refundable, so if they can't make it to the event in time, you'll miss out on the Simoleons! Maximum Profit: §300,000.	City Hall, Department of Tourism	N/A	§225,000	§600
	Pro Stadium Sign	With a Pro Stadium, it's all about branding.	Expo Center	1	§3,000	§100

CITY SPECIALIZATION BUILDINGS

Image	Name	Description	Prerequisites	Max. Modules	Cost	Hourly Cost
		LANDMARKS				
	Arc de Triomphe	Perfect for the Francophiles, lend your city a touch of Gallic class! Origin: Paris, France. Maximum Tourists per Day: 2,400. Attraction: High.	City Hall, Department of Tourism	1	§280,000	§1,755
	Cinquantenaire Arch	This imposing arcade celebrates your city's independence! Watch as tourists are drawn to take photos of the famous landmark. Origin: Brussels, Belgium. Maximum Tourists per Day: 2,400. Attraction: Medium.	City Hall, Department of Tourism	1	§50,000	§610
	Dutch Windmill	The Netherlands are famous for their beautiful pastoral windmills. Origin: The Netherlands. Maximum Tourists per Day: 600. Attraction: Medium.	City Hall, Department of Tourism	1	§50,000	§610
	Edifício Copan	This wavy residential building adds a flowing sense of movement to even the densest urban cityscape. Origin: São Paulo, Brazil. Maximum Tourists per Day: 150. Attraction: Medium.	City Hall, Department of Tourism	1	§50,000	§612
	Empire State Building	It's not the tallest building in the world (anymore), but this impressive building can be said to be the core of the Big Apple. Origin: New York City, USA. Maximum Tourists per Day: 504. Attraction: High.	City Hall, Department of Tourism	1	§575,000	§4,050
	Giralda	This bell tower is a former minaret for the Cathedral of Seville. Origin: Seville, Spain. Maximum Tourists per Day: 2,400. Attraction: Medium.	City Hall, Department of Tourism	1	§50,000	§610
	Globe Theatre	All the world's a stage, and now you can bring yet another replica of The Globe Theatre to your city! Origin: London, England. Maximum Profit: §189,000. Maximum Attendance: 1,557. Attraction: High.	City Hall, Department of Tourism	1	§48,000	§1,000
	Kölner Dom	Towering spires crown this famous gothic church from Cologne. Origin: Cologne, Germany. Maximum Tourists per Day: 2,400. Attraction: Medium.	City Hall, Department of Tourism	1	§50,000	§610
	Królewski W Warszawie	The Royal Castle of Warsaw is the historical home to the royal family of Poland. Origin: Warsaw, Poland. Maximum Tourists per Day: 2,400. Attraction: High.	City Hall, Department of Tourism	1	§280,000	§1,755
	Leaning Tower of Pisa	Tilting 3.99 degrees, Sims will be hard pressed to walk in a straight line after visiting this famous tower. Origin: Pisa, Italy. Maximum Tourists per Day: 600. Attraction: High.	City Hall, Department of Tourism	1	§280,000	§1,755
	Oslo Opera House	This angular modern opera house hosts opera and ballet performances. Origin: Oslo, Norway. Maximum Profit: §189,000. Maximum Attendance: 1,364. Attraction: High.	City Hall, Department of Tourism	1	§150,000	§2,000

CITY SPECIALIZATION BUILDINGS

Image	Name	Description	Prerequisites	Max. Modules	Cost	Hourly Cost
	Rundetårn	The "Round Tower" of Copenhagen is a historical monument and a public astronomical observatory. Maximum Tourists per Day: 480. Attraction: Medium.	City Hall, Department of Tourism	1	§140,000	§1,755
	Statue of Liberty	Where else can you stand in a lady's head? This giant statue is undeniable proof that France loves the United States. Add it to your city! Origin: New York City, USA. Maximum Tourists per Day: 5,000. Attraction: High.	City Hall, Department of Tourism	1	§575,000	§4,050
	St. Basil's Cathedral	The official name of this Red Square cathedral is far too long to get into. Origin: Moscow, Russia. Maximum Tourists per Day: 2,400. Attraction: Medium.	City Hall, Department of Tourism	1	§140,000	§1,755
	Stockholm City Hall	Don't be jealous that your City Hall's not as cool as Stockholm's. Now you can have it in your city as well. Origin: Stockholm, Sweden. Maximum Tourists per Day: 100. Attraction: Medium.	City Hall, Department of Tourism	1	§50,000	§575
	Sydney Opera House	Add the distinctive silhouette of the Sydney Opera House to your city and watch droves of wealthy tourists flock to your city! Origin: Sydney, Australia. Maximum Profit: §189,000. Maximum Attendance: 2,679. Attraction: High.	City Hall, Department of Tourism	1	§200,000	§2,000
	Tokyo Tower	This tall lattice tower broadcasts J-dramas and anime to all the homes in your city. Origin: Tokyo, Japan. Maximum Tourists per Day: 504. Attraction: Medium.	City Hall, Department of Tourism	1	§50,000	§575
	Washington Monument	One of the most recognizable obelisks in the world, the Washington Monument stands erect at 169.294 meters. Origin: Washington D.C., USA. Maximum Tourists per Day: 2,400. Attraction: Medium.	City Hall, Department of Tourism	1	§50,000	§575
	Willis Tower	This 108-story-tall building is the tallest building in the United States. Origin: Chicago, USA. Maximum Tourists per Day: 504. Attraction: Medium.	City Hall, Department of Tourism	1	§140,000	§1,755

GAMBLING

Image	Name	Description	Prerequisites	Max. Modules	Cost	Hourly Cost
	Gambling House	Tourists will wheel their oxygen tanks to this simple casino to blow their hard-earned Simoleons. Maximize profits with Gambling Hall improvements. Criminals turn up at casinos like bad pennies. Low Wealth Gambler Capacity: 100. Income per Low Wealth Gambler/Hour: §10. Medium Wealth Gambler Capacity: 50. Income per Medium Wealth Gambler/Hour: §14.	Working water and power service and seven commercial buildings	N/A	§15,000	§260
	Casino Marquee	Like moths to a flame, tourists will flit on in to your casino. Increases casino tourist attraction. Maximum Tourists per Day: 25.	Gambling House	1	§1,000	§50

CITY SPECIALIZATION BUILDINGS

Image	Name	Description	Prerequisites	Max. Modules	Cost	Hourly Cost
	Casino Marquee	Like moths to a flame, tourists will flit on in to your casino. Increases casino tourist attraction. Maximum Tourists per Day: 25.	Gambling House	1	§1,000	§50
	Casino Marquee	Like moths to a flame, tourists will flit on in to your casino. Increases casino tourist attraction. Maximum Tourists per Day: 25.	Gambling House	1	§1,000	§50
	Cheap Rooms	No-frills lodging for less than discerning tourists. Tourists will stay in lodging to spend any remaining Simoleons in the casino the next day. Low Wealth Rooms: 60.	Gambling House	4	§3,500	§115
	Nice Rooms	These rooms aren't great, but at least they're "nice". Tourists will stay in lodging to spend any remaining Simoleons in the casino the next day. Medium Wealth Rooms: 30.	Gambling House	4	§4,000	§135
	Nickel Slots	It's just a nickel at a time. How fast could that add up? Low Wealth Gambler Capacity: 45.	Gambling House	4	§4,500	§40
	Blackjack Tables	Your casino won't bust if you get enough tourists into the casino. Try for at least 21... Medium Wealth Gambler Capacity: 30.	Gambling House	4	§5,500	§75
	Comedy Club	The Laughs Per Minute (LPM) are low, but any distraction from how much money Sims are losing at the slots is welcome. Low Wealth Gambler Capacity: 45. Maximum Tourists per Day: 25.	Gambling House	4	§4,000	§75
	Lounge	Now Featuring! Fernando and Don! Magic Motion! Tony T.! Weak drinks and lounge acts serve as a tourism draw. Medium Wealth Gambler Capacity: 45. Maximum Tourists per Day: 25.	Gambling House	4	§4,000	§225
	Gambling HQ	The lights! The glitz! The glamor! Rake in the Simoleons from your casinos. Just look out for criminal activity! Use the success of your casinos to gain improvements to your casinos' entertainment, lodging, or gaming. Upgrades available based on Casino Daily Profits.	Earn §50,000 in a day from gambling	N/A	§37,500	§450
	Gambling HQ Sign	Assure the city that this is a totally legitimate business establishment.	Gambling HQ	1	§200	None
	Entertainment Division	Tourists are more attracted to casinos that provide entertainment. Local Access Granted: Celebrity Stage, Disco Club, and Exclusive Club.	Pick one new Division each time your Gambling HQ receives an upgrade	1	§20,000	§400

CITY SPECIALIZATION BUILDINGS

Image	Name	Description	Prerequisites	Max. Modules	Cost	Hourly Cost
	Gaming Division	Enables new gaming modules that favor the house even more, providing more income per gambler. Local Access Granted: Poker Parlor, Craps Parlor, and Roulette House.	Pick one new Division each time your Gambling HQ receives an upgrade	1	§20,000	§400
	Lodging Division	With lodging in the casino, your gamblers can stay until they spend all their hard-earned money. Local Access Granted: Tower Rooms, Classy Rooms, Penthouse, and Penthouse Suite.	Pick one new Division each time your Gambling HQ receives an upgrade	1	§20,000	§400
	Sleek Casino	Glass and steel highlight the sweeping lines of this modern casino. Attracts medium wealth tourists. Low Wealth Gambler Capacity: 100. Income per Low Wealth Gambler/Hour: §10. Medium Wealth Gambler Capacity: 200. Income per Medium Wealth Gambler/Hour: §20. High Wealth Gambler Capacity: 100. Income per High Wealth Gambler/Hour: §40.	Casino HQ	N/A	§140,000	§1,500
	Flashy Casino Sign	With this flashy sign on top of your casino, Sims from all over will seek your Sleek Casino! Maximum Tourists per Day: 50	Sleek Casino	1	§4,000	§100
	Casino Marquee	Don't be a square! Get this sleek, modern marquee sign and show the world you have style! Maximum Tourists per Day: 100	Sleek Casino	1	§5,000	§1,000
	Sleek Rooms (Ground Floor)	Entice your gambling tourists to stay in your Sleek Casino. These rooms are close to the ground for quick access to the casino. Tourists will stay in lodging to spend any remaining Simoleons in the casino the next day. Low Wealth Rooms: 120	Sleek Casino, Casino HQ with Lodging Division	4	§7,000	§560
	Sleek Rooms (Tower)	Trap, er, host your gamblers in this shiny tower. Tourists will stay in lodging to spend any remaining Simoleons in the casino the next day. Medium Wealth Rooms: 60.	Sleek Casino, Casino HQ with Lodging Division	4	§9,000	§560
	Penthouse	This exclusive penthouse suite is a block of rooms that can only be plopped at the top of other rooms. High Wealth Rooms: 40	Sleek Casino, Casino HQ with Lodging Division	4	§9,000	§850
	Poker Parlor	If you can get a full house to play in your poker games, you'll be flush with cash! Low Wealth Gambler Capacity: 180.	Sleek Casino, Casino HQ with Gaming Division	4	§10,000	§675
	Craps Parlor	Roll the hard six! Craps is a cheap game to maintain and makes your casino even more money. Medium Wealth Gambler Capacity: 120.	Sleek Casino, Casino HQ with Gaming Division	4	§15,000	§900

CITY SPECIALIZATION BUILDINGS

Image	Name	Description	Prerequisites	Max. Modules	Cost	Hourly Cost
	Sci-Fi Casino	Take me to your dealer! Land your shuttlecraft at the rear docking bay of this medium wealth sci-fi-themed casino. Watch out for unsavory characters around the casino. Low Wealth Gambler Capacity: 200. Income per Low Wealth Gambler/Hour: §10. Medium Wealth Gambler Capacity: 200. Income per Medium Wealth Gambler/Hour: §20.	Casino HQ	N/A	§120,000	§1,125
	Holo Sign	Draw earthlings to your Sci-Fi Casino with this holographic sign! Maximum Tourists per Day: 50.	Sci-Fi Casino	1	§3,000	§100
	Casino Marquee	Attract gambling humans to your Sci-Fi Casino with this imposing sign. Maximum Tourists per Day: 50.	Sci-Fi Casino	1	§3,000	§100
	Rocket Rooms (Ground Floor)	This casino hotel launch pad features an umbilical tube to allow easy reentry to your Sci-Fi Casino. Low Wealth Rooms: 120	Sci-Fi Casino, Casino HQ with Lodging Division	4	§7,000	§600
	Rocket Rooms (Tower)	Extend your hotel tower rocket and achieve maximum lodger capacity! Low Wealth Rooms: 120.	Sci-Fi Casino, Casino HQ with Lodging Division	4	§7,000	§600
	Penthouse	This penthouse allows rich Sims to live like they are the captain of their very own rocket ship. Medium Wealth Rooms: 60.	Sci-Fi Casino, Casino HQ with Lodging Division	4	§10,000	§900
	Celebrity Stage	The Celebrity Stage attracts only the finest B- and C-grade celebrities. Remember that one guy, from that show? Check out his new one-man show! And that one gal, with the song? She's got a new one! Medium Wealth Gambler Capacity: 120. Maximum Tourists per Day: 50.	Sci-Fi Casino, Casino HQ with Entertainment Division	4	§15,000	§1,125
	Disco Club	Thought disco was dead? Well not any more! Disco has hustled from its grave with a high-grade disco fever and is jive-talkin' in your casino! Low Wealth Gambler Capacity: 180. Maximum Tourists per Day: 50.	Sci-Fi Casino, Casino HQ with Entertainment Division	N/A	§45,000	§375
	Elegant Casino	This stylish casino is evocative of a quaint Italian villa that caters solely to the nouveau riche. This expensive casino is only for the most discerning of cities. You'll need to entice high wealth tourists to meet the demanding maintenance costs. Medium Wealth Gambler Capacity: 100. Income per Medium Wealth Gambler/Hour: §28. High Wealth Gambler Capacity: 300. Income per High Wealth Gambler/Hour: §56.	Casino HQ	N/A	§300,000	§6,000

CITY SPECIALIZATION BUILDINGS

Image	Name	Description	Prerequisites	Max. Modules	Cost	Hourly Cost
	Decorative Sign	This elegantly understated sign in a fan motif is for the sophisticated casino mogul. Maximum Tourists per Day: 100.	Elegant Casino	1	§6,000	§500
	Casino Marquee	It's an exclusive casino, but drivers for the wealthy will still need to know where the place is. With this sign, they can see it from miles away! Maximum Tourists per Day: 100.	Elegant Casino	1	§6,000	§500
	Classy Rooms (Ground Floor)	The literal base of your Elegant Casino's classy hotel tower! Tourists will stay in lodging to spend any remaining Simoleons in the casino the next day. Medium Wealth Rooms: 60.	Elegant Casino, Casino HQ with Lodging Division	8	§10,000	§565
	Classy Rooms (Tower)	Use this tower of classy rooms to create a hotel-casino. Tourists will stay in lodging to spend any remaining Simoleons in the casino the next day. Medium Wealth Rooms: 60.	Elegant Casino, Casino HQ with Lodging Division	8	§10,000	§565
	Penthouse Suite	The most exclusive lodging in the most exclusive casino. No, you can't see a list of who stayed here before. High Wealth Rooms: 40.	Elegant Casino, Casino HQ with Lodging Division	8	§20,000	§845
	Exclusive Club	Casino patrons will be drawn to your casino to chill with celebrities and superstar athletes. Just please, no autographs! High Wealth Gambler Capacity: 60. Maximum Tourists per Day: 100.	Elegant Casino, Casino HQ with Entertainment Division	8	§40,000	§1,500
	Roulette House	Remember what Lesley Snypes said, "Always bet on black. No, wait, red!" High wealth tourists love to watch that wheel go 'round and 'round with the hope they won't lose their money. High Wealth Gambler Capacity: 80.	Elegant Casino, Casino HQ with Gaming Division	8	§50,000	§1,875

ⓘ NOTE

Only missions with a monetary reward are shown in this chart. In addition to these, there are a variety of other instructional missions, guiding you through the various steps necessary to complete basic tasks related to city management and specializations. Click on blue request bubbles to start a mission.

MISSIONS

Name	Criteria 1	Criteria 2	Criteria 3	Results
CIVIC				
Top Simoleon	Raise taxes to increase hourly earnings by §10	Turn off some buildings to decrease hourly expenses by §10	Increase hourly earnings by §100	§10,000
Moving In!	Achieve a 70% approval rating	Have 10,000 residents in your city	Build a house for yourself, Mayor!	§5,000
Mayor of the Year!	Achieve a 75% approval rating	Have 40,000 residents in your city	Build your dream mansion!	§15,000
Become a Small City!	Have 2,500 residents in your city	—	—	§2,500
Become a Suburban City!	Have 15,000 residents in your city	—	—	§15,000
Become a Medium-Sized City!	Have 40,000 residents in your city	—	—	§40,000
Become a Large City!	Have 80,000 residents in your city	—	—	§80,000
Become a Small Metropolis!	Have 100,000 residents in your city	—	—	§100,000
Become a Metropolis!	Have 200,000 residents in your city	—	—	§200,000
Become a Megalopolis!	Have 400,000 residents in your city	—	—	§400,000
Become a MEGA City!	Have 600,000 residents in your city	—	—	§600,000
MAGNASANTI!!!!!	Have 1,000,000 residents in your city	—	—	§1,000,000
A Walk in the Park	Have 100 Sims visit your parks within the next 72 hours	—	—	§5,200
Top of the Hour (Deluxe Edition only)	Build Big Ben	—	—	§10,000
The Grand Gate (Deluxe Edition only)	Build Brandenburg Gate	—	—	§10,000
La Tour (Deluxe Edition only)	Build Eiffel Tower	—	—	§10,000
Petit Tour Architectural de l'Europe!	Build a landmark in your city	—	—	§10,000
Tourist Trap	Increase the number of tourists coming to your city by 200	—	—	§1,000
CITY SERVICES				
Arsonist!	Arrest the arsonist	—	—	§25,000
Firework Fun!	Have less than 5 fires	—	—	§50,000
Fanning the Flame	No rubble in your city in the last 24 hours	—	—	§25,000
You're Fired!	Eliminate all rubble from your city	Put out 5 fires	—	§12,000
Day After New Year's	Collect 250 garbage cans	Pick up all garbage in 24 hours	—	§25,000
Bombing Run	Add a Detective Wing to the Police Precinct	Find the bomb and disarm it!	Your detectives have 10 hours to diffuse the situation	§50,000
EDUCATION				
College Town: Educayshun	Build a Town Hall	Build a Grade School	Have 50 students attending classes	§1,000
College Town: Bus Riders	Add a second School Bus Lot to the Grade School	Build two School Bus Stops	Have both School Buses bring students to the Grade School	§15,000
College Town: Making the Grade	Add a Classroom to the Grade School	Increase number of students attending classes at the Grade School by 80	—	§20,000

MISSIONS

Name	Criteria 1	Criteria 2	Criteria 3	Results
College Town: Head of the Class	Upgrade Town Hall to City Hall	Add a Department of Education to the City Hall	Have 500 students attend school in one day	§20,000
College Town: Sophomore Effort	Build a High School	Add a School Bus Lot to the High School	Build two more School Bus Stops	§30,000
College Town: Extra-Curricular	Add a Gymnasium to the High School	Build a Public Library in your city	Have 800 students attend class in one day	§30,000
College Town: Elective Education	Build a Community College	Add an Extension Wing to the Community College	Have 1,200 students attend class in one day	§40,000
College Town: Ivy League	Build a University	Add a Dormitory to the University	Have 100 students attend classes	§40,000
College Town: Higher Education	Increase the number of students enrolled in higher education by 25	Increase the number of graduates with college degrees by 25	—	§50,000
College Town: Go Team Nuclear!	Build a Nuclear Power Plant	Have no unpowered buildings in your city	—	§25,000
SimUniversity	Build a University	—	—	§12,000
Now Hiring: Smart People	Have no unskilled workers at the Nuclear Power Plant	Build a High School	Build a Public Library	§2,000
SPECIALIZATION: METALS				
Coal Town: Digging Deep	Build a Coal Mine	Add a Coal Shaft to the Coal Mine	Extract 48 tons of coal from the Coal Mine in one day	§5,000
Coal Town: Coal Miner's Niece	Build a Clinic	Your Clinic successfully treats 4 sick patients	—	§7,500
Coal Town: Coal to Go	Build a Trade Depot	Build a Coal Storage Lot at the Trade Depot	Sell 20 tons of coal on the global market	§10,000
Coal Town: Burning Coal	Add 3 more Coal Shafts to the Coal Mine	Mine 96 tons of coal in one day	Build a Metals HQ	§12,500
Coal Town: Heart & Coal	Upgrade Town Hall to City Hall	Add a Department of Safety to your City Hall	—	§12,000
Coal Town: Coal Lapse!	Build a Hospital	Add an Emergency Center to the Hospital	Successfully treat 5 injured Sims	§15,000
Coal Town: Coal Research	Increase your daily profits from metals sales by §350,000	Upgrade the Metals HQ to a Metals, Co.	Add the Engineering Division to the Metals HQ	§15,000
Coal Town: Be Mine	Build an Advanced Coal Mine	Extract 96 tons of coal from the new mine	Sell 60 tons of coal	§17,500
Coal Town: Big Coal Business	Increase your daily profits from metals sales by §700,000	Upgrade the Metals HQ to Metals, Inc.	Add the Smelting Division to the Metals HQ	§20,000
Coal Town: Imported Ore	Add a Raw Ore Storage Lot to the Trade Depot	Import 5 tons of raw ore	—	§15,000
Coal Town: Test Your Metal	Earn §2,000,000 more in daily profits from metals import/export	Upgrade the Metals HQ to a Metals Global	Add the Commerce Division to the Metals HQ	§20,000
Coal Town: Stop the World and Smelt With You	Build a Smelting Factory	Smelt 24 tons of alloy per hour	Sell 40 tons of alloy	§22,500
Coal Town: Coal No More?	Build a Trade Port	Add a Coal Storage Lot to the Trade Port	Sell 100 tons of coal	§25,000
Coal Town: Heavy Metal Truckin'	Add a Delivery Truck Garage to the Trade Port	Sell 100 tons of coal	Sell 100 tons of alloy	§27,500
Coal Town: Metal on the Rails	Add a Freight Rail Terminal to the Trade Port	Sell 60 tons of coal	Sell 60 tons of alloy	§20,000
Coal Town: Ship It!	Add a Cargo Ship Dock to the Trade Port	Sell 200 tons of coal	Sell 200 tons of alloy	§20,000

MISSIONS

Name	Criteria 1	Criteria 2	Criteria 3	Results
SPECIALIZATION: PETROLEUM				
Oil Fields: Purely Crude	Build an Oil Well	Build 4 Oil Pumpjacks for your Oil Well	Pump 2,000 barrels of crude oil in one day	§5,000
Oil Fields: Petrol Patrol	Build a Trade Depot	Add a Crude Oil Storage Lot to the Trade Depot	Earn §60,000 in crude oil sales on the global market	§10,000
Oil Fields: Fill 'er Up!	Have 10 Oil Pumpjacks at your Oil Well	Extract 9,600 barrels of crude oil in one day	Build a Petroleum HQ	§15,000
Oil Fields: Darkest Rain	Build an Oil Well	Add 2 more Oil Pumpjacks to the Oil Well	Extract 4,800 barrels of crude oil in one day	§50,000
Oil Fields: Safety First	Upgrade Town Hall to City Hall	Add Department of Safety to the City Hall	—	§50,000
Oil Fields: The Sound… of Sirens	Build a Large Fire Station	Put out all fires	—	§50,000
Oil Fields: Crude, Refined	Increase daily profit from crude oil sales on the global market by §200,000	Upgrade the Petroleum HQ to a Petroleum, Co.	Add the Refining Division to the Petroleum HQ	§60,000
Oil Fields: Give Me Fuel	Add a Fuel Distillation Unit to the Oil Refinery	Refine 2,400 barrels of fuel	—	§60,000
Oil Fields: Fantastic Plastic	Build an Oil Refinery	Refine 2,400 crates of plastic	Earn §54,000 in global market plastics sales	§65,000
Oil Fields: Really Big Business	Increase daily profits on the global market in crude oil sales by §2,000,000	Upgrade the Petroleum HQ to a Petroleum, Inc.	Add the Commerce Division to the Petroleum HQ	§70,000
Oil Fields: Get the Unleaded Out	Build a Trade Port	Add a Delivery Truck Garage to the Trade Port	Earn §200,000 in global market crude oil sales	§75,000
Oil Fields: Plastic Toy Train	Add a Freight Rail Terminal to the Trade Port	Export 50 more crates of plastic	Export 50 more barrels of fuel	§50,000
Oil Fields: Thicker Than Water	Add a Cargo Ship Dock to the Trade Port	Export 500 more barrels of fuel	—	§50,000
Drillin' Down	Build an Oil Well	Extract 100 barrels of crude oil	—	§10,000
Fuel for the Fire	Build an Oil Refinery	Refine 50 barrels of fuel per hour	—	§8,000
SPECIALIZATION: TRADE				
Free Market: Trade's Fair	Build a Town Hall	Build a Trade Depot	Build 3 different kinds of storage lots at the Trade Depot	§10,000
Free Market: Important/Exportant	Earn §72,000 in trade daily profits on the global market	Build a Trade HQ	—	§10,000
Free Market: Port in a Storm	Build a Trade Port	Add a Coal Storage Lot to the Trade Port	Add a Crude Oil Storage Lot to the Trade Port	§10,000
Free Market: Upgrade	Earn §250,000 in trade daily profits on the global market	Upgrade the Trade HQ to a Trading, Co.	Add a Metals Division to the Trade HQ	§10,000
Free Market: So Metal	Add a Raw Ore Storage Lot to the Trade Port	Add a Metal Storage Lot to the Trade Port	Increase earnings by §40,000 from exports to the global market	§12,000
Free Market: Truckin'	Add a Delivery Truck Garage to the Trade Port	Earn §60,000 in raw ore sales to the global market	—	§12,000
Free Market: Trading Up	Earn §2,000,000 in trade daily profits on the global market	Upgrade the Trade HQ to a Trading, Inc.	Add the Electronics Division to the Trade HQ	§15,000
Free Market: High-Tech Trading	Add a Processors Storage Lot to the Trade Depot	Earn §280,000 in processor sales on the global market	Earn §450,000 in TV sales on the global market	§18,000
Free Market: Millions Traded	Earn §4,000,000 trade daily profits on the global market	Upgrade the Trade HQ to a Trading Global	Add the Petroleum Division to the Trade HQ	§25,000

MISSIONS

Name	Criteria 1	Criteria 2	Criteria 3	Results
Free Market: Petrol Trader	Add a Crude Oil Storage Lot to the Trade Port	Earn §72,000 in crude oil sales on the global market	Earn §200,000 in fuel sales on the global market	§25,000
Free Market: Empire	Import 50 truckloads of resources from the global market	Export 50 truckloads of resources to the global market	Trade §5,000,000 in resources on the global market	§50,000
Free Market: Soul Coal	Add a Freight Rail Terminal to the Trade Port	Earn §32,000 in coal sales on the global market	Earn §116,000 in metal sales on the global market	§12,000
Free Market: Oil Tanker	Add a Cargo Ship Dock to the Trade Port	Earn §50,000 in crude oil sales on the global market	—	§15,000
TRADE: IMPORT/EXPORT				
Allez Alloy!	Build a Trade Depot	Add an Alloy Storage Lot to the Trade Depot	Export 10 tons of alloy	§2,500
Alloy Ally	Import §10,000 in alloy	—	—	§2,500
Coal Shipping	Build a Trade Depot	Add a Coal Storage Lot to the Trade Depot	Export 10 tons of coal	§2,500
Coal Stocking	Import §10,000 in coal	—	—	§2,500
Shipping Computers	Build a Trade Depot	Add a Computer Storage Lot to the Trade Depot	Export 1,000 crates of computers	§2,500
Export Excess Electronics!	Build a Trade Depot	Add a Processors Storage Lot to the Trade Depot	Export 1,000 crates of processors	§2,500
Hard to Process	Import 1,000 crates of processors	—	—	§2,500
Fill'er Up!	Build a Trade Depot	Add a Fuel Storage Lot to the Trade Depot	Export 1,000 barrels of fuel	§2,500
Muster Your Metal	Build a Trade Depot	Add a Metal Storage Lot to the Trade Depot	Export 10 tons of metal	§2,500
Bubblin' Crude	Build a Trade Depot	Add an Oil Storage Lot to the Trade Depot	Export 1,000 barrels of oil	§2,500
Needs More Oil!	Import 1,000 barrels of oil	—	—	§2,500
Raw Shipping	Build a Trade Depot	Add a Raw Ore Storage Lot to the Trade Depot	Export 10 tons of raw ore	§2,500
Ore or Else!	Import 10 tons of raw ore	—	—	§2,500
The Future is Plastic	Build a Trade Depot	Add a Plastics Storage Lot to the Trade Depot	Export 1,000 crates of plastic	§2,500
Need More Plastic	Import 1,000 crates of plastic	—	—	§2,500
Must Watch TV!	Build a Trade Depot	Add a TV Storage Lot to the Trade Depot	Export 1,000 crates of TVs	§2,500
Expand Your Trading Empire!	Build a Trade Depot	Receive deliveries from 25 trucks loaded with any global resource	Send out 25 trucks loaded with any global resource to the global market	§8,000
SPECIALIZATION: ELECTRONICS				
ZTronix: Electronics Art	Have 5 medium-tech industrial buildings in your city	Build a Processor Factory	Build a Trade Depot	§10,000
ZTronix: Fabrication	Import 9 tons of alloy	Import 900 crates of plastic	Manufacture 3,600 crates of processors	§10,000
ZTronix: Ship It!	Add a Processors Storage Lot to the Trade Depot	Increase earnings by §20,000 from global market in processor sales	—	§10,000
ZTronix: ZTronix HQ	Manufacture 7,200 crates of processors	Build an Electronics HQ	—	§50,000
ZTronix: Upgrades	Earn more than §1,500,000 in daily profit from electronics sales	Upgrade your Electronics HQ to an Electronics, Co.	Add the Consumer Electronics Division to the Electronics HQ	§10,000

MISSIONS

Name	Criteria 1	Criteria 2	Criteria 3	Results
ZTronix: Mike TV	Build a Consumer Electronics Factory	Manufacture 3,600 crates of TVs	Earn §400,000 on the global market in TV sales	§10,000
ZTronix: Power of Positive Computing	Research Computer Manufacturing at the Electronics HQ	Manufacture 3,600 crates of computers	Earn §450,000 on the global market in computer sales	§10,000
ZTronix: It's a Process	Earn more than §5,000,000 in daily profit from electronics sales	Upgrade the Electronics HQ to an Electronics, Inc.	Add the Commerce Division to the Electronics HQ	§10,000
ZTronix: Exports	Build a Trade Port	Add a Processors Storage Lot to the Trade Port	Export 10,000 crates of processors	§10,000
ZTronix: Exports	Add a Delivery Truck Garage to the Trade Port	Add a TV Storage Lot to the Trade Port	Export 10,000 crates of TVs	§25,000
ZTronix: Train to Zone	Add a Freight Rail Terminal to the Trade Port	Add a Computer Storage Lot to the Trade Port	Export 10,000 crates of computers	§25,000
ZTronix: Bulk Cargo	Add a Cargo Ship Dock to the Trade Port	Export 10,000 crates of processors	—	§25,000
ZTronix: Massive Profits	Export 1,000,000 crates of processors	Export 100,000 crates of TVs	Export 100,000 crates of computers	§50,000

MANUFACTURING

Name	Criteria 1	Criteria 2	Criteria 3	Results
Industrial Action!	Develop an additional Industrial Zone	Add 100 new jobs	—	§5,000
The Power of Computing I	Build a Processor Factory	Assemble 100 crates of processors	—	§2,500
The Power of Computing II	Build a Consumer Electronics Factory	Assemble 100 crates of TVs	—	§2,500

SPECIALIZATION: GAMBLING

Name	Criteria 1	Criteria 2	Criteria 3	Results
The Big Gamble: Ante Up!	Build a Gambling House	Have 80 gamblers visit the Gambling House	Earn §1,000 from your Gambling House	§1,000
The Big Gamble: Neon Boogaloo	Earn §20,000 from your Gambling House	Build a sign for your Gambling House	Increase commercial zoning to attract 10 new businesses near the Gambling House	§1,500
The Big Gamble: Head Honcho	Earn §50,000 in a day from your Gambling House	Build a Gambling HQ	Have 200 low wealth gamblers visit your casinos	§1,750
The Big Gamble: Cop Up	Build a Police Station	Your police force arrests 2 criminals	—	§1,000
The Big Gamble: Cashing In	Earn §100,000 more in daily profits from casinos	Upgrade the Gambling HQ to a Gambling, Co.	Add the Gaming Division to the upgraded Gambling HQ	§2,000
The Big Gamble: Games Sims Play	Add a Nickel Slots to the Gambling House	Add Blackjack Tables to the Gambling House	Increase your earnings from casinos by §5,000	§2,500
The Big Gamble: Gamification	Increase your earnings from casinos by §10,000	Build a Sleek Casino	Add a Craps Parlor to the Sleek Casino	§2,750
The Big Gamble: Heist!	Add a Patrol Car Lot to the Police Station	At least 3 criminals are arrested	—	§1,400
The Big Gamble: Showbiz!	Earn more than §400,000 in daily profits from casinos	Upgrade the Gambling HQ to a Gambling, Inc.	Add the Entertainment Division to the upgraded Gambling HQ	§2,800
The Big Gamble: Everyone Loves a Show	Add a Comedy Club to the Gambling House	Have 1,500 low wealth gamblers visit your casinos	—	§1,750
The Big Gamble: Top of the Heap	Earn §1,000,000 more in daily profit from casinos	Upgrade the Gambling HQ to a Gambling Global	Add the Lodging Division to the upgraded Gambling HQ	§2,850
The Big Gamble: Fancy Pants	Build an Elegant Casino	Add Classy Rooms to the Elegant Casino	Have 400 tourists stay overnight in casinos	§1,850
The Big Gamble: Improving Upon Excellence	Add a Roulette House to the Elegant Casino	Add an Exclusive Club to the Elegant Casino	Add 50 high wealth rooms to the Elegant Casino	§1,900
The Big Gamble: Debts	Have 5,000 low wealth gamblers in your casinos	Increase income by §10,000 from your casinos	You have 24 hours to reach these objectives!	§50,000
The Big Gamble: Bus 'Em In!	Upgrade Town Hall to City Hall	Add a Department of Transportation to your City Hall	Build a Bus Terminal	§1,200

MISSIONS

Name	Criteria 1	Criteria 2	Criteria 3	Results
The Big Gamble: Take Them for a Ride	Build a Passenger Train Station	Have two train trips made in one day	—	§1,250
The Big Gamble: Flights of Fun	Build a Municipal Airport	Have 500 tourists arrive by air in one day	Add a Passenger Terminal to the Municipal Airport	§1,800
GREAT WORKS				
The Great Arcology	Have 1,179 residents in your city	Unlock the Arcology Great Works	—	§5,000
Go International!	Build a Municipal Airport in the region	Increase tourist attractions in the region by a capacity of 100 tourists	Have 100 tourists arrive by air at the Municipal Airport in one day	§1,000
A Place to Land	Work with your neighbors to send at least 300 construction workers to the International Airport site	Construction begins on the International Airport	—	§1,000
Rays of Light, From the Sun	Add the School of Science to the University	Research the Solar Farm Project at the University	—	§1,000
Build a Satellite!	Send computers, fuel, and alloy to the Space Center	Send workers to the Space Center	—	§100
Building the Future	Work with your neighbors to send at least 300 construction workers to the Space Center site	Construction begins on the Space Center	—	§1,000
Into...Spaaaaaace!!!	Add the Consumer Electronics Division to the Electronics HQ	Research the Space Center Project at the University	—	§1,000
Plague From The Arcology!!	Save 500 plague-stricken Sims in 24 hours	—	—	§30,000
Build Arcology	Connect your city to the Great Works site and send at least 20 workers	Send resources: metal, processors, crude oil, alloy	Complete construction of the Arcology	§1,000
Build International Airport	Connect your city to the Great Works site and send at least 20 workers	Send resources: metal, crude oil, alloy	Complete construction of the International Airport	§1,000
Build Solar Farm	Connect your city to the Great Works site and send at least 20 workers	Send resources: plastic and alloy	Complete construction of the Solar Farm	§1,000
Build Space Center	Connect your city to the Great Works site and send at least 20 workers	Send resources: metal, alloy, processors, crude oil	Complete construction of the Space Center	§1,000
Build A Satellite	Send 20 workers to the Space Center site	Send resources: alloy, electronics, fuel	Complete construction of a satellite	§1,000
Get Arcology Operating	Collectively supply at least 120 kGal/hr water	Collectively supply at least 300 MW/hr power	Increase population of Arcology	§10,000
Get International Airport Operating	Collectively supply at least 300 workers to the Airport	Collectively supply at least 100 MW/hr power	Collectively increase tourist attraction capacity by 100	§10,000
Get Solar Farm Operating	Collectively supply at least 300 workers to the Solar Farm	Turn on the power	—	§10,000
Airport Closed Due to Security Breach	Catch 5 escaped criminals in 24 hours	—	—	§10,000
The (Not So) Final Countdown	Launch a satellite in 12 hours	—	—	§100,000
Solar Farm Closed by Fire	Extinguish the fire completely in 24 hours	—	—	§10,000
Space Center Computers Infected by Virus! Send Replacements Right Away!	Send 20 crates of computers to the Space Center within 24 hours	—	—	§10,000
HEROES AND VILLAINS				
Crime Pays: Go Evil!	Have 5 more industrial businesses built in your city	Have at least 5 criminals at large in your city	Build Vu Tower!	§10,000
Crime Pays: Keep Calm. Commit Crimes.	Unleash at least one henchman from Vu Tower	10 new crimes are committed	—	§20,000

MISSIONS

Name	Criteria 1	Criteria 2	Criteria 3	Results
Crime Pays: VuMobile...Not Just a Phone Service!	Dr. Vu acquires §10,000 more in ill-gained loot	Add the VuMobile Garage to Vu Tower	—	§30,000
Crime Pays: Criminal Mastermind	Unleash 20 henchmen from Vu Tower	20 new crimes are committed	—	§40,000
Crime Pays: Paging Dr. Vu	Dr. Vu acquires §10,000 more in ill-gained loot	Add Dr. Vu's Laboratory to Vu Tower	—	§50,000
Crime Pays: VuBot Attack!	Dr. Vu acquires §10,000 more in ill-gained loot	Unleash the VuBot! Bwahahahaha!!!	—	§60,000
No Regrets: You Won't Regret This	Have at least 1,065 residents in your city	Build Maxis Manor	Send MaxisMan out on patrol	§5,000
No Regrets: Dr. MaxisMan	Dispatch MaxisMan to heal injured Sims	MaxisMan heals 3 injured Sims	—	§10,000
No Regrets: Turbo Time!	MaxisMan earns §500 in rewards	Add the Turbo Machine Garage to Maxis Manor	Arrest 3 more criminals	§30,000
No Regrets: Reticulate my Splines	MaxisMan earns §2,500 in rewards	Add the Reticulator Landing Pad to Maxis Manor	Send MaxisMan out to extinguish 5 fires	§50,000
No Regrets: MaxisMan vs. Dr. Vu	MaxisMan earns §5,000 in rewards	Capture the nefarious Dr. Vu!	—	§100,000

Diagrams

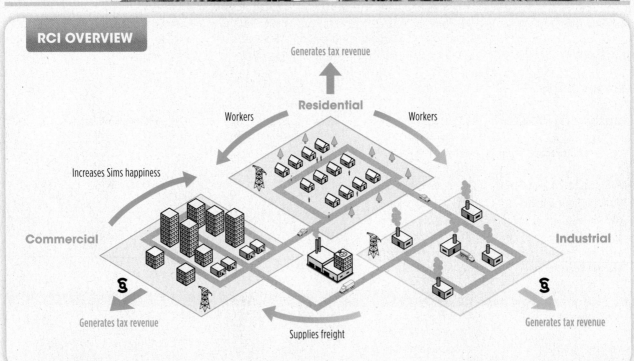

RCI OVERVIEW

Residential Flow

 Happy new Sims attempt to enter the City at a fixed rate.

This rate can be increased (per wealth class) by transportation networks (roads connected to the edges of a region, boat docks, train stations and airports).

Demand

C
I
T

Low wealth jobs **Mid wealth jobs** **High wealth jobs**

The number of new residents allowed into the city is capped based on the demand for jobs.

max residents per building

daily positive output per resident

tax revenue

crime/garbage

water
power

daily needs per resident

daily negative output per resident

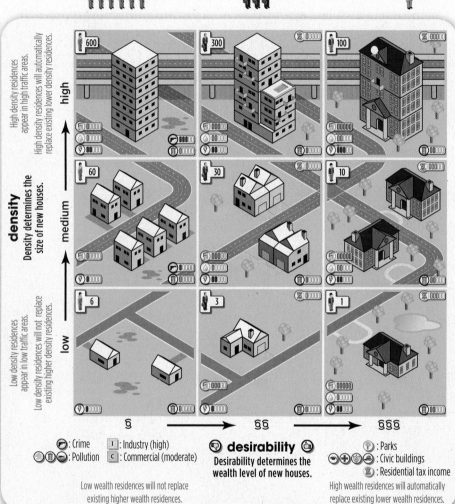

high

High density residences appear in high traffic areas.

High density residences will automatically replace existing lower density residences.

density
Density determines the size of new houses.

medium

Low density residences appear in low traffic areas.

Low density residences will not replace existing higher density residences.

low

600 | 300 | 100
60 | 30 | 10
6 | 3 | 1

 : Crime
: Pollution
I : Industry (high)
C : Commercial (moderate)

 desirability
Desirability determines the wealth level of new houses.

: Parks
: Civic buildings
: Residential tax income

Low wealth residences will not replace existing higher wealth residences.

High wealth residences will automatically replace existing lower wealth residences.

Every residential building contains the following information:

Needs

Job | Power | Water | Desirability

Every house keeps track of how many residents are employed and whether the building has enough water and power.

Unhappiness

Unhappy | Normal | Happy

Sims near Commercial entertainment buildings become increasingly happy.

Sims with unmet needs become increasingly unhappy.

Sickness

= 😞

As pollution grows the chance of sickness increases. Sickness will also be caused by random events.

Sick citizens are still employed. However, they don't contribute to their workplaces' production.

Sick citizens do not get any Commercial entertainment benefits.

Education

Low | High School | College | PhD

Residential buildings near schools increase in education level over time. (A lack of schools causes a decrease.) The education level determines the tech level of the industrial buildings.

New citizens enter the box with an education level that matches their residential building. (New buildings have an education value of 0.)

Unhappy Sims abandon their houses and leave the city.

: Increased crime
: Increased fire hazard
: Counts as garbage

Abandoned houses decrease desirability.

You can bulldoze an abandoned house, wait for it to burn down, or fix the issues that caused the abandonment (this allows Sims to move back in).

Commercial Flow

Happy new commercial buildings attempt to enter the city at a fixed rate.

This rate can be increased (per wealth class) by transportation networks (roads connected to the edges of a region, boat docks, train stations and airports).

Demand

R →

Low wealth shoppers | Medium wealth shoppers | High wealth shoppers

The number of new commercial buildings built in the box is capped based on the demand from shoppers

max workers per building
- low wealth: 6
- mid wealth: 3
- high wealth: 1

daily positive output per actual income

tax revenue

desired income (total for all sales): 100

water — daily needs per worker/shopper
power

garbage — daily negative output per worker/shopper

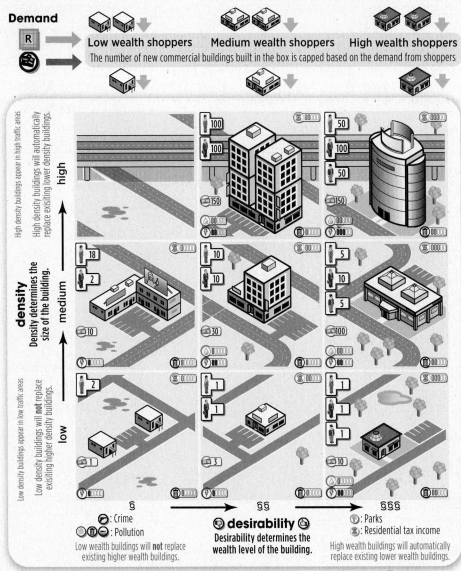

density — Density determines the size of the building.

high — High density buildings appear in high traffic areas. High density buildings will automatically replace existing lower density buildings.

medium

low — Low density buildings appear in low traffic areas. Low density buildings will **not** replace existing higher density buildings.

(a): Crime
(b)(c)(d): Pollution

Low wealth buildings will **not** replace existing higher wealth buildings.

desirability — Desirability determines the wealth level of the building.

(T): Parks
(S): Residential tax income

High wealth buildings will automatically replace existing lower wealth buildings.

Special Functions

Attraction — Increases visitors to the city.

Hotel — Can house visitors
+1 income per low wealth, +3 income per mid wealth, +10 income per high wealth

Entertainment — Distributes happiness to R.
+1 income per happiness.

Crime — Increases crime locally.

Parking — Can hold cars.
+1 income per car.

Every commercial building contains the following information:

Desired Income

20 — Commercial buildings need to make a certain amount of money each day. Each building makes §1 each time it makes a sale.

A commercial building can make 1 sale per employee per day.

Low Wealth: All shoppers. §
Medium Wealth: Mid-wealth and wealthy shoppers. §§
High Wealth: Only wealthy shoppers. §§§

Needs

Workers | Water | Power | Desirability

Commercial Buildings without any workers, water, power, or in an undesirable zone will make no income.

Unhappiness

Unhappy | Normal | Happy

Buildings that make less than the desired income become increasingly unhappy.

Desired income

Buildings that make more than the desired income become increasingly happy.

Workers/Shoppers

Employed Sims that don't work in a commercial zone will attempt to shop there.

Each morning workers leave the residential zones and go to work in nearby commercial zones.

R

 Unemployed workers stay home for the day.

Visitors

Each visitor makes one purchase and then leaves the box.

The number of visitors in the city is capped to the number of hotel rooms.

 New visitors enter the city at a fixed rate. Attractions and transportation networks increase the flow of visitors into the city.

Unhappy commercial buildings become abandoned

(a): increased crime
(b): increased fire hazard
(c): counts as garbage

Abandoned commercial buildings decrease desirability.

You can bulldoze an abandoned or commercial building, wait for it to burn down, or fix the issues that caused the abandonment (this allows it to open again).

Industrial Flow

I

Happy new industrial buildings attempt to enter the city at a fixed rate.

This rate can be increased (per wealth class) by transportation networks (roads connected to the edges of a region, boat docks, train strations and airports).

Demand

R → Low education | High-school education | College education

🎓 : Education

The number of new industrial buildings built in the city is capped based on the demand from residents.

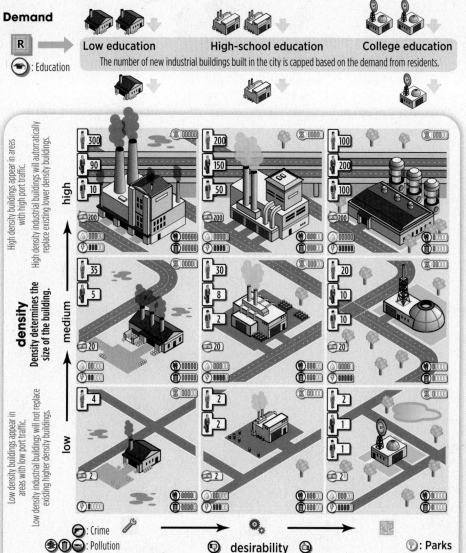

Left margin (top): High density buildings appear in areas with high port traffic.

High density industrial buildings will automatically replace existing lower density buildings.

density
Density determines the size of the building.

Left margin (bottom): Low density buildings appear in areas with low port traffic.

Low density industrial buildings will not replace existing higher density buildings.

high / **medium** / **low**

🚬 : Crime

⚙️ : Pollution

Low tech industrial buildings will not replace existing higher tech buildings.

→ desirability →
Desirability determines the tech level of the building.

High tech industrial buildings will automatically replace existing lower tech buildings.

🌳 : Parks

---

max workers per building | daily positive output per actual income

low wealth 👷 6
mid wealth 👷 3   **tax revenue** 💰
high wealth 👷

desired income 💰 100 | **air pollution/garbage**
total for all shipments

water 💧 | 👥
power ⚡ | 🗑️
daily needs per worker | daily negative output per worker

Every industrial building contains the following information:

Desired Income

💰 20 Industrial buildings need to make a certain amount of money each day. Each building makes money each time it makes a shipment

👥 An industrial building can make 1 shipment per employee per day.

Commercial Shipping

Every commercial building will buy shipments based on their density:

High Density: 200 units per day

Medium Density: 20 units per day

Low Density: 2 units per day

Global Shipping

Every time a transport unit arrives at a port it buys shipments from connected industrial buildings:

— Truck Stop: 10 units per truck.

⚓ Sea Port: 1000 units per boat.

▦ Train Station: 100 units per train car.

✈ Airport: 100 units per airplane.

Needs

Workers | Water | Power | Desirability

Industrial Buildings without any workers, water, power, or in an undesirable zone will make no income.

Unhappiness

😞 Unhappy 😐 Normal 😊 Happy

Buildings that make less than the desired income become increasingly unhappy. | Desired income | Buildings that make more than the desired income become increasingly happy.

Workers

Each morning workers leave the residential zones and go to work in nearby industrial zones.

R

🚭😞 Unemployed workers stay home for the day.

😞 Unhappy industrial buildings become abandoned.

🚬 : Increased crime

🔥 : Increased fire hazard

🗑️ : Counts as garbage

Abandoned industrial buildings decrease desirability.

You can bulldoze an abandoned industrial building, wait for it to burn down, or fix the issues that caused the abandonment (this allows it to open again).

UNDERSTANDING FIRE

Before

No Fire
Sims safe inside.

During

building locked, no new Sims can enter

**Smoke
(level 1)**

Uninjured Sims run out of the building at a steady rate.

They become Gawkers when they reach the street.

Saved

If a fire truck arrives during this time then the building and its remaining occupants will be saved.

heat radiates out to nearby structures

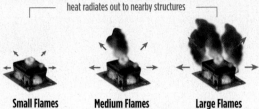

**Small Flames
(level 2)**

**Medium Flames
(level 3)**

**Large Flames
(level 4)**

Injured Sims run out of the flaming building at a steady rate

If there is a waiting ambulance then the Sim will be saved and taken to the Hospital.

If there is no ambulance then the Sim will die.

After

Abandoned

The fire truck put out the fire. The building is lost but the remaining Sims are saved.

Uninjured Sims run out of the building at a steady rate until it is empty.

They look for a new house when they reach the street.

-OR-

Rubble

The fire truck did not put out the fire. The building collapses and all the remaining Sims die.

CRIME FLOW

Criminal creation
Criminal starts at Level 0

Criminal at Home → **Arrested**
Evidence

Travel to Target

Suppressed
Too Hot

Arrive at Scene
Play pre-crime vignette → **Arrested**
Crime Prevented

Crime Committed
Criminal gains +1 Level → **Arrested**
Caught in the Act

Travel back Home
Hot pursuit event if seen → **Arrested**
Hot Pursuit

Jailed

Released Early
Due to overcrowding

Escaped
Random mini-disaster

Rehabilitation
Criminal Reduced -1 Level

Served Sentence
Crime Level 0

"Processed"
One less criminal in the city

 Police Assets:
All police buildings and vehicles suppress crime in a local area.

 Helicopter:
Can track criminals trying to escape.

 Detective Wing:
Arrest criminals while they are still in their houses.

 Dispatch Tower:
Automatically sends police units to a building as soon as the criminal arrives.

 Patrol Car:
Can catch criminals and return them to jail.

 Jail Cell:
Holds criminals until they serve their "sentence."

TRANSPORTING CARGO

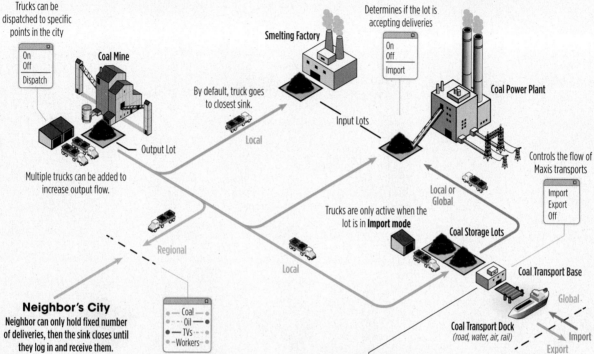

SOURCE
Sources use trucks to deliver resources to Input Lots in the city.

SINK
Sinks have no garages/trucks. They rely on Output Lots for transportation.

Trucks can be dispatched to specific points in the city

On / Off / Dispatch

Coal Mine

By default, truck goes to closest sink.

Local

Output Lot

Multiple trucks can be added to increase output flow.

Regional

Determines if the lot is accepting deliveries

On / Off / Import

Smelting Factory

Input Lots

Coal Power Plant

Controls the flow of Maxis transports

Import / Export / Off

Local or Global

Trucks are only active when the lot is in **Import mode**

Local

Coal Storage Lots

Coal Transport Base

Global

Import

Export

Coal Transport Dock
(road, water, air, rail)

Neighbor's City
Neighbor can only hold fixed number of deliveries, then the sink closes until they log in and receive them.

— Coal —
— Oil —
— TVs —
— Workers—

Both sides can control the resources that are allowed across the border.

Trade Depot/Trade Port
(Road, Rail, Water)
Can act as a source (Import mode) or a sink (Export mode), depending on player's needs. Can transfer cargo from one transportation network to another. (i.e., from trucks to boats)

Global Market
All Global Market vehicles are owned by Maxis.

TOURISTS FROM REGION

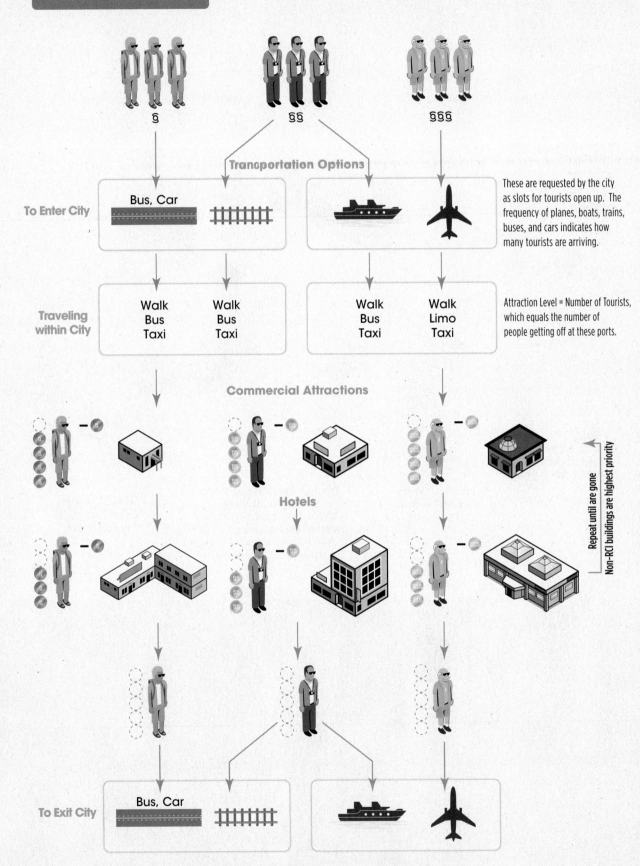

Transportation Options

To Enter City

Bus, Car

These are requested by the city as slots for tourists open up. The frequency of planes, boats, trains, buses, and cars indicates how many tourists are arriving.

Traveling within City

Walk Bus Taxi | Walk Bus Taxi | Walk Bus Taxi | Walk Limo Taxi

Attraction Level = Number of Tourists, which equals the number of people getting off at these ports.

Commercial Attractions

Hotels

Repeat until are gone
Non-RCI buildings are highest priority

To Exit City

Bus, Car

EFFECTS ON HAPPINESS

Causes	Residential			Commercial			Industrial		
	Low Wealth	Medium Wealth	High Wealth	Low Wealth	Medium Wealth	High Wealth	Low Tech	Medium Tech	High Tech
Low Land Value	–	😞	😞	–	😞	😞	–	–	–
No Power	😞	😞	😞	😐	😞	😞	😐	😞	😞
No Water	😞	😞	😞	😐	😞	😞	😐	😞	😞
Can't Pay Rent	😞	😞	😞	😞	😞	😞	😞	😞	😞
Garbage Uncollected	–	😐	😞	–	😐	😞	–	😐	😞
Sewage Back-up	–	😐	😞	–	😐	😞	–	😐	😞
Pollution	–	–	😐	–	–	😐	–	–	–
Germs	–	😐	😐	–	😐	😐	–	–	–
Sickness	😐	😞	😞	–	–	–	–	–	–
Injury	😐	😐	😐	–	–	–	😐	😞	😞
Death	😞	😞	😞	😞	😞	😞	😞	😞	😞
Successful Shopping	🙂	🙂	🙂	🙂	🙂	🙂	–	–	–
Tourist Shopping	–	–	–	🙂	🙂	🙂	–	–	–
Student Shopping	–	–	–	🙂	🙂	🙂	–	–	–
Visiting Parks	🙂	🙂	🙂	–	–	–	–	–	–
Lack of Any Education	–	😐	😞	–	–	–	–	😞	😞
Traffic	😐	😐	–	😐	😐	😐	–	–	–
Mass Transit	😐	😐	–	😐	😐	😐	–	–	–
Crime at Building	😞	😞	😞	😞	😞	😞	😞	😞	😞
Crime in Area	😐	😞	😞	😐	😞	😞	–	😐	😞
Crime Suppression	–	–	🙂	–	–	🙂	–	–	–
Low Taxes	🙂	🙂	–	🙂	🙂	–	🙂	🙂	–
Medium Taxes	–	–	😞	–	–	😞	–	–	😞
High Taxes	😞	😞	😞	😞	😞	😞	😞	😞	😞
Low Wealth Plops	🙂	–	–	🙂	–	–	–	–	–
Medium Wealth Plops	–	🙂	–	–	🙂	–	–	–	–
High Wealth Plops	–	🙂	🙂	–	🙂	🙂	–	–	–
Fire Marshal Visits	–	–	🙂	–	–	🙂	–	–	🙂
Health Outreach Visits	–	–	🙂	–	–	🙂	–	–	🙂
Police Outreach Visits	–	–	🙂	–	–	🙂	–	–	–
Homeless	–	–	–	–	😐	😞	–	–	–
Freight Deliveries	–	–	–	–	–	–	🙂	🙂	🙂

● Complaints and happiness lost   😐 Complaints but no happiness lost   🙂 Happiness gained and explained

ⓘ NOTE

These are just a few of the challenges you can expect after launch. New challenges are released regularly, so check the game or www.primagames.com for details on past and current challenges. And remember, these optional tasks are timed—you need to finish in the top 10% to earn the achievement associated with each challenge, so don't waste any time.

CHALLENGES

Icon	Name	Criteria
	500 Alarm Fire	Watch out, it's dry out there. Extreme fire hazard! Extinguish 500 fires in the region.
	Another Sim Rides the Bus	Not everyone can take a limo to work, Moneybags. Some honest, hard workin' Sims have to take the bus. Pick up 100,000 Sims on buses in the region.
	Black Gold	Get those other regions over a barrel with your oil empire! Sell 100,000 barrels of the region's crude oil.
	Blinded by Science	Build the region of tomorrow, today! Have 100 high tech industry buildings in the region.
	Gone Fission	Split the atom to harness the ultimate power! Maintain 10 gigawatts of power in the region using only Nuclear Power Plants.
	Heavy Metal Finish	Muster your mettle to master metal! Upgrade a Metals HQ to a Metals Global in a city in the region.
	Lockdown!	There are too many criminals on the loose! Time to crack down on crime! Lock up 500 criminals in holding cells throughout the region.

CHALLENGES

Icon	Name	Criteria
	Population Explosion	Encourage a baby boom in the region! Reach 150,000 population in the region.
	Soak the Rich	Concerned the wealthy aren't paying their fair share? Bleed §1,000,000 in tax revenue from the rich throughout the region!
	Soot Yourself	Environment schmenvironment, coal is plentiful. Let it burn! Burn 1,000,000 tons of coal in Coal Power Plants throughout the region.
	The Final Frontier	Build some expensive technology and launch it into orbit! Launch a satellite!
	Time to Crate	Let's get SimWorld working again. Ship 100,000 crates from industry throughout the region.
	Vacation Destination	It's vacation time! Get ready for busloads of out of place tourists! Welcome the 100,000th tourist to the region.
	What a Waste	It smells, it's gross, but you have to deal with it. Treat 1,000,000 gallons of the region's sewage.

ACHIEVEMENTS

Icon	Name	Criteria
	CITY MANAGEMENT	
	Best Mayor Ever!	Have an approval rating of 95% or more.
	Big Government	Place one of each of the City Hall departments on a single City Hall.
	Busy Downtown	Have at least 100 commercial buildings in your city.
	Good Credit	Pay off §1,000,000 in bond debt.
	Industrial Revolution	Have 100 industrial buildings in your city.
	Jumbo Region!	Have 1,000,000 residents living in a region.
	Mega-Region!	Have 2,000,000 residents living in a region.
	Metropolis!	Have 100,000 residents living in your city.
	Money Cube	Have a total income of §15,000+ per hour.
	Multi-Millionaire City	Have §10,000,000 in your treasury.
	My Favorite Mayor	Have 24 hours of a 75% or better approval rating.
	Population Boom	Have 50,000 residents living in your city.
	Quid Pro Quo	Place one each of all the modules on a single Mayor's Mansion.
	Sand Through My Fingers	Have total expenses of §15,000+ per hour.
	Suburb City	Have 10,000 residents living in your city.

ACHIEVEMENTS

Icon	Name	Criteria
	Suburbtopia	Have 500 residential buildings in your city.
	Worst. Mayor. Ever.	Hold an approval rating of below 50% for 24 hours.
	CITY SPECIALIZATION	
	A Lot of Lots	Place 6 unique storage lot types on any Trade Depot or Trade Port.
	All Oiled Up	Pump 10,000 barrels of crude oil in a day.
	Blast Furnace	Smelt a total of 100 tons of metal.
	Electrical Magic	Assemble 4,000 crates of processors in a day.
	King Coal	Extract a total of 100 tons of coal.
	Moving Pictures	Assemble 100 crates of TVs in one day in a single city.
	Penny Slots	Generate §200,000 in total revenue from casinos.
	Refined Tastes	Refine 40 barrels of fuel and 40 crates of plastic in a single city in one hour.
	Sin City	Place one of each type of casino in a single city.
	Specialist First Class	Select "Guide Me" for any city specialization.
	To Be, Ore Not To Be	Extract a total of 100 tons of raw ore.
	Trading Empire	Ship 250,000 global market export shipments.
	You Mean Business!	Plop every City Specialization HQ in the game.

ACHIEVEMENTS

RCI

Icon	Name	Criteria
	Apartment Rows	Have 50 high density, low wealth residential buildings in your city.
	Billionaire's Playground	Have 10 high density, high wealth residential buildings in your city.
	Elite Estates	Have 50 low density, high wealth residential buildings in your city.
	Office Parks	Have 50 low density, high wealth commercial buildings in your city.
	Skyscraper Magnet	Have 10 high density, high wealth commercial buildings.
	Technophile	Have 40 high density, high tech industrial buildings in your city.
	The Big (Insert Fruit Here)	Have 50 high density, low wealth commercial buildings in your city.

CITY SERVICES

Icon	Name	Criteria
	A Streetcar Named SimCity	Have 1,000 Sims travel by streetcar in a day.
	All Aboard!	Have 1,000 Sims take the train in a day.
	Aqua Max	Have a city that has over 100 kgal of water needed per hour.
	Bad Move, Creeps	Have your police capture their first criminal.
	Cruisin' Along	Have 2,000 Sims take a cruise in a day.
	Dump City!	Have 560 tons of garbage in your Garbage Dumps.
	EMT ASAP	Pick up and treat 50 injured Sims in one day.
	Garbage Man!	Pick up 10 tons of garbage in a day.

ACHIEVEMENTS

Icon	Name	Criteria
	Green Plumbobs	Pick up 10 tons of recyclables in your city in a day.
	High Tech Fire Fightin'	Add the hazmat Garage, the Fire Helipad, and the Fire Marshal Office to a Large Fire Station in your city.
	Ick or Treat!	Treat 200 kgal/hr of sewage at a Sewage Treatment Plant.
	Main Attraction	Have 300 low wealth tourists leave your city satisfied in one day.
	Medical Miracle	Plop a Hospital and treat 200 sick Sims in a day.
	No Child Left Behind	Plop 20 School Bus Stops in one city.
	Only You Can Prevent City Fires	Put out more than 10 fires in a day.
	Redemption of the Sims	Rehabilitate 50 Criminals in a day.
	Revolving Doors	Have 25 criminals released from jail cells in one day due to overcrowding.
	Sewage Stuffing	With 10,000 or more residents, prevent sewage issues using only Sewage Outlet Pipes.
	SimCity University!	Have a University with each School module.
	Sludge-free H-2-0!	Pump 500 kgal of fresh, clean water in an hour.
	Sunday! Sunday! Sunday!	Run a successful stadium event in your city.
	Super-Powered	Have a city that has over 300 MW of power needed per hour.
	You're on Fire!	Extinguish 1 Hazmat fire in your city in a day!

ACHIEVEMENTS

Icon	Name	Criteria
	REGION	
	A Burning Region of Fire	Have 50 fires extinguished in your region in a day.
	All-Powerful City	Produce power from one of each type of power plant in a city in the region (Coal, Oil, Wind, Solar and Nuclear).
	Extraditions	Have your police capture 50 criminals in neighbors' cities.
	Godfather	Have 50 crimes in one month in a region of 5,000+ residents.
	Llamahound	Have a municipal bus from a neighbor make 100 trips into your city within a year.
	Make Sure You're Grounded...	Provide both power and water to a neighbor, at the same time.
	Team Mayor	Grant approvals for 10 buildings for the region.
	The Philanthropist	Gift §200,000 or more to a neighbor.
	Time to Relocate	Have 200+ garbage issues at once in a region.

ACHIEVEMENTS

Icon	Name	Criteria
	SECRET	
	2 Kilometer Island!	Have a nuclear meltdown in your city.
	Blowin' in the Wind	Have 24 Wind Turbines at Wind Power Plants in your city to gain access to the Tornado disaster.
	Bronze Anniversary	Play a city for 10 years!
	Dug Too Greedily and Too Deep	Mine 100 tons of coal or raw ore in your city to gain access to the Earthquake disaster.
	Golden Anniversary	Play a city for 50 years! Take a break!
	Laboratory Outbreak	Add a Diagnostic Lab to a Hospital and have 15 Sims die in a day to gain access to the Zombie Attack disaster.
	Mayor Yuck	Have 500 Sims complaining about dirty water in a day.
	Silver Anniversary	Play a city for 25 years!
	We Are Not Alone	Ship any resource to a Space Center Great Work to gain access to the UFO Encounter disaster.
	What Goes Up Must Come Down	Have 200 tourists arrive on flights at the Municipal Airport in a day to gain access to the Meteor Strike disaster.
	What's Cookin'?	Burn 100 tons of garbage in an Incinerator at the Garbage Dump to gain access to the Big Lizard disaster.
	DELUXE EDITION	
	French Authority	Lock up 10 criminals at the French Police Station.
	German Efficiency	Have 5,000 Sims take trips on trains from the German High-Speed Rail Station.
	UK Character	Have 1,000 Sims get picked up by buses from the Bus Terminal.

SIMCITY™

OFFICIAL GAME GUIDE

WRITTEN BY:

David Knight & Dorothy Bradshaw

Prima Games

An Imprint of Random House, Inc.

3000 Lava Ridge Court, Suite 100

Roseville, CA 95661

www.primagames.com

SENIOR PRODUCT MARKETING MANAGER: Donato Tica

DESIGN & LAYOUT: Sara Jean Kunz, Page Design Group

COPYEDIT: Julia Mascardo

Prima Games and the authors would like to thank the following people for their support throughout this amazing project:

George Pigula, Lucy Bradshaw, Ocean Quigley, Stone Librande, Tammy Sauer, Kip Katsarelis, Chris Schmidt, Christian Stratton, Shawn Stone, John Giordano, Guillaume Pierre, Jason Haber, Kyle Brown, John Scott Clarke, Brian Bartram, Jeremy Dale, Jon Lee, Tyler Thompson, Kent Jolly, Alex Peck, Meghan McDowell, Dan Moskowitz, Mike Khoury, Brian Ford, Robert Perry, Greg Eng, Joel Eckert, Jason Halvorson, Kadet Kuhne, Brian Jennings, Russ Treyz, Ali Jamalzadeh, Michael Donahoe, Karen Tong, Lorraine Honrada, and Jim Stadelman.

IMPORTANT:

Prima Games has made every effort to determine that the information contained in this book is accurate. However, the publisher makes no warranty, either expressed or implied, as to the accuracy, effectiveness, or completeness of the material in this book; nor does the publisher assume liability for damages, either incidental or consequential, that may result from using the information in this book. The publisher cannot provide any additional information or support regarding gameplay, hints and strategies, or problems with hardware or software. Such questions should be directed to the support numbers provided by the game and/or device manufacturers as set forth in their documentation. Some game tricks require precise timing and may require repeated attempts before the desired result is achieved.

Standard Edition ISBN 978-0-307-89540-0

Mini-Edition ISBN 978-0-804-16119-0

Printed in the United States of America.

AUSTRALIAN WARRANTY STATEMENT:

This product comes with guarantees that cannot be excluded under the Australian Consumer Law. You are entitled to a replacement or refund for a major failure and for compensation for any other reasonably foreseeable loss or damage. You are also entitled to have the goods repaired or replaced if the goods fail to be of acceptable quality and the failure does not amount to a major failure.

This product comes with a 1 year warranty from date of purchase. Defects in the product must have appeared within 1-year, from date of purchase in order to claim the warranty.

All warranty claims must be facilitated back through the retailer of purchase, in accordance with the retailer's returns policies and procedures. Any cost incurred, as a result of returning the product to the retailer of purchase – are the full responsibility of the consumer.

AU wholesale distributor: Bluemouth Interactive Pty Ltd, Suite 1502, 9 Yarra Street, South Yarra, Victoria, 3141. (+613 9646 4011)

Email: support@bluemouth.com.au